The New Right in the New Europe

Czech transformation and right-wing politics, 1989–2006

Seán Hanley

Routledge
Taylor & Francis Group

LONDON AND NEW YORK

First published 2008
by Routledge
2 Park Square, Milton Park, Abingdon, Oxon, OX14 4RN

Simultaneously published in the USA and Canada
by Routledge
711 Third Avenue, New York, NY 10017

Routledge is an imprint of the Taylor & Francis Group, an informa business

First issued in paperback 2011

© 2008 Seán Hanley

Typeset in Times by Wearset Ltd, Boldon, Tyne and Wear

British Library Cataloguing in Publication Data
A catalogue record for this book is available from the British Library

Library of Congress Cataloging in Publication Data
A catalog record for this book has been requested

ISBN10: 0–415–34135–3 (hbk)
ISBN10: 0–415–67489–1 (pbk)
ISBN10: 0–203–47935–1 (ebk)

ISBN13: 978–0–415–34135–6 (hbk)
ISBN13: 978–0–415–67489–8 (pbk)
ISBN13: 978–0–203–47935–3 (ebk)

Contents

Tables

Preface

When I first lived in the Czech Republic I was dismayed to discover that its politics were dominated by right-wing parties which seemingly modelled themselves on the British Conservatives. I was also perplexed. Despite undergoing far reaching post-communist transformation, the Czech Republic was far removed from the polarized electoral and social confrontation of British politics I remembered from the 1980s. As I also discovered, sometimes to my frustration, the Czech Republic was a far more bureaucratic, less market-governed society than post-Thatcherite Britain. When I began to research Czech politics more seriously, I found myself repeatedly returning to the Czech right and its paradoxes. Although the country with perhaps the strongest social democratic traditions in Central and Eastern Europe, in Václav Klaus's Civic Democratic Party (ODS), the Czech Republic also gave rise to the region's strongest and most stable free market party. Despite an initial period of dominance in the decade after 1996 both the Civic Democrats and the broader Czech centre-right have repeatedly failed to regain a parliamentary majority, even in 2006 after ODS had triumphantly won parliamentary elections with its highest ever share of the vote. This book, which draws together research on Czech and Central European politics written over a number of years, is an attempt to unravel and explain some of these paradoxes.

Academic treatments of the Czech right have often been highly critical, sometimes partisan. While some writers have written in hyperbolic terms of Klaus as a 'Lenin for the bourgeoisie' leading a 'vanguardist party' (Innes 2001: 175, 174), others have shown more subtle biases in, for example, a sometimes uncritical reliance of Klaus's former political opponents as sources of information and interpretation. Much writing on the Czech right has also centred, sometimes to exclusion of all other considerations on the personality and career of one man, the former Czech Prime Minister and current President, Václav Klaus, overlooking other political actors and the wider social and historical background of Klaus and his party. This book seeks to offer a mild corrective to both trends, offering a balanced and historically grounded study that is neither a vindication of the Czech centre-right nor an academic exposé of its deficiencies and failings. I also seek through the Czech case to highlight some of the broader issues surrounding the development of centre-right forces in Central and Eastern

Europe since 1989 which have often been overshadowed in both media coverage and academic research by accounts of extreme nationalism, sinister populism and the afterlife of former ruling parties. All translations from Czech sources are my own unless otherwise stated.

Acknowledgements

Many people helped and supported me when I was researching and writing this book. I would particularly like to thank staff at both the Institute for Contemporary History in Prague and the Unijazz Archive in 1996–7 for their unfailing politeness and help and officials and archivists at the Civic Democratic Party (ODS), the Civic Democratic Alliance (ODA) and the Czechoslovak People's Party (KDU-ČSL) for providing access to internal party bulletins and newsletters. I should also like to thank to Aleks Szczerbiak, Brigid Fowler and Tim Haughton for many interesting discussions about the politics of the right in their countries of expertise and also their collaboration on a special issue of the *Journal of Communist Studies and Transition Politics* on the centre-right in East Central Europe and other ongoing projects. I also thank Tim Bale and the participants in ESRC workshops on The Right in Contemporary Europe for wide-ranging discussions, which helped set the politics of the Czech and Central European right in still wider context for me. Lastly, I am particularly grateful to Kieran Williams, the quality and clarity of whose research on Czech and Central European politics I have always taken as a benchmark, for his insightful comments on earlier drafts of several chapters in this book. I would also like to thank Peter Sowden for being a most patient and supportive editor.

Versions of several chapters in this book have been previously published. Parts of Chapter 1 were previously published in the *Journal of Communist Studies and Transition Politics* (20: 9–27 and 28–54) in September 2004 as 'Getting the Right Right: Redefining the Centre-Right in Post Communist Europe' and 'Blue Velvet: The Rise and Decline of the New Czech Right'. Parts of Chapters 3 and 7 first appeared in June 1999 as 'The New Right in the New Europe: Unravelling the Ideology of "Czech Thatcherism"' in the *Journal of Political Ideologies* (4: 169–89). Material from these articles is reproduced by kind permission of Taylor & Francis (www.tandf.co.uk/journals). Parts of Chapter 8 were previously published in 2003 as a Chatham House briefing paper on 'The Context of EU Accession in the Czech Republic' and in 2004 in *East European Politics and Societies* (18: 513–48) as 'From Neo-Liberalism to National Interests: Ideology, Strategy, and Party Development in the Euroscepticism of the Czech Right'. Material from the latter is reproduced by kind permission of SAGE Publications. A small section in Chapter 8 was first published in

'A Nation of Sceptics? The Czech EU Accession Referendum of 13–14 June 2003' in *West European Politics* (27: 691–715).

Last but not least, I would like thank my family: my parents-in-law in Brno, Mr Knotek and Mrs Knotková for all manner of practical help; my own parents for still greater help and support over the years; and, of course, my patient and long-suffering wife and children. My daughter Darja will be especially glad that the book about a 'man with a moustache who lives in a castle' has finally been completed. It is dedicated to her.

Czech and Slovak abbreviations

4K	*Čtyřkoalice*	Quad-Coalition
ČSDI	*Československá demokratická iniciativa*	Czechoslovak Democratic Initiative (=Democratic Initiative)
ČSL	*Československá strana lidová*	Czechoslovak People's Party
ČSS	*Československá strana socialistická*	Czechoslovak Socialist Party
ČSSD	*Československá sociální demokracie* (from February 1993) *Česká strana sociálně demokratická*	Czechoslovak Social Democracy (*from February 1993*) Czech Social Democratic Party
DEU	*Demokratická unie*	Democratic Union
DI	*Demokratická iniciativa*	Democratic Initiative
ED-SNK	*Evropští demokraté – Sdružení nezávislých kandidatek*	European Democrats – Association of Independent Electoral Lists
HOS	*Hnutí za občanskou svobodu*	Movement for Civil Liberty
HSD-SMS	*Hnutí za samosprávnou demokracii – Společnost pro Moravu a Slezsko*	Movement for Self-Governing Democracy – Society for Moravia and Silesia
HZDS	*Hnutie za demokratické Slovensko*	Movement for a Democratic Slovakia
KAN	*Klub angažovaných nestraníků*	Club of Committed Non-Party Members
KDH	*Kresťansko-demokratické hnutie*	Christian Democratic Movement (*Slovakia*)
KDS	*Křesťansko-demokratická strana*	Christian Democratic Party

KDU-ČSL	*Křesťanská a demokratická unie– Československá strana lidová*	Christian Democratic Union–Czechoslovak People's Party
KSČM	*Komunistická strana Čech a Moravy*	Communist Party of Bohemia and Moravia
KSČ	*Komunistická strana Československa*	Communist Party of Czechoslovakia
KSD OF	*Klub sociálních demokratů při OF*	Club of Social Democrats in Civic Forum
LA	*Levá alternativa*	Left Alternative
LB	*Levý blok*	Left Bloc
LDS	*Liberálně demokratická strana*	Liberal Democratic Party
LK	*Liberální klub*	Liberal Club
LSNS	*Liberální strana národně sociální*	Liberal National Social Party
LSU	*Liberálně-sociální unie*	Liberal Social Union
MKDP	*Meziparlamentní klub demokratické pravice*	Inter-Parliamentary Club of the Democratic Right
ODA	*Občanská demokratická aliance*	Civic Democratic Alliance
ODS	*Občanská demokratická strana*	Civic Democratic Party
OF	*Občanské fórum*	Civic Forum
OH	*Občanské hnutí*	Civic Movement
SB-KS	*Svobodný blok – Konzervativní strana*	Free Bloc – Conservative Party
SČPŽR	*Strana československých podnikatelů, živnostníků a rolníků*	Party of Czechoslovak Businesspeople and Farmers
SKS	*Strana konzervativní smlouvy*	Party of Conservative Accord
SPR-RSČ	*Sdružení pro republiku – Republikánská strana Československa*	Association For the Republic – Republican Party of Czechoslovakia
SRS	*Svobodná rolnická strana*	Free Peasants Party
SZ	*Strana zelených*	Green Party
US	*Unie svobody*	Freedom Union
US-DEU	*Unie svobody- Demokratická unie*	Freedom Union – Democratic Union
VPN	*Verejnosť proti násiliu*	Public Against Violence (*Slovakia*)
VPN-ODÚ	*Verejnosť proti násiliu- Občianská demokratická únia*	Public Against Violence – Civic Democratic Union (*Slovakia*)
ZS	*Zemědělská strana*	Agricultural Party

1 Getting the right right in post-communist Europe

Despite their importance in contemporary European politics, parties of the centre-right remain an under-researched area. This is particularly the case of the mainstream right in the new democracies of Central and Eastern Europe, where centre-right parties in almost all countries held office for significant periods in the years following 1989 (see Table 1.1). The existing literature on the centre-right in Eastern and Central Europe is, therefore, small and fragmentary. In the immediate aftermath of the fall of communism in Central and Eastern Europe, discussion of the re-emergence of the right centred on concerns that it would take the form of ultra-nationalism or Peronist anti-market populism leading to a possible breakdown of democracy in the region (Andor: 1991; Przeworski 1991; Tismaneanu 1996). However, when such predictions proved erroneous (for a critique see Greskovits 1998: 1–34), scholarly interest rapidly moved elsewhere.

After more than a decade of competitive party politics in the region, published research barely amounted to a book-length treatment (Hellen 1996), which largely reviewed prospects for democratization, and short monographs on national cases (Schöpflin 1991; Held 1993; Roper 1998; Wenzel 1998; Kiss 2003; Sharman and Phillips 2004; Szczerbiak and Hanley 2006). Comparative perspectives on the right in the region amounted to two conference papers, one of which remained unpublished (Chan 2001; Vachudova 2001). A number of more general works discussed the centre-right in the region, often dealing with it as a subsidiary theme within accounts of economic transformation (see, for example, Orenstein 2002). Critical, left-wing scholarship also sometimes focused on East and Central European centre-right as the key political vehicle for the restoration of capitalism (Callinicos 1991; Gowan 1996; Saxonberg 2001: 387–95). However, while such analyses raised important issues, they often lacked plausibility, sophistication and empirical grounding. As Ganev (2005) notes, many sweepingly depicted all post-communist societies and their citizens as passive victims of external manipulation by transnational capital, Western-led international organizations or local intellectual and technocratic (ex-*nomenklatura*) elites with a hidden pro-capitalist agenda (Andor 1991: Callinicos 1991; Gowan 1996; Saxonberg 2001: 387–95; Shields 2003).[1] Such analyses tended to underestimate not only the vitality of social forces resisting such pressures but also the role of domestic social and political forces in creating the East and Central European centre-right and supplying it with broader legitimacy. The relative paucity of literature on the centre-right in post-communist Europe contrasted markedly with the voluminous, detailed and often sophisticated comparative literatures on the left – usually focused on communist successor parties (Grzymala-Busse 2002; Bozóki and Ishiyama 2002) – and on the extreme right (Hockenos 1993; Cheles 1995; Ramet 1999; Minkenberg 2003).

The right in post-communist Europe

Lewis (2003: 160) suggests that '[b]y and large similar kinds of parties in terms of ideological orientation have developed in CEE as in Western Europe' and groups them empirically according to their membership of transnational party groupings such as the European People's Party (EPP) and the Liberal International (Lewis 2003: 162–3). Although important in highlighting the recent role of European integration in (re-)shaping party identity in Central and Eastern Europe, membership in groupings like the EPP is, however, now so wide-ranging that it obscures as much as it reveals. Early comparative work identified three groups of parties in post-communist Europe as 'right-wing or 'conservative' on the basis of their origins or ideology: (1) mainstream centre-right parties with ties to the West European centre-right, which Vachudova (2001) terms the 'moderate right' and others subdivide into traditionalist conservatives (including parties with a 'Christian democractic orientation') and liberal-conservatives (Lewis 2000a, 2003; Chan 2001); (2) broad populist-nationalist groupings, which played a dominant role in the politics of new nation-states, such as Slovakia and Croatia in the 1990s – termed the 'independence right' by Vachudova (2001); and (3) former ruling communist parties, with a 'chauvino-communist position', combining nationalism, social conservatism and economic populism – termed the 'communist right' by Vachudova (2001) and 'communist conservatives' by Chan (2001). Lang (2005) introduces a further set of sub-divisions, distinguishing large moderate conservative parties, such as Hungary's FIDESZ, whom he terms 'neo-traditionalists', from niche-based, Christian-oriented 'particularist traditionalist' parties, such as the League of Polish Families (LPR) or Slovakia's Christian Democratic Movement (KDH).[2] He also distinguishes full-fledged market modernizing parties, such as New Era and the People's Party in Latvia or *Res Publica* in Estonia, from more nationally oriented neo-liberal parties such as the Czech ODS. As Peter Učeň (2003) has argued, however, such parties can, also be regarded as part of a broader phenomenon of pro-market '-anti-establishment right',[3] sometimes shading into the wider phenomenon of 'centrist populism', which emerges in response to the failures and compromise of established centre-right parties in the transformation process. The Czech Freedom Union (US) and Bulgaria's Simeon II National Movement can both be seen in this light.

The identification of such a variety of 'right-wing' forces is valuable in pointing up different patterns of post-communist development (see also Snyder and

Table 1.1 Typologies of 'right-wing' parties in post-communist Europe 1989–2001

| Vachudova (2001) | 'Communist right' | 'Moderate right' | 'Liberal conservatives' | 'Independence right' |
| Chan (2001) | 'Communist-conservatives' | 'Traditional conservatives' | 'Liberal conservatives' | 'Nationalist' |
Lewis (2000)	'Post-communist'	'Conservative'	'Liberal-conservative'	'Nationalist'
Hungary		Hungarian Democratic Forum (1990–4) FIDESZ – Hungarian Civic Party[1]		none
Poland		Solidarity Election Action (1996–2001)		
Czech Republic			Civic Democratic Party (ODS)	
Slovakia				Movement for a Democratic Slovakia (HZDS)
Croatia				Croatian Democratic Union (HDZ)
Serbia	Serbian Socialist Party (SPS)			
Romania	Social Democracy of Romania (PSDR)		Romanian Democratic Convention (CDR)[2]	
Bulgaria	Bulgarian Socialist Party (BSP)		Union of Democratic Forces (SDS)[2]	
Russia	Communist Party of the Russian Federation (KPRF)			

Notes
1 Categorized by Lewis as 'liberal-conservative'.
2 Lewis (2001).

Vachudova 1997; Vachudova 2005) and the way nationalist and conservative discourses were appropriated by different political forces in different national contexts. However, in other respects it is confusing and unsatisfactory. 'Chauvino-communist' former ruling parties, for example, while clearly 'conservative' in reacting against change, fall most comfortably within the comparative study of communist successor parties. Parties of the 'independence right' such as the Croatian HDZ and Slovak HDZS – despite the nostalgia of a radical nationalist fringe for wartime clerico-fascism – are regarded by most other scholars as simply populist or nationalist (see, for example, Lewis 2000a, 2003; Mudde 2001). This reflects their inconsistency or indifference towards issues unrelated to state-building and the possibility that their dominance may prove transitory, ultimately giving way to more conventional patterns of programmatic competition (Vachudova 2005). Moreover, these typologies imply, in certain party systems in the region, that all major parties and blocs, even when separated by clear ideological and political divisions, are in some sense 'right-wing' or 'conservative'. For this reason this study excludes parties of the 'communist right' and 'independence right' from discussion of the centre-right.[4]

The most recognizable centre-right forces from a West European perspective are the group of 'moderate right' or liberal-conservative parties. These parties define themselves as (centre) right formations and have been accepted into the main EU-level groupings, such as the European Peoples Party (EPP) and European Democrats (ED), founded by the West European centre-right. Both anecdotal and survey-based research (Kitschelt *et al.* 1999; Tworzecki 2002) suggest that in these cases understandings of 'right-wing' politics, at both elite and mass level, are consistent and have real programmatic and ideological content. However, even with this group of 'moderate right' parties, there is significant variation. In states such as Hungary and Poland 'right-wing' politics are understood in terms of Christian, conservative-national, national-populist or radical anti-communist positions (McManus-Czubińska *et al.* 2003; Fowler 2004; Szczerbiak 2004).[5] As we will see, in the Czech Republic, by contrast, the centre-right largely defined itself in terms of economic liberalism and anti-communism, seeing its 'conservatism' in its commitment to bringing the 'tried and tested' neo-liberalism of the West to a provincial society overly inclined towards collectivism. In Romania and Bulgaria the initial dominance after 1989 of 'chauvino-communist' former ruling parties – or groupings that emerged from them – saw the 'moderate right' emerge as heterogeneous 'democratic' alliances of traditionalist nationalists, historic parties, liberals and radical anti-communists (Roper 1998; Tismaneanu and Klingman 2001; Peeva 2001).[6] In new national states such as Slovakia and Croatia, despite the existence of strong nationalist, liberal and Christian forces, a self-identifying discourse of the right was largely absent from party politics during much of the 1990s. Here, political competition was polarized around a single set of issues relating to national statehood and its stewardship by Vladimír Mečiar's Movement for Democratic Slovakia (HZDS) and Franjo Tudjman's Croatian Democratic Community (HDZ) (Fisher 2000), what Vachudova terms the 'independence right'. Only since the electoral defeat of these movements in 1998 and 2000 by broad coalitions of parties with more conventional ideologies of left and right has a moderate right akin to that elsewhere in Central Europe begun to emerge. Both HZDS and HDZ have expressed a desire to reinvent themselves as West-European-style, Christian Democratic parties (Cvijetic 2000; Haughton 2001; Hipkins 2002; *RFE/RL Newsline* 22, 23 April 2002). At the same time, however, Christian Democratic and liberal groupings in the opposition alliances, which displaced them, also claim to be on the centre-right and have links with centre-right groupings in Western Europe. A similar pattern can be detected in the Baltic states, where, despite not enjoying the degree of dominance of HZDS or HDZ, conservative nationalists have tended to present themselves as champions of recovered national independence against a Russophone 'left' (Zake 2002). In such states a number of *new* centre-right parties with conventional programmatic appeals, such as the neo-liberal People's Party (TP) (Zake 2002) and later the 'New Era' party (Raubisko 2003) in Latvia, the business-oriented Alliance for the New Citizen (ANO) in Slovakia (Haughton 2003; Kopeček 2006) or the conservative NGO-cum-party Res Publica in Estonia (Taagepera 2006), have made electoral breakthroughs, although few have consolidated such early gains.

Defining the centre-right

As the discussion above suggests, scholars working on parties and party systems have produced the most coherent accounts of the re-emergence of left and right in East and Central Europe. However, these analyses tend to stress the historical and cultural specificity of parties of the 'right' and the patterns of variation that underlie this without considering how the right or centre-right should be conceptualized and defined. At bottom, the 'right' is a culturally and historically contingent category – part of a 'spatial metaphor' which can be applied to many types of political competition – the meaning of which has varied across different contexts. Nevertheless the term is rooted in the political discourse of most West European states and, since the fall of communism, has re-rooted itself in that of many, but not all, post-communist societies – in the main those geographically and historically closest to core West European states. However, for conceptual clarity a more worked-out definition of the right and centre-right in Central and Eastern Europe, however provisional, is clearly necessary.

Some definitions view the right in essentialist terms as a set of enduring philosophical tenets or inherent psychological predispositions (Eatwell and O'Sullivan 1989). However, these are often both abstract and largely struggle to account for variation and change on the right or to relate it to its social context (Kitschelt and McGann 1995). Other political scientists have sought to define the 'right' in terms of defined locations in political space, often depicted in two dimensions with crosscutting axes for socio-economic positions and 'values' issues (Kitschelt 1994; Kitschelt and McGann 1995; Krouwel 2005). However, despite their methodological rigour and usefulness for tracking changes in political alignments and patterns of competition, such analyses do little to explain the nature of political space, unless bolstered with additional sociological theories (Kitschelt 1994; Kitschelt and McGann 1995), and tend to identify the centre-right arbitrarily as a certain portion of political space (Wellhofer 1990).

The literature on 'party families' in Western Europe groups parties on the basis of shared social and historical origins and a common set of values and ideological predispositions (Lipset and Rokkan 1967; Mair and Mudde 1998). West European Christian Democratic parties, for example, emerged after 1945 on the basis of reformed Catholic confessional parties, which had themselves emerged in the late nineteenth century on the basis of social movements mobilized to resist the encroachments of secularizing liberal states in countries with an unresolved Church–state cleavage (Kalyvas 1996).[7] The 'centre-right' in a contemporary West European context thus comprises several party families: Christian Democracy, the conservative parties of Great Britain and Scandinavia, pro-market liberal parties such as the Dutch VVD, and, some would add, more recently formed 'national movements' such as the French Gaullists (Marks and Wilson 2000).

Adapting this methodology to identify parties of the right in CEE at first seems problematic.

Historically, the emergence of the political right in Western Europe and North and South America was associated the rise of distinct property-owning classes and a bourgeois civil society linked to the development of capitalism (Lipset and Rokkan 1967; Middlebrook 2000). The same is true of the re-emergence of the right in new or restored democracies such as West Germany, Italy and France after 1945 or Spain after 1975 (Wilson 1998). However, in East Central European countries the emergence of an organized political right after 1989 largely *preceded* the laying of social bases and the 'transition to capitalism'. Moreover, in one case, that of Poland, the right had a substantial working-class base, having largely emerged through the Solidarity movement (Wenzel 1998).

Moreover, whereas communist successor parties in Cental and Eastern Europe, despite their very different political trajectories since 1989, can be easily identified through their clear organizational continuities with former ruling parties and nominally socialist or social democratic ideology, parties of the right pose considerably greater problems of classification. However, as Vachudova (2001, 2005) notes, while their relationship with pre-communist right-wing traditions varies (see Held 1993), the most successful and electorally appealing parties of *the CEE centre-right do have a common historical and organizational origin, namely opposition to communist regimes before 1989 or mobilization against them in 1989–90*. Only in Romania, where intense repression, the implosion of Ceauşescu's personalistic regime in 1989 and the management of the transition from above by old elites as 'pre-emptive strike' closed down initial opportunities for a 'new' party of the centre-right, is this not the case. Here, historic parties of the right did play a significant role as the core of a centre-right bloc. However, this bloc was weak (Siani-Davies 1998) and required expansion beyond the historic parties that lay at its foundation to gain any degree of effectiveness.[8] Indeed, in most but not all states in the region, the left–right split in party competition post-1989 largely reflects the regime–opposition divide before 1989. The Czech Republic constitutes a partial exception in that the principal Czech communist successor party, the hard-line Communist Party of Bohemia and Moravia (KSČM), did not become the main party of the left. This implies that the centre-right in CEE must *be understood as essentially 'new' political forces, shaped by late communism and the subsequent politics of post-communist transformation*, rather than a simple throwback to the authoritarian conservatisms and integral nationalisms of the past.

Agrarians and liberals – the right's lost relations?

The need, in some cases, to consider (social-)liberal and agrarian parties as distinct third forces appears a complicating factor in defining the East Central European centre-right. In many West European party systems both the defence of agricultural interests and economic liberalism are components of broad centre-right blocs. In a number of countries in the region, small free market parties have constituted a 'West of centre', liberal camp, distinct from the more nationalist, conservative and statist positions of larger centre-right formations. Small agrarian parties were a feature of both the Hungarian and Polish party systems during 1990s, and similar parties made electoral gains in Croatia, Estonia and Latvia. As the Scandinavian experience demonstrates, agrarian formations have the potential to evolve into ideologically distinct, centre parties (Sitter and Batory 2004). To some extent this problem is offset by the limited electoral support of such parties (Lang 2000; Sitter and Batory 2003) and the trend, over time, for them to become aligned with (or absorbed into) broader centre-right or centre-left blocs, Hungary being the clearest example of this tendency. Here, the Independent Smallholders (FKGP) have disappeared as an electoral force and been absorbed into the dominant centre-right grouping FIDESZ (Fowler 2004), while the liberal Free Democrats are an increasingly established ally of the Hungarian Socialist Party. However, we should note that very often *new* centrist, liberal groupings have rapidly reoccupied the political space vacated by older, discredited (neo-)liberal groupings. Such newly ascendant liberal centrist parties included the Freedom Union (US) in the Czech Republic which entered parliament in 1998 (discussed in more detail in Chapter 6), and the Civic Platform (PO) in Poland, which became a parliamentary force in 2001. Moreover, after this 'unexpected earthquake' election, the unstable Polish party system contained *two* agrarian parties, the Polish Peasants' Party (PSL) and the radical-populist protest party, Self-Defence (Szczerbiak 2002). This suggests that patterns of competition that separate the liberals and agrarians from the broader centre-right are more durable than individual parties themselves (see Sitter 2002). The underlying pattern of party and party system formation in the region is therefore one in which the centre-right, in the absence of a strong class base, lacks the broad appeal and integrative ability of its West European counterparts. In certain respects, this is comparable to the historic pattern of party formation in Scandinavia, where a weak, sectorally and regionally divided bourgeoisie produced an array of weak conservative liberal, agrarian and denominational parties, rather than a unified centre-right (Luebbert 1991; Hancock 1998; Svasand 1998).

The centre-right and the extreme right

A further issue of definition is that of delineating the centre-right from the extreme right. In West European party systems, although the nature of the extreme right is disputed, this distinction seems empirically and conceptually clear. Most West European centre-right parties draw on the historic cleavages identified by Lipset and Rokkan (1967) and on the experience of post-1945 re-democratization. Extreme right, 'new populist' parties, by contrast, emerged only in the 1970s in response to cultural and social shifts in advanced capitalist societies (Betz 1994; Taggart 1995; Kitschelt and McGann 1995). It is, therefore, possible to define the extreme right in terms of a family of parties with its own distinct origins and characteristics (Mair and Mudde 2000). In post-communist East and Central Europe, it has been suggested, the distinction between the centre-right and the far-right is conceptually considerably less clear. This reflects both the legacy of the integral nationalism, authoritarian conservatism and collaboration with fascism that historically defined the right in many states of the region (Rogger and Weber 1966; Wolff and Hoensch 1987; Blinkhorn 1990) and the fact that both centre-right and extreme-right are products of post-1989 democratization. In many cases, however, it appears possible to make a clear *empirical* distinction, identifying the centre-right by its larger and broader electorate (generally in the range of 20–45 per cent), status as a (potential) participant in government and membership in European groupings of mainstream conservative and Christian Democratic parties. However, in Poland, where the dominant centre-right grouping, Solidarity Election Action (AWS) collapsed as an electoral force in 2001, to be effectively replaced by a number of new conservative/Christian parties with a more radical rhetoric of protest and medium-sized electorates of around 10 per cent (McManus-Czubińska *et al.* 2003; Szczerbiak 2004), such empirical yardsticks seem difficult to apply. This offers us one further conceptualization: to view the *centre-right as seeking to reconcile liberal-capitalist modernization with traditional moral values and specific local and national identities*, and the extreme right as seeking alternatives to such modernization (Minkelburg 2003; see also Schöpflin 2002).

The rise and decline of the new Czech right

This book seeks to give an analytical overview of the origins, development and success since 1989 of one national case, that of the centre-right in the Czech Republic. Although it will present the Czech right in a broadly comparative context, its principal concern will be to identify the mechanisms and processes through which new centre-right forces have emerged and sustained themselves in contemporary Central and Eastern Europe. In empirical terms the book will focus principally on the most successful party of the Czech right, the Civic Democratic Party (ODS) of the former Czech prime minister (and current president), Václav Klaus, which has been the principal party of the centre-right in the Czech Republic since its formation in early 1991 on the basis of the free market, anti-communist right wing of the broad Civic Forum movement that oversaw Czechoslovakia's transition to democracy in 1989–90. After convincingly winning the 1992 parliamentary elections in the Czech lands, ODS emerged as the dominant force in Czech politics and formed the linchpin of the - centre-right coalition governments that negotiated the division of Czechoslovakia in late 1992 and implemented many key policies of post-communist transformation in the Czech Republic before losing office in 1997. However, the book will also discuss the fortunes of a number of smaller Christian Democratic, liberal and anti-communist groupings to ODS which, with varying degrees of success, sought to provide right-wing alternatives to Klaus's party. These include both its junior coalition partners in the 1992–7 Czech governments, the Civic Democratic Alliance (ODA) and the Christian Democrats and more peripheral groups on the populist and anti-communist right such as the Republican Party (SPR-RSČ) and the Democratic Union (DEU). Whereas ODA, which initially shared many of ODS's neo-liberal positions, emerged from the pre-1989 dissident movement, the Christian Democratic Union – Czechoslovak People's Party (KDU-ČSL) had existed as a 'satellite' party under communism and had existed as an independent mass party before communism.

The Czech case in comparative context

The Czech centre-right stands out from others in the region because of its strong initial commitment to free market economics; identification as a Western-style conservative party defined by issues of post-communist transformation making little reference to historical traditions; and rapid early electoral and organizational success. In these respects it contrasts markedly with the position of dominant centre-right formations in neighbouring states such as Hungary and Poland, which emerged as conservative-nationalist groupings sceptical of the free market and preoccupied with social and moral issues and identity politics, which underwent more tortuous and difficult consolidation processes.

Indeed, although crosscutting issues such as civil society, national identity or European integration have often dominated Czech elite debates, left–right competition at the party system level in the Czech Republic has since the early 1990s been predominantly structured by divisions over the role of the state and the market. This has, moreover, been underpinned by growing correlation between social class and party choice. Although parties on the Czech centre-right (and centre-left) draw support from a range of social groups, there has been a clear tendency for better-educated, more urban and more prosperous groups of 'transition winners' to support the centre-right, and 'losers' to support the left and centre-left. This again contrasts with the position in states such as Hungary and Poland, where the electorate of the principal centre-right and centre-left forces are hetereogeneous cross-class alliances defined more by region, values or religiosity, which combine groups of marked economic 'winners' and 'losers'.

However, as in Poland and Hungary, there is an ideological and cultural division between neo-liberals and conservatives, although, in the Czech case, the neo-liberal right was the dominant partner and the conservative Christian Democrats the more minor player. Despite close ideological and organizational links with sister parties in Western Europe, the Czech Christian Democrats' minority status and pivotal position in the Czech party system often saw them assume the role of a centrist 'third force' balancing between the main blocs of right and left. For historical reasons relating both to the prewar social structure of the Czech lands and the post-1945 'restructuring' of the old bourgeois right (discussed in Chapter 2), post-communist Czech politics had neither a historic agrarian party nor large, distinct social constituencies of rural voters.[9] The incorporation of agrarian and rural interests into the re-emergent right was thus not a relevant issue in a Czech context. In terms of political success the Czech centre-right in the period 1991 to 2002 represents an intermediate case. Although in Klaus's ODS the Czech centre-right was represented from an early stage by a large, stable and well-institutionalized party, avoiding the fragmentation and instability of the Polish right, it failed to achieve the degree of ideological and organizational concentration seen in Hungary and for more than a decade after 1996 lacked both the cohesion and the breadth of support needed for either a majority centre-right government or even a durable minority administration (Fowler 2004; Szczerbiak 2004).[10]

The origins of the Czech New Right

In many ways, the Czech lands were an unlikely historical setting for the emergence of a strong 'Thatcherite' neo-liberal centre-right. In contrast to Hungary and Poland, where the post-1989 right was able to draw on powerful traditions of populism, conservative nationalism and political Catholicism dating back to the nineteenth century, 'right-wing' forces in the Czech lands were historically weak and divided. Kitschelt and his collaborators have argued that the dominance of traditional distributional issues in left–right competition in the Czech Republic was conditioned by the repressive, reform averse, nature of the 'bureaucratic-authoritarian' form of communism in Czechoslovakia. This in turn is seen as a product of relatively high levels of pre-communist socio-economic modernity in the Czech lands, which, it is argued, furnished the communist regime with both an effective state apparatus and mass support from a sizeable and well-organized working class. Left–right division after 1989, it is argued, thus centred on distributive issues, rather than moral or social issues, producing a free market, liberal-conservative centre-right, rather than a national-populist bloc. In Chapter 2, such legacy approaches are critically examined through the Czech case. The chapter argues that models of 'deep' historical causation tracing the nature of the right and of left–right party competition to pre-communist patterns of socio-economic modernization and state–society relations are unsustainable. It suggests that in a Czech and Central European context, the power of class and state–society relations to determine long-term historical pathways was overridden and disrupted by geo-politics, the crosscutting effect of nationalism in domestic politics and the imperatives of building and rebuilding new national states. Such legacy approaches, it is argued, are also too rigid in their analysis of communist regime types and overlook the contradictory nature of Czechoslovakia's communist regime, which generated powerful reformist forces as well as Stalinist and neo-Stalinist authoritarianism, and the 'critical juncture' opened by the conflict of such forces in 1968 during the 'Prague Spring' crisis.

The role of counter-elites after 1968

Rather than 'deep' patterns of causation rooted patterns of historical modernisation or state-society relations, Chapter 3 suggests that we should look to a more proximate cause for explanation of the emergence of the Czech new right after 1989: the nature of the counter-elite groupings and debates during the 1969–89 'normalization' era that followed the failure of Czechoslovakia Prague Spring reform movement of the 1960s. Drawing on earlier work on the importance of elites and their origins in the transformation of communist successor parties (Grzymala-Busse 2002) and the break-up of Czechoslovakia (Eyal 2003) as well as the wider literature on the role of ideas in politics, it examines the formation, realignment and discussions of counter-elites in late communist Czechoslovakia which laid the basis for the post-1989 Czech right. Like other analyses, it identifies dissident intellectuals and marginalized neo-liberal technocrats as key counter-elite groups.

The political thought of Czech dissidence has usually been analysed in terms of its supposedly anti-political philosophical conceptions, reflections on the nature of politics and totalitarianism, and notions of civic and Central European identity. Its political consequences are usually seen only in relation to the shared struggle to resist the communist regime and the carrying over of anti-political biases into democratic politics during the 1990s. Despite this, important elements of a proto-'right-wing' discourse can be identified in the thinking of dissidents who placed themselves outside the reform communist and 'democratic socialist' traditions. Václav Havel's critique of modernity and stress on authenticity and transcendence had some affinities with Western conservative thought. Elements of the traditional conservative Catholic critique of the left-liberal progressive cast of Czech non-communist thought informed Charter 77 documents and the intellectual development of more secular dissident thinkers on conservatism such as Petr Pithart and the dissident grouping around Pavel Bratinka and Daniel Kroupa. An equally significant counter-elite can be found in the generation of younger neo-liberal technocrats, including future Prime Minister and President Václav Klaus, who emerged on the margins of the 'Prague Spring'. Rather than being co-opted into the reformist wing of the regime or marginalized in opposition milieux strongly defined by the historical nationalism, as in Hungary and Poland, under Czechoslovakia's repressive post-1968 'normalization' this group formed part of an outwardly uncommitted 'grey zone' standing between official power structures and independent political opposition. Although they did not coalesce into politically distinct conservative or liberal groupings until 1988–9, the intellectual and political realignment of Czech counter-elites during the 'normalization' period, it is argued, created the potential for the emergence of a Czech right after 1989, which had already rejected many traditions of the historic Czech right and begun to adopt a range of Anglo-American models as a means of re-inventing a modern non-socialist Czech political discourse.

From civic movement to right-wing party

Moderate centre-right formations in contemporary Central and Eastern Europe are typically the 'successor parties' of opposition movements. The Czech Civic Democratic Party (ODS) was no exception. ODS emerged from the mass Civic Forum (OF) movement formed in Prague in November 1989 by dissidents, actors, students, social scientists and economists. However, the emergence of stable parties of the centre-right from social movements, both historically and in contemporary Central and Eastern Europe, cannot be regarded as the automatic outcome of successful democratization, historical legacies or underlying social cleavages. Much research on civic mobilization in Eastern Europe attests to the difficulty of transforming broad movement organizations into durable party structures. However, the Civic Democratic Party emerged on precisely this basis. Chapter 4 seeks to identify the reasons for its relative success in party building. It focuses on the formation of the 'right' within a fragmenting Civic Forum in 1990–1 which united around Federal Finance Minister Václav Klaus under the banner of conventional, hierarchical party organization, the primacy of rapid economic reform, radical decommunization and resistance to Slovak demands for greater autonomy within the Czechoslovak federation. The chapter locates the origins of the Civic Forum right wing in policy divisions between rival elite groups, elite–grassroots tensions and the Forum's unresolved efforts to reconcile contradictory organizational and political imperatives of acting as both governing 'party' and inclusive social movement.

The temporary dominance of the right

Having convincingly won the June 1992 parliamentary elections in the Czech lands, Klaus's ODS – and those parties and politicians inspired by the Anglo-American New Right more generally – seemed to enjoy an unassailable intellectual and political dominance. Whilst the combined electoral support of Klaus's Civic Democrats and the smaller, neo-liberal coalition partner the Civic Democratic Alliance never exceeded 35–36 per cent, their political power was extensive. The two parties controlled key economic ministries and exercised considerable influence in the Czech state bureaucracy. They faced a largely supportive and uncritical media and a fragmented opposition seemingly unable to offer any coherent alternative policies. After the split of Czechoslovakia in 1992, the independent Czech Republic thus appeared to be an island of conservatism and free market radicalism in a sea of nationalism, populism and post-communism. To many, the strength of right-wing forces at such an early stage in the transition process when economic and political institutions and administrative structures were in flux suggested that the Czech right would 'lock-in' its dominance over the longer term. Chapter 5 analyses the consolidation of centre-right parties as political organizations in 1991–2 and analyses the role of transformation policies such as privatization, decommunization and the reform of public administration as resources for party-building and political competition. The chapter argues that although Klaus's ODS quickly achieved an unusual measure of dominance on the right, based largely on organizational and political resources inherited from Civic Forum and a stable 'stratarchical' division of power between elite and grassroots, it failed to incorporate smaller liberal and anti-communist groupings or fully choke off their resources. The electoral breakthrough achieved in 1992 by the Civic Democratic Alliance (ODA) institutionalized the division of the Czech liberal right, providing a framework for competition between rival right-wing transformation policies in government. The relative success of the Christian Democrats (KDU-ČSL), the third partner in the coalition, in reinventing themselves as champions of a German-style 'social market', rather than remaining a moribund former satellite party with an essentially confessional worldview, added to the growing dynamic of right-wing disunity. In the June 1996 elections, the centre-right coalition narrowly failed to retain its parliamentary majority and was forced to continue as a minority administration 'tolerated' by the opposition Social Democrats, who had consolidated the electorates of a number of failing centrist, centre-left and regionalist groupings around themselves. The rise of the Social Democrats, the chapter argues, highlights both the relative balance between liberal and social-market-oriented voters and the fact that the numerous advantages of incumbency enjoyed by right-wing parties failed to generate the 'increasing returns' necessary to translate the right's early dominance into a lasting outcome.

Decline and deadlock

By the late 1990s it had became evident that, despite the rapidity and scope of Czech market reforms, the policies of the Klaus government had created an under-regulated, under-capitalized, inefficient private sector, dominated by politically connected, rent-seeking groups. The resultant economic malaise both added to the political momentum of the Czech Social Democrats and aggravated relations between Klaus's party and its two smaller coalition partners, the Christian Democrats and the Civic Democratic Alliance (ODA), both of which developed programmatic positions strongly critical of the perceived failings of ODS. In November 1997 Klaus's alleged complicity in a major party financing scandal finally prompted his coalition partners to withdraw from the government and caused a split in ODS itself. Similar irregularities in the smaller Civic Democratic Alliance ignited factional tensions so explosively that ODA rapidly disintegrated as a political force. Claiming to have been unaware of the irregularities, Václav Klaus successfully mobilized grassroots party members to resist pressure for his resignation, prompting his defeated opponents ODS to found a new party, the Freedom Union (US).

In early parliamentary elections in June 1998, despite recovering support apparently lost to the Freedom Union, ODS was out-polled by the Social Democrats, who, for the first time, became the largest Czech party. Although centre-right parties regained a theoretical parliamentary majority because of the collapse of the far right, such were the tensions between them that Klaus unexpectedly opted to allow a minority Social Democratic government to take office on the basis of a written pact, the 'Opposition Agreement'. Galvanized by the two larger parties' plans for electoral reform, the Christian Democrats and Freedom Union responded by founding a new electoral alliance, the Quad-Coalition (4K), with the rump Civic Democratic Alliance and the small Democratic Union (DEU) party. By 1999–2000, the Quad-Coalition seemed to be emerging as a powerful moderate conservative bloc, in tune with public dissatisfaction over the cartel-like character of the 'Opposition Agreement', which might be able displace ODS as the principal force on the Czech right. Klaus's party, however, underwent its own form of realignment, combining its traditional neo-liberal demands with the new theme of defending 'national interests' against the EU, immigration and Western-style multi-culturalism. The Social Democrats won the June 2002 parliamentary under a new leader, Vladimír Špidla, confirming the electoral eclipse of the ODS under Klaus as well as the minority status of the Freedom Union and the Christian Democrats, whose Quad-Coalition alliance collapsed shortly before the elections. Špidla abandoned cooperation with the ODS to work with its two centre-right rivals, who became junior partners in a coalition government with a narrow parliamentary majority united by a common commitment to rapid EU membership. In the face of recriminations from his party's increasingly powerful regional organizations, Klaus announced in October 2002 that he would step down as ODS leader to campaign for the Czech presidency due to be vacated by Václav Havel after a final term of office. In February 2003, against expectations, Klaus was narrowly elected President by the Czech parliament with the support of Communist deputies and dissident Social Democrats. In a further unexpected development, the ODS congress elected Senator Miroslav Topolánek, a pragmatic politician with a regional power base, to replace Klaus as leader. Although he was a politically weaker figure than Klaus, under Topolánek ODS developed a raft of policies for further domestic reforms including proposals for flat taxation and welfare reform and seemed well placed to displace a disunited and politically accident prone Social-Democrat-led administration, which saw two Prime Ministers depart in rapid succession – Vladimír Špidla in 2004 after disastrous European election results, and his successor Stanislav Gross in 2005 after revelations of financial impropriety. In 2005–6, however, the tougher, more populist campaigning of Gross's successor, Jiří Paroubek, allowed the Social Democrats to make a significant electoral revival. The 2006 elections, although won by ODS, once again produced parliamentary deadlock with no viable parliamentary majority of either right or left.

Chapter 6 surveys the decline and realignment of the Czech centre-right in this period through the internal politics of the Civic Democratic Party and other groupings and the internal debates of the right about its own role, identity and strategy. Tensions over issues such as the transition from the extraordinary politics of economic transformation to more balanced 'everyday politics'; the relationship of the right to civil society, the middle class and the nation; the relative importance of national and local party elites; the role of ideology; and the extent to which the right could (and should) ideologically and organizationally unify against the left can be traced back to the very earliest days of the first Klaus government. The disintegration of the right in 1996–8 – and its failure to rebuild a centre-right majority coalition – it is argued, owes as much to the failure to resolve these issues and the ensuing break-down of elite and party cohesion as it does to the corruption scandals and policy failures of the 1990s or the resilience of the Czech centre-left.

The ideology of the Czech New Right

Ideology plays an important role in both framing political action and giving cohesion and identity to political organizations. This is particularly the case in periods of far-reaching change such as post-communist transformation. Successful centre-right parties in East and Central Europe have formulated distinct new right-wing ideologies drawing on historic conservative and nationalist discourses, ideas familiar from Western contexts and issues of post-communist transition. For much of the 1990s the Civic Democratic Party (ODS) presented itself as a neo-liberal party inspired by the British and US New Right, albeit with a nationalist subtext stressing the congruence of the Czech national character and the free market. Its early ideological discourse argued that the free market, political parties and ideologies of left and right were 'tried and tested' and 'standard' forms of organization, which could, and should, be quickly re-established in the Czech lands. However, it explicitly rejected traditional Czech political thought, including its conservative, liberal and nationalist strands, as too provincial, collectivist, messianistic to be relevant to contemporary Czech society, stressing the 'revolutionary' character of its conservatism in breaking with the immediate past.

Like other centre-right formations in CEE, the ideology of ODS also incorporated early calls for radical decommunization, which were linked, as elsewhere in the region, to aspirations for a speeding up or radicalization of reform. In the Czech case these conflicts were partly played out in the disintegration of the Civic Forum movement and the foundation of ODS in 1990–1. However, the imperatives of historical justice central to decommunization frequently conflict with those of liberal market reform, making them a potentially divisive issue *within* the emergent CEE centre-right if not combined in a coherent ideological narrative able to pre-empt populist anti-communist right-wing alternatives.

However, like other successful centre-right parties in the region, as well as accommodating radical anti-communist populism, ODS used anti-communism in more sustained and sophisticated ways as an ideological device to frame post-communist transformation as a continuation of the struggle against communism and the communist *nomenklatura*. Unlike the centre-right in Poland and Hungary, the Czech right did not face a reformed communist successor party as its principal competitor. It thus presented its centrist and social democratic opponents more subtly as proponents of 'Third Ways' between Soviet-style communism and the West European mainstream in a way reminiscent of the failed reform communism of the 1960s.

A further ideological fault line running through the right across Europe is that between liberalism and conservatisms stressing the centrality of the Nation (or the People) as a historic or moral community. Most large, established centre-right parties in Western Europe successfully combine these conflicting elements in both their ideologies and their electoral constituencies. However, in Central and Eastern Europe the centre-right is typically more fractured. In states in the region such as Hungary and Poland there is a historic cleavage between a dominant conservative-national (national-populist) camp and a weaker liberal camp, which has often weakened the post-1989 right.[11] This division was also present in the Czech context, albeit in reverse. The bulk of the Czech centre-right was liberal or neo-liberal in outlook. However, the small, but well-established Christian Democratic party formed a small, but distinct moderate conservative camp. The positions developed by the Christian Democrats and sympathetic secular thinkers outside the party offered an alternative reading of Czech national identity and post-communist transformation, stressing the long-term, organic nature of political and social change and the role of civic values and local civil society in underpinning it. With the development of the Quad-Coalition (4K), this ideological rapprochement between liberalism and the moderate conservatism of Czech Christian Democracy gathered pace, but failed to develop a durable alternative synthesis. A somewhat different rearticulation of liberalism and conservatism can be found in the Civic Democrats' revival in the late 1990s of traditional Czech nationalist paradigms juxtaposing the interests of the Czech nation to those of Germany and the German-speaking world and the exploration by Klaus and others of themes such as the defence of 'national cohesion' against multi-culturalism and Europeanization.

The Czech right, Europeanization and globalization

Many centre-right parties in Western Europe emerged on the basis of cleavages associated with classical socio-economic modernization and national state formation. Centre-right parties in post-communist East and Central Europe have, by contrast, formed against a background of social, cultural and technological changes that can broadly be termed 'post-modernization', many of which call into question the importance of the national state (Inglehart 1997; Giddens 2002). Of these, globalization and the related process of European integration (Bieler 2000), which led to the accession to the European Union of ten CEE states in 2004–7, are by far the most significant. These processes not only aggravated historical sensitivities in a region where the formation of national states was historically belated, contested or incomplete, but posed particular challenges to many parties of the centre-right in the region.[12] Although few centre-right formations were actively opposed to EU membership, early comparative research on party-based euroscepticism highlighted a tendency for them to be more eurosceptic than their counterparts in Western Europe (Taggart and Szczerbiak 2002; see also Kopecký and Mudde 2002). Many disliked the far-reaching transferral and restriction of national sovereignty required by EU membership; the bureaucratic centralization and likely power of large West European states (in particular, Germany) in an enlarged EU; the marginalization of local businesses and elites; and the erosion of national and local identities under the competitive pressures of the Single Market. Parties with strong free market commitments, such as the Czech Civic Democrats (ODS) have also argued that the EU is over-regulated and 'socialist' or 'collectivist' in its economic thinking.

Beyond a loosely shared set of eurosceptic concerns, however, centre-right parties in the region seemed to have differing geo-political and European orientations, reflecting both ideological differences and older historical alignments. Both the Czech ODS and the Bulgarian ODS tended to view themselves as conservative parties on British or US lines and are strongly Atlanticist. In the Czech case this arguably reflects historic anxieties about German domination of the Central European region at the expense of Czech interests. Conservative national parties, by contrast – if they have a vision going beyond the preservation of national distinctness and independence – have closer affinities with Gaullism and German Christian Democracy. They are more suspicious of the US role in Europe and, notwithstanding reservations over European political integration, show a greater willingness to accept the Franco-German axis.[13]

Chapter 8 traces the evolving views of the Civic Democratic Party on European integration from Václav Klaus's vaguely formulated critiques of the early 1990s, combining neo-liberalism and a sense of smallness and geo-political vulnerability, to the more elaborated 'eurorealist' positions critiquing the accession process developed by younger figures around Jan Zahradil in 2000–2, which centred on the concept of 'national interests'. It notes how, following accession to the Union in 2004 and the foundering of the EU Constitution in 2005, ODS eurosceptics focused on wider projects to remake the EU through 'flexible integration' or the creation of a new 'Organization of European States', but were increasingly marginalized by a party leadership preoccupied with domestic issues. Although comparatively 'soft', Czech centre-right euroscepticism is, nevertheless, puzzling, given the generally pro-integration stance of most of its electorate and the Europhile positions of liberal and pro-market parties elsewhere in the CEE. The chapter argues that the ideology versus strategy debates informing much of the literature on party euroscepticism difficult to apply to new centre-right parties in CEE such as ODS. It concludes, however, that ODS's euroscepticism can be seen as in part an elite-driven ideological project with little wider resonance and in part a mobilization strategy intended to recapture the right's role as a vehicle for broad national goals.

2   Historical legacies and the Czech right

Introduction

Almost from the very outset, analysts sought to explain emerging patterns of political competition after the fall of communism in Central and Eastern Europe as a product of history and historical legacies. Early hypotheses included the 'unfreezing' of pre-communist traditions and divisions; an unstable politics of populism and anomie rooted in the social levelling and culture of distrust engendered by failed one-party regimes (Jowitt 1992); or a varied set of sub-cultures each shaped by different aspects of the pre-communist and communist past (Korosényi 1991; Schöpflin 1993; Janos 1994). In this chapter, I seek to examine the historical origins of the post-1989 Czech right and to relate them to such analyses. In doing so, I will suggest that even the most sophisticated historical legacy approach, that developed by Herbert Kitschelt and his collaborators, faces significant difficulties in formulating a convincingly 'deep' historical explanation linking historical pathways and legacies to post-communist party politics. Kitschelt's work, I will suggest, tends to overemphasize aspects of classical political and social modernization familiar from a West European context, neglecting the impact of external, geo-political influences and the crosscutting effects of ethnicity and nationalism. Moreover, I will argue, detailed examination of the historical record highlights important historical breaks and moments of contingency that Kitschelt's account glosses over. Ultimately, I will suggest, the case of the Czech right demonstrates that a strongly determined historical path to patterns of left–right politics after 1989 can sometimes only convincingly be traced from the late communist period following the collapse of Czechoslovak reform communism in 1968–9.

Regime legacies and the origins of right and left

Many early models relating party political patterns of left–right competition in post-communist democracies to historical and structural factors (Jowitt 1992; Schöpflin 1994; Janos 1994) were plagued with limitations and inconsistencies. Leaving aside the erroneous expectations of atavistic extreme right-wing nationalism noted in Chapter 1, almost all failed convincingly to explain the relative influence of different historical periods, account for the marked variation in the post-1989 politics of different post-communist states or clearly explain *how* the influence of the past shaped outcomes in the post-communist present. Most also failed to consider the impact on patterns of left–right competition of political processes occurring *after* the fall of communism such as different models of transition from communism (Werning 1996); the emergence of divisions between 'winners and losers' in post-communist economic reform (Kitschelt 1992a); or the break-up of multinational federation such as Yugoslavia and Czechoslovakia (Evans and Whitefield 1993).

The work of Herbert Kitschelt and his collaborators (Kitschelt 1995, 2002; Kitschelt *et al.* 1999) represented a major breakthrough in the comparative study of post-communist party politics. Not only did it measure different patterns of left–right competition in several East Central European states, it also presented a wide-ranging comparative explanation for such variation, elegantly integrating a range of historical and social factors. Like earlier analysts of West European party development (Lipset and Rokkan 1967), Kitschelt and his co-authors (1999: 27–8) took as their starting point the varying patterns of socio-economic and political modernization that emerged across Europe during nineteenth and early twentieth centuries. These, it was suggested, established distinct patterns of state–society relations which set the societies of Central and East Europe on varying historical pathways, which influenced both the nature of the communist regimes that emerged from the late 1940s, the nature of their demise in 1989 and, ultimately, the types of left and right that emerged under post-communist democracy. The operation of these pathways has been traced in more detail in relation to the development of communist successor parties (Grzymala-Busse 2002; Kitschelt 2002; March 2006).

Kitschelt's framework can, however, easily be redescribed with a focus on centre-right parties. For Hungary and Poland, for example, Kitschelt and his collaborators take as their starting point the incomplete nature of social modern-ization in gentry-dominated semi-agrarian societies before communism. Such social structures, it is argued, ultimately saw peasant and agrarian parties rather than socialist or bourgeois parties emerge as the dominant political forces in 1945. Strong agrarian populist traditions combined with the coercive nature of modernization imposed under communism led to the conservation of populist, ruralist and conservative discourses in the opposition circles and movements that developed from 1960s. These discourses constituted a cultural and ideological reservoir for reconstituting a conservative-national right after 1989, but pre-served the historical division with liberal forces committed to free markets and lifestyle pluralism, historically represented by the weak urban middle class and later, under communism, by the nonconformist intelligentsia. Moreover, Kitschelt and his co-thinkers suggest, the lack of social support for communism in such semi-modern societies created 'national-accommodationist' communist regimes, whose ruling parties permitted a degree of freedom to the traditional intelligentsia and the Catholic Church and embraced elements of market reform. After 1989 communist successor parties in these countries themselves initiated and embraced economic reform, blurring the socio-economic dimension of left–right competition, reinforcing the emergence of a nationalistic, morally conservative right inclined to etatism and social protection.

In the Czech lands, by contrast, Kitschelt and his collaborators claimed, the existence of relatively modern social and political structures before communism set Czech society on path towards post-communist party competition between a free market centre-right and a social-democratic centre-left. By the late nineteenth century, the Czech provinces of Bohemia and, to a lesser extent, Moravia had undergone considerable industrial and urban development, emerging as two of the most developed regions in the Austrian Empire. This led to a pattern of political and social mobilization before communism that Kitschelt and his collaborators characterize as 'the simultaneous mobilization of bourgeois and proletarian political forces around class-based parties' (1999: 26). When a communist regime was established in Czechoslovakia in 1948, the traditions of a modern mass labour movement and a legal mass communist party resulted in a communist regime with relatively high levels of popular support and social embeddedness. Mass socialist and communist traditions, combined with the administrative effectiveness of a modern state apparatus as a tool for repression and the threat from historically strong bourgeois and non-Marxist socialist parties, produced what Kitschelt and his collaborators term a 'bureaucratic-authoritarian' communist regime that was both repressive and averse to any element of market reform.[1] When Czechoslovakia's communist regime finally collapsed in November 1989, its 'bureaucratic-authoritarian' legacies, it is argued, produced a pattern of left–right party politics centring on issues of economic transformation. Issues of morality, national identity and religion that informed right-wing politics elsewhere in the region had largely been resolved through modernization processes that took place *before* communism. By contrast, the absence of economic reform in Czechoslovakia during the communist period, and the deeply rooted historic identity of both the largely unreconstructed Czech Communists and the more moderate Czech Social Democrats as defenders of the working class, made marketization the defining issue separating left and right. This division was reinforced by a widespread, if not entirely historically accurate, sense among Czechs that they had fallen behind societies once less developed than their own.

Despite its success in integrating causal factors and establishing a clear cause and effect, often absent in 'shallower' analyses focusing on more immediate causes (Kitschelt 2003), the Kitschelt framework suffered a number of apparent weaknesses. First, although ostensibly based on the legacies of *communist* regimes, on closer examination it was *pre-communist* patterns of modernization that emerged as the key variable shaping the historical pathways that led to varying patterns of left–right competition after 1989 (Hanley 2000a; Munck 2001; Kopstein 2003). Despite their seemingly radical transformation of states and societies in the region, communist regimes, it appeared, were thus merely 'mirrors of the pre-communist order' which had not fundamentally altered the underlying trajectories of their societies (Kopstein 2003: 233, 238–9). Second, although the empirical measurement and mapping of patterns of party competition in East Central Europe after 1989 conducted by Kitschelt and his co-researcher was detailed and rigorous, the historical research presented to identify the historical paths of causation for these patterns was much less extensive.[2] Finally, some critics objected, Kitschelt's stress on the domestic dynamics of state and society overlooked the impact of contemporary geo-political factors such as the proximity of Western Europe and processes of European integration (Kopstein 2003).[3]

There is therefore a strong case for re-examining and reassessing Kitschelt's framework. The Czech case – and in particular the case of the Czech right – provides a useful test of the theory. The Czech case is the only fully developed example of the 'bureaucratic-authoritarian' path through communism and should present a close empirical fit to the comparative category outlined.[4] When compared with the closed oligarchical pre-communist political systems found elsewhere in the region, the more open character of political competition in the Czech lands also provides a clearer, more accessible historical record against which the mechanisms of 'deep' causation postulated by Kitschelt *et al.* can be tested. Retracing the historical pathways leading to the Czech party system of 1990s through a focus on parties of the right also represents a more challenging test for legacy approaches than earlier studies of communist successor parties, because the post-1989 right lacked the obvious institutional or ideological continuities enjoyed by former ruling parties and their satellites.

The historical weakness of the Czech right

On first examination, Czech political history seems to confirm the linkage between pre-communist modernization and receptiveness to right-wing (neo-)liberalism after 1989 identified by Kitschelt and his collaborators. Historically, 'conservatism' had little historical resonance in the Czech lands except as a synonym for reactionary nineteenth-century Austrian rulers, whom traditional Czech national historiography traditionally depicted as holding back the Czech nation. Moreover, the social forces that formed the bases of the conservative right in many European countries, such as conservative aristocratic landowners and the Catholic Church were politically weak or absent in the Czech case.

The (re-)emergence of the Czechs as a political nation from the early nineteenth century onwards largely excluded the aristocracy from the Czech nation; instead, this key social force was largely perceived as a pro-Habsburg interest. Similarly, the Catholic Church, although institutionally and numerically dominant in the Czech lands, came to be viewed as a pro-Austrian body, ambivalent or indifferent to the aspirations of the nation for political and cultural self-determination. Key intellectual and political figures such as Tomáš Masaryk, Czechoslovakia's first President, argued that Czech national traditions were essentially rooted in Protestantism and its Hussite precursor, rather than Catholicism. Estrangement from the Catholic Church and the loss of a native aristocracy were widely viewed as making the Czech nation inherently 'plebeian' and democratic. Thus, by the late nineteenth century economic and political liberalism was firmly rooted in the Czech lands, drawing support from an increasingly important Czech commercial and industrial bourgeoisie (Urban 1982). As in much of nineteenth-century Europe, Czechs looked to advanced free market democracies of Britain and the United States for both practical and intellectual models of liberalism (Pfaff 1996: 19–30, 69–88, 205–41).

In many ways, Czech party development before 1938 also broadly conforms to classic West European models (Duverger 1954; Lipset and Rokkan 1967; see also Rokkan 1970; Flora *et al.* 1999). In organizational terms, Czech parties followed a broadly West European pattern in moving from small elite groupings to mass parties. The first Czech political parties, formed in the 1860s, were thus loose-knit liberal and conservative groupings of 'notables' based on upper-class networks and factions in provincial assemblies elected on a restricted and indirect franchise (Garver 1978; Malíř 1996). As in Western Europe by the late nineteenth century, the modernization and differentiation of society and the progressive extension of the franchise saw once dominant elite and upper-class groupings such as the 'Old Czechs' and liberal-nationalist 'Young Czech' Party challenged by mass class- and interest-based parties (Garver 1978). As elsewhere in Europe (Lipset and Rokkan 1967), these mass parties reflected both new and historic cleavages which were opened up and politicized by modernization and democratization. The rise of the Social Democrats and National Socialists reflected the growing cleavage between capital and labour produced by industrialization. The emergence of Agrarians and Christian Socials reflected urban–rural cleavages and the estrangement of the Catholic Church from an increasingly secular society and political establishment (Garver 1978; Dostal 1998).[5]

However, despite reflecting the classic cleavages generated by the modernization of state and society, Czech party development was also strongly *crosscut* by the struggle for national self-determination and by the need to 'build' and defend the Czech(oslovak) national state belatedly founded in 1918 (Kopeček 2002; Hloušek 2002). Czech liberalism was thus always historically highly 'impure', suffused and intertwined with nationalism (Urban 1995: 15–27). Liberal institutions – parliamentarianism, constitutionalism, free trade, the free market – were thus often viewed as a *means* to achieving national autonomy and related social goals rather than ends in themselves. Political forces that might have coalesced into a broad conservative or liberal Czech 'right wing' were impeded to a considerable extent from doing so by the prominence of the 'National Question', a pattern of fragmentation also detectable on the Czech left. The landowning and liberal middle-class elites, which formed the first Czech political parties from the mid nineteenth century onwards created 'national' formations primarily defined as vehicles for achieving national autonomy. The centrality of the National Question and Czech parties' lack of access to real political power in the semi-authoritarian 'dual track' Austrian Imperial political system (Garver 1978) limited their ability to integrate class and group interests in a durable, broad liberal or conservative formation. This tendency was reinforced by the growing trend, particularly after 1918, for the Czech intelligentsia and liberal professions to support the left-wing National Socialist Party whose mix of progressive social policies, liberal humanitarianism and Czech(oslovak) nationalism, arguably best reflected their interests and preoccupations.

The 'right wing' of the historic Czech party system, formed in the nineteenth century and inherited by the Czechoslovak Republic, was thus represented by an array of parties with different historical and social roots, a pattern of party system development, which, to some extent, paralleled that in Scandinavia, rather than core West European states (Luebbert 1991).[6] The three most significant of these were: Czechoslovak National Democracy, formed in 1918 from the merger of a number of the declining traditional nationalist groupings (Blackwood 1990; Čechurová 1999);[7] the Catholic-based People's Party, whose support was concentrated in rural Catholic regions; and the Agrarian Party which, of the three, came closest to being a broad party of the right and, in the mid-1930s, even adopted a conscious strategy of creating a right-wing conservative bloc (Dostal 1998). However, these efforts met with little success and, despite being the largest party for much of the interwar period, the Agrarian vote never exceeded 15 per cent of the Czechoslovak electorate (Dostal 1998). At the ideological level, the closest equivalents to a broad historic ideology of the right were a line of Catholic-oriented, political thought associated with Josef Pekař (1870–1937) and forms of right-wing integral nationalism (Blackwood 1990; Čechurová 1999).

The crosscutting effect of the 'National Question' in Czech politics continued to make itself felt in the governing coalitions in interwar Czechoslovakia. Although shifting in composition, these coalitions tended to oppose 'state-forming' (*státotvorné*) Czech-based parties to German and Slovak parties critical of the new state, rather than blocs of left or right, or bourgeois and socialist parties. Only with the short-lived entry into Czechoslovak coalition politics of German Christian Socials and German Agrarians in 1927–8 did a recognizably 'right-wing' government, excluding parties of the left, take office, the so-called Gentleman's Coalition. The intense 'partification' of the state that resulted from its more or less permanent occupancy by five 'state-forming' Czech parties (the *pětka*) further undercut the programmatic class politics characteristic of modern left and right competition in Western Europe, promoting party clientelism and the extensive 'partification' of the state apparatus (Hruby 1984). Historically, therefore, the Czech 'right wing' remained politically fragmented, organizationally underdeveloped and intellectually marginalized, failing to develop the broad appeal of bourgeois parties elsewhere in Europe. Indeed, for this reason Luebbert (1991: 291–5) characterizes prewar Czechoslovakia's regime as a 'social democracy', rather than a 'liberal democracy'.

The impact of war on the historic right

Although long-term changes in the international economy can slowly bring about domestic political realignments (Rogowski 1989), in most contexts the changing international *political* environment is regarded as a secondary influence, which essentially complements historically rooted patterns of domestic development (Collier 1993). In a Central and East European context, however, the international geo-political context shaped patterns of competition between domestic social and political forces far more profoundly. As one historian has noted, the Second World War in Central and Eastern Europe 'constituted and spawned a 'social, economic and cultural revolution', which 'ripped the fabric of interwar societies, reconfigured social hierarchies, reorganized economies, [and] reshuffled political allegiances' (Abrams 1995: 624, 629; see also Gross 1989). In the Czech case, the 1938–48 period saw semi-authoritarian experiments in 'managed' party competition alternating with full-blown totalitarianism which undermined and partially eliminated the historic Czech right, ideologically, organizationally and socially. Among the key impacts of the period were a weakening of the Czech bourgeoisie and a strengthening of the working class, a strengthening of the state against society, and a re-articulation of patterns of left-wing collaboration in a form which ultimately disadvantaged the right.

In September 1938 at Munich, France, Britain and Italy agreed to Hitler's demands for the immediate annexation of Czechoslovakia's ethnically German border regions (the Sudetenland) to Germany. Deserted by its international allies, the Czechoslovak government pragmatically acquiesced to the agreement. The Munich Agreement not only deprived Czechoslovakia of much of its economic potential, population and military defences, but led to the collapse and the restructuring of its political and party system. During the so-called 'Second Republic', the new government of the rump 'Czecho-Slovakia' sought to create a pro-German, ethnically defined Slav state based on a system of 'authoritarian democracy' (Rataj 1997) under which the Communist Party was banned and all remaining Czech parties, more or less voluntarily, merged into two broad parties: a ruling Party of National Unity (SNJ) on the right and the National Labour Party (NSP) on the left as a 'loyal opposition'. The SNJ was based on the Agrarians, National Democrats, the People's Party and the small Tradesmen's Party. The NSP was formed by the Social Democrats and parts of the National Socialist Party (Rataj 1998: 32–5). Although for the first time Czech politics was formally organized into blocs of left and right, the political system of the short-lived Second Republic was wholly non-competitive and the merging of pre-1938 parties into larger groupings was motivated by a desire for national unity, rather than a clearer left–right division.

On 15 March 1939 the Czech lands were occupied by the German army and incorporated into Nazi Germany as the Protectorate of Bohemia and Moravia. Under the Protectorate all representative bodies, including political parties, were dissolved and Czech political organizations were replaced by a single all-embracing, mass organization, the National Fellowship (NS) (*Národní souručenství*), which, after 1942, functioned only as a cultural and educational trust. Efforts by Czech collaborators, such as Emanuel Moravec, to legitimize the Protectorate by developing the ideas of the 'Second Republic' into a radical totalitarian, pro-German Czech 'national' ideology foundered on the absence of any meaningful political sphere for Czechs and the clearly coercive nature of the Protectorate regime. More sophisticated later attempts during the war to co-opt Czech middle-class anti-communism through front organizations such as the League Against Bolshevism failed for similar reasons, arguably serving only to delegitimize traditional right-wing anti-communist discourses.

The social and economic policies of the occupation replaced the balanced class structure and regulated market economy of interwar Czechoslovakia with a 'caste-like system' based on racial and occupational categories and an etatistic war economy with extensive German ownership and control. In social terms the interregnum of the 'Second Republic' and German occupation weakened the traditional Czech middle class and intelligentsia through a mix of policies, such as the closure of Czech universities in 1939, intended to undermine national identity and solidarity, and social and economic policies, which transferred ownership and control of capital away from Czechs, but expanded industrial production, and hence the industrial working class. By 1944 the number of industrial workers in the Czech lands had increased by 53 per cent since 1939 (Krejčí and Machonin 1996: 140–2). The numerical growth of the working class combined with wage, social and rationing policies that gave preferential treatment to industrial workers produced a radical proletarianization and egalitarianization of Czech society. The experience of wartime occupation saw '... a social structure already eroded in the 1930s by ... economic recession shattered under the pressure of war and the foreign totalitarian regime' (Krejčí and Machonin 1996: 145).

Postwar 'People's Democracy' and the remnants of the right

In the Czech lands, as in much of postwar Europe, the demise of the pro-Nazi occupation regime in 1945 saw an initial post-war settlement based on a broad national coalition, which included both communists and non-communists. However, in contrast to West European states such as Italy, Germany and France where new, broad-based democratic centre-right forces, such as Christian Democracy and Gaullism, emerged to replace the divided and discredited prewar right and share power with the left, in the Czech lands right-wing forces were largely excluded from the postwar political settlement. Instead of the 'mixed economies', welfare capitalism and democratic corporatism adopted across much of Western Europe after 1945, Czechoslovakia adopted a semi-authoritarian political system of 'People's Democracy' and a set of social and economic policies, which continued and reinforced wartime trends towards the proletarianization and etatization of Czech society. The effect of this regime was to exclude the bulk of the historic right from power, to close the bourgeois, non-socialist part of the political field to new entrants and to undermine the social bases of the Czech right.

Wartime discussions between non-communist Czech resistance groups and politicians in the Czechoslovak government in exile in the London and the United States had concentrated on how prewar democratic and social structures could be re-engineered to prevent any repetition of ignominious state collapse seen in 1938. The most widely shared set of responses, articulated most eloquently by Czechoslovakia's exiled President Edvard Beneš (1941), proposed: a state-regulated party system from which the core elites of the Second Republic would be excluded; the adoption of radical social or socialist measures in the economy, including the creation of an extensive nationalized sector; the exclusion of the German minority from political life; and a close foreign policy alliance with the USSR (Kural 1994: 80–5; 116–25). As the Czechoslovak state was re-established in 1944–5, a political system of this type was enacted by presidential decree. Balancing communist aspirations for a unified political structure with the more pluralistic designs of non-communists in London, the new system of 'People's Democracy' permitted only five legal political parties: the Communists, National Socialists, Social Democrats and the Catholic-oriented People's Party, the only survivor of the historic Czech right-wing parties, and the newly created Democratic Party in Slovakia.[8] Other pre-1938 parties, including other key parties of the historic Czech right such the Agrarians, National Democrats and the Party of Small Businessmen and Tradesmen were banned for alleged betrayal of national interests after Munich. The surviving assets and organizational resources of these parties were redistributed or nationalized. However, with the exception of alleged collaborators, former members of the banned parties of the historic right were able to join legal parties. The formation of new parties was, however, forbidden, institutionalizing the preponderance of left-wing parties in the Czech lands.

Political and social pluralism was also regulated through the creation of a National Front of Czechs and Slovaks, which all legal political parties and recognized social organizations were required to join. All National Front member organizations were guaranteed a share in political office in exchange for co-operating in government on the basis of a shared programme. There was thus little formal role for political opposition or competition outside elections. As elsewhere in Europe, the perceived collaboration of traditional right-wing parties and the failure of the prewar regime prompted the Czech electorate to swing markedly to the left after 1945. Elections held in 1946 on the basis of the National Front system were won by the Communists, who polled 40 per cent of the vote in the Czech lands and quickly came to dominate both the National Front and the state apparatus (Kaplan 1987; Rupnik 1981).

The People's Party 1945–8: a last outpost of the right?

Despite the dominance of the left, the one surviving representative of the prewar Czech right, the Catholic-oriented Czechoslovak People's Party, seemed well placed to become the nucleus of a new centre-right bloc, as had occurred in Italy and Germany where traditionally Catholic parties had expanded into broad Christian Democratic formations. Despite polling 20 per cent of the vote in 1946 – almost twice its highest share of the vote in prewar Czechoslovakia – the People's Party failed to gain votes outside its historic heartlands or to gain significant additional votes from either secular middle-class former supporters of the National Democrats or the more rural electorate of the Agrarians. The People's Party and its officially sponsored publications did, however, provide a temporary political home to a range of 'right-wing' non-socialists critical of the system of 'People's Democracy'. These included anti-communist Catholic traditionalists such as Bohumil Chudoba and more liberal, proto-Christian-Democratic figures such as the campaigning journalist Helena Koželuhová, whose explicit defence of capitalism and entrepreneurialism and arguments for a broader, less clerical People's Party struck a surprisingly modern note (Drápala 2000: 17–102).[9]

Such 'right-wing' elements were politically marginal in the People's Party. Despite grassroots popularity Koželuhová's unfashionable views and quixotic challenge to the party leadership rapidly led to her expulsion. Although the People's Party was sceptical of the prevailing socialist, pro-Soviet consensus; questioned the implementation of policies such as the postwar 'transfer' (*odsun*) of Czechoslovakia's Sudeten German population; and actively resisted those with direct impact on Catholics and the Catholic Church (Abrams 2004), its leadership remained committed to the progressive, consensual politics of the National Front system. Contrary to its own post-1989 history (Daněk 1990), this position reflected less the influence of pro-communist factions infiltrating the People's Party – a tactic, which proved relatively ineffective against the party – than its leaders' strategy of seeking to wait out the tide of left-wing radicalism, rather than confront it (Abrams 2002). More recognizable 'right-wing' politics subsisted among marginal groups abroad. Exiled Agrarians, for example, meeting in mid-1948 adopted a pro-market and anti-Soviet programme, equating Nazi and Soviet totalitarianism, which prefigured later Czech right-wing discourse (Dostal 1998). Émigré Catholic and conservative groupings were also critical of the 'transfer' of the Sudeten Germans. However, such exile groups and the views they articulated rapidly declined into fractious obscurity.[10]

The eroding social bases of the right

Postwar policies which promoted a more socially and ethnically homogeneous society further undercut the historic Czech right. As elsewhere in the region the number of self-employed property owners was briefly boosted by land redistribution, but the nationalization in 1945 of industrial and media companies with more than 500 employees created a large public section employing 61 per cent of the industrial workforce. In combination with wage and price policies favouring industrial and unskilled workers, radical land redistribution and the confiscation or punitive taxation of large individual bank deposits (assumed to be the product of wartime profiteering) effectively eliminated the upper bourgeoisie as a social and political force (Krejčí and Machonin 1996: 153–4). The wartime genocide of East Central Europe's Jewish population and 'transfers' from the region after 1945 of ethnic Germans and, to a lesser extent, ethnic Hungarians, also weakened the bourgeoisie, historic bourgeois parties and respect for bourgeois property rights.

Despite the strongly ideological character of postwar party discourses, the political and social changes implemented after 1945 further diluted the programmatic character of Czech party politics and bolstered party patronage and party clientelism. As in 1918, the postwar refounding of the Czechoslovak state and its occupancy by a fixed coalition of 'state-building' parties within the National Front offered few incentives for conventional electoral competition, but extensive opportunities for party patronage. In this respect, the postwar party system during the 1945–8 period was in many ways more problematic than the prewar system it replaced. Not only had the authoritarianism of the 1938–45 period weakened the constraints of constitutionality and the rule of law, but the National Front principle of limited pluralism and economic etatism stifled a civil society and public sphere already devastated during the Second Republic and the Protectorate. Almost all aspects of economic management, public administration and social life became patronage resources, which were allocated on a party-political basis. There was little scope for independent, non-party-controlled media. Some contemporary reports even suggest that performers at poetry readings were selected by officials to maintain party-political balance (Peroutka 1991: 538).

Far from the balanced configuration of bourgeois and socialist forces suggested by Kitschelt and his co-authors, by the eve of communism the historically divided Czech bourgeois right was virtually extinct. Similarly, the 'abundance of competing models of socio-economic modernization advanced by competing political forces in the interwar period' (Kitschelt *et al.* 1999: 27) identified by these authors as a legacy paving the way for conventional left–right competition after 1989, seems to have exhausted itself by 1945. Leaving aside the strength of party clientelism, evident even before 1938, the ideological 'models' that existed in Czech politics after 1945 consisted of a series of variants on the left-wing 'People's Democracy' regime described above. Even if we discount its formal endorsement of the socially progressive, pro-Soviet programme of the National Front, the traditionalist Catholic politics of the People's Party hardly amounted to an alternative model of social modernization. Indeed, unlike newly founded Christian Democratic parties elsewhere in postwar Europe, People's Party leaders privately resented the ecumenism forced on it in 1945 as a condition of National Front participation. The balance of political and social forces in the Czech lands on the eve of communism was skewed leftwards. Czech bourgeois parties, however broadly we define the term, were considerably weaker than briefly resurgent peasant parties that held office in 'national' coalitions in Poland and Hungary after 1945, or even than the artificially created Democratic Party in Slovakia which had won 62 per cent of the Slovak vote in the 1946 election.

The key reason for the rapid sapping of the strength of the historic Czech right after 1945 can again be found in nationalism and geo-politics. During the 1945–8 interregnum, the logic of political development implicit in the Czech lands' modern social structure was once again crosscut by a logic of state-building and national survival. After 1945, large numbers of Czechs on the prewar right or centre – and rising generations who might once have gravitated towards the historic right – embraced the left-leaning, Soviet-oriented agenda as an acceptable and necessary price for re-establishing a strong, secure and cohesive national state. This political calculus was brutally summed up as early as 1940 by General Homola, leader of the right-leaning Defence of the Nation resistance group, who commented prophetically that 'Moscow will not take our language or our land, Berlin will take both ... in 30–50 years there will be no communism, but the nation will still be here, while German rule would destroy it within 20 years' (cited in Kural 1994: 190).

The nature of Czechoslovak communism

Drawing on the literature on Latin America's would-be developmental dictatorships, Kitschelt's influential typology identifies Czechoslovakia's communist regime along with that of the German Democratic Republic as a 'bureaucratic authoritarian' variant of communism. Such regimes are said to be characterized by a powerful professionalized party-state bureaucracy with significant technocratic elements; a sharp demarcation between the 'ideological' and technocratic *nomenklatura*, with the latter playing a subordinate role; dense mass party organization; and a degree of popular legitimacy based on the traditions of earlier mass labour movements (Kitschelt 1995, 2002: 15–18; Kitschelt *et al.* 1999: 25–6, 70–1; Grzymala-Busse 2002, 2003). These features, in conjunction with relatively high living standards enjoyed by historically industrialized societies, it is argued, enabled these regimes to retain a high degree of social control by simultaneously repressing and placating society. The Czechoslovak regime was thus able to avert the explosive regime crises of 1950s which affected Hungary and Poland and the subsequent reforms these 'national-accommodative' regimes were forced to concede. Neither did the Czechoslovak regime need to make use of pre-existing patronage structures present in more agrarian societies as did the 'patrimonial communist' regimes established in south-eastern Europe.

There are, however, a number of significant flaws with this model, which significantly undermine Kitschelt's account of 'deep' historical causation for the emergence of the pro-market, Czech right and traditionally social democratic Czech centre-left after 1989. First, as the foregoing analysis suggests, any account viewing 'bureaucratic-authoritarian' Czechoslovak communism as primarily the product of a historically modern state and society is misleading if it does not consider the crosscutting effect of nationalism and state-building. As most historians agree, the foundation of communist one-party rule in Czechoslovakia in February 1948 was not merely the victory of an authoritarian pro-Soviet movement rooted in the working-class movement and possessed of superior repressive apparatus. It was also largely, indeed some would argue primarily, a product of the Communist Party's successful appropriation of Czech nationalism and its assumption of the role of a broad national party defending the refounded Czechoslovak state (Kaplan 1987; Abrams 2004; Sayer 1998; Rupnik 1981).

Victors and vanquished after 1948

There is, however, considerable evidence of the 'class' character of the regime and its policies *after* it had established its monopoly of power in 1948 in the more settled geo-political environment of Cold War Europe. By the late 1950s, through further waves of nationalization of small businesses and a policy of radical agricultural collectivization, the regime had wholly eliminated both bourgeois and petty bourgeois property owners as social groups, producing one of the most heavily centralized, state-owned economies in the Soviet bloc. Some sociologists have thus argued that Czechoslovak communism should be interpreted less in terms of the state–society conflict – the paradigm which informs much writing on communist regimes including Kitschelt's – than as a *social* system in which privileged *nomenklatura* groups allied with less skilled, less well educated strata to maintain egalitarian anti-meritocratic norms of remuneration at the expense of better educated and more entrepreneurial groups, including both the old intelligentsia and middle class and newer groups of specialists (Krejčí and Machonin 1996: 156–7, 160–5). We will return to this point in the next chapter. With the partial exception of the People's Party and the Catholic Church discussed below, such 'class' measures of social transformation finally eliminated the social and ideological basis of the historic Czech right. At the same time they laid the basis for newer right-wing forces by creating a constituency of the politically vanquished and economically dispossessed and frustrating the aspirations of better educated groups.

First, the social and political changes enforced by the Communist Party of Czechoslovakia after it assumed an effective monopoly of power in February 1948 inevitably generated distinct groups of direct losers. Statistics relating to judicial rehabilitations, which were complied after 1989, indicate that 107,000 people were imprisoned or subject to other criminal sanction for political reasons between 1948 and 1956. For the 1948–89 period as a whole the equivalent figure is 257,000 (Blaive 2001: 189, 187–90).[11] These included members and supporters of non-communist parties, those (alleged to be) resisting policies of nationalization and collectivization, and individuals whose class background or ties to the West made them perceived opponents of the regime. This group of imprisoned and expropriated citizens formed an important anti-communist constituency, which emerged at an organized level in the form of ex-political-prisoners' organizations both in 1968 and during the 1990s.

The size and significance of this constituency of the vanquished, formed from the historic bourgeoisie and participants in non-communist civil society, should, however, not be overstated. Notwithstanding further economic measures against the old propertied classes and their more prominent representatives after 1948, the Communist Party, consistent with its earlier electoral appeal to such groups, rapidly *absorbed* middle-class elements (Blaive 2001: 259–60). Moreover, recent research has suggested that, contrary to both anti-communist and ex-reform communist historiographies, repression in Czechoslovakia in 1950s was *less intense* and *less widespread* than in neighbouring Hungary and Poland

(Blaive 2001). Rejecting the notion that a powerful, socially rooted 'democratic tradition' needed to be suppressed, Blaive (2001) argues that, in the absence of prolonged or severe economic privation, the bulk of Czech society, as early as the 1950s, was largely passive towards the regime. Such organized resistance as did take place was small-scale, poorly co-ordinated and confined to activities such as *samizdat*, fundraising, organizing communications networks and illegal border crossings, and isolated acts of, usually symbolic, armed resistance. Anti-regime groups lacked any clear unifying political perspective beyond anti-communism and an appeal to earlier democratic traditions of prewar Czechoslovakia. Almost all had been suppressed by communist security services by the end of 1954 (Radosta 1993).

The Catholic Church under communist rule

As in many other states in Central and Eastern Europe, the Catholic Church in the Czech lands was the most powerful single non-state actor in 1945. It possessed significant economic resources, extensive networks of affiliated social organizations and a formal membership that included the majority of the population. As such it was an obvious potential focus for non-socialist and right-wing politics. Moreover, despite the fraught relationship between the historically pro-Habsburg Church and wider Czech society – and the attraction of the authoritarian corporatism for some Catholic ultra-conservatives during the 'Second Republic' – the Church's reluctance to collaborate with the Protectorate, and the engagement of many clergy in resistance, had regained it much moral credit. In the People's Party the Church also had a political representative in the new political order.

Many of the National Front policies of the 1945–8 period such as the incorporation of Catholic schools into a single state-run education system or the confiscation of German-speaking religious orders' land threatened the Church's power and autonomy. Yet, it was largely able to maintain its position during the 'People's Democracy' period. After the communist takeover in February 1948, despite early hopes of a similar accommodation, the Church–state relationship became one of clear (and one-sided) confrontation. Although attempts by the regime to create a 'progressive' pro-regime lay movement outside the control of the Church hierarchy, and to reduce levels of religious observance, foundered, by the mid-1950s state repression had reduced the Czech Catholic Church to a state of political and social paralysis and impotence (Kaplan 1993; Cuhra 2001). This situation contrasted markedly with that in Poland and, to a lesser extent, Hungary. It arguably reflected both the isolation of the Church and its limited legitimacy as a 'national' body in a passive and demobilized society,

A further side effect of the regime's failure to co-opt any significant section of Czech Catholicism was a downgrading of the importance of the People's Party, which had continued to exist as a much diminished satellite organization within a 'renewed' National Front. Passive resistance to the regime's co-optation strategy among lay Catholics in the early 1950s saw the party's already severely reduced organizational networks partially disintegrate (Taborsky 1959; Kaplan 1993). While in Hungary and Poland the traditional intelligentsia remained sufficiently socially and culturally intact to continue pre-communist conservative and nationalist discourses, albeit in attenuated and modified form, the Czech intelligentsia largely confined itself to a socialist or 'People's Democratic' idiom. Discussion of right-wing or conservative elements in Czech political history, other than those assimilating them to fascism or reactionary foreign rule, remained a taboo subject in official historiography (Křen 1990: 95–101) and, even after 1968, was only belatedly and sporadically taken up by *samizdat* writers and dissident historians. Such debates are reviewed in more detail in Chapter 3.[12]

Such social passivity raises questions as to the real strength and efficiency of the regime's 'bureaucratic authoritarian' apparatus. Although there is a lack of detailed research on the day-to-day functioning of bureaucratic structures under communism, Williams's (1997a) archival research on the Czechoslovak security services, a key institution for regime monitoring, control and repression of society, is instructive. Williams (1997a: 210, 214) concludes that in the early 1960s the State Security (StB) police in Czechoslovakia was fragmented, overloaded with unnecessary command structures, had an ineffective network of informers and was hampered by its officers' inadequate levels of education. He concludes that the StB '[as] an example of bureaucracy ... was neither rational nor routinised: it encompassed many autonomous branches and was racked by countless turf battles, so that it rarely produced results commensurate to its expense or expanse' (Williams 1997a: 225). Only in early 1970s did the StB become a more effective tool for repressing internal dissent, although attempts to rationalize and streamline its structures were to continue until its dissolution in 1990 (Williams and Deletant 2000: 39, 46).

Communist regime crises as critical junctures

However, Kitschelt and his co-thinkers' analysis of Czechoslovak 'bureaucratic authoritarian communism' as link in a chain of 'deep' causation has more fundamental flaws. Most analysts of communism in the region tend to identify *changes* in patterns of communist rule across Central and Eastern Europe between the 1950s and 1980s as a historically salient feature. Some write of a shift from 'totalitarianism' to 'post-totalitarianism' (Linz and Stepan 1996) while others merely note the 'decay' of communist regimes (Schöpflin 1993). Kitschelt and his collaborators, by contrast, present an essentially fixed and static model of communist regime types, which tends to gloss over both long-term political and social changes and short-term political crises. Such static models are to some extent necessary to pick out patterns of cross-national variation. Nevertheless, the implication that the essential character of these regimes remained frozen from the early 1950s until the eve of multi-party politics reflects an underlying determinism. Despite their stress on legacies, in their discussion of *post-communist politics* of 1990s, Kitschelt and his co-thinkers

(1999: 33–4, 53) have little difficulty accepting the widely shared view that out-comes *after* the collapse of communism in Eastern Europe were uncertain and thus to some extent shaped by actors' choices. However, in their *historical* account of national pathways they seem unwilling to concede that any periods of regime change in the past were similarly 'partially path dependent' in allowing actors' choices some scope to determine subsequent events. This marks them out from other analysts of path dependency (Collier and Collier 1991; Mahoney 2000: 513–15; Pierson 2004: 17–53) who stress that there may be *many* such 'critical junctures' at points in a historical chain, when actors are able to choose one option, rather than another.[13]

Scholars applying the Kitschelt framework in more detail to CEE have some-times introduced the idea of critical junctures into their historical accounts. In her work on communist successor parties, Grzymala-Busse (2002: 26–8), for example, suggests that the late 1940s when communist regimes were established was a critical juncture, when the key organizational practices of different com-munist regimes were 'locked-in'. Even her account, however, pays relatively little attention to *subsequent* regime crises, such as the events of October 1956 in Poland, the Hungarian Revolution or the culmination and collapse of the 'Prague Spring' reform process in Czechoslovakia in 1968–9. In so far as these crises are examined by legacy theorists, they are seen as illustrating, confirming and rein-forcing the logic laid down when communist regimes were established in the region.

The Prague Spring as historical crossroads

Accordingly, such authors downplay the strength of reform communist forces in both the party-state and wider Czech society and exaggerate the strength of both conservative communists and non-communist mobilization before August 1968. Kitschelt *et al.* (1999: 40), for example, speak of a 'weak technocratic reform current' whose 'technocratic experiments were short-lived because they trig-gered an almost instant re-awakening of a massive opposition to communism' (Kitschelt *et al.* 1999: 27; see also Kitschelt 2002: 17).[14] In fact, the reform coalition that coalesced in January 1968 was a powerful one, which drew on a diverse set of interests within the party-state and had a eclectic programme, embracing political themes which went far beyond the usual technocratic con-cerns over economic under-performance and efficient governance. As Williams's (1997a) detailed archival research makes clear, both the factional balance within the Czechoslovak communist leadership and the broader balance of power within the party-state were complex and finely balanced. Nevertheless, before the invasion conservative Communists dominated neither in the leader-ship nor in the broader nomenklatura and *precisely for this reason* were ulti-mately forced to seek external intervention. Moreover, consistent with findings of a passive, demobilized society facing a repressive apparatus of patchy effec-tiveness outlined earlier, and despite increasingly vocal criticism from the intel-ligentsia and well-defined groups such ex-Social Democrats or former political prisoners, social pressure and wider social mobilization remained weak before the invasion and lacked any clear non-communist ideological focus. It was only *after* the 1968 invasion that spontaneous mass mobilization occurred in Czechoslovakia. Given this and the fact that such public protests articulated mass *support* for reform communist leaders, it is difficult to view Czechoslovak society as expressing 'massive opposition to communism' and perhaps still more difficult to speak of its 'reawakening'.

The outcome of the Prague Spring was thus far from predetermined – or overdetermined – by the nature of the regime. Ekiert (1996) suggests that the period can best be seen as analogous to earlier crises of communist rule in Hungary and Poland in 1956. In both cases, regime destabilization was followed by 'political re-equilibrium' which restored a stable form of party-state control. In 1968–9 Czechoslovakia's more entrenched party-state institutions faced a more limited challenge from society and did not collapse as was the case in Hungary and Poland in 1956. The period was, Ekiert suggests, a critical juncture from which a number of different political settlements might have emerged. There were, to use the language of rational choice theory favoured by Ekiert, 'multiple re-equilibria'. Detailed examination of the historical record suggests that two key aspects of the period can be regarded as contingent: (1) the formulation and content of the initial reform strategy itself and; (2) Czech–Soviet relationships during 1968. First, the decision to launch the Prague Spring reforms was a 'strategic choice taken by a faction of the incumbent communist elite' (Williams 1997a: 10) and the reforms themselves were a policy amalgam reflecting a variety of – often contradictory – interests and strategies which could have emerged with a number of different emphases. Second, the USSR's decision to intervene militarily can also be regarded as a politically contingent outcome. As Williams (1997a) has established, contrary to earlier scholarship (Valenta 1979), there seems ultimately to have been little dispute within the Soviet political elite over the need for military intervention. However, his work suggests, intervention turned on the *Czechoslovak* communist elite's decisions in response to Soviet pressure and the shifting factional balance within the Czechoslovak leadership. Dubček and other 'centrists' in the Czechoslovak leadership overestimated Soviet understanding of and willingness to tolerate the re-establishment of one-party rule on the basis of limited pluralism. They also repeatedly failed to respond to Soviet demands for the enactment of agreed measures to curb liberalization or see invasion as a realistic eventuality (Williams 1997a: 29–38, 37–8). Although such misunderstandings were in part influenced by differences of political culture,[15] they reflected much more an accumulation of political misjudgements on the part of Czechoslovak leaders and the difficulties of co-ordinating a divided and finely balanced collective leadership than the inherent logic of reform-averse 'bureaucratic authoritarian' communism.

Alternative paths to Czech multi-party politics?

The inherently contradictory nature of the Prague Spring reforms in attempting to introduce elements of social and political pluralism within the framework of a one-party state would in all probability have led to some form of internally generated 'normalization' project to delimit and police the limits of reform. Indeed, there is evidence that by June 1968 the Dubček leadership was actively contemplating the reintroduction of censorship, curbs on the right of assembly and the dissolution of independent groupings, measures finally introduced under apparent Soviet pressure *after* the invasion.

Williams suggests that, without Soviet intervention in August 1968, Czechoslovakia would have experienced a pattern of political instability characteristic of failing communist liberalization elsewhere in the region: a loss of initiative by reformers, mobilization of both non-communist 'independents' and communist conservatives, a revival of ethno-nationalist politics, growing economic problems resulting from the loosening of central authority and the contradictions of the 'socialist market'; and competition between bureaucratic power centres to recentralize power. Such a scenario might have resembled developments in Yugoslavia in the period 1964–73, where similar economic reforms and political liberalization took place, before power was effectively centralized within national republics (Williams 1997a: 27–8). The 'stop-go' nature of reform in Kadár's Hungary in 1970s and 1980s (Swain 1992; Tőkés 1996) and *perestroika* in the Soviet Union, where external guarantees of regime survival were absent, offer further examples of similar dynamics. Such an alternative 'normalization' would, however, have preserved substantial elements of the reformist coalition and reform project, albeit in diluted and discredited form, making the Czechoslovakia of 1970s and 1980s a freer, more open, if probably more unstable and economically more blighted, society. Despite the 'bureaucratic authoritarian' nature of the regime's origins, a very different set of opportunity structures would have shaped an eventual transition to democracy which, given the corporatist logic underpinning much of the Prague Spring reform, might have taken the form of a negotiated exit on the Polish or Hungarian model. In the absence of a cultural divide between liberals and national-populists of the type that existed in Hungary or Poland, the resultant pattern of party competition after 1989 might well have opposed a broad liberal centrist bloc drawn from both reformist ex-regime forces and co-opted independent groups to a weak Catholic-conservative right and a radical socialist left. Political competition would have been likely to centre on shallow divisions over social and economic policy. This is approximately the pattern detectable in Slovenia, where reform-inclined communist elites ruled over a historically modern society without deep cultural cleavages (Fink-Hafner 2002; Toš and Miheljak 2002). In the event, the uncertain politics of the Prague Spring triggered what path dependence theorists term a 'reactive sequence' (Mahoney 2000: 291–5), an opposite reaction changing and counteracting the earlier reformist trajectory of the Czechoslovak regime.

Conclusions

Broad structural-historical frameworks, which locate the origins of left–right party competition after 1989 in East Central Europe in pre-communist state–society relations and levels of modernization, have done much to integrate thinking about the impact of the past on contemporary party politics. Careful re-examination of the historical forces shaping the case of the Czech right suggests that neither these broad frameworks nor their more detailed empirical application give a fully convincing account of such 'deep' causation. Such structural-historical regime legacy accounts, the case of the Czech right suggests, have three principal flaws. First, they underestimate the extent to which the politics of national development, national autonomy and at times national survival have *crosscut patterns of modernization* familiar from a West European context. Re-examination of the Czech case, therefore, suggests that the Czech historical pathway was less a direct product of social modernity, class politics or the tradition of mass labour movement than a consequence of the way the 'modernity' of Czech society was filtered through the politics of nationalism. In the nineteenth and early twentieth centuries the crosscutting pressures of the National Question inhibited the formation of a broad Czech conservative or bourgeois party with a programmatic orientation going beyond nationalism or the defence of sectional interests and produced a consensus-based pattern of competition that overrode and reduced the salience of class and left/right ideological divisions. The creation of a Czechoslovak state in 1918 and its occupancy by Czech parties – as well as the state's refoundation in 1945 – further diluted the potential for broad politics of right and left based on programmatic difference by providing much greater opportunities for party patronage than the basic historical sequence of bureaucratic development before party formation would suggest (Shefter 1977/1994). Although legacy theorists accept that ethnic pluralism and new state-building may modify state-society relations – and crosscut patterns of competition they produce – in *a post-communist* context (Kitschelt *et al.* 1999: 42; Kitschelt 2002: 23),[16] their failure to consider how such factors have shaped politics and societies in the region *historically* is a crucial omission.

A second and related problem with legacy accounts is their failure to take systematic account of the impact of geo-political factors in Central Europe on the logic of domestic development. Austrian Habsburg, Nazi and then Soviet hegemony and their constraining effect are thus largely taken for granted and presented as background narrative rather than causal factors in Kitschelt's account.[17] Accordingly, the abrupt changes of regime are treated merely as exogenous 'external shocks' to self-contained national systems, which do not fundamentally modify the composition of domestic social forces or the trajectory of political development (Kitschelt 2002: 39). However, the social, ethnic and party-institutional re-engineering of the Czech polity in 1938, 1939 and 1945, which progressively undercut and eroded the historic Czech right, shows that geo-politically driven regime change can remake domestic social forces in significant ways.

In addition, such periods of regime change can themselves lay down important legacies.

For the development of the post-1989 Central and Eastern European right two moments of the postwar settlement of late 1940s seem significant. First, the way in which bourgeois and peasant parties were 'managed' by emerging communist-led regimes after 1945 had important consequences for the structure of the centre right after 1989.[18] Some were banned outright after 1945; others were eliminated under pressure in the course of communist takeovers in the late 1940s, while others were incorporated into communist regimes as satellites. In the Czech case, although it was anticipated until a very late stage that a 'party of agricultural people' would be created (Kocian 1994; Dostal 1998: 220–30, 232–6), the Catholic People's Party (ČSL) was the only non-socialist party permitted. The survival of the People's Party, first as a member of the post-1945 National Front and subsequently as a satellite party, contributed to its emergence after 1989. Second, and perhaps equally significant in the longer term, was the reshaping of the region's 'ethnic geography' as a result of the population transfers and redrawing of borders mandated by the postwar settlement of 1945–6. The absence of significant national minorities in the Czech Republic, as well as in states such as Poland and Hungary, after 1989 and the division and elimination of Germany as a dominant regional power during the Cold War (Garton Ash 1993), represented a crucial modification to the political opportunity structure, which was to weaken the appeal of ethnic populism and populist nationalism and allow the emergence of programmatic left–right politics (Snyder and Vachudova 1997). Although later the subject of much anguished reassessment among Czech *samizdat* authors, by removing the historic focus for radical Czech nationalism the 'transfer' of the Sudeten German minority in 1945–6 undermined the prospects of the revival of the Czech right on the basis of integral nationalism.

Finally, the case of the Czech right suggests that legacy-based approaches give a static and thus deterministic account of the communist regimes in Central Europe that fails to consider the evolution (and gradual decline) of these regimes and the regime crises that punctuated their existence. Such crises were moments of indeterminacy, or critical junctures, when several paths of development were briefly possible. As such, they represent breaks in the deterministic chain of 'deep' historical causation driven by patterns of pre-communist modernization postulated by Kitschelt and his collaborators. In the Czech case, communism's major regime crisis was the 'Prague Spring' and its aftermath. Here it appears that the modern social and political structures that produced Czechoslovakia's 'bureaucratic authoritarian' communist regime generated *contradictory pressures* within that regime, which created powerful constituencies for reform within the party-state. The reform communist project that such forces championed, although unlikely to have been fully realizable, arguably represented a form of 'national accommodation' comparable to those unfolding in Hungary and Poland. In sum this suggests that, while not discounting the historical background factors identified by Kitschelt and his collaborators, we need to identify a shorter and less tenuous chain of causation to explain the origins of the new, post-1989 Czech right. As the identification of Czechoslovakia's 'Prague Spring' as a critical juncture in this chapter suggests, it is in the failed reform communist project of 1960s and reactions to that failure that the roots of the new Czech right of 1990s are to be found.

3 'Normalization' and the elite origins of the Czech right

Despite the limitations of the historical-structural approaches discussed in Chapter 2, few would argue that right-wing politics in post-communist Central Europe developed on a *tabula rasa*. Instead, this chapter will suggest, the influence of the past on the post-1989 right was felt in a complex and diffuse way through the nature of elite groups that founded right-wing parties and defined right-wing politics after 1989. Such groups had in almost all cases already formed as counter-elites under late communism, developing a range of intellectual and political responses to the decline of communist rule.

Theorists who stress the role of regime legacies and other structural factors have tended to view elites in communist polities essentially as mechanisms through which legacies are transmitted (Grzymala-Busse 2002; Kitschelt 1992a, 2003). Such approaches, however, underestimate the autonomy of elites under communism both to make and remake strategic alliances. 'New class' and sociological literatures have been more sensitive to the strategic choices involved in elite formation (Szelenyi *et al.* 1999) whilst political science studies of democratization have very effectively foregrounded the role of elites as decision-makers in the uncertain immediate transition period from communism (Linz and Stepan 1996; see also Bozóki 2003). Few studies, however, have focused in detail on the importance of elite groups' abilities *consciously* to rethink both their goals and wider understandings of politics under late communism.

Those studies of marginalized counter-elites under late communism which have been undertaken suggest that the processes of learning and strategic realignment that their debates give rise to can have a significant impact on both the mode of transition from communism and subsequent party alignments. Renwick's (2006) empirically grounded study of dissident debates in Hungary and Poland, for example, highlights how opposition groups in the two cases pursued contrasting strategies, which cannot be explained fully by differences in timing or different opportunity structures. Similarly, in a single-country study of late communist Hungary, Hall (2003) argues that, although partisan divisions between liberals and national-populists drew on historical cleavages, attempts at political and intellectual *rapprochement* during 1980s came close to achieving a significant realignment that might have created a unified liberal-national bloc.[1]

A similar logic is followed by Gil Eyal (2000, 2003), who analyses the origins of the counter-elite groups that formed the post-1989 political class in the Czech lands and Slovakia after 1989. While the post-1989 Czech political elite was formed of ex-dissident anti-politicians and neo-liberal technocrats from the 'grey zone', Eyal argues, Slovakia's post-1989 political class was composed of communist-era managers, ex-reform communists and co-opted nationalist intellectuals. The two national elites' divergent understandings of power and authority, Eyal claims, underlay the 1992 Czech–Slovak split. In the Czech case, Eyal suggests, dissidents and monetarist economists were united by a shared anti-political commitment to self-regulating social systems allowing government 'at a distance' and claimed 'pastoral power' for themselves as confessors and educators for a citizenry morally corrupted by communism. While the dissidents stressed personal integrity and the creation of an authentic social sphere, neo-liberals, Eyal notes, saw the free market as a natural and morally beneficial order. Despite ostensible political differences, in his view the two groups' shift towards moralism and anti-communism drew them towards a common set of '-'right-wing' policies whose essence was ritual renunciation of the communist past, marking them off from ex-reform communists and social democrats in the dissident movement.[2]

This chapter will argue that although Eyal's central insight – that Czech right-wing elites emerged from counter-elites' responses to the failure of reform communism in 1968 – is compelling, his case study analysis of the origins of the Czech right is deeply flawed. There was not as he suggests a straightforward dichotomy between anti-political 'right-wing' monetarists and dissidents on one hand and ex-reform communists on the other. Nor with certain individual excep-tions can the former be labelled 'anti-political' in any meaningful sense. Rather, this chapter will argue, dissident and other counter-elites contained an array of sub-groups developing different – and sometimes contradictory – sets of ideas and strategies. Within this loose and shifting network it is, however, possible to identify several sub-groups whose intellectual concerns and subsequent traject-ories marked them out a dissident 'proto-right'. In many cases, their concerns centred not on ideologies of anti-statist, anti-political Foucaultian-inflected liber-alism as suggested by Eyal, but on Christianity, conservatism and nationalism and the application of Anglo-American political models to the Czech experience

Elites and society under late communism

The political limits of the 'Prague Spring'

The 'Prague Spring' reform movement of 1960s saw a brief period of open debate about pluralism, democratic competition, market reform and the failings of the communist regime. While official reformers wished to steer pluralism through the existing institutions of the National Front (Kusin 1971: 106–23), critical intellectuals both inside and outside the Party pressed for more thorough-going democratization based on unrestricted pluralism and the institutionaliza-tion of political competition. Ludvík Vaculík, for example, urged the public to act independently to monitor the party-state, and writers such as Václav Havel (1968/1989) and Petr Pithart (1968) advocated the foundation of new socialist political parties and the institution of competitive elections for parliament, rather than agreed National Front candidates.[3] However, such debates always took place within the self-imposed limit of not considering alternatives to socialism in Czechoslovakia, either historically or in the present. Such self-limitation reflected both non-communists' appreciation of the reality of Czechoslovakia's Cold War position in the Soviet bloc and, for some sections of the Czech intelligentsia, the residual appeal of democratic socialism (Hruby 1980; Abrams 2004). Nevertheless, some new non-socialist organizations were founded, which sought to compensate for failings of the communist regime. Drawing on the distinction in official theory between a Communist (*straník*) and a non-party member (*nestraník*), the Club of Committed Non-Party Members (KAN) sought to provide an avenue for the 80 per cent of citizens who were not members of the Communist Party (or its satellites) to participate in politics. The formation of the K231 club of former political prisoners, although it focused on welfare and the process of legal rehabilitation, highlighted the divide between the regime and (parts of) Czechoslovak society. Both organizations were at pains to stress that they were supportive of official reform, not anti-socialist, and did not intend to function as opposition parties in embryo (Kusin 1972: 176–91). Public opinion polls carried out in 1968 also found that an overwhelming majority of Czechs favoured socialism and pluralism within the bounds of the National Front and would support the Communist Party under the reformist leadership of Dubček in hypothetical competitive elections (Piekalkiewicz 1972: 4–14, 246).

The 'normalization' regime

The 'normalization' of Czechoslovakia that followed the Soviet-led invasion of August 1968 established a repressive reform-averse regime, which enjoyed considerable stability and succeeded in stifling and containing political opposition for almost two decades. Despite limited research on the period, the 'normalization' regime's principal strategies for restoring and maintaining social control are well documented: mass purges of those associated with the reform movement followed by a carefully graduated strategy of intimidation and repression (Kusin 1978); and social and economic policies intended to demobilize and depoliticize society by promoting outward conformity and a retreat into private life. However, despite maintaining relatively high living standards in comparison with other East European states, 'normalization' saw the acceleration of long-term economic stagnation and an accumulation of social problems such as pollution (Sobell 1988).

In 1968–9 there were mass protests against the invasion and, in its immediate aftermath, a relatively large network of 'reform communist' groups, which sought to organize a mass underground party or broad opposition movement (Pelikan 1976; Kusin 1979; Suk 1982; Otáhal 1993a). By the 1970s such groups had disappeared partly because of state repression but also because of a mood of public resignation, which came to reject the reform era as one of naive and misplaced hopes. When independent activism did re-emerge in Czechoslovakia in the mid-1970s, it took the form of small isolated groups of 'dissident' intellectuals within groupings like Charter 77 who were primarily embraced in discussion, the publication of *samizdat* and appeals to the authorities to observe civic and human rights (Kusin 1979; Otáhal 1994). For much of 1970s and 1980s 'dissent' consisted only of small, closely monitored networks of intellectuals, numbering at most a few hundred, concentrated in Prague and Brno.

In contrast to the relative economic and social openness of Hungary and mass social protests in Poland, wider Czechoslovak society seemed indifferent, immobile and passive. Western visitors to Czechoslovakia in the mid-1980s wrote of a society which 'can be compared to a lake permanently covered by a thick layer of ice' where 'the tide of life seems to be barely moving' (Selbourne 1990: 3). Polling undertaken both by the regime itself and clandestinely by Western researchers suggested a more complex picture, showing the high audiences for Western radio stations, wide circulation of *samizdat* and exile publications, and quite high levels of interest in political and social developments (Novák 1990: 294; Vaněk 1994; Williams 2006). However, although there was widespread dissatisfaction with – and disengagement from – the official political system, when asked in clandestine polling to label their views most respondents were vague, claiming to be 'democrats' in the political centre or rejecting any ideological label (Strmiska 1986).

In the 1970s some sections of Czech society became more actively nonconformist and by the late 1980s some independent social and political activities had begun to develop outside the dissident movement. There was a growth in religious activity and a growing assertiveness on the part of both the Catholic Church and independent religious activists. By the mid-1980s this religious revival had gained visible public expression and begun to acquire some characteristics of a social movement. In the Czech lands its most significant manifestations were arguably the mass pilgrimage to Velehrad in July 1985 marking the eleven hundredth anniversary of the death of St Methodius and the 'Petition of Moravian Catholics' demanding greater religious freedom initiated by the religious activists, which attracted more than 600,000 signatures after being distributed at Catholic churches.[4]

The mid-1980s also saw the emergence of embryonic student activism and a more open critical attitude towards the regime among university students, especially in arts and humanities faculties in Prague and Brno. Some students used the structures of the official youth organization, the Union of Socialist Youth (SSM), to publish semi-independent student magazines and organize discussion fora, which were invariably critical of the *status quo* and frequently strayed on to unapproved topics. Other students sought to organize independent activities, sometimes in collaboration with established dissident networks (Otáhal 2003: 57–120). Students and young people were also prominent in the first sizeable anti-regime demonstration since 1969–70 – a protest of some 10,000 people in

Prague on 20 August 1988, the twentieth anniversary of the 1968 invasion – as well as in smaller demonstrations on 28 October 1988 and 15–20 January 1989 marking the seventieth anniversary of Czechoslovak independence and the self-immolation of the student Jan Palach in 1969 in protest against 'normalization'.[5] Yet, the nascent Czech student movement of late 1980s did not develop a distinct *political* stance of its own comparable to that of Hungary's Federation of Young Democrats (FIDESZ), but remained confined to practical activism. Moreover, those few students who did seek more developed political alternatives remained intellectually dependent on established dissident intellectuals for their ideological cues (Dufek 2001).[6]

The dissident 'proto-right'

The political thought of Czech and Slovak dissent has usually been analysed in terms of its philosophical conceptions of the civic and the nature of politics or its articulation of Central European identity (Laruelle 1996; Tucker 2000; Krapfl 2000). Studies of its longer term political consequences have usually been restricted to the events of the 'Velvet Revolution' and the carrying over of anti-political attitudes into post-1989 democratic politics (Tucker 2000). Little, if any attention has been paid to the emergence of prototypical right-wing discourses within Czech dissent and other counter-elite groups or the implications of these for developments on the Czech right after 1989.

The notion of a Czech dissident 'right-wing' or 'proto-right'[7] is in some ways problematic. Outside radical left and reform communist circles, most unofficially organized activity in Czechoslovakia after the onset of 'normalization' took the form of philosophical, historical or literary discussion at informal 'home seminars' (*bytové semináře*), rather than openly political debates. In 1976 Czechoslovakia's formal ratification of international civil and political rights conventions and the trial of the 'Plastic People of the Universe' rock group spurred some intellectuals to take a public stand that led directly to the foundation of Charter 77. The Charter united individuals of diverse backgrounds and views around basic questions of legality, human rights and citizenship. The repressive nature of the regime and the strong ties of friendship and solidarity that developed between members of the small and isolated community of Chartists thus blurred earlier political divisions (Garton Ash 1991).[8] For the majority of Czech dissidents the key political division throughout 'normalization' was that between democracy and totalitarianism and the key task was the common struggle to resist and ultimately displace Czechoslovakia's communist regime.

Nevertheless, political and ideological divisions did exist within Czech dissent and were evident to both to external observers and to Chartists themselves from the outset,[9] as well as to the Czechoslovak security police which actively sought to exacerbate them (Nová 1994). Indeed overcoming such divisions was part of the very rationale for the foundation of Charter 77. Most accounts identify three main sub-groupings within the Charter: former reform communists and democratic socialists; Christian-oriented intellectuals who had never identified with Marxism; and a looser group of 'liberals' drawn from the creative intelligentsia and cultural underground (Kusin 1978; Skilling 1981; Day 1999: 16–17). One means of identifying the 'right' within Czech dissent is, therefore, to do so negatively by contrasting them with the several currents in Charter 77 which identified with the socialist tradition. The most prominent of these were the group of former reform communists, some formerly holding high-ranking posts before 1968; a small group of radical leftists influenced by the Western 'New Left', the best known of whom was Petr Uhl; and a social-democratically oriented group of 'independent socialists' with links to the Socialist International centring on the former KAN activist Rudolf Battěk.[10] Although reform communists and leftists such as Zdeněk Mlynář or Petr Uhl played a prominent role in the Charter, their commitment to forms of democratic socialist politics marked them out from the majority of dissidents and generated tensions. The former 'reform communists' were, however, torn between developing independent opposition activity, on one hand, and, on the other, seeking openings to the regime in the hope of spurring change from within. This strategic dilemma became acute after the launch of *perestroika* in the USSR and of Czechoslovakia's own parallel, but much more cosmetic, programme of 'restructuring' (*přestavba*) in 1987 (Bloem 2002). Such lingering ambiguity towards the regime generated suspicion among other Chartists. Similarly, Uhl's overt criticism of capitalism and liberal parliamentary democracy as models for Czechoslovakia drew many sharp ripostes in the *samizdat* press (Hlušičková and Císařovská 1994: 110–23; 202–8).

Politics and anti-politics in Czech dissent

The concept of a dissident proto-right challenges both the widespread notion of Czech dissent as essentially anti-political and Eyal's related interpretation of the post-1989 Czech right as a product of liberal anti-politics. Eyal does not explicitly define 'anti-politics' and his understanding of the term is, confusingly, filtered through Foucault's conceptions of power, knowledge and self and 'new class' debates about the role of intellectuals. More straightforwardly, we might view anti-politics *either* as the radical rejection of the political sphere as redundant or unnecessary *or* as efforts to redraw the boundaries of the political or replace the conventional logics of politics – competition over binding collective decisions – with mechanisms or principles drawn from fields such as morality, aesthetics, science or economics (Schedler 1997). Eyal's views embrace both senses but tend to stress the second, seeing Czech counter-elites' anti-politics mainly in their supposed retreat from a conventional intellectual commitment to using state power to a belief in ethically acquired 'pastoral power' or the technocratic authority of economists (2003: 29, 67–71, 86–7). Such a retreat to 'non-teleological' forms of power, he suggests, also entailed a rejection of means–ends rationality and goal-oriented action by Czech counter-elites in communist Czechoslovakia (Eyal 2003: xvii).

However, even as a somewhat abstracted study of dissident 'problematiza-tion' strategies (Eyal 2003: 65), such an analysis bears little relationship to the realities of Czech dissent. Many Czech dissidents' thinking *was* anti-political in one or several of these senses described above. The writings of Jan Patočka, the author of Charter 77's founding texts, or Václav Havel, the best-known (and most widely translated) Czech dissident, *were* often radically anti-political in their negation of the political sphere. Other dissidents merely wished to narrow the boundaries of the political, which extended (in theory) to all aspects of social and economic life in communist Czechoslovakia.[11] Many, however, remained intellectually committed to traditional concepts of politics, which allowed for and anticipated partisan divisions. Although sharing Havel's preoccupations with establishing 'civic' values by acting 'as if' formal rights and freedoms were observed, they did so because they saw 'normal' politics as temporarily distorted or blocked by communism, not because they saw all forms of politics – includ-ing Western parliamentary democracy – as existentially exhausted (see also Szacki 1995: 78–80). Petr Pithart, for example, whom Eyal (2003: 70) presents as an anti-political thinker, argued that establishing a sense of civic community was 'the only viable road to take to the establishment of normal, that is political, conditions' (Pithart 1990a: 338).[12] Similar views were expressed by the leading former reform communist and Charter signatory Zdeněk Mlynář (1978), who stressed that developing shared values and mutual understanding between Chris-tians and democratic socialists was a prerequisite for eventual democratic competition. Such thinking, which was more pre-political than anti-political, was arguably more typical of Czech dissidents than the radically anti-political positions of Patočka in 1977–8 or Havel's writings of the late 1970s.

Furthermore, in the decade following Patočka's death in March 1977 the Charter evolved away from radical anti-politics. Václav Benda's (1980) essay on the 'parallel polis' which advocated building the Charter into an autonomous civil society in embryo was an explicit response to the perceived deficiencies of Patočka's radical anti-politics, which centred on the individual.[13] In the course of the 1980s the changing political and social climate in Czechoslovakia and the playing out of 'generational' conflicts in Czech dissent saw the further dilution of dissident anti-politics. Indeed, by the late 1980s, even Václav Havel had come to advocate the rehabilitation of the political sphere and preparation for political action. The emergence of a Czech dissident proto-right was less a product of dissident anti-politics than a reflection of its limits and gradual decline.

It is also questionable whether dissident activity was 'anti-political' in expressing a 'non-teleological' rejection of means–ends rationality in political action. Many strands of dissident thinking undoubtedly saw moral imperatives and the assertion of values and identity as sufficient in themselves to justify dissent. Most dissidents were, however, also aware that their actions were implicitly concerned with bringing about political and social change over the longer term, even if the mechanisms for such change remained unclear. This was especially true of dissidents on the proto-right. As the neo-conservative dissident

Pavel Bratinka recalled '[t]here were only a few people who consciously hoped for ultimate victory, but there were many of us who did on a subconscious level' (Bratinka 1991). On occasion, even anti-political thinkers such as Havel intuitively sensed a connection between anti-politics in the present and future political outcomes. Writing in his seminal 1978 essay *Power of the Powerless*, which developed the idea of 'living in truth' as an alternative to formal politics, Havel accurately anticipated the regime's potential for sudden implosion, writing that from

> [t]he hidden movement it ['living in truth'] gives rise to there can issue forth (when, where, under what circumstances and to what extent are difficult to predict) in something visible: a real political act or event, a social movement, a sudden explosion of civil unrest, a sharp conflict inside an apparently monolithic power structure, [...] it is never quite clear when the last straw will fall or what the last straw will be.
>
> (Havel 1989: 58–9)[14]

The 'anti-politics' of Czech dissent should therefore be viewed not in essential or absolute terms but as an uneven and inconsistent mix of anti-political elements, combined with a range of more conventional understandings of politics, including elements of the proto-right, which shifted over time.

Conservative sensibilities of dissent?

Philosophical projects became gradually more political during the course of the 'normalization' period, and markedly so from the mid-1980s when Czech dissidents came into contact with British right-wing intellectuals such as Roger Scruton, editor of the *Salisbury Review*, one of the leading voices on the 'social authoritarian' wing of the British New Right (Seidal 1986). As a result of contacts established by Scruton and others in the Jan Hus Educational Foundation, a series of underground seminars with Western academics and intellectuals ran in Prague and Brno between 1980 and 1989 (Oslzlý 1993; Day 1999). Many (but not all) of the Western visitors were politically on the right. Scruton's *Salisbury Review* and other Western conservative journals were widely known (sometimes in translated *samizdat*) among dissident intellectuals in Czechoslovakia. In the 1980s sections of the Czech dissident intelligentsia became more consciously 'right-wing'. In February 1988, Václav Havel, for example, told an English visitor of 'new moods' in dissent and a drift to the right reflecting a 'worldwide wave of neo-conservatism, which has reached here also. Such moods have mainly affected Catholics of the younger generation' (cited in Selbourne 1990: 81). These 'moods' were reflected in the founding during the 1980s of a number of new, more self-consciously conservative journals such as the *samizdat* publications *Prostor* or *Střední Evropa* and the Catholic-oriented *Rozmluvy* based in Munich and London.

While some Western intellectuals and activists saw East European dissidents as a counterpart to West European peace movements (Kaldor 1990) or a source of inspiration for reflection a new 'civic' socialism (Keane 1988), the British New Right rushed to claim Václav Havel as a conservative thinker (de Candole 1988) and took any interest in market economics, private property, civil society or transcendent values as a manifestation of a dissident 'New Right' in Central Europe (Scruton 1988a, 1988b). Despite the sweeping nature of such claims, a number of distinctly conservative *concerns*, with questions of social order, historical continuity, public morality and/or a sense of the particular can readily be identified in Czech dissident thought. In political terms they resolved into two broad themes: (1) the need to restore 'natural' social forms and 'traditional values'; and (2) a suspicion of populism and mass democratic politics.

First, both dissident and Western conservatives thought of their respective societies as natural communities threatened by the aggressive and artificial impositions of modern politics. Many dissidents, including 'anti-political' thinkers such as Havel, saw the communist regime as promoting soulless modern consumerism and moral decay and longed for an authentic, 'natural' society and a return of 'decency' (*slušnost*), public spiritedness and spiritual values. This vein of romantic anti-modernism was influenced by the phenomenological philosophy of Jan Patočka, the Czech lands' most prominent non-Marxist philosopher who later became one of Charter 77's first 'speakers'. His work drew indirectly on the work of Heidegger, albeit humanized and shorn of its totalitarian bent, in examining the 'natural world' or 'life world' undistorted by power, ideology or technology (Blecha 1997; Tucker 2000).[15] The adoption after 1968 by many dissidents of 'totalitarianism' (or 'post-totalitarianism') as a frame for understanding the communist system at a time when the concept was in decline among Western specialists on Eastern Europe (Rupnik 1988) provided a further point of affinity with Western conservatives.

Second, throughout virtually the whole of the communist regime most Czechoslovak dissidents lived in a tiny ghetto of opposition intellectuals. Despite their commitment to democracy, many regarded the possible mass entry of the Czech public into politics with distinct apprehension. A sudden collapse of the regime, they feared, would bring not meaningful democracy but an out-break of vengeful demagogic anti-communist populism. Indeed, Ludvík Vaculík (1990: 80–2) went so far as to argue that, because the Czech public largely shared the values of the communist regime, the principal advantage of a democratic regime would not be that it reflected the will of the majority, but that it would guarantee and protect the rights of educated minorities violated under communism. Such views echoed both British conservatism's historical scepticism of democracy and the anxieties of liberals that freedom would prove incompatible with democratic majority rule.

Nevertheless, the affinities of Western conservatism and Czech dissent should not be exaggerated. Preoccupations with moral decline, the alienating effects of the modern world and the need to shore up the pre-political (moral, cultural) bases of politics and state authority have animated many Western neo-conservatives. However, dissident concerns were more communitarian than conservative. The 'traditional values' whose loss many mourned were more those of the 'civic culture' – traditions of co-operation and trust – than those of patriarchy and a monolithic, organic national culture. These, paradoxically had been well maintained in socialist Czechoslovakia where communist authoritarianism had enforced social and cultural conformity and insulated the country from much of the cultural pluralization and 'permissiveness' of the West (Heitlinger 1996; Šiklová 1997; Saxonberg 2003). Like many traditional conservative ideologies, much dissident thought linked authenticity and human identity with the renewal of the local, parochial and small-scale. In the Czech context, however, such concerns reflected less a preoccupation with authority than a reaction against communist gigantism and strong traditions of localism, which identified the community (*obec*) with the commune (*obec*).

Similarly, although many Western conservatives, both historically and in the present, have been sceptical of democracy – Scruton (1989: 59, for example, referred to it as a 'contagion' – they have typically been more concerned with preserving traditional (unelected) authority than with stemming popular mobilization. Thus, while Czech dissident (anti-)political thought *did* have certain common preoccupations with the conservative Western New Right, these affinities should not be overstated.[16] Close affinities were confined, in fact, to a relatively distinct groups and individuals who were, more or less consciously, developing proto-'right-wing' discourses.

Catholic conservatism in Charter 77

From the early 1960s a range of underground Catholic networks and religious communities emerged in Czechoslovakia and, despite repression, grew slowly in strength through the 1970s and 1980s. Most were concerned with the survival of Catholic doctrine and the organization of activities banned or obstructed by the regime such as religious education and the ordination of clergy (Corley 1993: Luxmoore and Babiuch 1992). Despite the initial disapproval of the Church hierarchy, a number of Catholic clergy and lay intellectuals signed or publicly supported Charter 77, the human rights demands of which fitted with the religious and the political ecumenicalism fostered by the liberalization of communist rule in the 1960s and the climate in the Roman Catholic Church after the Second Vatican Council (Luxmoore and Babiuch 1992: 110–13; 1995).

At the same time, a significant Catholic-conservative current emerged only slowly within Czech dissent. The thinking of the most prominent Catholic dissident with Charter 77, Václav Benda, initially echoed that of Havel in its desire to find new – but not specifically Catholic or Christian – ways of thinking about politics and society (Benda 1985: 112).

However, like others on the 'proto-right', Benda was less anti-political than Havel and more preoccupied with the specific pathologies of communism and socialism, than with the condition of modernity or modern civilization (of which Havel viewed communism as an extreme example). He also explicitly rejected Havel's view that Eastern and Western modernity were in some sense equivalent, seeing communism as a 'malignant tumour' far more grave than the more minor ailments afflicting the essentially healthy political systems of the West. Ignoring the vast differences between totalitarianism and democracy, he claimed, was a wilful error of the Western left (Benda 1985: 111). By the late 1980s Benda had come to share the view of other dissidents on the 'proto-right' – such as the 'realist' group and Petr Pithart – that the dissident 'parallel polis' should be seen not as an invitation for individuals to 'live in truth' outside society but as a form of Masarykian 'small-scale work' (*drobná práce*) focused on renewing the national community and rebuilding social bonds severed by the incursions of the totalitarian party state (Benda *et al.* 1988: 217–18). Although as early as 1979 Benda labelled himself 'conservatively radical' (*konzervativně radikální*),[17] in the 1980s other dissidents developed more recognizably Catholic-conservative positions.

The Střední Evropa group: Catholic conservatism versus the nation

On 20 May 1984, Charter 77 issued a document entitled 'A Right to History' (no. 11/84 reprinted in Prečan 1990: 254–7). It called for a national history undistorted by communist ideology which would reconcile different aspects of the Czech experience by recognizing the positive role of Catholic Church and Habsburg rule. In an implicit criticism of the Charter's usual abstract, legalistic stress on human rights, the document also argued that, given the regime's totalitarian efforts to control historical memory, only those able to recover a sense of Czech history would be able to assert their rights effectively. 'A Right to History' was immediately criticized by dissident historians with a reform communist background. Many objected to its oversimplification of historical fact[18] and sweeping dismissal of research by 'official' historians (Hajek *et al.* 1984; Kohout 1984). However, it was the document's suggestions for re-evaluating Czech history that generated the greatest controversy. The suggested areas for rethinking, critics noted (Hajek *et al.* 1984; Hübl 1984; Kohout 1984), were essentially a restatement in more circumspect form of conservative Catholic arguments of the 1920s calling into question the foundation of the Czechoslovak state (Paces 1999). Critics on the Charter's left thus criticized 'A Right to History' as itself misusing the past by trying to impose a single meaning on Czech history in a manner uncomfortably reminiscent of the communist regime (Kohout 1984). At the same time, however, they defended the factual basis of established Czech interpretations of the role of the Church and Habsburg dynasty as impediments to Czech national development (Kohout 1984).

The controversy over 'A Right to History' opened up one of the clearest splits between 'left' and 'right' and marked the emergence of a new Catholic-oriented dissident 'right', drawing inspiration both from the religious revival in Czech society in the 1980s and from the 'conservative moods' observed by Havel. Although signed by the Charter's three 'speakers', Václav Benda, Jiří Ruml and Jana Sternová, 'A Right to History' was written by Jan P. Kučera and Rudolf Kučera, the editors of the *samizdat* journal *Střední Evropa* ('Central Europe'), which had been founded in 1984. Despite its title, the journal's conception of 'Central Europe' differed from the familiar dissident trope of the region as a 'kidnapped West' (Kundera 1984), whose culture and spirit transcended the political realities of Cold War Europe (Garton Ash 1991: 161–91; Schöpflin and Wood 1989). Instead, it saw the region as defined by Catholicism (Hradec 1985). *Střední Evropa* contributors assertively presented the interwar Catholic revisionist view that Czechs had steadily prospered under Habsburg tutelage and that the establishment of an independent, Czechoslovak state in 1918 had been a historical error. The nationalistic, egalitarian and secular ethos of interwar Czechoslovakia and above all its antagonistic, unresolved relationship with its German minority, argued *Střední Evropa,* led directly to its destruction in 1938 and paved the way for communism. Communism was, in their view, the logical and inevitable outcome of almost a century of progressively oriented liberal Czech nationalism, which thus failed to serve the interests of Czechs (Laruelle 1996: 7–8).[19] As an alternative, *Střední Evropa* posited a vision of Czechs without a national state co-existing alongside ethnic Germans in territorially defined historic provinces as part of a supranational 'Central Europe' united by Catholicism, territorial patriotism, a cosmopolitan aristocracy and supranational monarchy (Laruelle 1996: 6–7). Indeed such co-existence appeared a precondition of the Czech identity. For this reason *Střední Evropa*'s rejection of the 'transfer' (*odsun*) of ethnic Germans from Czechoslovakia in 1945–6, which some contributors characterized as 'genocide' and a 'crime against humanity', was particularly marked (Laruelle 1996: 9–10).

On first examination, *Střední Evropa*'s intellectual conservatism seems part of a widely shared nostalgia for the pre-1918 Habsburg Empire which suffused much of the region in late 1980s. However, as Laruelle (1996 12–16) notes, its underlying points of reference were often more premodern than *fin de siècle.*[20] The group's reworking of Czech Catholic conservatism critiques extended, in fact, to a radical deconstruction of Czech national identity as it had evolved since the mid nineteenth century. Indeed so marked was this questioning of the Czech nation that some of the group's themes such as its reappraisal of St Wenceslas or the distinct identity of Moravia echoed the ideology of the Nazi Protectorate (Kohout 1984; Laruelle 1996: 8–9).

In search of national liberalism: the 'realist' group

The 'realist' or 'constructive' grouping, like Charter 77, emerged during the 1970s on the basis of intellectual networks formed during the Prague Spring – in this case those around Bohumil Doležal, Emanual Mandler and contributors to the short-lived radical cultural and political magazine *Tvář.* Although the group had contacts with neo-liberal economists such as Václav Klaus, Tomáš Ježek and Jan Straský, who had written for *Tvář* during the 1960s and occasionally contributed pseudonymously to its *samizdat* journal *Ineditní sborníky* in the mid-1980s, the group remained deliberately aloof from Charter 77 and developed an intellectual agenda understood as an alternative to the weaknesses of Chartist thinking (Otáhal 1993b).[21]

The group's 'realism' was expressed in its view of politics as understandable only in terms of power and contending interests and as a social phenomenon rooted in (Czech) history and culture. This analysis led the group both to highlight the role of Soviet (Russian) hegemony in maintaining the political *status quo*, rather than the moral crisis of the individual or of society, and to see communism less as an unnatural totalitarian ideological project than as the wholesale importation of Russian political practices, which were gradually eroding Czech political identity (Hlušičková and Otáhal 1993).

Like the philosopher Karel Kosík (*Listy*, 7 November 1968), whose interest in the nineteenth-century radical democratic writers of the Czech National Revival they shared (Kusin 1971: 37–9), the 'realists' viewed 1968 and post-1968 'normalization' as presaging the degeneration of the Czechs from being a self-conscious political nation with clear national goals into a Czech-speaking populace of workers and producers. The key task, they concluded, was to articulate a political strategy capable of reconstituting the Czech nation as a political subject by revisiting the ideas of Czech nationalist thinkers such as Masaryk and Havlíček, who had undertaken a similar task in the nineteenth century. Central to this strategy was the vaguely defined concept of 'national reconciliation', which would see communists and non-communists come together within existing institutions around shared national goals. Although the 'realists' had no commitment to socialism, this search for a politically defined, new national project seemed to amount to hopes for a gradual Kádárization of Czechoslovak society.

However, from the mid-1980s, perceiving that Gorbachev's policies could lead to more permissive environment for independent activity in Czechoslovakia, the 'realists' turned to a more activist strategy. In 1987 they founded the Democratic Initiative (DI), the first attempt to build alternative political movement since the 1970s. DI was intended in the longer term to lay the basis of 'strong popular movement' along Polish lines rooted in socio-economic as well as political grievances. Despite launching regional branches as well as consumer and student groups, as an organization DI was quickly stifled by official repression and was, in practice, no more successful than groupings linked to Charter 77.

The dissident 'Toryism' of Petr Pithart

The jurist and historian Petr Pithart represented a further strain of dissident conservatism. The son of a prominent Communist diplomat and himself a Communist Party member until 1968, Pithart was a law lecturer at Charles University during the 1960s and also served as secretary to the interdisciplinary team at the Czechoslovak Academy of Sciences preparing plans for political reform. He first came to public attention during the Prague Spring as a contributor to the flagship reformist journal *Literární noviny*, when he emerged as a critic of the limitations of official political reform. By the early 1970s Pithart had been purged from academia and relegated to the first in a series of menial occupations. He was later among the first Charter 77 signatories. Pithart used the 'normalization' period largely as an opportunity to write and reflect upon Czech politics and history in *samizdat*, including co-authored contributions to the *odsun* debate and a jointly written reinterpretation of modern Czech history ('Podiven' 1991). In common with others on the proto-right, Pithart was seeking alternatives to the socialist and Marxist discourses predominant in Czech intellectual life since 1945. Like Havel, he quickly came to see his earlier arguments for institutional reforms to the communist party-state as superficial and naive (Pithart 1990e: 124–8), sceptically dissecting the illusions of both reform communists and radical democrats during the Prague Spring in an influential *samizdat* work (Pithart 1990b).

Pithart found the alternative he sought in an intellectual scepticism strongly influenced by traditional British conservatism and what he termed the 'British political style', which he had discovered in a moment of revelation on a study visit to St Antony's College, Oxford, in 1969 (Pithart 1992: 49). Pithart developed his dissident intellectual 'conservatism' more consciously in the 1980s when he came directly into contact with right-wing British intellectuals such as Roger Scruton, whose *The Meaning of Conservatism* he translated into Czech (Oslzlý 1993; Day 1999: 119–20). However, as emerged in his earliest *samizdat* writings (Pithart 1990c), it was traditional British Tory ideas, such as the importance of historical continuity, the immutability of human nature, the need for social cohesion rooted in a sense of place, the importance of law and pragmatic non-ideological statecraft, which attracted him, rather than the illiberal social-authoritarianism characteristic of Scruton's contributions to British debates of the 1980s (Seidal 1986).

In contrast to both genuinely anti-political thinkers and those who identified with conventional ideologies of left and right, Pithart embraced the Tory belief that politics should exist as a separate sphere, but one governed by pragmatism and realism rather than 'ideology' (Pithart 1990c).

Unlike thinkers such as Havel, who focused on the individual as a philosophical subject and neo-liberals views of a Czech *homo economicus*, Pithart's conservatism led him from the very outset to a concern with issues of social cohesion and collective (usually national or historical) identity (Pithart 1990a: 327–38). He shared a widely held dissident view in seeing the communist authorities as 'creating a social climate characterized by the social decay (*pokleslosti*) of traditional values of human solidarity, honesty (*poctivosti*) and decency' as a means to reinforce social control (Pithart 1990d). However, Pithart's emphasis on the need to rebuild civic values was concerned not so much with 'living in truth' but, like Benda, with re-establishing *social* bonds through a renewed sense of a decency and public duty and, like the 'realist' group, through a renewed awareness of the Czech 'homeland' (*vlast*) as a civic *and* national community (Pithart 1990d).[22]

In contrast to religiously inclined dissidents or Hayekian liberals, Pithart was thus deeply concerned with understanding the continuities and discontinuities of Czech history. In particular he was concerned with understanding the mass appeal for Czechs of radical ideologies, such as communism, which promised to break with and 'undo' the past. Like the Catholic conservative revisionists of *Rozmluvy* and the *Střední Evropa* group, Pithart questioned the secular, left-liberal progressive mainstream Czech national tradition, which had been co-opted by the Communists in 1945–8. Like them, he too sought to re-examine historical alternatives to this national-liberal mainstream tradition, although for him the Czech nation or homeland remained central. The *samizdat* reinterpretation of modern Czech history that he co-wrote in the late 1970s ('Podiven' 1991; Bryant 2000) thus paralleled the Catholic interpretations of Czech national identity as forged *through*, rather than against, Catholicism and Habsburg rule. Czechs' provincialism, flawed democratic tradition and inclination to populism, and lack of respect for political institutions, rather than the action of a determined minority, had, Pithart and his co-authors suggested, led to the dead end of communism.

In later writings, Pithart critically reassessed aspects of Czech interwar conservative and right-wing thought opposed to Masaryk and the Czech political establishment of the time in *samizdat* studies of the historian Josef Pekař (1870–1937) and Czech integral nationalist intellectuals of the 1920s. Although at heart a secular nationalist, Pekař had challenged the progressive democratically oriented Czech nationalist ideology developed by Masaryk and was critical of the new Czechoslovak state's policy of demonstratively breaking with the Austrian past through, for example, land reform and hostility to the Catholic Church. Pithart broadly endorsed these criticisms. Rather than stressing the importance of Catholicism to Czech national life,[23] or nostalgically regretting the passing of the Austro-Hungarian Empire, he drew a different, 'Tory' lesson: that evolutionary political change was preferable to the illusory revolutionary breaks with which modern Czech history was punctuated. Such thinking also informed Pithart's contribution to the dissident *odsun* debate. Writing as 'Bohemus' (1990), Pithart and a group of co-authors argued that the post-1945 *odsun* of the Sudeten Germans was not only unacceptable on moral and human rights grounds but had damaged Czech society by undermining the rule of law, private property rights and entrepreneurial culture.[24] Pithart was less sympathetic in his assessment of Czech interwar integral nationalists, whose crude chauvinism he did not share, but valued their prophetic warnings about the potential for the Czechoslovak state to collapse undefended, which he agreed stemmed from the liberal-nationalist vision of Czech statehood as a standard bearer for democracy, progress and Western values, whose existence was in some sense historically guaranteed (Pithart 1990a: 105–64).[25]

Pithart's conservative commitment to evolutionary change, social and civic cohesion and the primary need to re-establish the rule of law and legitimate state authority, combined with his view of the Czech democratic tradition as flawed, led him to regard a future transition from communism with some trepidation. He was acutely concerned that post-communist transition, if and when it came, should not take the form of an 'anti-1948', populist anti-Communist purges masquerading as parliamentary democracy but in reality ignoring the rule of law.

Given the erosion of ethical and moral norms, Pithart also regarded the potential release of market forces in a future post-communist society with trepidation. In a *samizdat* interview in May 1988, he surprised his interlocutor by stressing the need for strong legal safeguards and state regulation in any new regime, warning that 'in the first years [private] business may appear in such a form, that we may be robbed even more than we are today by the [communist] state' (Pithart 1990e: 20).

Dissident neo-conservatives

Western-derived neo-conservative orientations in the Czech lands originate largely from a group centred on Pavel Bratinka and Daniel Kroupa, part of a generation of young Catholic-oriented intellectuals who shunned the reform politics of the 1960s and chose to study technical subjects, rather than follow official Marxist-oriented curricula on philosophy and politics. The Kroupa–Bratinka grouping appears to have emerged as an indirect product of the 'Kampademia' philosophical seminar organized in the early 1970s by Kroupa and Martin Palouš (which Bratinka joined in 1974) and also of Kroupa's own philosophical seminar (Kroupa n.d.; Palouš 2003; Day 1999: 10–11, 21–2, 78–83). Its initial informal political discussions continued debates of the 1960s reform era and reacted to the collapse of the reform communist project and the onset of 'normalization'. Kroupa (1996: 9), for example, has recalled the formative influence on him of the 1968–9 polemic between Václav Havel and Milan Kundera about the meaning of the Prague Spring. While Kundera (1968; 1968–9) considered the reform communist project of 'democratic socialism' a unique and heroic Czech contribution to world politics, Havel (1969) saw it as a failed and half-hearted attempt to return to political normality.[26] Endorsing Havel's view of the Prague Spring as the failure of socialism, the small, isolated group around Bratinka and Kroupa made a conscious effort to find a wholly non-socialist social and political philosophy. From an early stage, however, the Bratinka–Kroupa group drew on the thinking of the American New Right, which appears to have initially been an interest of Bratinka, a regular reader at the US embassy library since the mid-1960s (Day 1999: 112). Kroupa recalls how 'Bratinka studied Anglo-Saxon literature and was enchanted by the American neo-conservatives. At the beginning of the 1970s he used to translate articles, which we pored over, as we were left to our own lonely reflections, because there was no one to talk to and virtually no literature which might have guided us' (Kroupa 1996: 11–12). Hayek and the American Catholic neo-conservative Michael Novak were important influences, as were G.K. Chesterton and the Austro-American philosopher Eric Voegelin.

American neo-conservatives' tendency to define themselves in terms of hawkish positions towards the Soviet Union and actively seek inroads into the 'Soviet Empire' made them an attractive point of reference for East European dissidents at a time when many Western politicians overlooked (the possibility of) opposition in the region and focused on East–West *détente*. Despite an almost complete absence of personal contact between North American neo-conservatives and Czech dissidents before 1989,[27] even in the 1980s neo-conservatism had greater intellectual currency than the Toryism of Scruton and others in the British *Salisbury Review* group, who visited Czechoslovakia frequently and whose work was widely translated in *samizdat* and exile journals. There were a number of reasons for this. Many key philosophers influencing US neo-conservatism – as well as some key neo-conservative writers themselves – were of Central European origin and had been more directly affected, both personally and intellectually, by the experience of totalitarianism than thinkers on the British New Right. Moreover, given its origins in Cold War liberalism, US neo-conservatism consciously embraced universal civil and human rights and democratic politics, distancing itself from traditionalist and anti-democratic variants of conservatism (Wolfson 2005). Notwithstanding its founders' stress on US exceptionalism (Kristol 1995: 373–86), this universalism made neo-conservatism less susceptible to the limitations of context that affected British Toryism. The US's own origins as a new and egalitarian democratic republic also offered parallels to the Czech experience not present in the aristocratic origins of British conservatism and the British state's supposed centuries of historical continuity.

Despite the personal ties of Scruton and other British right-wing thinkers with Czech dissidents, British Toryism, by contrast, seemed intellectually problematic or of little relevance to many dissidents (Benda 1984; Kroupa 1996, 2003). As a Tory thinker Scruton, for example, was critical of the concept of social justice which was important to Catholic Chartists such as Václav Benda, and rejected the notion of universal human rights on which Charter 77 had been founded for a view of individual freedom as guaranteed by cultural tradition and traditional institutions upholding the rule of law (Scruton 1981: 205–9). Ultimately, as Scruton himself conceded, the differences between the defence of a semi-traditional social order embodied in institutions such as private schools, the House of Lords and English common law and the 'inner life of a destroyed social order' represented by dissident thought (Scruton 1990: 87) were unbridgeable.[28]

Other aspects of US neo-conservatism also resonated with the Czech dissident experience. Much US neo-conservative writing was directed not against the conventional 'Communist threat' but against the New Left, echoing Czechoslovak dissidents' preoccupation with the failure of reform communism and 'socialism with a human face' rather than Stalinism or orthodox Marxism.[29] A further source of attraction was American neo-conservatism's vision of spreading 'democratic capitalism', which echoed Masaryk's idea of Czechoslovak statehood as linked to a democratic 'world revolution' (Gellner 1995), but challenged both the well-established equation of socialism and democracy in Czech political discourse. Similarly, the neo-conservative stress on the potential of capitalism to promote civic good provided it was rooted in religious morality and traditional values (Younkins 1999) represented an antidote to Czech Catholicism's traditional scepticism towards market forces.[30]

Technocrats and the 'grey zone'

A further significant counter-elite on the Czech proto-right can be found outside dissident networks in a generation of neo-liberal technocrats who emerged on the margins of the 'Prague Spring'. Rather than being co-opted into the reformist wing of the regime or marginalized in opposition milieux defined by historical nationalism, as in Hungary and Poland, this group formed part of an outwardly uncommitted 'grey zone' between official power structures and independent groups. This 'grey zone' of economists, sociologists, social scientists and other 'qualified, professionally erudite people' used their professional resources and opportunities to engage in 'crypto-opposition' without openly opposing the regime (Šiklová 1990). Such activity usually took the form of 'non-political' research on social and economic problems or technical and theoretical discussions, highlighting the unsustainability of 'normalization' policies and the need for fundamental reform.

Such 'grey zone' activities were concentrated in specialized institutions such as the State Bank, technical research institutes or the research departments of some state entreprises, exploiting the regime's desire to use sub-fields such as mathematical modelling and industrial sociology to generate greater efficiency without implementing structural reforms (Smith 2003a; Machonin 2004). With the increasing stagnation of the Czechoslovak economy in the 1980s and the onset of Soviet *perestroika*, opportunities for 'grey zone' elites increased and they developed networks in institutions such as the Institute of Economics and the new Forecasting Institute (ProgÚ), established in March 1986 to produce long-term, interdisciplinary forecasts of Czechoslovak's social and economic development until the year 2000 (later 2010). The organization of the institute was entrusted to Valtr Komárek, an economic administrator who had headed the Czechoslovak government's Economic Council in 1968–71 before suffering demotion and re-emerging as a researcher at the Economics Institute of the Czech Academy of Sciences in 1978. Komárek skilfully built up the Forecasting Institute's staff, resources and autonomy, gaining permission to employ staff regardless of the usual political criteria, to freely import books and journals from the West and to maintain contacts with Western researchers (Burian 1997). Although it subsequently gained legendary status as the seedbed of post-1989 reform, the Institute appears to have been a disorganized and inefficient organization, reportedly driven more by Komárek's empire-building and self-aggrandizing personality than any coherent project (Ježek 1997: 54–61). The Institute's main significance seems to have been that it offered 'grey zone' elites greater freedom and opportunities to pursue personal research projects which ranged from market economics to Marxist philosophy.

Neo-liberalism and the 'Young Economists' of the 1960s

Within the 'grey zone' there was a distinct sub-group of neo-liberal economists centring on a generation of 'Young Economists' who emerged on the margins of the 1960s reform movement. This group included such subsequently important figures on the Czech centre-right politics as Václav Klaus and Tomáš Ježek. The 'Young Economists' had discovered the free market liberalism of the Austrian and Chicago schools as young researchers in the Academy of Sciences in the mid to late 1960s, when they were given access to previously unavailable Western social science literature and allowed to participate in conferences, seminars and study visits in Western countries. The group embraced a range of pro-market views,[31] but by the late 1960s all had come to reject not only orthodox Marxist central planning but also officially backed ideas of a 'socialist market' being developed by Ota Šik and his team at the Institute of Economics.[32] In time many gravitated from the Keynesian 'neo-classical synthesis' towards neo-liberalism of the Austrian and Chicago schools (Klaus 1996: 15–16).[33]

Klaus, Ježek and other 'Young Economists' were attracted to neo-liberalism and monetarism for a range of reasons. First the Austrian School of Hayek and Von Mises had, from the 1930s, elaborated a critique of the idea of planning, and in particular of the idea of socialist central planning which it rejected as an impossibility given the nature of human knowledge. Monetarists such as Friedman focused on the dangers of inflation, which, Klaus and others believed, was a major, but hidden, feature of socialist economies given the distortions, shortages and 'monetary overhang' created by administratively fixed prices (Batt 1988).[34] However, as Bockman and Eyal (2002) suggest, the relationship between Western and Eastern neo-liberals was more than a simple one-way transfer of neo-liberal ideas from Western teachers to Eastern pupils. Instead Western and Eastern neo-liberals formed a transnational 'actor network' with similar levels of expertise engaged in discrete academic dialogue. The outcome was a view of 'real socialism' as a 'laboratory of economic knowledge' which could serve both to empirically validate the ideas of thinkers such as von Mises, Hayek and Friedman about planning and markets in Western debates and to strengthen the technocratic legitimacy of Eastern neo-liberals in their own economics and policy communities.[35]

In 1968 the 'Young Economists' were organized in the Club of Young Economists (KMEN), which had 300–400 members. Klaus and others also wrote, sometimes pseudonymously, for reformist political-cultural journals such as *Kulturní život* and *Tvář*, popularizing previously taboo ideas about Czechoslovakia's economy, such as the role of trade unions as defenders of sectional interests or the possibility of inflation, as well as commenting on current events (Klaus 1996 14; Ježek 1997; Klaus 2001b: 27). The political impact of the young neo-liberals was minimal and their existence went largely unrecorded and unnoticed by historians of the 'Prague Spring' (Kusin 1971, 1972; Skilling 1976).[36] Following the 1968 invasion some 'Young Economists' including Klaus were dismissed from academic posts. However, their relative youth, lack of association with reform communism, and lingering plans among some regime politicians for Hungarian-style technocratic economic reform, allowed many 'Young Economists' to escape the worst of the post-1968 purges. Most were merely demoted or relegated to technical roles in financial and economic institutions, not excluded from all professional activity as were leading reform communists or liberal intellectuals such as Pithart and Havel (Ježek 1997: 50–1). Klaus, for example, worked in the State Bank between 1969 and 1989. Others were untouched by the post-1968 purges. Despite resigning his Communist Party membership in 1968, Tomáš Ježek, for example, remained at the Institute of Economics of the Academy of Sciences throughout the 'normalization period' until he joined the Forecasting Institute in 1988. Like other 'grey zone' elites, Czech neo-liberals were able to make use of the resources and opportunities these institutions afforded to engage in patterns of 'crypto-opposition' described above. Klaus was able to organize a series of economic seminars under the auspices of the Czechoslovak Science and Technology Society, which resulted in a series of internal papers published in editions of between 100 and 200 copies (Stráský 1993; Klaus 1996: 18–20; Blejer and Coricelli 1995: 9–39). Klaus, Ježek and other neo-liberals were also able to publish in domestic (and by the late 1980s foreign) academic journals on technical and theoretical issues in economics relating to the Czechoslovak economy.

The politics of Czech neo-liberalism

As with other 'grey zone' elites, the neo-liberals' activities had ramifications going beyond possible economic reform. As Klaus himself later recalled, the internal seminars he organized when at the State Bank 'were clearly a political matter (*politikum*). And everyone understood that they were a political matter. Both for those taking part in them, and those carefully keeping track of them' (Klaus 1996: 22). There is little available archival evidence concerning the exact nature of such discussions, but participants' subsequent recollections broadly confirmed that they obliquely addressed wider issues relating to capitalism and socialism and the role of the state and the individual (Stráský 1993; Klaus 1996: 13–28; Ježek 1997). Nevertheless, neo-liberals faced contradictory political incentives under late communism. On one hand, they viewed the political institutions of socialism as an obstacle to market forces, which in their view operated – albeit in distorted form – even in a planned, state-controlled economy such as that of Czechoslovakia. On the other hand, their commitment to free markets and private property did not automatically imply support for democratization,[37] although neo-liberal economists' writings of the late 1980s, which began to discuss the social and political prerequisites of economic reform, did highlight the need for broad social and political consensus (Klaus 1989: 42).

Of greater significance for the subsequent development of right-wing politics, however, were the fact that 'grey zone' elites represented a source of political thinking quite different from that of dissent. Indeed Hayekian views of intellectuals as self-interested 'second-hand dealers in ideas' inclined towards etatism and detached from the everyday life directly challenged the traditional Central European notion of the intelligentsia as conscience and moral leaders of the nation (Klaus 2005d). Neo-liberals drew their inspiration almost exclusively from foreign sources – mainly from Hayek and Friedman, but also from writers such as Michael Novak or James Buchanan (Klaus 1993b: 31; 1996 14–28). Klaus consciously dismissed traditional Czech social, political and economic thought (including that of the democratic interwar Czechoslovak Republic) as uninteresting, unproductive and parochial, and recalled, for example, that the approach of James Buchanan was

> very close to mine, and to that of the small group of people around me, who used to meet in the 1980s. We never romanticized politics. I believe that the view of our leading dissident elites on political matters drew on completely different intellectual sources and roots. It drew on a much more traditional view of the problem, or came out of a not very pragmatic philosophy. It certainly did not draw on the more rigorous, exact and markedly liberal standpoint which culminated in the Public Choice school.
>
> (Klaus 1993a: 49)

The philosophy of Jan Patočka was a formative influence on both Havel and neo-conservative dissidents such as Kroupa. Klaus, by contrast, dismissed Patočka as 'indisputably one of the blind alleys of Czech philosophy' (Klaus 1996: 22).

However, Anglo-American neo-liberal ideas – and especially those of Hayek – had a wider normative appeal than mere abstract economic efficiency. Ježek, for example, recalled his pre-1989 vision of a Czech 'market society' thus:

> I personally dreamt of a little, clean, orderly Austrian town with white houses, small inns and a sense of spiritual balance. I imagined people coming out of church on fine Sundays, all the houses whitewashed, all the fences mended and all the lawns mown. There was nothing there that wasn't carefully looked after by someone – simply boring old Europe (*ta nudná Evropa*).
>
> (Ježek 1997: 15)

Unlike many Anglo-American liberals, Hayek was less interested in the nature of individual freedom than in the problem of *social order* (Gamble 1996). The Hayekian idea of the market and market society as a 'spontaneous order' guaranteeing the emergence of a stable, well-ordered and moral society – with morality promoted by individual choice not state coercion – was deeply appealing to many Czechs who had retained both a Central European sense of petit-bourgeois propriety *and* a suspicion of the state, rooted in the experience of both communism and foreign rule before 1918 (Holy 1996: 180–94).[38]

Reviving the People's Party?

While most counter-elites in late communist Czechoslovakia were informal networks united by a shared intellectual or professional background, one group, which played an important role in the politics of the after 1989, emerged in a more institutionalized setting: reformists within the People's Party (ČSL). Following the communist takeover in 1948, the People's Party was restructured from a mass Catholic-oriented party into a satellite organization under a compliant pro-communist leadership. Like the other two Czechoslovak satellite parties, the satellite People's Party had a reduced membership; a residual organizational network; and a small number of deputies both in parliament and in the system of 'National Committees' which administered local government.[39] Unlike other mass organizations within the National Front, satellite parties had little function other than to act as auxiliary mobilizing structures and ideological transmission belts (Taborsky 1959).[40] The People's Party's main impact on public life in Czechoslovakia was through its daily newspaper, *Lidová demokracie*, and publishing house, Vyšehrad. Although its publications rarely overstepped permitted political boundaries, their relative lack of political propaganda and readers' sense of them as residually non-communist gave them a popularity out of all proportion to the People's Party's marginal status. Although the satellite parties played a relatively minor role in the politics of the 1960s reform era, under the system of 'socialist pluralism' proposed by communist reformers, it was envisaged that they would be transformed from façade organizations into active partners of the Communist Party with real autonomy and an influence in policy-making. In 1968 the People's Party happily embraced this new role, displacing its long-serving pro-Communist leader Fr Plojar, positively re-evaluating its pre-1948 history and adopting a new provisional programme stressing its distinctness, and began to explore distinct policies, such as the concept of a 'family wage' (an idea it had championed in 1945–8), the reform of Church–state relations and the development of individual private businesses and producer co-operatives. Like all political forces during the period, the party stressed its commitment to working within the socialist system and firmly rejected 'anti-socialist' positions for which, as a historically Catholic party, it might be an obvious vehicle (Kusin 1972: 167–70). Opinion polls carried out in 1968, it should be noted, indicated that ČSL had retained a significant base of support in Czech society and, in the same period, party membership grew significantly (Kusin 1972: 163, fn2, 169; Piekalkiewicz 1972: 246–51; Pecka *et al.* 1995: 9–11).[41] With the onset of 'normalization', ČSL resumed its role as bureaucratic shell organization under the close supervision of Communist officials in the National Front apparatus. The party's formal representation in government was scaled back and membership once again declined. Nevertheless, the party did provide an institutional focus for Catholics and a refuge for professionals who did not wish to (or could not) join the Communist Party. In a few localities in Moravia, the party also retained aspects of a 'real', socially rooted party and exercised some local influence (Daněk 1990).

After the advent of *perestroika* in 1985, reformist factions based in the People's Party's South Moravian branches and party training centre began to organize against the part leadership under the cover of officially sanctioned discussions on 'restructuring', demanding that the party should explicitly identify itself as Christian in outlook and seek to represent Christians, rather than merely transmit official policy.[42] Despite much bureaucratic infighting, the party's 'normalized' leadership blocked these efforts until October 1989, when reformists finally coalesced into a nationally organized 'Revival current' and agreed an alternative programme demanding competitive elections; the removal of the Communist Party's 'leading role'; the end of state supervision of the Church and the recognition of religious bodies as public organizations; the legalization of small-scale private enterprise; and restrictions on abortion and the use of the death penalty (Daněk 1990: 100–1). Reformist leaders in the People's Party were also linked to wider counter-elite networks, maintaining discreet links with Catholic dissidents, especially in Brno, from the early 1980s, and in some instances, providing practical assistance to them, such as access to duplicating machinery or copies of draft laws about to be presented to parliament (Daněk 1990: 52, 62–3). However, ČSL reformists' thinking differed fundamentally from those of Catholic conservative dissidents. Although both shared the view that Catholic values should influence politics, ČSL politicians saw political Catholicism as a democratic force loyal to the Czechoslovak state, rather than one calling the state and nation radically into question.[43] The 'revival current' finally displaced the People's Party's normalization era leadership on 26 November 1989, a week after the outbreak of the Velvet Revolution that marked the collapse of communist rule.

Charter 77's turn to politics: the emergence of right-wing proto-parties

As late as 1988–9 some Czech counter-elite figures and foreign observers saw little or no prospect of rapid or meaningful change in Czechoslovakia (Pithart 1990a: 364–5; Garton Ash 1991: 196). However, the gathering pace of reforms in the USSR, Hungary and Poland and a perceptible weakening of Czechoslovak regime control of society led others to begin to contemplate its demise. Some including the 'Revival current' of the People's Party anticipated a prolonged disengagement from socialism offering opportunities for once unimportant regime organizations to gain influence, as had occurred in the USSR and Hungary. Others such as Václav Benda, Pavel Bratinka and the 'grey zone' economist Josef Zieleniec foresaw the possibility that the regime might collapse in the face of a revolutionary situation which could propel new elites to power (Benda *et al.* 1988: 221; Day 1999: 113, 218–19). The changed social and political climate led Charter 77 to agree a strategy of actively creating independent social organizations and of founding a broad political grouping, the Movement for Civil Liberty (HOS), to rehabilitate politics and press for change. HOS's 'Democracy for All' manifesto thus articulated a broad liberal-democratic consensus for parliamentary democracy and a market economy (Hlušičková 1994: 10).

However, HOS also came to be a 'seedbed of political parties' (Dobal 1995) in which dissident political currents belatedly organized themselves into proto-parties. On the left former reform communists created *Obroda* ('Revival') as a

'Club for Socialist Restructuring' in February 1989 (Kokošková and Kokoška 1997), while the social-democratically oriented 'independent socialists', around Rudolf Battěk, developed open co-ordination structures in Prague and Brno, exploiting links with the satellite Czechoslovak Socialist Party (ČSS). The proto-right organized only in the latter part of 1989. The 'realist' group of Mandler and Dolezal, which had always embraced politics, had first formed an organized political movement, the Democratic Initiative (DI) in 1987. This early attempt at national political organization – the first since the 1970s – was quickly stifled by police repression and DI was able to reconstitute itself as an organized group only in spring 1989. It formally declared itself a political party, the Czechoslovak Democratic Initiative (ČSDI), in October 1989. A less ambitious but smoother course was followed by Christians in the Charter. The Christian Human Rights Union (KULP) was formed on 1 June 1989 as an ecumenical grouping campaigning for Christian conceptions of human rights neglected by other independent groups, such as the rights of the unborn child. An explicitly political Christian proto-party did not emerge until November 1989 when Václav Benda formed a Christian Democratic Club within the Movement for Civil Liberty, refounded shortly afterwards as the Christian Democratic Party (KDS) during the first days of the Velvet Revolution. In December 1989 dissident neo-conservatives around Daniel Kroupa and Pavel Bratinka who saw themselves as part of a 'civic current' and rejected political organization on the basis of group interests signed the founding declaration of another new political party – the Civic Democratic Alliance (ODA). The Catholic conservatives around *Střední Evropa* followed up links with Otto von Habsburg's Christian-Democrat-linked Paneuropa movement by founding the Pan-European Union of Bohemia and Moravia (PEUČM).

Despite the personal prominence of their founders, such proto-parties were a marginal and belated addition to a Czech dissident movement, which had itself always been weak and socially isolated. In neighbouring countries, opposition movements were stronger and proto-parties emerged more quickly, established themselves more easily and started to define the likely contours of post-communist political competition more clearly than in the Czech case. In Hungary, well-resourced liberal and neo-populist proto-parties emerged in 1987–8, (Tőkes 1996: 181–91, 195–202, 311–12) while in Poland, despite the unifying experience of Solidarity, distinct nationwide liberal, nationalist and Catholic political networks functioned throughout the 1980s (Szacki 1995).

Conclusions

In the wake of collapse of the 'Prague Spring' in 1968–9 a number of counter-elite groups formed in the Czech lands. By the mid-1970s, these groups had coalesced into an open dissident movement and a less visible 'grey zone' of technocrats and professionals. Although linked by common networks, these groups were intellectually and politically heterogeneous and generated diverse intellectual agendas. Circumscribed by repression and the absence of clear prospects of political change, none amounted to a coherent political project. As repression in Czechoslovakia moderated in the late 1980s, many moved towards more overtly political programmes and forms of organization. Although many Czech dissidents inclined towards an anti-modernism, moralism and elitism redolent of traditional conservatism, only limited numbers of dissident and 'grey zone' technocrats can be identified as forming a Czech 'proto-right'. These groupings rejected both the *status quo* of 'real socialism' and any notion of democratic socialism, by consciously seeking to think in new, wholly non-socialist political categories.

The appeal of free market economics and independent civic activity reflected a common desire to replace the bureaucratic power of the party-state with decen-tralized, autonomous social systems. Eyal's view of a 'right-wing' alliance of monetarists and dissident counter-elites united by moralistic, liberal anti-politics is, however, unsustainable. Notwithstanding his questionable view of ex-reform communists as external to dissent, few non-socialist dissidents embraced the 'non-teleological' anti-political view committing them to the 'renunciation of political power in favor of pastoral power' or rendering them always 'not inter-ested in formulating political programs' which he ascribes to them (Eyal 2000: 65). Proto-right groups were more concerned with identifying deeper historical foundations for liberal concepts of human rights and citizenship than in recon-ceptualising power in terms of liberal anti-politics.

In Hungary and Poland, non-socialist dissident discourses had strong continu-ities with debates in the pre-war period. With the exception of the Catholic con-servatism of *Středni Evropa* little such continuity can be found in the Czech case. Instead, most emergent proto-right views were based upon explicit *rejec-tion* and critique of the national past, variously seen as too collectivist, too egalitarian, too liberal or too statist. These critiques varied in focus and depth. While the Catholic conservatives of *Středni Evropa* challenged the very basis of Czech nationhood, a 'Tory' thinker such as Pithart merely highlighted the nation's perceived failings. Neo-conservatives and neo-liberals, by contrast, whilst not insensitive to the 'problem' of the Czech progressive and social democratic tradition, focused more narrowly on communist political and eco-nomic institutions in both their reform communist and their 'normalized' forms. These critical stances towards the past often led proto-right elites to adapt foreign models as a means of inventing or modernizing non-socialist political discourse.

In the Czech case, the sharp division of the dissident intelligentsia between Western-oriented liberals and national-populist conservatives found elsewhere in Central and Eastern Europe was less marked. Catholic counter-elites tended to eschew overt anti-liberalism, either focusing on history and Czech national tra-dition or linking themselves with broader demands for human rights and demo-cratic reform. More subtle tensions between liberalism and conservatism did, however, divide the Czech proto-right. While both Catholic conservatives and Pithart's more secular brand of dissident 'Toryism' stressed the importance of identity, history and legitimate state authority as the key to change, neo-liberals focused instead on the problems of the economy and the need to free economic actors. Dissident neo-conservatives occupied an intermediate position, sharing the concern of other dissident conservatives with moral values and civic cohesion, but seeing the renewal of the market as the key means to effect this transformation.

Compared with developments in Poland and Hungary, distinct 'proto-right' positions among Czech counter-elites emerged slowly and incompletely and, when finally formed, Czech right proto-parties lagged behind their Central European neighbours organizationally and politically. All were essentially Prague-based, had no meaningful organization and, at best, had a few dozen loosely affiliated supporters. The underdevelopment of the Czech dissident right was to have important consequences for the patterns of right-wing party formation after 1989 and ensured that the elite and ideas that had developed under late communism fed into the transition in fragmentary and unpredictable ways.

4 From civic movement to right-wing party

The emergence of the Civic Democratic Party 1990–1

Introduction

Both legacy-based approaches and discussions of post-communist elites tend to take the formation of political parties in post-communist Central and Eastern Europe as unproblematic. The same is also true of broader institutional approaches stressing the importance of constitutional design or electoral systems. However, as the literature on party development makes clear, party formation is a complex and uncertain process which requires the carefully crafted mobilization of resources and the making of alliances, as well as powerful underlying social conflicts or favourable electoral incentives. Much writing on party development in Central and Eastern Europe since 1989, although acknowledging this in general terms, has overlooked issues of party formation, tending to assume that – other than communist successor parties or 'historic' parties with links to the pre-communist period – most parties in the region are simply elite creations which emerged 'from scratch' in the early 1990s. This implies that new centre-right parties such as the Civic Democratic Party (ODS) in the Czech Republic were formed 'internally' by parliamentary and governmental elites with few pre-existing organizational resources in place in a pattern reminiscent of the top-down emergence of conservative and liberal 'cadre' parties in nineteenth-century Western Europe.[1]

This chapter critically reappraises these assumptions through a detailed examination of the formation of ODS in 1990–1 from the fragmenting Civic Forum movement, which led the early stages of Czechoslovakia's transition from communism. ODS's emergence as a successful new centre-right party, it will suggest, did not take place through the creation of a latter-day cadre party but through the successful *transformation* of the pre-existing mass grassroots organization of the Civic Forum movement. However, as several well-researched studies have shown, despite the efforts of ambitious and charismatic politicians in comparable cases in Poland, Russia or East Germany (Grabowski 1996; Brudny 1993; Fish 1995; Kamenitsa 1998; Dale 2004), similar mass civic movements yielded no significant liberal or right-wing 'successor party', but quickly fragmented and dissipated. This chapter also therefore seeks to analyse the formation of ODS in a broadly comparative perspective, seeking to identify the distinct factors that enabled the successful formation of a right-wing 'successor party' from a mass civic movement in the Czech Republic.

It begins by reviewing the formation of Civic Forum during the 'Velvet Revolution' of November–December 1989 and its ambiguous organizational structure and political identity. After reviewing the June 1990 elections from which the Forum emerged as the leading Czech 'party', it then considers conflicting organizational interests within the movement and the growing political divisions over economic reform, decommunization and Czech–Slovak relations, which saw a distinct 'right-wing' coalesce. Finally, it reviews rival elites' efforts to transform the Forum into a more durable and politically effective structure, contrasting the unsuccessful attempts of the Forum's centrist ex-dissident leaders to create a 'party-movement'; the failure of neo-conservative former dissidents in the Civic Democratic Alliance (ODA) to build a right-wing bloc in parliament; and the success of neo-liberal elites around Václav Klaus in mobilizing grassroots support for the creation of a 'standard party' of the right.

The formation of Civic Forum

The emergence of mass civic movements is characteristic of transitions from communism in which an outgoing regime seeks to resist social pressures for change, either by initiating the transition process itself as a 'pre-emptive strike' or by remaining intransigent until swept aside by popular protest. Czechoslovakia's 'Velvet Revolution' of November–December 1989 was a clear case of the second, 'revolutionary' mode of transition (Linz and Stepan 1996: 316–28). On 17 November 1989 the police's brutal response to a student demonstration in Prague triggered a wave of mass protest in Czechoslovakia on a scale not seen since 1968–9. It began among students, actors and intellectuals in Prague but rapidly took in regional centres and other social groups.

'Civic Forum' was formed in Prague on 19 November 1989 as an ad hoc committee bringing together Prague-based dissidents and dissident groupings, representatives of striking actors, student activists, writers and intellectuals and economists and social scientists from the Forecasting Institute, including neo-liberals such as Klaus and Ježek. As mobilization against the regime gathered momentum in the first three weeks of December 1989, 'civic fora' were created in workplaces and localities across the Czech lands and on 24 November 1989 the Prague 'Civic Forum' restyled itself the Co-ordinating Centre of Civic Forum and became a more structured body with sub-committees and a press service. On 27 November the Co-ordinating Centre agreed to co-ordinate the activity of local civic fora throughout the Czech Republic and, with its Slovak sister movement, Public Against Violence (VPN), began to negotiate on their behalf for the dismantling of the one-party system (Suk 1995: 41; 1997a: 23–8).[2]

The changing role of Civic Forum

It was initially very unclear what the structure of the movement was, or even whether one should speak of 'Civic Forum' as a national organization, or merely 'civic fora' in the sense of ad hoc assemblies for public discussion or a form of quasi-revolutionary local government (Marada 1997). In its early public declarations of November 1989, its Co-ordinating Centre defined Civic Forum (OF) as 'not a political party ... [or] an organization which accepts members ... an open community of those who feel a responsibility to find positive solutions in an intolerable political situation' (Suk 1998: 14, document 2). In so far as Václav Havel and the prominent dissidents who had founded OF in Prague had *any* conception of Civic Forum's role, it was that of representative of society in a prolonged 'pacted' transition based on opposition-regime negotiations of the kind that had already occurred in Hungary and Poland.

By mid-December 1989 the speed and scope of the regime's collapse meant that this conception of Civic Forum had been rapidly overtaken by events. Politically wrong-footed by the resignation of Prime Minister Adamec (Čalda 1996: 135–77; Glenn 2001: 167–90) and concerned lest a vacuum of power result in social disorder, OF leaders decided that the movement should shift from representing society and overseeing the communist authorities to heading a transitional government (Suk 2003: 37–79). The Government of National Understanding, formed on 12 December 1989 included a majority of OF and VPN nominees and marked the Communists' effective relinquishing of power. In coalition with Public Against Violence (VPN), Civic Forum thus rapidly became a dominant political actor with a nationwide organization (Suk 1995: 41) and a powerful role in government. Two other important decisions were taken at this time: first, that OF would put forward Václav Havel as its candidate for President, symbolically taking over the state but depriving the Forum of its effective leader; and, second, that the Forum would not merely 'guarantee' the free elections scheduled for June 1990 but would also *contest* them as a single organization with a common programme and would continue to exist after the elections.[3]

Civic Forum's uncertain organizational identity

Civic Forum's emergence as a *mass movement* marked a shift away from dissident ideas of the 'civic' as a self-enclosed 'parallel polis' to a concept of popular mobilization close to that of critics of Charter 77 such as the Democratic Initiative. There was, however, particular ambiguity as to whether (and in what sense) Civic Forum was a 'party' or a political organization. On 10–11 December 1989, members of the 'action group' of the Prague Co-ordinating Centre had defined OF as a 'civic political movement ... not a political party' but a 'coalition of democratic forces' (Suk 1998: 207–8, document 67), blurring the issue of whether the Forum was a *coalition* of political forces or a vehicle for non-partisan citizens to enter politics. However, Havel and other leading figures in the Co-ordinating Centre were determined that the Forum should be seen neither as a party nor as a coalition of parties.

The Forum's first statutes, passed in January 1990, settled on the description of the organization as a 'spontaneously arisen civic political movement' rather than a political party ('Stanovy OF', *Införum* 8/90, article 1). As a 'loose association of citizens' rejecting the Communist principle of democratic centralism, Civic Forum would, according to its January 1990 Statutes, develop 'a self-managed horizontal structure ... based on the autonomy of individual civic fora' with only a minor element of vertical structuring and 'small professional units' rather than a large bureaucratic apparatus ('Stanovy OF', *Införum* 8/90 articles 3 and 2a). Participation and affiliation were to be informal and open to all those who actively supported its programme of transition to democracy, the rule of law and a market economy (Suk 1998: 28–31, document 18), including members of 'democratically oriented political parties'. There was to be no formal membership for individuals, membership cards or membership dues ('Stanovy OF', *Införum* 8/90, article 2).[4] Local civic fora were to promote civic activism, bring people together to discuss politics and clarify their differing views as had occurred when they had come together in November and December 1989. Local Fora would also pressurize and transform existing official structures, organizing protests if necessary, acting as a 'means of civic self-defence' in defending citizens' rights and resolving local problems (Suk 1998, 159–60, document 57, articles 6b, 6c and 6d). The Civic Forum Co-ordinating Centre in Prague, effectively its national headquarters, was to provide a co-ordination and information service, and 'represent' OF nationally and internationally. It would not, however, give orders to fora at lower levels. Civic Forum was governed by an Assembly (*sněm*)[5] meeting every two weeks at which different components and institutions of the movement, including regional Civic Fora, were represented. Delegates to the Assembly elected the Civic Forum Council and other executive bodies in the movement. The Forum was to be headed by a collective leadership of three to five 'representatives' (or 'speakers') elected from within the OF Council.[6]

Organizational tensions in Civic Forum

A democratic deficit?

Conflicts between different levels of organization were endemic in loose civic movements that formed in Eastern Europe in 1988–9. In Civic Forum, local fora sometimes rejected the authority and legitimacy of district and regional bodies (Suk 2003: 303–6). Regional bodies in turn challenged the national leadership's control of resources and right to allocate 50 per cent of the places on the OF list for the June 1990 elections to national leaders and 'personalities' ('Jednání sněmu OF, *Införum* 19/90, 7 March 1990; 'Zpráva o zasedání Sněmu KC OF dne 21. dubna', *Införum* 25/90, 29 April 1990). As internal critics quickly noted, while Civic Forum proclaimed itself an entirely non-hierarchical organization, a de facto hierarchy existed. Such a fiction, they argued, was dangerous and implied a lack of leadership accountability and internal democracy (Hekrdla 1990). Later critics remarked on a growing gap between OF's Prague leadership which was 'assuming more and more the character of the apparatus of a political party' preoccupied with 'high politics' and 'OF as a movement, as a network of local fora' restricted to local problems (Chudomel *et al.* 1990). In the longer term, they feared, this democratic deficit risked either the emergence of a new political oligarchy – Civic Forum becoming in effect a new 'ruling party' – or, conversely, the movement's sudden disintegration, which could seriously destabilize reform (Kavan *et al.* 1990; see also Suk 2003: 321–6).

The marginalization of proto-parties

Civic Forum's ethos as a non-party social movement espousing non-ideological 'civic' values and rejection of organizational hierarchy and discipline was shared by mass civic movements in other transitions from communism (Brudny 1993; Fish 1995; Grabowski 1996). However, unlike movements such as Democratic Russia, Bulgaria's Union of Democratic Forces (SDS) or Romania's Democratic Convention (CD) (Roper 1998), Civic Forum was less a coalitional 'organization of organizations' than a single united, if loosely integrated, structure. A number of groupings and 'parties' based on the main dissident currents of 1988–9 did, however, participate in the founding of the Forum and had the status of collective members. Proto-parties such as the Club of Social Democrats (KSD) led by Rudolf Battěk, the Obroda club of former reform communists and the 'New Left' group Left Alternative (LA), as well as right-wing groupings such as the Czechoslovak Democratic Initiative (ČSDI) soon renamed the Liberal Democratic Party (LDS), the Civic Democratic Alliance (ODA), founded in November 1989 by the dissident neo-conservatives around Bratinka and Kroupa, and Václav Benda's Christian Democratic Party (KDS), were represented in the Prague Co-ordinating Centre's 'Political Commission'.

The Political Commission was initially conceived as one of the OF policy committees (Suk 1995: 20–1),[7] reflecting Havel's conception of parties as centres for discussion not decision-making (Havel 1990: 19–20). The Commission quickly came to function as a means of quarantining small proto-parties within the Forum, which, nevertheless, depended on it for delegates to the Civic Forum Assembly, funding and other resources such as 'electable' places on the OF electoral list.[8] Parties in the Forum were thus quickly relegated to the status of a minor interest group, and, from spring 1990, started to leave the Forum to seek alliances elsewhere or build independent party organizations. The Forum's parliamentary election campaign reinforced their marginalization, playing heavily on public anti-party sentiment using the (in)famous slogan 'Parties are for party hacks, Civic Forum is for everyone'.[9] Of the 535 candidates fielded by Civic Forum in the Czech and federal parliamentary elections of June 1990, only 42 (7.9 per cent of the total) were members of political parties (Suk 2003: 318).[10] This fell far short of the 30–40 per cent demanded by the Civic Forum's member parties, a level of representation which might have provided the nucleus of a meaningfully sized party groups in parliament (Suk 2003: 315–18).

The emergence of organizational interests

Before the June 1990 elections, across the Civic Forum movement as a whole organizational tension were arguably more important than factional divisions. As Hadjiisky (1996, 2001) has convincingly shown, the development of organizational interests in Civic Forum must be understood in terms of the professionalization of politics and the 'local dimension' of the movement. The main actors in both processes represented a 'second generation' of participants in OF mobilized in late 1989 and 1990, usually lacking any earlier involvement in dissident politics (or the moral authority that accompanied it): local councillors, OF parliamentary deputies, who had emerged through district and regional fora, full-time paid 'electoral managers' working in district Civic Forum Co-ordinating Centres, who wanted increasingly to secure their personal futures and establish their political identity and legitimacy as political professionals working within a well-structured, efficient political organization (Hadjiisky 1996: 14–16).[11]

Compromises over OF's campaign strategy and organization in spring 1990 meant that Civic Forum's district managers occupied a pivotal but ambiguous role in the movement (Suk 2003: 312–14).[12] Managers worked at district level and were elected by district Fora, but were responsible to regional structures and were paid by the Co-ordinating Centre in Prague.[13] Such confused lines of responsibility and the unique position of managers as the only real vertical link in the movement, made this 'group of actors living for and by politics, emerging from the regions but in constant communication with the centre' (Hadjiisky 1996: 16) an increasingly powerful and self-conscious force with an interest in both the further professionalization of OF and a reduction in the power of the Prague Co-ordinating Centre in favour of the regions. Despite these tensions, the June 1990 elections, which were, in effect, a referendum on four decades of communist rule, were a triumph for Civic Forum. In the vote for the Federal Assembly – for which separate national ballots were held in the Czech lands and Slovakia – the Forum received over 53 per cent of Czech vote (see Tables 4.1 and 4.2). In the parallel vote for the Czech parliament (the Czech National Council) it received just under half of all votes cast (see Table 4.3).

The failure of Christian Democracy

Despite Civic Forum's role in leading the transition, before the elections most Czech observers had anticipated relatively strong performances by 'historic' parties of left and right, which had played an important role in Czechoslovakia's successful interwar democracy and subsequently survived as 'satellite' parties or exile groups. Many had expected a renewed Social Democratic Party to emerge

Table 4.1 Czech elections of 8–9 June 1990 to the Czechoslovak Federal Assembly – Chamber of the People (lower house)

Party	No. of votes	% of vote	No. of seats
Civic Forum (OF)	3,851,172	53.15	68
Communist Party (KSČS)	976,996	13.48	15
Christian Democratic Union (KDU)[1]	629,359	8.69	9
Movement for Self-Governing Democracy– Society for Moravia and Silesia (HSD-SMS)	572,015	7.89	9
Czechoslovak Social Democracy (ČSSD)	278,280	3.84	0
Alliance of Countryside and Farmers (SZV)	273,175	3.77	0
Green Party (SZ)	224,432	3.10	0
Czechoslovak Socialist Party (ČSS)	199,446	2.75	0
All-People's Democratic Party/Association for the Republic–Republican Party of Czechoslovakia (VDSPR)	67,781	0.94	0
Free Bloc (SB)	57,925	0.80	0
Interest Associations of the Czech Republic (VSZS)	47,971	0.66	0
Czechoslovak Democratic Forum (ČSDF)	22,866	0.32	0
Movement for Civil Liberty (HOS)	21,585	0.30	0
Friends of Beer Party (SPP)	8,943	0.12	0
Movement For Czech-Slovak Understanding (HČSP)	8,032	0.11	0
Co-Existence (ESWMK)	5,472	0.08	0
Total	7,254,450	100.00	101

Source: *Statistická ročenka ČSFR 1991.*

Note
1 Coalition of Czechoslovak People's Party (ČSL), Christian Democratic Party (KDS) and Slovak Christian Democratic Movement (KDH).

quickly as the main force on the left and saw the likely future of the Czech right in a conservative or Christian Democratic bloc based on the Czechoslovak People's Party (ČSL). Yet, despite the adoption of a list-based system of proportional representation with a low (5 per cent) threshold for both Czech and federal parliaments, 'historic' parties fared poorly and were outpolled not only by Civic Forum but also by the Communist Party and the hastily created Moravian regionalist movement, HSD-SMS. The two main parties of the 'historic' Czech left, Czechoslovak Social Democracy (ČSSD) and the Czechoslovak Socialist Party (ČSS) fell below the 5 per cent threshold and failed to enter parliament, while the Christian and Democratic Union (KDU) coalition led by the Czechoslovak People's Party polled less than 9 per cent in the Czech lands.[14] As analyses by political geographers confirmed, in the Czech lands the KDU coalition drew strongly on Catholic voters and localities with pre-1948 traditions of voting for the People's Party for its support (Kostelecký 1994, 1995), but made few inroads elsewhere.

Table 4.2 Czech elections of 8–9 June 1990 to the Czechoslovak Federal Assembly – Chamber of Nations (upper house)

Party	No. of votes	% of vote	No. of seats
Civic Forum (OF)	3,613,513	49.96	50
Communist Party (KSČS)	997,919	13.80	12
Movement for Self-Governing Democracy– Society for Moravia and Silesia (HSD-SMS)	658,477	9.10	7
Christian Democratic Union (KDU)[1]	633,053	8.75	6
Czechoslovak Social Democracy (ČSSD)	301,445	4.17	0
Alliance of Countryside and Farmers (SZV)	288,270	3.99	0
Green Party (SZ)	248,270	3.44	0
Czechoslovak Socialist Party (ČSS)	208,662	2.89	0
Free Bloc (SB)	78,910	1.09	0
All-People's Democratic Party/Association for the Republic-Republican Party of Czechoslovakia (VDSPR)	72,155	1.00	0
Interest Associations of the Czech Republic (VSZS)	54,196	0.76	0
Friends of Beer Party (SPP)	13,869	0.19	0
Czechoslovak Democratic Forum (ČSDF)	32,044	0.44	0
Movement for Civil Liberty (HOS)	21,210	0.29	0
Movement for Czech-Slovak Understanding (HČSP)	8,738	0.12	0
Total	7,232,125	100.00	75

Source: *Statistická ročenka ČSFR 1991.*

Note
1 Coalition of Czechoslovak People's Party (ČSL), Christian Democratic Party (KDS) and Slovak Christian Democratic Movement (KDH).

The failure of a strong Christian Democratic bloc to emerge in the Czech lands in 1990 can be explained largely by the strategy adopted by People's Party leaders after November 1989. Although happy to use the Christian Democratic label, ČSL did not present itself as right-wing but, like many other parties at this time, merely stressed its democratic character. Moreover, ČSL leaders saw their party as representing a sizeable Catholic and Christian constituency and campaigned under the slogan 'Believers Vote for Their Faith' (*Věřící volí víru*) and sought to re-establish a mass party of some 100,000–150,000 members with a network of affiliated social organizations of the type ČSL had been before 1948 (*Lidová demokracie*, 19 January 1990, 2).[15] The other main plank of the party's appeal to voters was a vague anti-communism, which, notwithstanding its status as a former satellite party, depicted ČSL as a victim of communist repression and bulwark of non-communist values before 1989. Such anti-communism provided the party's only real engagement with the issues of the transition period.

Although the Socialist and Social Democratic parties' strategies of mass

Table 4.3 Elections to the Czech National Council of 8–9 June 1990

Party	No. of votes	% of vote	No. of seats
Civic Forum (OF)	3,569,201	49.50	127
Communist Party (KSČS)	954,690	13.24	32
Movement for Self-Governing Democracy– Society for Moravia and Silesia (HSD-SMS)	723,609	10.03	22
Christian Democratic Union (KDU)[1]	607,134	8.62	19
Alliance of Countryside and Farmers (SZV)[2]	296,547	4.11	0
Czechoslovak Social Democracy (ČSSD)	296,165	4.11	0
Green Party (SZ)	295,844	4.10	0
Czechoslovak Socialist Party (ČSS)	192,922	2.68	0
Free Bloc (SB)	75,242	1.04	0
All-People's Democratic Party/Association for the Republic-Republican Party of Czechoslovakia (VDSPR)	72,048	1.00	0
Interest Associations of the Czech Republic (VSZS)	60,453	0.84	0
Friends of Beer Party (SPP)	43,632	0.61	0
Czechoslovak Democratic Forum	23,659	0.33	0
Total	6,473,250	100.00	200

Source: *Statistická ročenka ČSFR 1991.*

Notes
1 Coalition of Czechoslovak People's Party (ČSL), Christian Democratic Party (KDS) and Slovak Christian Democratic Movement (KDH).
2 Coalition of Czechoslovak Agricultural Party (ČSZ), Party of Czechoslovak Integration, Party of the Moravian Countryside, Movement for the Equality of Women, Political Movement of Co-operative Farmers, Pensioners for a Secure Life (DŽJ), Nationwide Citizens' Activist Group (CAO).

party building and historic revival rapidly faltered (Hanley 2001), the People's Party (ČSL) and the KDU coalition initially appeared to enjoy good electoral prospects. ČSL had a united leadership, significant material advantages and a groundswell of popular support. Party membership grew spectacularly after November 1989, more than doubling in the first three months of 1990 with a membership of just under 100,000 and marked growth in Catholic regions such as South Moravia and East Bohemia. ČSL had a paid nationwide apparatus and organizational infrastructure, significant real estate, a publishing company and a national newspaper, *Lidová demokracie.* As Civic Forum's popularity began to flag in spring 1990, support for KDU was increasing and the bloc appeared well placed to emerge as the second most powerful force in the Czech lands. According to IVVM polling, its support reached a peak of 15 per cent in April 1990 compared with 21 per cent for OF and remained at over 10 per cent until the eve of polling (cited in Krejčí 1994: 239).

However, it quickly became clear that the party's organizational and material advantages were more apparent than real. Given its moribund, bureaucratic 'shell' organization as a satellite party before 1989, the 'renewed' party's leadership was an isolated, self-selected group reliant on a party apparatus, which lacked the skills and energy to co-ordinate political activity, mobilize grassroots support or cope with the influx of new members effectively. The abolition in April 1990 of the National Front, through which state funding had been channelled to the party under the old regime, and the temporary freezing in the same month by the Federal Assembly of parties' right to dispose of their property or use it for commercial ends (*Svobodné slovo*, 25 October 1990, 7) significantly disrupted the party's finances, as did new tax legislation increasing the liabilities of its two publishing houses (*Bulletin* no. 1, 7 September 1990, 7–8).[16] As its support rose in March–April 1990, the People's Party became a target of Civic Forum's election campaigning which highlighted ČSL's internal divisions and its leaders' links with the former regime. Much criticism focused on the employment of former members of communist secret police by Federal Interior Minister Richard Sacher who was a member of ČSL (Suk 2003: 355–72). More damaging still was the televised revelation two days before polling that the party's leader, Josef Bartončík, was listed as an informer in the records of the former communist secret police.

The relative failure of KDU confirmed the real, but limited nature of 'historic' parties' constituencies and the difficulty of reviving traditional mass party organization in a post-communist society. It also confirmed the historical status of Czech political Catholicism as a minority force, slightly removed from the political mainstream, a pattern seen in 1918–38 and 1945–8, in a society undergoing long-term secularization (Spousta 2002). KDU's emergence as a minor political player ruled out the emergence of the anticipated Christian Democratic right, ensuring that, if the strong centre-right was to emerge in Czech politics, it would do so through Civic Forum.

Political divisions in Civic Forum

The struggle against 'old structures'

There was a widespread perception across much of East Central Europe in the early 1990s that powerful hidden forces from the former *nomenklatura* were destabilizing or perverting democracy, leaving the abuses of the communist past unpunished. Such sentiments were especially strong in the Czech lands, where an intransigent and repressive regime had collapsed with surprisingly little resistance. Divisions over decommunization were present in Civic Forum at local level from its inception. The Civic Forum in Brno, the Czech lands' second city, had, for example, acrimoniously split over the issue as early as February 1990 ('Parlament rozhodl', *Infórum* 18/90, 28 February 1990, citing VIA news agency, and 'Přehled událostí v Brně', *Infórum* 24/90, 2 April 1990; see also Suk 2003: 326–37) leaving the Forum 'paralysed' in the region ('Zpráva o zasedání Sněmu OF 17.3', *Infórum* 21/90, 2 April 1990). In spring 1990, demands for sweeping decommunization, including the banning of the Communist Party itself, were voiced by a number of small political groups and parties, some of which organized demonstrations and public protests. These included the Movement for Civil Liberty (HOS) and Club of Committed Non-Party Members (KAN) which were collective members of Civic Forum, as well the Confederation of Political Prisoners (KPV) which organized a demonstration on 23 April 1990, attended by 10,000 people, demanding the banning of the Communist Party (Suk 2003: 386–90). Anti-communists were also sharply critical of OF leaders who were sceptical of demands for radical decommunization, claiming that their (assumed) backgrounds as reform communists in the 1960s had left them with an indelible sympathy with Communists and the Communist Party ('Vystoupení představitele KAN', *Införum* 33/90, 31 July 1990).

It was only after the elections that such divisions appeared at national level. Post-election disappointment over the slowness of change and the apparently continuing power of 'old structures' and '*nomenklatura* brotherhoods' was especially strong in local and district Civic Fora. Although many OF-endorsed figures had been 'co-opted' into national positions of authority as part of the 'round table' agreements between representatives of Civic Forum, Public Against Violence, the Communist Party and its satellites in early 1990, the process of replacing discredited communist-era managers and administrators at local level was far less advanced. The post-election radicalization of grassroots anti-communism brought regional activists directly into conflict with the OF leadership in Prague which, consistent with its attempts at a negotiated transition, 'did not want to drive the Communist Party into a corner' ('Sněm OF', *Införum* 32/90, 16 July 1990). One such *cause célèbre* was the conflict between the Czech Prime Minister, Petr Pithart, and district Civic Forum leaders in Hodonín, who had drawn up lists of discredited figures for removal from office in their district. Pithart, whose conservative rejection of political radicalism had led him to speak out repeatedly against proposals for anti-communist purges (Hovoří P. Pithart', *Införum* 7/90, 9 January 1990 and 'Projev P. Pitharta v čs. televizi', *Införum* 11/90, 21 January 1990) quickly condemned the Hodonín initiative.[17] This prompted an angry public protest by Hodonín OF (*Lidové noviny*, 17 July 1990: 1) and was quickly endorsed by other district Fora (*Lidové noviny*, 23 July 1990: 1) which accused Pithart of ignorance of the situation 'far from Prague' and indifference to the activists who had campaigned to get him and other OF leaders elected. Radical decommunization measures were also supported by OF organizations in major cities, such the Prague Regional Civic Fora (PROF), as well as by deputies in the Czech parliament with a background in district Civic Fora ('Vladimír Šuman: postupovat radikálněji', *Införum* 36/90, 21 August 1990).

This mood of post-election frustration with the pace of change was, surprisingly, most effectively articulated by President Havel in a speech in Wenceslas Square on 21 August 1990, the anniversary of the 1968 invasion.[18] Havel noted that, despite the Velvet Revolution

> In many communities the same people rule, who ruled them before. They are linked to the management of economic enterprises. Enormous bureau-

cratic colossuses still exist, which prevent the rational economic behaviour of individual enterprises and plants.

(Havel 1992: 17)

The antidote to 'the tentacles (*chapadla*) of invisible mafias' was, the President told his listeners, to create a reinvigorated and remobilized civic and social movement to pressurize the state apparatus to complete the Velvet Revolution. Havel's apparent call for a second revolution was enthusiastically taken up by moderate former dissidents on the Civic Forum Council ('Petr Kučera: období druhé revoluce' and 'Ivan Fišera: Občanské fórum – stav a východiska', *Infórum* 36/90, 21 August 1990). However, the speech also lent itself to more radical anti-communist interpretations. More significantly, it also publicly reframed political debate around the question of *how* post-communist reform could be implemented by linking issues of decommunization, economic reform and the future of OF into a single discourse. This same triad of issues was later to define the Czech right.

By September 1990 decommunization had become an issue openly dividing Civic Forum. Government ministers with a *nomenklatura* background such as Federal Prime Minister Marian Čalfa increasingly came under attack from grass-roots activists. Many right-wing delegates left the Assembly of 15 September 1990, making it inquorate, rather than discuss a motion sponsored by the OF leadership condemning 'tendencies to condemn, label and discriminate against whole groups of citizens' (i.e. ex-communists) (Usnesení Sněmu OF ze dne 15.9.90', *Infórum* 40/90, 18 September 1990) and 'primitive anti-communism' ('Zpráva z jednání kolegia Občanského fóra 19.9.90', *Infórum* 41/90, 25 September 1990). By 13 October 1990, the OF Assembly was debating a motion (finally rejected) that Petr Pithart, a *bête noire* of radical anti-communists, should be removed as Czech Prime Minister.

The politics of economic transformation

From late 1989 opinion polls had shown that for both the Czech public and Czech political elites the most urgent political issue was economic reform (Rak 1992; Boguszak *et al.* 1996). While favouring Civic Forum's loose non-party style of organization, voters also expected the movement to be the main engine of economic reform. It was widely expected that, when implemented, economic reform would be a shock and would give rise to social unrest (Boguszak *et al.* 1990a). Moreover, opinion polling in May 1990 uncovered ambiguous attitudes to economic reform. There was, on one hand, a widespread feeling among the public that 'something must be done' about the economy and strong support for the principle of privatization. On the other hand, there was much less support for (or understanding of) the most likely privatization measures such as the sale of large industries or the participation of foreign capital in privatization (Boguszak and Rak 1990; Boguszak *et al.* 1996). Analysis of underlying public attitudes suggested that 52 per cent of the Czechoslovak population was either 'consistently' or 'mildly' anti-reformist in outlook, while another 30 per cent held 'inconsistent' views on economic reform (Boguszak *et al.* 1996: 106–8). By September 1990 polling experts were warning that the public's essentially 'political' support for economic reform – support based on a rejection of socialism, rather than well-defined socio-economic interests – had peaked and noted 'a growing distance between the government's expert based policies and everyday life, where a dangerous "them and us" relationship is developing' (Boguszak *et al.* 1990b; see also Pehe 1991a).

Although there were ineffectual attempts by small left-wing parties, such as the Social Democrats (ČSSD), to present alternative reform proposals, much of the policy debate took place between groups of technocrats holding political office at the behest of Civic Forum. The specialist knowledge and presumed ability to address Czechoslovakia's economic problems that such figures possessed was an important asset enabling them to gain access to political power. The more high-profile, assertive and ambitious amongst them, such as Václav Klaus, Miloš Zeman or Valtr Komárek, the Director of the Forecasting Institute, had rapidly gained important posts in the OF Co-ordinating Centre or the Government of National Understanding and quickly became well-known public figures. Klaus, for example, became Federal Finance Minister and Komárek Deputy Prime Minister in the Government of National Understanding. Zeman became a Civic Forum MP and wrote much of the movement's electoral programme. While many former dissidents envisaged a social market economy based on small businesses and many left-wing technocrats favoured privatization after state-led restructuring, the neo-liberal economists around Václav Klaus were committed to free market approaches.

Czech responses to Slovak nationalism

In the course of 1990, the emergence of Slovak nationalism and, to a lesser extent, Moravian regionalism (Obrman 1991), propelled the issue of reform of Czechoslovak federalism onto the Czech political agenda. Like other 'politically strong, institutionally weak' national groups in multinational communist federations (Bunce 1999a), Czech politicians and public initially failed to see the issue as important, but, having no strong preferences, were prepared to engage with Slovak demands. After initial dispute between Czech and Slovak politicians over the new official name of non-communist Czechoslovakia (the so-called 'Hyphen War'), bilateral negotiations on restructuring the federation between the governments of the Czech and Slovak Republics (later joined by the President and the federal government) began in April 1990. Despite sometimes tense negotiations and occasional difficulties negotiating with the mercurial Slovak Prime Minister, Vladimír Mečiar, during the period of OF's disintegration Czech–Slovak relations seemed an issue of manageable proportions. Indeed, in December 1990, it appeared to have been resolved through the passing of an agreed Competence Law reallocating some powers from the federal centre to the two national republics (Stein 1997: 57–85; Suk 2003: 351–5).

However, even at this early stage the issue served to divide some groups in Civic Forum from the movement's leadership and the majority of the Czech government, who saw the accommodation of Slovak demands and the negotiation of a new federal settlement as a matter of priority. The retention of a strong federal centre – and hence a strong Federal Finance Ministry – was important to Václav Klaus and his team both because the Ministry was their main vehicle for influencing policy and because the decentralization of economic power threatened to delay and complicate the implementation of the market-led reform strategy which they had co-formulated.[19] Some Czech parliamentarians also became increasingly hostile towards efforts by the Federal and Czech government to accommodate Slovak demands at the apparent expense of Czech interests. In November 1990, the right-wing Chair of the Czech parliament's Constitutional Committee, Jan Kalvoda, was instrumental in bringing about the Committee's rejection of the draft Competence Law and later that month right-wing OF deputies led efforts to amend the Competence Law against the wishes of both the Czech and federal governments.

Reorganizing Civic Forum

Conflicts over transformation became increasingly enmeshed with issues of the internal organizational reform within Civic Forum and the wider question of if, when and how new broad-based political parties would emerge in Czechoslovakia. Some former dissidents in Civic Forum saw the movement as the harbinger of a 'new politics' of non-ideological civic participation superseding traditional ideologies of left and right and conventional party politics (Urban 1990a: 126, 134–5). In the event, most politicians from all wings of Civic Forum were happy to accept that their movement would ultimately become a conventional programmatic party (or coalition) of the centre or break into two or three equal-sized parties representing different parts of the traditional spectrum (Urban 1990b; Hajek 1990; Zeman 1990). Although politicians on the ex-dissident right and former reform communist left favoured a quicker and more decisive transformation of the movement, the OF leadership envisaged a gradual process, which would take place once key transformation policies had been consensually agreed and implemented. However, in July 1990, even for well-informed observers, the mechanism for the ultimate division of OF into parties was still 'a very big "if"' (Garton Ash 1991: 281) and the political direction of a transformed OF was still uncertain. Given the social-liberal leanings of the OF leadership, many inclined towards the view that 'the constituent elements of Civic Forum are likely to crystallize around some novel form of social democracy' (Glenny 1990: 48).

There was, it seems, a growing realisation among OF elites, particularly those in government or parliamentary office, that although the Forum's self-definition, rhetoric and organization remained largely those of an inclusive civic movement, the roles it already performed – contesting elections, producing policy and co-ordinating executive and legislature – were largely those of a political party.[20] Following its unexpectedly sweeping election victory, a consensus emerged that, at a national level, Civic Forum could not function as a non-ideological vehicle for trusted 'personalities' but had to base its credibility and electoral appeal on a programme, and that it needed restructuring into a more integrated and effective national organization through the introduction of more hierarchical elements, more formalized participation and some means of recognizing the growing diversity of opinion within it.

Early organizational reform

In summer 1990, Civic Forum leaders – supported by Václav Havel – sought to introduce a series of incremental organizational reforms intended to make the movement more effective while retaining significant parts of the structure established after the Velvet Revolution. This reflected a view of Civic Forum as a uniquely successful organization of more than purely transitional significance because of its ability 'to unite quite different ideological currents (*ideové proudy*)' around a common programme ('I Fišera: Návrh připravené struktury OF', *Infórum* 31/90).[21] The first coherent set of such reorganization proposals were outlined at the Assembly of 16 June 1990 by Ivan Fišera, one of the four Civic Forum Council 'representatives' ('I Fišera: Návrh připravené struktury OF', *Infórum* 31/90, 29 June 1990). After discussion in the OF Assembly on 16 and 31 July 1990, a compromise version of these proposals was then adopted. New statutes passed in August 1990 described OF simply as '[t]he political movement "Civic Forum"', no longer mentioning its 'spontaneous' character. Adherence to OF was as previously to be based on supporting the November 1989 'Declaration of Civic Forum'. While the previous statutes had stressed the 'informal' character of participation in OF, the new document created forms of quasi-membership. OF supporters should 'allow themselves to be recorded (*evidováni*)' by local Civic Fora in a manner to be determined locally and could be asked to pay 'fees for record-keeping' (*evidenční poplatky*) on a purely voluntary basis ('Organizace a struktura Občanského fóra', *Infórum* 36/90, 21 August, supplement 2, article 1.1). The statutes also allowed OF supporters to form 'clubs attached to OF' (*kluby při OF*), which could *require* participants to pay 'regular one-off contributions (*pravidelných jednorázových příspěvků*)' providing a mechanism for the gradual grassroots formation of parties from within Civic Forum. The new statutes also reinforced the hierarchy of authority in Civic Forum by empowering local Civic Fora to 'remove from their records' supporters who had gone against the Civic Forum Declaration or violated the statutes ('Organizace a struktura Občanského fóra', *Infórum* 36/90, 21 August 1990, supplement 2) and allowed Civic Forum Assemblies from district level upwards to 'judge the legitimacy of lower units and organs of OF', and to 'adopt a resolution concerning the possible abolition of this organ or the recall of this organ' ('Organizace a struktura Občanského fóra', *Infórum* 36/90, 21 August

1990, supplement 2, article 2).[22] The new statutes created a national 'Collegium', an executive body bringing together representatives of Civic Forum's parliamentary deputies, government officeholders and internal leadership and recommended the creation of similar 'collegia' ('Organizace a struktura Občanského fóra', *Infórum* 36/90, 21 August 1990, supplement 2, articles 3.4 and 2).The statutes also recognized and outlined the role of a permanent, professional 'managerial network' but did not centralize control over it as Fišera had proposed.

A further round of organization reform was triggered by Václav Havel, who made a rare personal intervention in a speech to the Civic Forum Assembly of 15 September 1990. Havel argued that, although highly democratic, the Forum's traditions of decentralized loose organization inherited from the Velvet Revolution meant that authority was not clearly delimited or always respected. OF ministers, deputies and the OF Assembly did not co-ordinate their activities and regarded each other with mutual suspicion and the OF-led government was left uncertain as to whether the broader movement would support its policies. It was therefore necessary, argued Havel, for the Forum to have 'firmer leadership', by electing a Civic Forum Chairman[23] to give the 'firm and decisive leadership' needed to carry through the radical reform the public expected. The President's proposal was placed on the agenda of the OF Assembly and later passed.

For Havel, as for Fišera, such changes represented a compromise between the democratic ideal of a horizontal, inclusive movement and the political effectiveness of traditional party structures for policy-making and government co-ordination.[24] Even OF politicians such as Petr Pithart who did believe in conventional party models largely accepted the need for compromise as public hostility to traditional party politics seemed so strong that it would be unlikely to be rapidly overcome.[25]

The challenge of the Civic Forum right

In early 1990 a plethora of small self-styled 'right-wing' groups had emerged in the Czech lands.[26] However, few advanced a clear rationale as to what the 'right' stood for in the post-communist Czech context. Most confined themselves to vague anti-communist declarations and the argument that the right was necessary for a 'balanced' political spectrum. Only the small Civic Democratic Alliance (ODA) formed by Pavel Bratinka and Daniel Kroupa in December 1989 had a clear programmatic notion of the political right, which it defined somewhat abstractly as 'economic neo-liberalism and political neo-conservatism of a Western type' (Mašek and Žegklitz 1990). With the failure of the People's Party to create a strong Czech Christian Democratic bloc and the continuing uncertainty over the future of Civic Forum, the shape or strength of the right in OF was difficult to foresee. Like many civic movements in Eastern Europe in 1988–90, Civic Forum's loose decentralized structures, ambiguous identity and ongoing reorganization offered many 'zones of uncertainty' (Panebianco 1981) around which potential challengers to its existing leadership could mobilize. In the case of Civic Forum, there were a number of potential challengers. Some, such as the network of former reform communists in the Obroda club, had been marginalized by Havel and his allies at an early stage (Glenn 2001: 136–8, 184–5). Others, such as liberal technocrats, disaffected anti-communist grass-roots activists and the remaining proto-parties of the ex-dissident right, were to pose a more powerful challenge.

The Interparliamentary Club of the Democratic Right

The first formal attempt to organize the right within Civic Forum was the Interparliamentary Club of the Democratic Right (MKDP). The MKDP was a parliamentary caucus formed by right-wing Civic Forum deputies in the Federal Assembly and the Czech parliament. The Club met formally met for the first time on 25 September 1990 and by the time its existence was announced to the press on 12 October 1990 included 33 of the 118 federal deputies elected for Civic Forum and 33 of the 127 Civic Forum deputies in the Czech parliament. Although in part intended as a co-ordination device to facilitate negotiation within OF's large disparate parliamentary groups (Hadjiisky 1996: 27; Hamerský and Dimun 1999: 17–18), the MKDP was the first clear manifestation of an organized 'right wing' within the movement and the first public indication that the much anticipated process of 'differentiation' in OF was under way. The immediate impulse for the Club's formation seems to have come from a sense of frustration among right-wing OF deputies at their left-wing and centrist colleagues' more accommodating response to the Communist-led criticism of the government's economic reform strategy. However, in its Founding Declaration the MKDP presented a broader definition of 'the right', which centred on three issues: (1) support for the federal government's 'Scenario for Economic Reform' against 'social pressures'; (2) vigorous measures against 'old structures' and policies to punish the crimes of the communist past and enact historical justice through for example restitution of nationalized property to pre-1948 owners; and (3) defence of the powers of the federal state (Hamerský and Dimun 1999: 17–18).

The MKDP was more than an ad hoc grouping of disaffected legislators. It was also the first active political initiative by the Civic Democratic Alliance (ODA) – one of the few proto-parties of the ex-dissident right to have remained within Civic Forum – to shape the future of OF (Kroupa 1996: 29). The ODA Deputy-Chairman Daniel Kroupa chaired the Club and acted as its spokesperson, and three of ODA's seven parliamentary deputies were represented in the MKDP leadership. Although they publicly avoided the issue at the time (Hamerský and Dimun 1999: 19), there is some evidence that ODA leaders saw the MKDP as a means to create a broad-based 'Democratic Right' party or bloc around ODA (Stoniš and Havlík 1998: 23; see also Hadjiisky 1996: 38–9). Indeed, in autumn and winter 1990, a number of local and district Civic Fora passed resolutions associating themselves with the MKDP, suggesting that a right-wing party might emerge through a top-down 'cadre' model of party formation centring on a parliamentary caucus.

Despite its clearly defined brand of right-wing politics and the support it enjoyed from prominent former 'grey zone' economists such as newly appointed Czech Minister of Privatization Tomáš Ježek, ODA was too organizationally weak and publicly little known to make a significant immediate impact. Before Ježek's appointment as a minister in August 1990 and the foundation of the MKDP, none of its leaders had had a significant national profile. Indeed, as ODA Chairman Pavel Bratinka remarked in June 1990 its leaders were better known in Washington and London than in Czechoslovakia (Bratinka 1991: no pagination). More significantly ODA was regarded by many OF activists and legislators from the regions with the same scepticism they reserved for Prague-based, ex-dissident elites generally (Stoniš and Havlík 1998: 23).

The rise of Václav Klaus

Ultimately, it was not a group but an individual, the Finance Minister Václav Klaus, who was to emerge as focal point and standard-bearer of the Civic Forum right. As a central figure in disputes over economic policy earlier in the year, Klaus by summer 1990 had built a high public profile as 'architect of economic reform'. He had successfully co-ordinated the formulation of a coherent economic transformation strategy in the Finance Ministry and pro-moted it with some success as the basis of government policy. In the elections Klaus led the Civic Forum list in North Moravia, an area of heavy industry and a historic bastion of the Communist Party, to an unexpectedly high vote, impressing local OF activists with his energetic campaigning (Čermák and Sontona 1997: 37).

Klaus was also able to build up a personal following. He received the highest number of individual 'preference votes' cast for any OF candidate and, accord-ing to an AISA poll, was by autumn 1990 the second most trusted politician in Czechoslovakia (after Václav Havel) (Boguszak *et al.* 1990c). Klaus had, however, antagonized many Civic Forum leaders and ministers, as well as President Havel, with both his abrasive personality and his neo-liberal views which were at variance with the more social-liberal inclinations of many ex-dissident politicians including the President. Indeed, Klaus's suitability for office, arrogance and lack of collegiality were publicly debated at the OF Assembly in July 1990, where the Federal Finance Minister was vigorously defended by delegates from North Moravia. Klaus was also a divisive figure among the public. The same AISA polls cited above also indicated that the com-bined percentages of those who *distrusted* Klaus were the highest for any Czech politician (Boguszak *et al.* 1990c).

Before the June 1990 elections, Klaus had remained largely aloof from public debate on the future of Civic Forum. Most of his public statements were devoted to the need for economic reform and the role of social inequality and individual self-interest in a market economy (Klaus 1991: 21–5). He made only veiled crit-icism of the political situation, noting the disorganized nature of OF's election campaign (Klaus 1991: 138–40) and the need to adopt tried and tested solutions

based on the 'intellectual mainstream' rather than 'superfluous and sterile …
philosophizing' and a tendency in OF to 'praise amateurism over professionalism' (Klaus 1991: 19–21; see also Suk 2003: 410–12).

Trends in Czech public opinion and the problems experienced by Civic
Forum as a 'party of government' in late summer 1990 were a major source of
concern to the group around Klaus, who had become highly critical of Civic
Forum's ex-dissident leaders. The 'loose' character of Civic Forum, they feared,
could either lead to the modification of the agreed economic strategy or slow its
legislative and administrative implementation. Events in neighbouring Poland
also made a strong impression on them (Klaus 1993a, 3, 9–14; Stráský 1993:
81–2). The 'war at the top' between the leaders of Solidarity and Solidarity's
subsequent fragmentation were front-page news in the Czech press. Klaus
himself had been a frequent visitor to Poland before 1989, had close contact
with Polish liberal economists and was familiar with the post-communist economic reform strategy they were formulating (Suk 2003: 125). One of his close
collaborators, the economist Josef Zieleniec, a Czech of Polish origin, also had
an extensive knowledge of Polish politics (Ježek 1997: 74).[27] While Klaus and
Zieleniec agreed with Polish neo-liberals that the *formulation* of economic
reform should be the prerogative of small groups of technocrats, they regarded
their failure to campaign for popular backing for market reform as a grave error
(Klaus 1993a: 9).[28]

Grassroots discontent

By autumn 1990 there was a growing grassroots constituency in Civic Forum
disaffected with the movement's leadership. For many local activists, conflicts
over decommunization also raised questions about the representativeness and
legitimacy of ex-dissidents heading the Forum, who seemed an unrepresentative,
self-appointed group with neither the democratic legitimacy nor the charismatic
authority of prominent 'personalities' such as Havel. For such grassroots
participants, the autonomy of Civic Fora, far from making the movement 'more
democratic', as Havel had claimed in his September 1990 speech, represented a
denial of democracy. Incremental organizational reforms had also failed to
clarify the status of OF's elected representatives and its emergent political
bureaucracy. Civic Forum managers and local activists were thus increasingly
attracted to a more formalized, hierarchical 'party-like' organizational model
with clearly delineated rights and responsibilities. For elected legislators and
full-time employees such a structure offered a more secure environment and a
clearer career ladder, while for district activists it represented a means of exerting control on the Civic Forum leadership and the Co-ordinating Centre in
Prague and holding them to account. Fear of powerful and well-organized communist structures – either the Communist Party itself or 'old structures' working
through front groups – led many local and regional OF activists to the conclusion that they should be backed by a similarly professional national organization
in the November 1990 local elections (*Lidové noviny*, 20 July 1990, 1).

The right coalesces

The nascent coalition of disaffected neo-liberals, anti-communist activists and frustrated political professionals coalesced at the OF Assembly of 13 October 1990 during the election for the newly created post of Chairman of Civic Forum. Václav Klaus contested the election against the former dissident Martin Palouš, the favoured candidate of Václav Havel and the Forum's leadership. Despite his grassroots popularity, journalists familiar with the internal politics of Civic Forum considered Klaus a rank outsider. Czech Prime Minister Petr Pithart, Jan Urban, the former head of the OF Co-ordinating Centre, and the Federal Deputy Prime Minister, Pavel Rychetský were all considered stronger potential candidates (Vávra 1990). Evidence suggests that Klaus's own decision to stand was a last-minute one prompted by North Moravian delegates, who were already informally canvassing for him (Čermák and Sontona 1997: 40; Stoniš and Havlík 1998: 24–5).

Addressing the morning session of the Assembly in his capacity as Finance Minister, Klaus highlighted the Forum's divisions over economic policy which he linked to issues of accountability and internal democracy, complaining that he did not feel supported by OF leaders. Either, he suggested, this meant that his own commitment to radical economic reform was out of step with the prevailing view in OF or that 'today's leaders do not adequately reflect the views of their supporters'. If this was the case, Klaus argued, the future of Civic Forum should 'start on the basis of views coming from below, not from the views of a limited group in the centre' (cited in *Mladá fronta Dnes*, 15 October 1990, 1–2). Despite impassioned arguments by supporters of Palouš that the movement's leader should be a figure closely associated with resistance to communist rule before 1989, when the vote came Klaus was elected Chairman by a decisive majority of 115 to 52 votes. A subsequent vote defining the prerogatives and role of the Chairman gave Klaus extensive powers including the right to veto decisions of the Council and refer them back to the Assembly and stressed the role of the Chairman as 'leader' of the movement ('Sněm OF' and 'Předseda OF', *Infórum* 44/90, 17 October 1990). Klaus's election was a pivotal moment. It showed that the balance of forces in OF had shifted against its ex-dissident leaders and marked the further stage in the emergence of the right as a coherent force. However, it was far from clear if and how a strong right-wing party would emerge from the divided movement.

A 'break with the past': Klaus's plans for transforming Civic Forum

After his election as Chairman, Klaus at first said only that he wished to be seen as 'the symbol of a programme not yet written' ('Václav Klaus: Jakou roli bude hrát?', *Infórum* 44/90, 17 October 1990, 8) and that he had had thought through only 'certain contours of OF reform' (Klaus 1991: 178). He sought initially to consolidate his power as Chairman, making it clear that he would not follow a collegial style of leadership and saw the four OF 'representatives' as subordinate to the Chairman ('Zápis z Rady 16.10.90', *Infórum* 45/90, 25 October 1990, 1, and Klaus 1991: 168). He also sought to reduce the size and power of the Co-ordinating Centre (whose staff then numbered 120) and give a greater role to Civic Forum's regional offices, something which both fitted in with making OF a more integrated national organization and reinforced the position of his grass-roots allies (Hadjiisky 1996: 20).

It is not clear when or how the project of transforming Civic Forum into a right-wing political party emerged.[29] However, it was already clear to contemporary observers that, as Chairman, Václav Klaus would seek the wholesale transformation of the movement into a party (*Mladá fronta Dnes*, 15 October 1990, 1). Klaus initially spoke of OF 'gradually' becoming 'a party of the loose electoral type' retaining the essential structure of OF, including the Co-ordinating Centre (Klaus 1991: 167). However, it quickly became clear that, for Klaus, partification involved not merely organizational rationalization and 'differentiation' but a *qualitative* change in the political character and identity of the Forum.

Comments made to a journalist by Klaus's closest aide Petr Havlík suggested plans to transform the Forum within a year into a party with a single executive body largely elected by the regions and a network of district chairpersons supported by small professional teams (*Mladá fronta Dnes*, 22 October 1990, 2).[30] Organizational features which reflected the Forum's origins and founding ethos as a broad pluralistic movement with a consensual style of decision-making such as the Collegium, the Political Commission and the system of the four OF 'representatives' would be abolished. Havlík's suggestions, including his comments that the new leadership would seek to exclude left-wingers from positions of leadership in OF,[31] were rapidly confirmed by Klaus, who described opponents as 'people passing themselves off as OF, who basically have not been in OF for a long time' (Klaus 1991: 167–8). In accordance with the logic of this statement, on 30 October 1990 the Civic Forum Council – which had had a clear pro-Klaus majority since 13 October – declared that Obroda and the radical Left Alternative (LA) group had 'already abandoned OF's political line and are therefore no longer considered part of OF' (*Infórum* 46/90, 1 November 1990, 1).

Klaus at Olomouc – inventing the 'Civic Forum party'

Successful partification of Civic Forum required more than determined leadership and adroit coalition building. It also required a clear explanation and rationale of the role of the new party in the transformation process. In a series of speeches, articles and interviews in October–December 1990 Klaus elaborated his conception of a 'Civic Forum party', concluding with an address which encapsulated his thinking on the subject to OF representatives and managers at Olomouc on 8 December 1990.

Klaus took up many arguments previously aired by internal and external critics of Civic Forum. Klaus first argued that Civic Forum was too broad and too backward-looking to be politically viable, claiming that it is simply unrealistic to continue maintaining the all-embracing political umbrella movement (*všezastrašujícího politického hnutí*), which OF has up to now been, or rather tried to be ... [E]fforts to maintain OF ... as a broad coalition of the most diverse political views, constantly returning to and looking back at the magic date of 17 November 1989, a broad coalition, cemented together by only one element, resistance to the communist totalitarianism of the past, is not only unrealistic, but dangerous.

(Klaus 1991: 203–9)

Echoing Havel, he argued that the movement's 'boundless democracy (*demokracie bez břehů*)' while able to deliver united action 'for some short-lived revolution' could not do so for '"boring" everyday matters in the months and years to come' (Klaus 1991: 107). He also highlighted the problem of internal democracy and accountability that concerned local activists arguing that 'in its representatives and outward appearance, ... [Civic Forum] must come closer to its grassroots (*základna*) ... in political, organizational and personnel terms' (Klaus 1991: 166–7). Finally, he stressed the conservative argument, frequently made by right-wing ex-dissidents and historic parties in the course of 1990, that political parties were a 'standard', 'normal' tried-and-tested West European institution that Czechs *should* embrace as part of their return to Europe.

In contrast to Havel, Klaus argued that the ideas and organizational forms developed in dissent and during the 'Velvet Revolution' had exhausted their transitional role. Rather than organizational compromises reconciling the ethos of the Revolution with the demands of policy-making and organizational efficiency, the creation of a new party of the right would represent a clear 'break with the past' (Klaus 1991: 166–71). Indeed, in stressing the backward-looking nature of 'civic' politics and civic movements, Klaus made a further innovation by linking them to the discredited heritage of reform communism and the search for a 'Third Way' between socialism and established Western liberal-capitalist models. This discourse of 'Third Ways' is analysed at greater length in Chapter 7.

The solution to these problems, Klaus argued, was for Civic Forum, in accordance with the views of the majority of its supporters, to become a 'standard' right-wing political party, which would be broad-based and internally democratic, effective as a vehicle for transformation and culturally appropriate for Czechs. This would entail building a sizeable, integrated and permanent national organization with individual membership built 'from below' avoiding the supposed 'Pragocentrism' of the old Civic Forum or the makeshift solution of the 'electoral type party (*strana volebního typu*) ... a kind of electoral HQ, which meets from time to time to elect new or existing leaders' (Klaus 1991: 121–2). The party would have a clearly defined role – organizing support for the government and developing clear programmatic positions. Klaus presented the political differences in Czech politics in abstract Hayekian terms as opposing elitist, statist social engineers to his own 'more modest', 'genuinely democratic' and 'populist (in the good sense of the word)' outlook (Klaus 1991: 28–9).

However, he stressed much more that the new party he wanted to create would be a vehicle for the immediate tasks of social transformation following the agenda of the 'democratic right' outlined by the Civic Democratic Alliance. In Klaus's words, such a party should be

> functional *today*, ... related to the needs of the times (*časově podmíněné*) and clearly rooted in the reality of today ... on the one hand, the issue of constitutional arrangements, and the issue of transforming the Czechoslovak economy on the other.
>
> (Klaus 1991: 203–9; emphasis in the original)

The break-up of Civic Forum

Klaus's plans sharply divided the movement. The Olomouc meeting adopted majority and minority resolutions on OF's future organization ('Většinový návrh usnesení sekce pro organizační strukturu' and 'Varianta návrhu usnesení sekce', *Infórum* 52/90, 13 December 1990) as well as the outline of a new, radically right-wing, political programme (combining Klaus's critique of 'Third Ways' with a more strident anti-communist tone, which reflected the preoccupations of grassroots activists: *Občanský deník*, 11 December 1990).[32] The majority resolution advocated the transformation of OF into a political party with membership 'on an individual basis, delineated by a programmatic declaration' and a vertical organizational structure with clear competencies based on binding votes, headed by a Chairman who would be the party's national leader ('Většinový návrh usnesení sekce pro organizační strukturu', *Infórum* 52/90, 13 December 1990). The minority resolution sought only to 'introduce party features into OF', largely maintaining the *status quo* ('Varianta návrhu usnesení sekce', *Infórum* 52/90, 13 December 1990). The Civic Forum Assembly of 12–13 January 1991 overwhelmingly endorsed the project of transforming Civic Forum into a centre-right political party outlined at Olomouc ('Usnesení Sněmu OF 12. – 13.1.1991', *Infórum* 56/91, 17 January 1991, 1) and passed the outline programme previously agreed with slight amendments (*Infórum* 56/91, 17 January 1991, 2–5).[33] However, Klaus's centrist and centre-left opponents in OF, who had formed a parliamentary counter grouping, the Liberal Club (LK),[34] strongly objected to the Assembly's decision. They claimed that discussion at the Assembly had been inadequate and that it was dubious whether it was legally possible for a movement to transform itself into a party ('Briefing P Rychetského a J Dienstbiera – sobota 12.1 odpoledne', *Infórum* 56/91, 17 January 1991, 8–9). They particularly objected to the Assembly's resolution to 'pre-register' members of the new party before the next OF Assembly at which the party was formally to be founded and the OF Council's decision that only 'pre-registered members' could take part in elections for delegates to District Assemblies (which then elected delegates to the national Civic Forum Assembly).[35] Liberal Club leaders warned that, as they could support neither the proposed new structure nor the draft programme, a split in Civic Forum could no longer be excluded ('Briefing P. Rychetského a J. Dienstbiera – sobota 12.1 odpoledne', *Infórum* 56/91, 17 January 1991, 8–9).

By early February 1991 personal and political tensions were so great that they threatened Civic Forum's stability. While Civic Forum MPs were split approximately evenly, district activists solidly supported Klaus's position. Most district-level 'managers' also inclined towards Klaus.[36] However, staff at the Civic Forum Co-ordinating Centre in Prague overwhelmingly backed the Liberal Club and blocked the implementation of the partification project. In an effort to prevent any impending split President Havel had sent an open letter to delegates attending the January 1990 Assembly, urging them to agree upon a compromise that would prevent the division of Civic Forum. On 12 February 1991, he made a further attempt to broker a compromise, by calling talks between leaders of the two OF factions at his country residence in Lány ('Dopis Presidenta Václava Havla Sněmu OF 12.1.1991', *Infórum* 56/91, 17 January 1991, 5–6). So great were the political and personal differences that the talks produced not a compromise to maintain Civic Forum but an agreement on how it should be dissolved. Under the Lány agreement, Civic Forum was replaced by two new successor organizations, one a political party, the other a political movement. The two new organizations were to form a government coalition until scheduled parliamentary elections in June 1992. Civic Forum would be dissolved as a national organization, continuing only as a 'shell' within which the two new groups would co-ordinate their activities and oversee the dissolution of OF.[37] Assets at national level were to be split evenly between the two successor groups, with local and district Fora making their own arrangements for the division of their property. A settlement enacting the Lány accords was passed by a special Civic Forum Assembly on 23 February 1991 ('Usnesení mimořadného republikového sněmu OF ze dne 23. února 1991' and 'Stanovy Občanského fóra', *Infórum* 62/91, 23 February 1991, 5, 6).

The Civic Democratic Party (ODS) was formally founded at a congress in Olomouc on 20 and 21 April 1991 and overwhelmingly elected Václav Klaus its first Chairman. Centrist and centre-left politicians formed the Civic Movement (OH) a few days later.

Conclusions

Civic Forum was typical of many transitional civic movements that arose in Eastern Europe in 1988–9, in its origins, breadth, loose horizontal structures and stress on direct informal participation. As in other similar movements, the experience of political competition and office-holding after the collapse of communism soon laid bare organizational and political divisions which proved difficult to resolve given the range of forces, weak lines of authority and ambiguous identity of the movement. Civic Forum's rapid takeover of the state and the unitary (albeit unintegrated) organizational structure and accompanying low level of initial factionalization, do, however, seem to have militated in favour of the emergence of a single 'successor party'.

Václav Klaus and the group of neo-liberal economists from the former 'grey zone' around him were dissatisfied elite actors able to act strategically to attract the support of key internal constituencies, whose organizational, personal and political interests were compatible with Klaus's project for 'partifying' Civic Forum. Given the technocratic economic background of its leaders and its willingness to accommodate grassroots anti-communism, the group was also well placed to offer a distinct and attractive set of policies meeting the two key concerns of both the Czech public and much of OF grassroots: radical economic reform and decommunization. They were also able to reframe the political party as the most efficient democratic and culturally appropriate form of political organization for Czechs to adopt. Although they understood its organizational problems, the centrist ex-dissident leaders of the Forum saw moves towards programmatic politics and a more party-like organization as a necessary but regrettable trade-off between democracy and efficiency.

In comparative perspective, however, what is striking about the break-up of Civic Forum is not the existence of grassroots disillusion over the weakness of representative structures, or elites disaffected over the direction of reform, but the *success* of the Czech right in channelling these into an effective political challenge and founding a broad-based 'successor party'. The success of Klaus's project – despite his opponents' last-minute blocking of the formal process of transforming Civic Forum – stemmed from factors already highlighted in earlier accounts of party formation: the mobilization of broad support through effective coalition building to link diverse internal constituencies around a shared organizational and political project (Aldrich 1995; Hopkin 1996, 1999; Kitschelt 1989, 1993b). In addition to the anti-communist, pro-federal, free market politics of the 'democratic right', Klaus's personal prominence and charisma seem to have been an important focus for mobilization and coalition building. As an elite challenger, Václav Klaus also appeared unusual in combining both personal charisma and technocratic policy-based legitimacy (Orenstein 1998; Saxonberg 1999, 2003).[38] Despite its more marked anti-communism, the Interparliamentary Club of the Democratic Right initiative launched by the Civic Democratic Alliance (ODA) lacked such a leader figure and failed to align itself sufficiently with Civic Forum's grassroots activists and officials or to address their concerns about internal democracy and managerial efficiency.

5 'An unrepeatable chance'

The dominance of the new Czech right 1992–6

Introduction

Following the break-up of Civic Forum in 1991 and the federal and Czech elections of June 1992, the governing Czech coalition of ODS, the Czechoslovak People's Party – Christian and Democratic Union (KDU-ČSL), ODS and the Civic Democratic Alliance (ODA) emerged in a politically dominant position. They faced a largely supportive and uncritical media (Kettle 1995) and a fragmented opposition, controlled key economic ministries and exercised considerable influence in the Czech state bureaucracy. The independent Czech Republic appeared to some observers as an island of conservatism and free market radicalism in a sea of nationalism, populism and post-communism.

Some suggested that the nature of post-communist transformation implied a period of temporary dominance for the right which, as Klaus himself noted, offered an 'unrepeatable chance' for the right to shape politics and society (*Bulletin ODS* no. 37, 28 November 1991, 4; *Sobotní telegraf*, 4–10 December 1991, 1). A 'Japanese model' of protracted dominance by a powerful centre-right party combining clientelism and economic liberalism over a divided opposition (Terra 2002: 282) was widely anticipated in the Czech Republic. Indeed, in the early 1990s the idea of a Czech party system dominated by the right was even accepted by some figures on the centre-left. In the event, despite the rapid and apparently successful radical market reforms implemented with little social cost, by 1995 centre-left forces had coalesced around the Czech Social Democratic Party (ČSSD) under Miloš Zeman, which proved able to mount an electoral challenge strong enough to deprive the right-wing coalition of its majority at the 1996 elections.

The Czech right's short-lived dominance has often been explained purely as a consequence of the delayed formation of a credible Czech centre-left – itself rooted in the failure of the Czech Communists to transform themselves into a post-communist social democratic party and, more distantly, the hardline nature of Czechoslovakia's communist regime (Hanley 2001; Grzymala-Busse 2002; Vachudova 2005). Yet, the weakness of the centre-left does not logically imply the dominance of the centre-right.[1] Such explanations also fail to explain why the Czech right was unable to 'lock-in' the political dominance it enjoyed in such a crucial formative period. The chapter considers the Czech right's short-lived dominance by assessing the *mechanisms* through which the centre-right dominated the 1992–7 period, and the related process by which Klaus's Civic Democratic Party (ODS) came to dominate the centre-right.

Locking-in political dominance?

As argued in previous chapters, the initial dominance of a political party (or bloc of parties) in a new democracy cannot be reduced to the effect of historical legacies, but must also be seen as the product of unpredictable strategic choices made during the early democratization period. However, this does not address the question of how and why some parties or blocs remain dominant over a sustained period and others do not. We need to understand the *mechanisms* through which parties can 'lock-in' and extend initial advantages – a process which, as theorists of path dependence have noted, usually entails a logic of 'increasing returns' (Pierson 2000; see also Tilly 2001).

Although the 'problem of party system continuity and change' was a staple theme of West European party politics literature, many accounts of party and party system development in both new and established democracies paid little *explicit* attention to how such 'lock-in' mechanisms operate (or fail to operate). However, Peter Mair's (1997) exploration of Lipset and Rokkan's (1967) argument about the 'freezing' of the West European party systems in the early twentieth century identifies a range of mechanisms producing 'increasing returns' for political parties. These include the monopolization of pre-existing human and material resources, thus denied to weaker competitor parties and potential new entrants; organizational strategies which 'encapsulate' key social constituencies; the growth of party identification among members, voters and interest groups; and the development by them of rational 'adaptive expectations' – a recognition that small or newly founded parties have little prospect of success against large, well established parties, which then become a self-fulfilling prophecies.

The notion of mechanisms of political dominance overlaps with the better-established, if more contested, concept of party institutionalization. In participating in or supporting a new party, members, leaders, voters and interest groups contribute and exchange resources to generate political outcomes they could not achieve by acting on an individual or on an ad hoc basis. Such resources might include financial and material support, time and votes. In a post-communist context where social constituencies are relatively ill defined, levels of civic engagement low and distinctions between the public and private blurred, party-society links are often heavily supplemented by a heavily symbiotic relationship between parties and the state, which typically provides the bulk of party resources through public funding and the spoils of public office (Katz and Mair 1995; van Biezen 2003; Kopecký 2006).

A party becomes organizationally stable when such exchanges and flows of resources settle in some kind of equilibrium (Panebianco 1981; Aldrich 1995;

Hopkin 1996, 1999). Organizational stabilization may subsequently give way to a deeper sense of identification with the party by members, voters and supporters. When this occurs, the party becomes, to a lesser or greater extent, a part of their own identity and is seen as an end and value in itself extending beyond the instrumental goals of its founders. Institutionalization allows a party to manage its wider environment successfully and endure over time, generating an air of permanence and durability. It is also worth noting that parties' institutionalization processes also act as a mechanism to 'lock-in' parties' relative strength with regard to competitors, helping patterns of party competition settle into a changing but predictable equilibrium (Sartori 1976).

This chapter will focus on the mechanisms which seemed to allow the Czech right the possibility of institutionalizing itself as the predominant force in Czech politics: the nature of Klaus's ODS as a 'successor party' to Civic Forum; its internal balance of power; success in containing competitors on the liberal and Christian Democratic centre-right and the anti-communist radical right; the nature of the social interests, electorate and interest groups supporting the Czech right, its occupancy of the state and access to public resources; and its success in providing 'transformation goods' to the electorate. In the post-communist context, it will note, the resources and groups necessary to sustain a dominant party or bloc are not fixed, but emerge fluidly in and through transformation policies such as decommunization, privatization and the reform of public administration. After a discussion of initial party consolidation, each of these areas is examined in relation to the development of the Czech right.

ODS as successor party to Civic Forum

Despite the organizational and political changes introduced by the right, ODS received a substantial inheritance from Civic Forum, a substantial mass organization with significant material and human resources and with access to the powers of patronage that electoral success and incumbency bring. Civic Forum's 'farewell Assembly' of 23 February 1991 agreed that Civic Forum's assets at national level would be split evenly between Klaus's Civic Democratic Party and the liberal-centrist Civic Movement but would, partly on Klaus's insistence, exclude other political groups within the Forum. Local and district Civic Fora were to agree their own arrangements for the division of their property. Given Klaus's considerable grassroots support, the majority agreed that most or all of their assets should be passed to ODS. Moreover, in almost every district a majority of Civic Forum's full-time professional 'managers' (officials) – nationally approximately three-quarters of the total – joined ODS, many beginning the 'pre-registration' of ODS members even before Civic Forum had formally dissolved (Hanley 2000b: 188–214, 347–8; see also Pšeja 2004a).

With the exception of KAN, which received a small grant of 200,000 crowns (*Respekt*, 20 February 1991, 2) right-wing groups with roots in the pre-1989 opposition that had remained within the Civic Forum structure (see Chapter 4) gained no resources from the Forum's break-up. ODS's inheritance at parliamentary level was less decisive. In mid-1991, 44 of the 118 deputies elected to the Federal Assembly on the Civic Forum list had joined the ODS parliamentary group (*Lidové noviny*, 11 September 1991, 1). In the Czech parliament 38 of the 126 deputies elected for Civic Forum joined the party (*Občanský deník*, 12 June 1991, 1). In Klaus, ODS gained a trusted, well-known and charismatic leader, which many smaller groups lacked. However, other than Klaus, ODS had few nationally known politicians in its leadership, leading to accusations from critics that it was a 'one-man party'.

The dilemmas of the ex-dissident right

The early emergence of ODS as a dominant party of the right with a unitary structure posed particular problems for small right-wing groups with dissident origins. Already marginalized as collective members of Civic Forum (OF) and – if they remained within OF – excluded from the financial settlement dividing its assets, as Table 5.1 shows, all acutely lacked the financial, organizational and political resources. They thus faced a choice between three strategic options: long-term independent party-building; expansion by making alliances with other

Table 5.1 Assets of selected Czech political parties and movements

Name	Value of property 30 April 1990 (Czechoslovak crowns)	Value of property 1995 (Czech crowns)
Communist Party of Bohemia and Moravia (KSČM)	7,636,540,867	220,000,000
Czechoslovak People's Party (ČSL)[1]	43,868,000	39,347,000
– separate value of Lidová demokracie publishing house	52,125,000	n/a
Czechoslovak Socialist Party (ČSS)[2]	56,539,000	64,848,000
– separate value of Melantrich publishing house	21,076,000	n/a
Czechoslovak Social Democracy (ČSSD)	60,294,570	not stated
Civic Forum (OF)	26,883,900	n/a
Civic Democratic Party (ODS)	n/a	25,440,000
Obroda	397,720	n/a
Liberal Democratic Party (LDS)	388,980	n/a
Civic Democratic Alliance (ODA)	208,000	12,216,000
Association for the Republic–Republican Party of Czechoslovakia (SPR-RSČ)	200,530	7,092,000

Sources: *Svobodné slovo*, 25 October 1990, 7, and Reed (1996: 241) citing parties' annual financial reports for 1995.

Notes
1 Figures for 1995 for Christian Democratic Union–Czechoslovak People's Party (ČSL).
2 Figures for 1995 for Liberal National Social Party (LSNS).

small groups; or allying themselves on unequal terms with larger parties such as Klaus's ODS or the Czechoslovak People's Party (ČSL).

The experience of the Liberal Democratic Party (LDS), one of the better organized ex-dissident groups, rapidly demonstrated the difficulties of independent party-building. After quitting Civic Forum in June 1990, the party had two deputies in the Federal Assembly and five in the Czech parliament, 25 branches and a membership of between 1300 and 5000 (*Práce*, 23 August 1990; Hanley 2000b: 470). However, outside the Forum, LDS was cut off from potential supporters and dependent for resources on support from the German Free Democrats (FDP), which saw the party as a potential liberal partner in Czechoslovakia (Hamerský and Dimun 1999: 36; Mandler 2005: 159–74). LDS also lacked programmatic resources. Its 'right-wing' identity and liberalism were largely defined by its pre-1989 critique of dissident anti-politics and an anti-communist rhetoric then common across the Czech political spectrum. Moreover, its principal leaders, Emanuel Mandler and Bohumil Doležal, were little known and lacked the legal or technocratic skills necessary to formulate distinct transformation policies or gain ministerial office. As the November 1990 communal elections demonstrated, the party's grassroots organization was too weak even to mount even an effective local challenge. In November 1991 LDS split following the election as its new leader of Viktorie Hradská. Recognizing LDS's unviability, Hradská and her supporters quickly concluded a merger with the Civic Democratic Alliance (ODA).[2]

ODS and the politics of alliance making

Party mergers and the creation of loose electoral alliances were a common feature of early post-communist politics, acting as an important mechanism for party system consolidation across Eastern Europe (Bielasiak 1997). Such alliances both served to create larger, more competitive electoral blocs and offered discredited former regime parties a quick and effective way to 'modernize' themselves. Both considerations led the larger parties of the Czech centre-right to seek smaller allies. Despite its dominant position on the centre-right in 1991–2, Klaus's ODS was far from dominant in wider Czech politics. Despite Klaus's high personal profile, ODS was overshadowed in both the Czech and the federal government by representatives of Civic Movement and other parties.[3] With approximately 20 per cent support ODS's position in the Czech lands was considerably weaker than, for example, that of Slovakia's strongest party, Vladimír Mečiar's HZDS, and only some way ahead of the 14 per cent polled in the Czech lands in 1990 by the Communist Party. Opinion polls also suggested that, despite the plethora of small parties, left and right in the Czech Republic were evenly balanced in terms of electoral support (Novák 1997: 96–7).

ODS thus entered the process of right-wing alliance making, holding talks with a range of smaller groups. In early 1991 it had been widely assumed that the Civic Democratic Alliance (ODA), the motive force behind the foundation of Civic Forum's Interparliamentary Club of the Democratic Right (MDKP), would join Klaus's new centre-right party, but negotiations between ODA and Klaus's team quickly broke down. Although Klaus's notion of 'civic democracy' undoubtedly differed from ODA's neo-conservative thinking (Kroupa 1996: 15–20; see Chapters 3 and 7), the key stumbling block seems to have been Klaus's refusal to accept ODA's demand that groups with individual membership like ODA should be accepted as collective members of the new party (Klaus 1993b: 65; *Infórum* 54/91, 4 January 1991). ODA's status as a small independent party with a degree of political influence also generated conflicts with ODS.[4] There was also a sharp and public conflict between Klaus and the ODA Minister of Privatization, Tomáš Ježek, concerning privatization policy. In the event, ODS and ODA only concluded a 'non-aggression pact' signed on 21 November 1991, agreeing not to campaign again each other.[5] Other small right-wing parties were less wary of ODS. Klaus's party held talks with the tiny Free Bloc–Conservative Party (SB-KS) grouping of Jiří Kotlas and cultivated the Club of Committed Non-Party Members (KAN) with which it signed a joint declaration on 12 June 1991 agreeing (unspecified) future co-operation (Pšeja 2004b: 455–6). However, small ex-dissident parties, such as Václav Benda's small Christian Democratic Party (KDS) or the struggling LDS, whose intellectual leaders were a known quantity, appeared more likely political allies for ODS.

Unlike LDS, Benda's Christian Democrats had consistently pursued a strategy of allying with larger parties. It initially joined the Christian Democratic Union (KDU) coalition led by the Czechoslovak People's Party (ČSL), which welcomed the ex-dissident party as an indication of its anti-communism and modernization into a broader Christian Democratic grouping. KDS negotiated generous representation for its candidates on the Christian Democratic Union electoral list and gained five deputies in the Czechoslovak Federal Assembly and six in the Czech parliament in the June 1990 elections.[6] At the same time, KDS's intellectual anti-communist Catholic conservatism was at odds with the People's Party's more 'social' tradition and view of Christian Democracy as a force standing between anti-communist liberalism and socialism. Benda's grouping therefore left the KDU coalition on 8 July 1991 and sought allies among former Civic Forum parties. Benda entered negotiations with both the Liberal Democratic Party (LDS) of Mandler and Doležal and the Civic Democratic Alliance (ODA), hoping that the three small groupings could jointly negotiate an electoral alliance with Klaus's ODS.

Meanwhile, Klaus quickly turned against the policy of making alliances with smaller groups, a policy which he came to regard as a complication bringing little political benefit to ODS. In 1991–2, ODS's strategy for building a broad centre-right bloc focused on agreement for *post*-election co-operation with the People's Party and the extension of its own organization into Slovakia.[7] Klaus personally intervened to rule out any alliance with the faction-ridden Liberal Democratic Party (LDS) (Mandler 2005: 170), supporting a coalition only with Benda's small KDS, whose Christian orientation bolstered ODS's claims to be a conservative party fusing traditional values and market liberalism (see Chapter 7).[8]

Electoral ascendancy: the 1992 parliamentary elections

The June 1992 parliamentary elections in the Czech Republic were decisively won by the ODS-KDS coalition. ODS and KDS joined the Czechoslovak People's Party (KDU-ČSL) and the Civic Democratic Alliance (ODA) in a four-party Czech coalition government. The elections also established ODS as the dominant party on the Czech centre-right. As shown in Tables 5.2–5.4, with a vote of over 30 per cent in the elections to the Federal Assembly and support slightly below that level in the separate vote for the Czech national parliament, ODS emerged as by far the strongest Czech force electorally in the Czech party system, which was otherwise highly fragmented. Five Czech parties and groupings gained representation in the Federal Assembly and seven in the Czech National Council (Novák 1997: 93). With the exception of ODS and the Communist-led Left Bloc (LB), all received less than 10 per cent of the vote.

Despite its unconsolidated organization, in 1992 ODS successfully combined its distinct mix of local and national resources: the regional campaigning techniques developed by Klaus in North Moravia in 1990; the activism of local ODS members mobilized during the division of Civic Forum; advice on campaign management from US consultants supplied by the International Republican

Table 5.2 Czech elections of 5–6 June 1992 to the Czechoslovak Federal Assembly – Chamber of the People (lower house)

Party	No. of votes	% of vote	No. of seats
Civic Democratic Party–Christian Democratic Party coalition (ODS-KDS)	2,200,937	33.90	48
Left Bloc (LB)	926,228	14.27	19
Czechoslovak Social Democracy (ČSSD)	498,030	7.76	10
Association for the Republic–Republican Party of Czechoslovakia (SPR-RSČ)	420,848	6.48	8
Christian Democratic Union–Czechoslovak People's Party (KDU-ČSL)	388,122	5.98	7
Liberal Social Union (LSU)[1]	378,962	5.84	7
Civic Democratic Alliance (ODA)	323,614	4.98	0
Civic Movement (OH)	284,859	4.39	0
Society for Moravia and Silesia–Movement for Self-Governing Democracy (HSD-SMS)	274,489	4.23	0
Pensioners for a Secure Life (DŽJ)	214,681	3.31	0
Party of Czechoslovak Businesspeople and Farmers (SČPŽR)	166,135	2.56	0
Club of Committed Non-Party Members (KAN)	129,022	1.99	0
Others	286 350	4.31	0
Total	6,492,462	100.00	99[1]

Source: *Statistická ročenka Česke republiky 1993.*

Note
1 The Chamber also included 51 deputies elected in Slovakia.

Table 5.3 Czech elections of 5–6 June 1992 to the Federal Assembly – Chamber of Nations (upper house)

Party	No. of votes	% of vote	No. of seats
Civic Democratic Party–Christian Democratic Party coalition (ODS-KDS)	2,168,421	33.43	37
Left Bloc (LB)	939,197	14.48	15
Czechoslovak Social Democracy (ČSSD)	440,806	6.80	6
Association For The Republic–Republican Party of Czechoslovakia (SPR-RSČ)	413,459	6.37	6
Christian Democratic Union–Czechoslovak People's Party (KDU-ČSL)	394,296	6.08	6
Liberal Social Union (LSU)	393,182	6.06	5
Society for Moravia and Silesia–Movement for Self-Governing Democracy (HSD-SMS)	317,934	4.90	0
Civic Movement (OH)	307,334	4.74	0
Civic Democratic Alliance (ODA)	264,371	4.08	0
Pensioners for a Secure Life (DŽJ)	222,860	3.44	0
Party of Czechoslovak Businesspeople and Farmers (SČPŽR)	172,703	2.66	0
Club of Committed Non-Party Members (KAN)	140,045	2.16	0
Others	311,131	4.80	0
Total	6,485,739	100.00	75[1]

Source: *Statistická ročenka Češkě republiky 1993.*

Note
1 The Chamber also included 75 deputies elected in Slovakia.

Institution; and a well-financed professionally produced national advertising campaign that accurately caught the public mood by telling voters that 'the future is in the palm of your hand' (Pečinka 2003a: 42–7). At a more fundamental level, its success was rooted in its ability to win over the bulk of Civic Forum's pro-reform electorate. According to exit polling carried out by IVVM in June 1992, former Civic Forum voters gravitated towards the anti-communist, liberal pro-market parties by a margin of some three to one.[9] A large majority of these – 55 per cent of Civic Forum voters in June 1990 – voted for ODS (Krejčí 1994: 220). Put differently, 84 per cent of ODS's June 1992 electorate were former Civic Forum voters – the highest level of continuity found for any party, including the Communists (Fiala *et al.* 1999: 284; Kostelecký 1994).

However, ODS's electoral 'inheritance' from Civic Forum was less straightforward or immediate than the transfer of organizational, material and human resources. From autumn 1990 much of the Civic Forum electorate had started to drift away from the movement, frustrated at the apparent slowness of reform and the political infighting within the movement. ODS's initial support climbed rapidly from 12 per cent in March 1991 to 21 per cent at the time of the party's founding congress in April. In spite of the launch in late 1991 of the coupon pri-

Table 5.4 Elections of 5–6 June 1992 to the Czech National Council

Party	No. of votes	% of vote	No. of seats
Civic Democratic Alliance (ODA)	383,705	5.93	14
Civic Democratic Party–Christian Democratic Party (ODS-KDS)	1,924,483	29.73	76[1]
Christian Democratic Union–Czechoslovak People's Party (KDU-ČSL)	406,341	6.28	15
Czechoslovak Social Democracy (ČSSD)	422,736	6.53	16
Liberal Social Union (LSU)	421,988	6.52	16
Society for Moravia and Silesia–Movement for Self-Governing Democracy (HSD-SMS)	380,088	5.87	14
Left Bloc (LB)	909,490	14.05	35
Association for the Republic–Republican Party of Czechoslovakia (SPR-RSČ)	387,026	5.98	14
Civic Movement (OH)	297,988	4.59	0
Pensioners for a Secure Life (DŽJ)	244,319	3.77	0
Party of Czechoslovak Businesspeople and Farmers (SČPŽR)	203,654	3.15	0
Club of Committed Non-Party Members (KAN)	174,006	2.69	0
Total	6,473,250	100.00	200

Source: *Statistická ročenka České republiky 1993.*

Note
1 66 for ODS, 10 for KDS.
Turnout: 85.08%.

vatization programme closely identified with Federal Finance Minister Václav Klaus and the start of voucher auctions on 17 February 1992, ODS support remained relatively static at approximately 20 per cent. Only in the immediate run up to the elections did Klaus's party gain significant additional support from undecided voters, many of whom were former Civic Forum supporters (Novák 1997: 96–7).

Although undecided voters inclined towards ODS partly because it was the largest and best-known party, its growth in support also reflected the inroads that its vision of market-led transformation had made in Czech public opinion and the growth of partisan identification. ODS voters felt a higher than average sense of identification with their party.[10] By May 1992, 90 per cent of the party's supporters told pollsters that it satisfactorily represented their interests. Although ODS had only limited representation in the Czech and federal governments, polling found that the party's voters identified strongly with the reform process, which they saw as a continuation of post-1989 regime change. In June 1992, 86 per cent of ODS supporters were satisfied with the direction of political change and 78 per cent with that of economic change. The corresponding figures recorded for the Czech electorate as a whole were 33 per cent and 55 per cent. ODS supporters also tended to view transformation in strongly economic terms, removing the ambiguities found in 1990 when voters had expected both rapid and efficient economic reform, a cautious approach to privatization and participatory, decentralized politics (see Chapter 4) (AISA cited in Novák 1997: 104–5; *Mladá fronta Dnes*, 23 April 1992).[11] ODS supporters were overwhelmingly hostile to the Communist Party and in favour of the elimination of 'old structures' (86 per cent of ODS supporters).[12] The ODS thesis that there was little difference between the reform communists of 1968 and those of the 'normalization' era was also heavily supported both by its own voters and, more widely, even among centrist and centre-left voters (AISA data cited in *Lidové noviny*, 29 May 1992, 8–9).

The breakthrough of the Civic Democratic Alliance

Given its organizational assets and historic bastions of support in Catholic regions, the re-entry of the Czechoslovak People's Party (KDU-ČSL) into parliament was widely expected, but the success of the Civic Democratic Alliance (ODA), the only former dissident grouping to enter the Czech parliament independently, was less predictable. ODA was organizationally one of the weakest small right-wing groupings to emerge from Civic Forum. Like other smaller right-wing groupings it had few initial assets and gained no material resources from the break-up of Civic Forum. In June 1990 the party had a mere 70 members (almost all in Prague and Brno), three deputies to the Federal Assembly and four to the Czech parliament. In 1990–1, like LDS, the Alliance was dependent on international links for modest, but essential financial support.[13] In April 1991 when it relaunched itself as an independent political party (*Lidové noviny*, 22 April 1991, 3; *Fórum* 17/1991, 2), and despite its leaders' role in creating Civic Forum's Interparliamentaty Club of the Democratic Right (MKDP) (see Chapter 4), the Alliance still had only 150 members (Hamerský and Dimun 1999: 338) (*ZpraODAj*, August 1992, 2), a level of organizational weakness that reportedly led some individual supporters to join Klaus's ODS in the absence of a local ODA branch (*ZpraODAj*, August 1992, 2; *Respekt*, 2 September 1996).[14]

Following the break-up of Civic Forum and the failure of talks with Klaus, the Alliance sought to join with other small centre-right groups to create a 'Democratic Bloc'. However, although the Alliance gained members from the mergers negotiated with Viktorie Hradská's faction of the Liberal Democratic Party (LDS) in March 1992 and its absorption of the tiny Free Peasant Party (SRS), attempts to negotiate coalitions first with Klaus's ODS and then with smaller groups such as the Club of Committed Non-Party Members (KAN), the pro-business Party of Czechoslovak Entrepreneurs, Tradespeople and Farmers (SČPŽR) and Slovakia's Civic Democratic Union (VPN-ODÚ) all foundered (Hamerský and Dimun 1999: 37). As with other tentative alliances on the Czech right, conflicting interests and political priorities quickly combined to block effective collective action.[15]

ODA's electoral breakthrough owed less to alliance-making than to the accumulation of a critical mass of organizational, human and programmatic resources. First, ODA's clear orientation to Western neo-conservatism and pioneering concept of the 'democratic right' offered a distinct political vision, which made it attractive to members of the emergent technocratic elite. Tomáš Ježek, appointed Czech Minister of Privatization from August 1990, and his deputy, Roman Češka, were among the twelve signatories of the Alliance's founding declaration in December 1989. Following Civic Forum's break-up, other important technocrats such as Vladimír Dlouhý, the popular Federal Minister of the Economy, as well as a number of Civic Forum deputies with backgrounds in local politics, joined the Alliance.[16] ODA's growing political momentum and the contacts generated by its involvement in economic and privatization policy enabled the party to borrow 45 million crowns (approximately US$1.5 million) against the state funding it hoped to gain by entering parliament.

Finally, ODA was able to gain extra support sufficient to gain parliamentary representation by aligning itself with the increasingly assertive mood of Czech right-wing voters towards Slovakia. Reportedly frustrated at the collapse of latest Czech–Slovak understanding about a reformed federal state, on 7 March 1992 ODA issued a statement, rejecting Slovak demands for national autonomy within a loose confederal structure and condemned Slovak nationalism as a form of left-wing collectivism threatening civil rights, freedom and democracy. These demands, it argued, should be resisted even at the ultimate cost of splitting the federal state (*ZpravODAj*, March 1992, 1). ODA's newly elected leader, Jan Kalvoda, was already known as a vigorous defender of federal sovereignty Although not *advocating* the division of Czechoslovakia, the tenor of such remarks contrasted markedly with Klaus's cautious public assessments of Vladimír Mečiar and other Slovak leaders, his refusal to talk of Czech national interests and his efforts to build ODS into a Czechoslovakia-wide party. In the 1992 June election, ODA's small but critical mass of programmatic resources, financial resources and human resources enabled the party to exceed narrowly the 5 per cent threshold needed to enter the Czech parliament, although the Alliance's vote in the election Federal Assembly fell marginally below the threshold and it gained no federal deputies (see Tables 5.2 and 5.3).

ODS as a stratarchical party

Centre-right groupings in post-communist East Central Europe such as the Hungarian Democratic Forum (MDF) or Poland's Solidarity Election Action (AWS) enjoyed both early electoral success and initial political dominance, but quickly disintegrated under the pressure of internal tensions and external events (Szczerbiak 2004; Fowler 2004). ODS, however, proved able to stabilize and sustain itself as both a governing and an opposition party over more than a decade, surviving significant political splits in 1997–8 (see Chapter 6). In one of the more influential recent analyses of party organization, Katz and Mair (1993, 2002) argue that any cohesive party is sustained by a balance of power between three 'faces': the 'party on the ground' – its members and activists; the 'party in public office' – its elected representatives and parliamentary elites; and the 'party in central office' consisting of national officials and office-holders charged with running the party organization.

The dominant image of 'new' parties in post-communist Central and Eastern Europe – that is those that are not historic or former regime parties – is of elite-dominated, state-centred, low-membership formations, which are dependent on public funding and increasingly dominated by the 'party in public office' (Kopecký 1995; Mair 1997; Szczerbiak 1999) – a pattern loosely equivalent to the 'electoral professional party' (Panebianco 1981) or 'cartel party' in Western Europe, which has gradually displaced residual forms of mass party organization (Katz and Mair 1995). ODS's pattern of organizational development and organizational stabilization, however, qualifies some of these judgements. First, although limited by West European standards and less dense than that of the Czech Republic's two historic parties – the Communists and Christian Democrats – ODS had a significant grass-roots organizational network (see Table 5.5). In early 2005 ODS local associations existed in 76 per cent of communes with 2000 or more inhabitants (Kyloušek 2005). Such a degree of local organization is arguably denser and more extensive than that required for effective national electoral competition or elite recruitment. As Kyloušek (2005) notes, there is no automatic correlation between the density of ODS organization on the ground and the party's performance in national parliamentary elections.[17] However, such 'irrationalities' did enable ODS to mount a highly effective challenge in local government. In the communal and municipal elections of November 1994, for example, ODS-led coalitions took control of almost all larger urban municipalities, including the Czech Republic's second city Brno and other urban centres in Moravia, where the regionalist HSD-SMS party – now in rapid decline – had outpolled Civic Forum in 1990.

Table 5.5 Membership of the Civic Democratic Party 1991–2005

	Members	*No. of local branches*
1991	18,557	803
1992	21,615	n/a
1993	23,269	n/a
1994	21,984	1405
1995	21,355	1395
1996	22,899	1391
1997	22,095	n/a
1998	18,169	1372
1999	18,432	n/a
2000	18,908	1436
2002	20,412	1445
2003	21,641	1270
2004	21,138	1290
2005	26,155	1331

Sources: party records as cited in Hanley (2000b), Benešová (2001), Linek (2004).

Note
Data not available for 1992, 1993, 1997, 1999.

Second, the power relationships between the different 'faces', through which the ODS stabilized itself, were more complex than the straightforward dominance of the party in public office. As van Biezen (2003: 147, 150–2) points out, the ODS parliamentary group had a well-defined autonomy with the party; ODS parliamentarians and ministers overlapped with the national leadership; and elected representatives enjoyed ex officio rights to attend party congresses and district and regional assemblies as delegates. However, the bulk of the public subsidies on which ODS, like other Czech parties, relied were channelled to the party's national organization not to its parliamentary group.[18] In practice, and despite overlapping membership, the relationship between the 'party in central office' (the ODS Executive Council and the party's smaller national leadership committee (*gremium*)) and its ministers and parliamentarians was a confused one, which tended to empower the party leader, Václav Klaus, and a variety of informal elite sub-groups able to arbitrate between and co-ordinate the different power centres (*Respekt*, 9 May 1994, 7–9).

Third, the relationship between ODS's elite 'faces' and the grassroots 'party on the ground' raises questions about the image of a centralized, hierarchical dominated by national leaders through control of public funding and state resources party (van Biezen 2003: 147), whose local organization was essentially a redundant legacy of its origins in Civic Forum. Viewed in terms of *formal* organization, ODS does indeed appear as a four-tier hierarchy of local, district, regional and national bodies based on clear lines of democratic and bureaucratic accountability. Local associations are based purely on the voluntary activity of grassroots members, while associations at district level and above are run jointly by an elected leadership, delegate assemblies and professional managers. Although regional assemblies play an important role in selecting and ranking candidates on regional electoral lists used for parliamentary elections, district level organizations are a more important arena in the party. As well as playing an important role in candidate selection (Saxonberg 2003: 195–7)[19] and electing the party's national leadership by selecting congress delegates, they also co-ordinate much day-to-day activity and act as the key link between ODS elites and the party's grassroots.

In many ways the internal dynamics of ODS were less those of the hierarchically integrated 'standard party' than those of a looser, *stratarchical* alliance of local and national elites. In stratarchical power relationships – found historically in many US and Canadian parties – different party 'faces' enjoy considerable autonomy, whilst remaining interdependent by establishing a rough division of labour and thus organizational stability (Carty and Cross 2006). Carty (2004) suggests that stratarchical patterns can be summed up in ideal type as a 'franchise model' of party organization whereby

a central organization recognizable by its common brand, determines the product line and sets standards for its production and labelling, manages marketing and advertising strategy and provides management and training as well as arranging for the supplies needed by local outlets ... individual franchises exist to deliver the product to a particular market. To do so they invest local resources, both capital and personnel.

(Carty 2004: 10)

Many aspects of ODS's formation and functioning had the characteristics of the stratarchical 'franchise model'. In 1991–2, ODS local organizations were formally founded through the granting of 'licences' by the national leadership to local groups of pre-registered Klaus supporters. These 'licences' could be (and sometimes were) revoked for breaches of national party guidelines, which contradicted or undermined its national strategy and identity ('brand'), such as, for example, local co-operation with the Communist Party. In most respects, however, both formally and de facto local and district associations enjoyed very considerable autonomy in their day-to-day functioning. Despite numerous revisions in the course of 1990s, ODS statutes never stipulated any specific activities that members needed to undertake to meet the responsibilities of membership,[20] required local associations to meet only once a year and set no quorum for local associations' meetings.[21] These rules were far less prescriptive than those of other major Czech parties, which generally made (low) formal demands of their members (Linek 2004: 183, 184). From 1993 local ODS associations acquired the right to approve new membership applications and the exclusive right to expel members. Local ODS associations enjoyed full autonomy in selecting candidates for communal and municipal elections and broad latitude to conclude local-level coalitions with any parties other than the Communists or the far right. Although district managers' salaries were paid by ODS Head Office (as in Civic Forum), local and district organization were required to be financially autonomous, raising funds to meet their own running costs, and – despite occasional ad hoc provision of off-the-books cash payments to fight elections (Deloitte and Touche 1998) – neither made nor received significant regular transfers from party headquarters. Local autonomy was further reinforced by ODS elites' neglect of their party machine after the party won national office in 1992. Despite ritual appeals to increase party membership and a growing appreciation by regional party managers of the importance of membership growth for sustaining local party activity (Linek 2004), once in office, ODS leaders gave a low priority to building party organization (*Lidové noviny*, 19 May 1996, 8).

Such extensive autonomy meant that grassroots political influence in ODS was uneven and limited in scope. As the party's Executive Deputy Chairman Libor Novák reported in 1996, most ODS members did no more than pay party dues and most local party work was carried out by a handful of activists, holding multiple office (*Bulletin ODS* 18/1996, 9). As national ODS officials noted with frustration, grassroots members who were politically active were largely absorbed in parish pump politics and were ignorant of or uninterested in national politics (*Mladá fronta Dnes*, 3 November 1997).[22] Many used the party's local branches as little more than vehicles to advance personal or local interests (Novák 1996). The small, largely inactive memberships of ODS local associations, combined with district associations' constant need to find 'sponsorship' to cover running costs, created ideal preconditions for local interest coalitions or powerful individuals to take control of some ODS grassroots organizations (Smith 2003b). Local associations' prerogative to approve new members served as a mechanism for established interests to block any challengers.

Such localized, interest-centred grassroots politics not infrequently led ODS associations – including district associations in large cities such as Brno and Hradec Králové – to split into competing interest coalitions, requiring the intervention of higher units or national party leaders to re-establish functional local organizations (*Respekt*, 13 December 1993, 4; *Respekt*, 26 August 1996, 4). Arguably, such localism was central to the 'franchise contract' through which ODS stabilized itself. The active independence of franchisee and franchisor described by Carty (2004) was evident in local (and later regional and Senate elections) when the ODS national machine and parliamentary elites provided a national advertising campaign (sometimes with a considerable budget),[23] the support of nationally known politicians and an outline programme offering local organizations and candidates legitimacy and a clear political identity in exchange for their investment of local resources to deliver the ODS 'product' on the ground. In other respects, the ODS franchising relationship was one of *passive* interdependence based on respect for mutual autonomy. Local, and above all district, ODS organizations were free to pursue their own local strategies provided that they did not contradict the ODS 'brand' or destabilize the party's organization structures. In exchange, the formulation of national strategy and policy was left to Prague-based parliamentary and political elites, who crafted programmes which allowed scope for the local-level pursuit of business and other interests, thereby sustaining ODS organization on the ground.[24]

This division of labour was reflected in – and reinforced by – ODS's lack of formal structures for policy development. In 1991–2 ODS had relied on Klaus's teams of advisers from the Federal Finance Ministry and Civic Forum and on the informal 'advisory group' of ODS politicians and sympathetic intellectuals chaired by ODS Vice Chairman Josef Zieleniec, which drafted the party's 1992 election programme. On entering government in 1992, policy formation was transferred from these earlier informal structures within the party to government ministries with little objection from the 'party in central office' or the 'party on the ground'. As Zieleniec ruefully observed 'nobody … is breathing down the necks of our ministers trying to promote their ideas or [political] ambitions' (*Mladá fronta Dnes*, 5 August 1996, 4).

Transformation and the development of the Czech right

There is an extensive literature on Czech post-communist transformation covering marketization (Orenstein 2002; Myant 2003; Appel 2004), decommunization measures such as the restitution of confiscated property or the screening out from public office of individuals compromised by association with the former regime ('lustration') (Williams 2003), public administration reform (Yoder 2003) and the failed process of renegotiating the federal state in 1990–2 (Stein

1997; Innes 2001). Most examine the development of Czech parties and party politics as an institutional variable contributing to bigger outcomes such as democratic consolidation, the break-up of Czechoslovakia (Innes 1997; Olson 1993) or the effective implementation of liberal economic and political reforms (Terra 2003; Orenstein 2002; Vachudova 2005; Grzymala-Busse 2006).[25] The following section re-examines Czech transformation policies of the early 1990s from the standpoint of the development of the new Czech right, considering firstly the right's role in authoring the policies usually linked to it and secondly – and more importantly – the impact of these policies on the emergent parties of the Czech centre-right

The centre-right and the politics of decommunization

Although sometimes depicted as a source of blanket anti-communism (Innes 2001), in the early 1990s the Czech civic right had an ambiguous attitude towards decommunization programmes, which tended to divide it and distract from its liberal transformation goals. Although the Civic Forum right incorporated anti-communist demands into its challenge to the ex-dissidents heading Civic Forum in 1990–1, decommunization emerged on to the Czech political agenda in 1990 primarily as a result of grassroots pressure and public opinion – often radically articulated in protests by anti-communist activists and former political prisoners – and the unanticipated practical problems of managing the records of the StB, the former secret police (Williams 2003).

Czech decommunization *legislation* was thus pioneered, although not decisively shaped, by small parties of the ex-dissident right, marking one of the first points of political difference with Klaus and the future leaders of the Civic Democratic Party (ODS). The first general restitution legislation, the so-called 'small restitution' law (Law no. 403/1990) was initiated in August 1990 by Privatization Minister Tomáš Ježek (1997: 117–18) and introduced into parliament by fellow deputies of the Civic Democratic Alliance (ODA).[26] Similarly, after several cases of 'wild' lustration, such as the Bartončik affair discussed in Chapter 4, and the failure in early 1991 of informal attempts by the Federal Assembly to 'lustrate' its members discreetly, federal deputies for Václav Benda's Christian Democratic Party (KDS) and the Liberal Democratic Party (LDS) initiated the process that would result in a formal legal framework for 'lustration'.

Czech decommunization programmes in 1990–2 were, however, a compromise product of a general anti-communist consensus, rather than an expression of right-wing dominance. Although the period saw the emergence of the Civic Forum right and the foundation of ODS, until June 1992 the right fell far short of a parliamentary majority even in the Czech parliament.[27] Major legislation required careful coalition building. It was thus the federal government, in which the centrist Civic Movement was then the major party, which drafted the bill which formed the basis of lustration law passed by the Federal Assembly on 4 October 1991. Although the emergent right, now organized into cohesive parliamentary groups, undoubtedly inflected the legislation in a more anti-communist direction – extending the range of posts covered by lustration and the criteria for exclusion and making lustration findings potentially public, rather than legally confidential – it did not decisively shape it (Williams 2003).[28]

With the exception of KDS and LDS, and despite strong anti-communist discourses (see Chapter 7), decommunization *policies* were a secondary priority for the Czech centre-right, which viewed them as both constitutionally and legally problematic and a distraction from the tasks of rapid privatization, which was according to Václav Klaus 'the best and most direct solution to the problem of old structures' (*Sobotní telegraf*, 4–10 December 1991, 2). Even after gaining a parliamentary majority in the independent Czech Republic, centre-right politicians largely eschewed radical decommunization measures. Although a largely declarative Law on the Illegitimacy of the Communist Regime was passed in July 1993, on the whole, the centre-right coalition merely maintained existing lustration laws[29] and continued to justify them as a means of defending liberal democracy, rather settling accounts with the old regime. There were clearer international precedents for banning extremist parties to safeguard democracy. However, parties of the mainstream right showed little interest in banning the hard-line Communist Party of Bohemia and Moravia (KSČM). Even ODS's statutory conditions for membership, where there was more legal scope for imposing restrictions on former Communists, essentially tracked the provisions of the lustration law.[30]Any such blanket ban on former Communists holding public office or party membership would have excluded a number of prominent centre-right politicians such as future Czech Finance Minister Ivan Kočarník (ODS), Tomáš Ježek (ODA) and Vladimír Dlouhý (ODA), who, like many Czechs and Slovaks, had joined the Communist Party as a necessary precondition to pursing a career. Klaus's ODS was similarly lukewarm towards restitution. It opposed extensive restitution of Church property as an unacceptable attempt to empower the Catholic Church in Czech society, thereby setting a precedent for concessions to other special interests (Klaus 1996: 177–82) and, in May 1994, proposed to halt restitution claims under existing laws because it considered the legal complications and uncertainties restitution generated to be impeding privatization (Pehe 1994b).

Decommunization programmes are sometimes seen as a means of disabling anti-reformist groupings rooted in the old regime. However, there is little evidence that Czech decommunization programmes countered a distinct, concerted threat from 'old structures' that might otherwise have acted as a counterweight to the pro-market right (Williams 2003).[31] Between 1991 and 1997 303,504 screenings took place under the lustration law.[32] However, only 5 per cent of screenings produced a result of 'positive lustration' – proven secret police collaboration or having held proscribed office under the old regime – and the number of officials removed because of positive lustration appears negligible (Williams 1999).[33] The one institution clearly derived from 'old structures', the Communist Party of Bohemia and Moravia (KSČM), was isolated and had no significant access to political or economic power. The early passing of relatively tough lustration legislation in the Czech Republic may thus have reflected the growing strength of the centre-right and a wider anti-communist consensus, but did not reinforce that strength. Restitution laws, by contrast, had direct beneficiaries and seems also to have brought political benefits to the right. Despite its carefully drawn limits and the relatively small amount of property affected, the programme benefited some 18 per cent of the Czech adult population. As with those retaining shares acquired in voucher privatization, there was a clear correlation between being a restituent and pro-reform, right-leaning attitudes (Večerník 1999b; Earle and Gehlbach 2003). It is unclear, however, to what extent restitution policies merely reinforced the anti-communist family traditions of Czechs of bourgeois or peasant descent.

The challenge of the anti-communist right

The most important impact of decommunization policy on the Czech right was less its direct effect than its political side-effects in alienating a small, but electorally not unimportant anti-communist constituency. In comparative perspective, Czechoslovak restitution and lustration laws were among the earliest and toughest in post-communist Europe.[34] However, they fell far short of radical expectations of full historical justice and the mass exclusion of (former) Communists from public life which had been raised in 1990–1. Restitution excluded key categories of property and persons including religious and social organizations, property nationalized before 25 February 1948[35] and (former) Czechoslovak citizens resident abroad.[36] Lustration affected many *appointed* positions in the state administration and public bodies, but no elected offices; and only former higher-ranking Party officials, officers in the Communist Party's paramilitary 'People's Militia' and those working for the secret police were excluded from holding those posts (Williams 2003).

The main radical anti-communist group to emerge from Civic Forum, the Club of Committed Non-Party Members (KAN), declined after failing to agree an electoral alliance with other parties in 1992, but newer groupings based on moralistic and radical anti-communism emerged to challenge the legitimacy of the civic centre-right and Christian Democrats with new forms of right-wing politics. The two most significant were the Republicans (SPR-RSČ) and the Democratic Union (DEU). The Association For the Republic–Republican Party of Czechoslovakia (SPR-RSČ) was formed in February 1990 as of one of many small, obscure 'right-wing' groups with vague anti-communist platforms. The party and its leader Miroslav Sládek first came to wider public attention after the break-up of Civic Forum, when its weekly *Republika* started to promote the conspiracy theories alleging that the Velvet Revolution had been staged as a result of secret agreements between communist and dissident elites (*Lidová demokracie*, 15 March 1991. The party subsequently took up a range of populist issues, calling for larger social benefits; greater law and order; less bureaucracy; the defence of Czech national interests against supposed German revanchism; and special measures of social control to be targeted against the Roma – the racism for which the party became best known (Pehe 1991b). From spring 1991, the party's mix of outrageous rhetoric, provocative demonstrations and continual campaigning mobilized enough support to create a small national organisation of 2000–3000 active members,[37] and in the June 1992 elections the SPR-RSČ polled 6 per cent of the Czech vote and gained representation in the both Czech and Federal parliaments. Similar tactics allowed it to re-enter parliament in 1996, when it increased its share of the vote to 8 per cent.

A somewhat different anti-communist challenge was posed by the Democratic Union (DEU). DEU was initiated in February 1994 by newspaper publisher Josef Kudlácek, previously a supporter of both KAN and ODS, who like many returning émigrés had become disillusioned that the Klaus government had not broken more radically with the communist past (*Respekt*, 2 August 1993, 15 and 7 February 1994, 4). Intended as a new rallying point for anticommunists across the right, DEU eschewed the Republicans' blatant racism and economic populism and endorsed the civic right's goals of Europeanization and market reform. The new party attracted the support of the prominent former dissident Alena Hromádková, who became its leader. Although better known in the 1980s and early 1990s as a Christian conservative influenced by Roger Scruton (see Chapters 3 and 7), by the mid-1990s Hromádková came to embrace radical anti-communist critiques as an explanation for the failings of transition. Dismissing the Velvet Revolution as 'an StB-nomenklatura street carnival', she argued that Czech politics was 'a civil war between parasitical cynicism and decent hard-working people'. Only by purging the former *nomenklatura* and its (assumed) values from all positions of power and influence, she argued, could successful reforms take place (*Respekt*, 27 December 1994, 3).

The Democratic Union made a promising start, quickly recruiting 4000 members to become a larger, although not necessarily more effective, political organization than parliamentary parties such the Civic Democratic Alliance (ODA) and the Republicans (SPR-RSČ). In 1994, DEU's relatively strong performance in local elections – when it polled 5 per cent in Prague and Brno and had mayors elected in two smaller towns – and a national poll rating of 2 to 3 per cent suggested that it might have the potential to break into parliament by attracting KAN or ODS supporters, who identified with the goals of transformation but shared the sense of frustration articulated by Hromádková (*Lidové noviny*, 29 November 1994).

Economic transformation in the Czech Republic

Unlike decommunization, economic transformation was from the outset a key priority for the neo-liberal economists of the former 'grey zone' based around Václav Klaus in the Federal Finance Ministry. Although initially sceptical that rapid privatization was politically or economically feasible (Ježek 1997: 100–1), the neo-liberals around Klaus quickly gravitated towards a strategy of rapid economic liberalization and rapid mass voucher privatization (Myant 1993b: 168–78; Ježek 1997; Šulc 1998: 74–5). Under the voucher method shares in companies being privatized would be 'sold' to the public for points in a voucher book issued (for a nominal fee) to all resident Czechoslovaks aged 18 or over. For the neo-liberals voucher privatization had a combined political, economic and philosophical rationale: it would accomplish privatization rapidly during a short-lived period of 'extraordinary politics' when public toleration for reform was highest and anti-reform insider groups weakest (Balcerowicz 1994); it would bypass the problem of lack of domestic capital without resorting to extensive state financing or potentially unpopular foreign ownership; and it would build political support for reform by offering citizens a direct stake in privatization on an equal and inclusive basis, which would educate them about the emerging market economy.[38]

Like decommunization strategy Czechoslovak and Czech economic reform strategy was, however, essentially a compromise between the different groups within the Civic-Forum-led Czech and federal governments of 1990–2. Federal Deputy Prime Minister Komárek's proposals were quickly rejected by the Federal government as too conservative and etatistic (Šulc 1998: 74–5), marking Komárek's political eclipse. However, a group of economists and industrial managers in the Czech government – around Czech Industry Minister Tomáš Vrba – outlined a social-liberal strategy with greater credibility and greater political support. The 'Czech plan' centred on restructuring and finding investment for technologically outdated, inefficient state enterprises before privatization through 'standard' means such as direct sales (Šulc 1998; Orenstein 2002: 67–7; Myant 2003: 118–19; Appel 2004: 47–51).[39]

In May 1990 the Federal government asked that the Federal Finance Ministry's proposals and the 'Czech plan' be combined into a single strategy. The resultant 'Scenario for Economic Reform' was endorsed by the Federal Assembly in September 1990. Although sometimes seen as a neo-liberal blueprint, the Scenario combined radical macroeconomic and price liberalization with active social and employment policy and tripartite bargaining structures. Subsequent legislation passed in February 1991 (Law no. 92/1991) established a framework for the 'large privatization' programme envisaged in the Scenario for the privatization of state enterprises with over 500 employees, the vast bulk of the economy. As with subsequent lustration legislation, the February 1991 law still reflected the broad social liberal compromise of 1990 by providing for a mix of privatization methods decided on an enterprise by enterprise basis (Orenstein 2002: 66–76, 100–1).

The resultant privatization process centred on the submission for each enterprise of a detailed 'privatization project' by its managers and prospective buyers. Plans were assessed by the Czech Ministry of Privatization headed by Tomáš Ježek in conjunction with the 'founding ministry', which had created the state enterprise in question, and a winning project was agreed. The National Property Fund (FNM) founded in August 1991 was then responsible for implementing all 'standard' methods of privatization. Two overlapping 'waves' of computerized voucher privatization auctions, co-ordinated by the Federal Finance Ministry, took place in April 1992 to December 1993 and October 1993 to February 1995 to sell those shares allocated to the voucher scheme.

'Small privatization' and the grassroots right

In addition to 'large privatization', there were a number of parallel privatization programmes covering smaller or less productive assets. Some 350 billion crowns of property was to be directly transferred free to municipalities; 250 billion crowns of assets held by co-operatives were privatized through their transformation into new forms of co-operatives; between 70 and 120 billion crowns fell within the ambit of the restitution process; and there was 'small privatization' of retail and commercial businesses (Reed 1996: 90–1; Earle *et al.* 1994: 46–52). The privatization of small units of commercial property in cash auctions was relatively uncontroversial. After 'small privatization' was proposed by President Havel in August 1990, legislation was therefore rapidly agreed and passed. Property with a book value of 24 billion crowns was then sold under the programme between January 1991 and late 1993. The process was co-ordinated by the Czech Privatization Ministry through Local Privatization Commissions (LPCs) which proposed businesses – often sub-units of large state enterprises – for potential privatization and assessed proposals submitted by others. The Commissions were used in a similar role for the first wave of 'large privatization' (see below), which overlapped with 'small privatization' (Earle *et al.* 1994: 61–2; Reed 1996: 91).

Public criticism of small privatization centred on the exclusion of any element of employee shareholding and the apparently dubious origins of funds used to buy businesses: from the perspective of party-society relations, however, the Local Privatization Commissions are of most interest. Given the opportunities that membership could bring well-placed insiders, the LPCs were a logical focus both for local interest groups and for local party politicians. The LPCs' origins and the lack of clarity about their relationship to the Privatization Ministry made them attractive to local party activists to whom they offered a means of gaining resources and support through party patronage. Indeed, in a very real sense the LPCs were partly created through party structures. As Tomáš Ježek (1997: 134–5) later recalled, the 1600 members of the LPCs were recruited through local Civic Forum leaders and officials who 'always suggested a few reliable people who helped organize the others'. As noted earlier, many such 'reliable people' would later join Klaus's ODS and in some cases, as for example the dubious privatization of the ceramics producer Karlovarský porcelán in Karlovy Váry (Reed 1996: 174–80), formed an overlapping local power elite taking in LPCs, business organizations and local branches of right-wing parties.[40]

The possibility of exercising party influence in LPCs was particularly important in 1991–2, a period when all parties including ODS were experiencing severe financial difficulties and the precise forms of grassroots organization were still in flux. ODS leaders had initially rejected state funding of parties as inappropriate to a conservative party (*Bulletin ODS* no. 9, 6 May 1991, 3). However, by October 1991 the party had reconsidered its attitude towards state funding as it was experiencing such acute financial difficulties that its Executive

Council was appealing urgently to members at all levels to raise funds for the party (*Bulletin ODS* no. 31, 17 October 1991, 2 and 6, 9 January 1992, 3). In November 1991 Jiří Havlena, the ODS Head Office official responsible for financial management, went as far as to urge members to use 'available contacts, including personal contacts, friends and acquaintances and also contacts with local councillors, privatisation commissions, public authorities, institutions, sporting and cultural figures etc.' to canvass for information as to possible donors and appropriately sized donations (*Bulletin ODS* no. 35, 14 November 1991, 4). While the circular did warn against offering political favours, such strategies were a fertile soil for the development of patronage networks.

Similar issues were raised by the issue of ODS's relationship with wider society. Like other 'civic' right-wing parties, ODS rejected the notion that social interests should be institutionalized within the political system. Unlike the Social Democrats and the Christian Democrats, ODS therefore never created interest-based organizations affiliated to the party. In 1991, however, party leaders did sanction the spontaneously emerging 'professional clubs' of ODS members working in particular areas or professions, including railway employees, doctors, teachers and mayors, provided that they functioned within the party and did not include non-members. Some party leaders, such as Zieleniec, saw the clubs as a means of channelling members' expertise into policy-making. However, the clubs also extended to sensitive areas such as Local Privatization Committees and the state apparatus. ODS general secretary Petr Havlík expressed disapproval of party organization in such sensitive areas, which appears to have been officially discontinued (*Bulletin ODS* no. 29, October 1991). However, consistent with the stratarchical relationships within the party there is no evidence that the party took further measures to regulate the activities of its grassroots members in relation to privatization.

The right and the implementation of 'large privatization'

The implementation of 'large privatization', although a more bureaucratic top-down process, also had important consequence for the development of the Czech civic right.

By the end of 1997, 715 billion crowns' worth of assets had been privatized under the 'large privatization' programme (Myant 2003: 121). Although, as envisaged in the Scenario for Economic Reform, a range of privatization methods were used, the dominant method selected was voucher privatization.[41] The growing predominance of the voucher method in 1990–1 reflected the emergence of the Czech right as a political force. The ODS controlled Federal Finance Ministry backed by ODS's newly formed parliamentary groups exercised sustained, but ultimately unsuccessful, pressure on the Czech government ministries involved in the privatization to adopt the '97+3' formula, under which all but 3 per cent of shares (set aside for compensation to pre-1948 former property owners under restitution laws) would be privatized using vouchers (Ježek 1997: 153). It also made clear to managements of important enterprises that it would support only privatization projects which allocated significant assets for privatization by vouchers (Appel 2004).[42]

The implementation of 'large privatization' also reinforced the emerging divisions in the civic right. Despite its small size, until 1996 the Civic Democratic Alliance occupied key posts concerned with privatization generating both ideological and bureaucratic conflicts with Klaus's ODS. As a politician with a party base independent of ODS heading a poorly staffed new ministry with overwhelming administrative tasks (Reed 1996: chapter 3; Myant 2003: 122), the Minister of Privatization Tomáš Ježek had both the political incentive and the political ability to challenge Klaus over the implementation process. In late 1991, Ježek thus successfully sought a postponement of the period for submitting and assessing privatization projects because of the near impossibility of meeting the timetable set by the Finance Ministry. More significantly, partly in response to lobbying by the Czech private entrepreneurs' organization of Rudolf Baránek – with whose Entrepreneurs Party ODA later sought to ally itself – Ježek opposed Klaus's preference that only one privatization project – formulated by existing management – should be submitted for each state enterprise (Ježek 1997: 151–8). Instead, supported by social liberals in the Czech government, he successfully argued for a competitive process, which would allow the submission of alternative projects by outsiders. Reflecting the neo-conservatism of the Civic Democratic Alliance, Ježek also favoured a more balanced mix of privatization methods to allow for more thorough restitution, the development of small businesses and a fund for civil society development (Appel 2004: 57).

Both the design of 'large privatization' as a social-liberal compromise using a complex mixture of methods and its right-wing-inflected implementation created multiple opportunities for corrupt self-enrichment. As Reed's (1996) research highlights, opportunities for corruption were concentrated around a number of foci. First, the competitive process of selecting between rival projects allowed officials in the Privatization Ministry and those submitting privatization projects to demand and offer (thinly disguised) bribes. This in turn stemmed from a lack of clear criteria for assessing and selecting projects. 'Standard' formers of privatization involving the assessment of competing bids such as direct sale and tendering offered similar opportunities. Even the seemingly neutral computerized process of voucher privatization offered opportunities for corruption through information leakage about bids and sales in previous rounds of bidding and the use of discretionary administrative powers to modify prices produced by computer models simulating supply and demand.[43]

However, the rapid, complex and weakly regulated 'large privatization' process also offered opportunities for party corruption. Raising resources corruptly through the privatization process was attractive to political parties, whose large financial deficits and high running costs could not be met from membership fees or small donations made by party supporters. The financial pressures on the smaller the Civic Democratic Alliance (ODA) were particularly acute. Despite gaining state funding on entering parliament in its own right in June 1992, ODA was heavily indebted because of over-optimistic borrowing to fund its election campaign on the basis of exaggerated expectations of electoral success.

Although there is evidence of suspicious or corrupt dealings linked to Christian Democrats' control of the Defence Ministry (*Respekt*, 11 March 1996, 4 and 22 July 1996, 5; Reed 1996: 257–60) and the Agriculture Ministry (*Respekt*, 7 July 1995, 4 and 9 April 1996, 5), the two parties of the civic right which controlled the key economic ministries had the greatest opportunities to benefit illicitly from 'large privatization'. Press reports and academic research (Reed 1996) suggests that groups wishing to privatize state assets, win public contracts or influence government decisions regularly made concealed donations to both ODS and ODA on the understanding the that they would receive favourable treatment. There is also anecdotal evidence that in some cases politicians directly solicited corrupt donations or knowingly took decisions in exchange for them (Reed 1996: 248–9, 260–1) although the more implicit understanding highlighted in the 'Šrejber affair' discussed in Chapter 6 seems to been have typical.

There were, however, limits to how effectively or systematically corrupt exchanges with political parties could take place. Corrupt or dubious relationships could prove politically damaging if sufficiently exposed in the media. In 1994, for example, Václav Klaus publicly hosted a paid ODS fundraising dinner attended by representatives of privatized enterprises, many still partly owned by the state, which generated a storm of protest (*Respekt*, 5 December 1994, 2–3). Even when fully concealed, party corruption was not a straightforward process. Although highly centralized, privatization decisions, nevertheless, entailed a complex process involving many individuals and institutions and, not atypically, more than one political party.[44] The sums accessible through corporate and commercial donations were moreover too uncertain and too small to cover even parties' normal running costs.[45] In the non-election year of 1995 – the last before the levels of state subsidy significantly increased – ODS had declared expenditure of 74 million crowns and received 24.9 million crowns (31 per cent) of declared income in donations. Of its income 45.9 per cent came from state subsidies (*Respekt*, 9 April 1996, 5; van Biezen 2003: 191; Outlý 2003: 151). Even if we factor in a proportion of the 170 million crowns allegedly accumulated illicitly by ODS between 1992 and 1997 (see Chapter 6), private donations would only have covered about two-thirds of its expenditure in a non-election year, such as 1995. All parties thus came to rely increasingly on the system of state funding linked to election results established in 1990.

The longer-term consequences of 'large privatization'

Although slower than its designers had anticipated (Myant 2003: 147), 'large privatization' achieved its objective of rapid mass transfer of ownership. By 1995 estimates suggest that between 70 and 80 per cent of the Czech economy was privately owned compared to 12 per cent in 1990 (Reed 1996; Orenstein 2002: 98; Appel 2004).

As both academic and journalistic observers quickly noted, despite ODS's stridently neo-liberal rhetoric, the realities the Czech transformation economy were more complex. (Rutland 1992; Dangerfield 1997). The literature on Czech economic transformation generally highlights several principal problem areas.

First, despite extensive formal private ownership, the state retained extensive control over the economy, thereby distorting the working of the market. The Czech state retained substantial stakes in major banks and other strategic enterprises as well as large blocks of shares earmarked for privatization but not yet sold. State-owned banks owned the principal investment privatization funds (IPFs), which managed and invested citizens' voucher points in a way loosely analogous to a conventional mutual fund. Although they pursued different acquisition strategies, IPFs' bombastic advertising campaigns quickly saw them assume a central role in the voucher privatization process, controlling some 71 per cent of voucher points invested in the first round and 64 per cent from the second (Appel 2004: 61–3; Myant 2003: 120). This allowed them to control some 30 per cent of shares in privatized companies (Appel 2004: 67) which, researchers estimated, gained them 39 per cent representation on boards of directors and 30 per cent of seats on companies' supervisory boards (Myant 2003: 126).[46]

Second, even leaving aside sizeable state ownership in the banking sector, which persisted throughout the 1990s (Horowitz and Petráš 2003), the relationship between financial and industrial sectors was highly problematic. In dealing with companies in which their IPFs held large stakes, Czech banks played the role of both creditors and (proxy) owners, creating incentives to offer larger and looser credit. This not only led to a proliferation of bad debt – exacerbated by inexperience and corruption within banks – but reduced the availability of credit to potentially more dynamic small and medium enterprises.

Third, lack of adequate regulation and legislation, compounded by the collective action problems of co-ordinating the millions of micro-shareholders created by voucher privatization, prevented minority shareholders from asserting their rights against either majority shareholders or enterprise managements. This facilitated forms of post-privatization corruption such as the 'tunnelling out' of assets by powerful management or shareholder groups using a variety of methods, damaging both efficiency and competitiveness and, in effect, expropriating weaker shareholders. Such problems were particularly significant in relation to IPFs, which were not adequately regulated even by legislation (belatedly) introduced to oversee them, and banks which controlled both industrial assets through their IPFs and the huge sums of money in both loans and deposits. Among the more high-profile cases illustrating problems of corporate governance were Viktor Koženy's transformation of his HC&C group into an opaque offshore holding company (Myant 2003: 138–9); the collapse of Antonín Moravec's small, but politically well-connected KPB bank; the outright theft of the assets of the CS Fondy privatization fund; and the ease with which the obscure Motoinvest group targeted banks and IPFs for leveraged takeovers (Rona-Tas 1997).

Fourth, as research in the late 1990s highlighted, both enterprises privatized (largely) by the voucher method and those sold to domestic entrepreneurs by 'standard' methods significantly underperformed compared with firms sold to foreign buyers (*Právo*, 28 January 1999, 15). More damningly, in many cases, firms sold to domestic buyers either directly or through vouchers performed little better (and often worse) than enterprises that had remained predominantly state-owned. This resulted from a combination of factors including managements' conservatism and lack of experience operating in a market environment; more limited access to capital necessary for modernization; the difficulty of owners exerting effecting control over management; and, where privatization took the form of direct sale, the unsuitability (or criminality) of Czech entrepreneurs selected as majority shareholders, whose leveraged buyouts often relied on privatized firms' own assets to pay off debt. The failure of newly privatized industrial enterprises sold to domestic buyers – such as the Poldi Kladno steelworks, the engineering groups Škoda-Plzeň and ČKD and the Chemapol conglomerate created by Václav Junek – and the collapse of a raft of smaller management-controlled manufacturing companies vividly illustrated these pitfalls. Other companies survived but lacked profitability, becoming marginal in European and even domestic markets (Reed 1996: 200–4, Myant 2003: 188–200, 211–25, 238–44; Terra 2003: 190–7).

Transformation and the social bases of the right

The renewal of the middle class (*střední stav*) that had been such a prominent part of Czech society before communism was a recurrent theme after 1989 across much of the political spectrum. Although conflicting with its liberal emphasis on the individual citizen, the (re-)creation of the Czech middle class was also an explicit initial goal of ODS's vision of and a key rationale for the party's foundation (*Respekt*, 9 May 1994, 7–9). The emergence of what Klaus termed 'strong domestic capital … a class (*stav*) of small and medium businesspeople' (*Sobotní telegraf*, 4–10 December 1991, 2) would, it was believed, provide a solid constituency for the centre-right and for further reform, counterbalancing the large communist-era working class, thereby restoring the balanced social structure of interwar Czechoslovakia.

A preference for domestic over foreign ownership was, however, built in to most aspects of Czech privatization policy: non-citizens were excluded from both the first round of bidding in 'small privatization' and from the restitution process; voucher privatization was open only to Czech(oslovak) citizens; and – particularly during the 1992–6 Klaus government – many large enterprises privatized by direct sale were sold to would-be Czech entrepreneurs rather than to foreign investors. The extent to which Czech neo-liberals were at heart 'national-liberals', and the extent to which they merely adapted to the Czech public's inclination to view the economy as a *national* asset, are difficult to assess. However, the predilection of centre-right parties for leveraged sales of large industrial enterprises to domestic entrepreneurs with forceful personalities and grandiose visions of building home-grown industrial conglomerates can partly be explained as an effort to build the domestic capital spoken of by Klaus.

The reality of Czech post-communist 'domestic capital' was, however, somewhat different: it was a fragmented, sectorally divided set of property owners and beneficiaries from privatization, whose hybrid character and politically and socially uncertain status made it far removed from the strong supportive *střední stav* evoked by the early rhetoric of the right. The most palpable expression of such hybridism was the transformation of banks and groups of communist-era managers into the real or effective owners of large privatized companies. Despite the opening up of 'large privatization' to competing projects and the political pressure exerted to allocate sizeable blocs of shares to the voucher process, management groups' insider knowledge, technical expertise and contacts ensured that they were disproportionately successful in privatizing large enterprises. In addition, the fragmented ownership structure created by voucher privatization meant that, as under communism, managements could often exercise ownership rights, which nominally belonged elsewhere (Reed 1996; Kotrba 1997; Večerník 1999a).[47]

Some managers were 'red' or 'pink' in their approach to running enterprises, stressing paternalism and output rather than sales and profits, and politically etatistic in their more general attitude to transformation. However, younger, second-rank managers, who came to prominence after 1989, often embraced the free market ideology of the right, stressing their professionalism as Western-style company managers and quickly took on similar remuneration, lifestyle and perks (Clark and Soulsby 1996). Despite this, most usually sought direct access to policy-makers and office-holders through semi-formal networks, rather than open or institutionalized links with parties. Although some had close informal relationships with particular parties, as, for example, with the IPB bank's close links to ODS (Reed 1996: 253–4), such economic actors are perhaps best viewed as 'policy-takers' (Ost 1993) oriented towards whatever party or politicians were incumbent, rather than a distinct social or class group capable of forming a party–society relationship in the real sense of the term.

The liberalization of the Czech economy in the early 1990s also saw a rapid expansion of small business and self-employment. Although many licensed businesses merely represented a secondary source of income or a disguised form of employment, by 1998 an estimated 600,000 people – 9.2 per cent of the workforce – made a full-time living from independent business activities. Entrepreneurs with employees made up 4.2 per cent of the workforce (Večerník 1999b: 85). As opinion polling regularly confirmed, businesspeople and the self-employed *were* strongly supportive of right-wing parties. Overall, however employers in the emerging Czech market economy were divided by size, sector, ownership and origin and they gaining a coherent social identity only via the tri-partite bargaining structures established in 1990–1, which were quickly down-graded, then ignored, by the first Klaus government (Myant 2000; Myant *et al.* 2000).

At the aggregate level of individual voters and citizens, however, the Czech right did develop a distinct constituency through privatization and trans-formation. The 5.94 million and 6.17 million Czech citizens who participated in the first and second waves of voucher privatization hugely exceeded the

300,000–500,000 participants that policy-makers had planned for (Appel 2004: 60), creating less the small class of emergent private investors envisaged than a mass of citizen-shareholders. With the launch in 1995 of the so-called 'third wave of privatization' by financial groups seeking to buy up valuable majority stakes, many former voucher holders sold up. Nevertheless, despite this and a subsequent a steady decline in public confidence in the integrity of the privatization process, a clear correlation emerged between support for centre-right parties, *retention* of shares 'bought' in voucher privatization and perceived personal gains from privatization (Večerník 1999b; Earle and Gehlbach 2003).

The broader process of 'winning' or 'losing' in transformation also shaped the electoral constituency of the right. Notwithstanding the novelty of the 'right-wing' label in 1990–1, such conflicts were quickly understood by both Czech politicians and public in traditional left–right terms. Left–right self-placement by the Czech electorate since 1990 remained relatively stable, with most voters locating themselves in the political centre and the overall distribution skewed towards the right. Other studies found that, in the course of the 1990s, voting for parties of the right and self-placement on the 'right' by Czech voters became more closely linked with more meritocratic notions of social justice, an above average tolerance of inequality and a commitment to market forces (Šimoník 1996; Evans and Whitefield 1998; Matějů and Vlachová 1995, 1998; Vlachová 1999; Krause 2000; Vlachová 2001, 2002). This was, moreover, underpinned by growing correlation between social position and party choice (Vlachová 1997). Thus although the Civic Democratic Party and other (neo-)liberal groupings on the Czech centre-right drew electoral support from a range of social groups, there was a clear tendency for better-educated, more urban and more prosperous groups of 'transition winners' to back them (Matějů and Reháková 1997; Reháková 1999; Krause 2002).[48]

State transformation and the Czech right

In the post-communist context the state occupies a complex and ambiguous position. In addition to blurred distinctions between the public and the private (or the partisan) (Ganev 2001), it is simultaneously a means of implementing socio-economic transformation and itself an object of reforms intended to improve its capacity to administer a market society. As such it has often been less a vehicle for delivering policy or a framework for regulating interests than a battleground for political actors seeking to consolidate their power and obtain resources for political competition (Grzymala-Busse and Jones Luong 2002; O'Dwyer 2004; Kopecký 2006). Although such trends are less marked than in the former Soviet Union, the politics of state transformation in Central European states, such as the Czech Republic, also offered opportunities to early incumbents such as the Czech civic right.

Public administration reform as political resource

In contrast to economic reform, the transformation of the Czech state was complicated by the need to agree a new Czech–Slovak constitutional settlement and to a lesser extent the need to accommodate the regionalist movements seeking to make Moravia an autonomous historic 'land' on the Austrian or German model. Partial reforms implemented in 1990 thus created a centralized structure amenable to party politicization.

From 1960 until 1989 the Czech Republic had been organized into 76 administrative districts (*okresy*) grouped into seven regions administered through a hierarchical system of National Committees and parallel Communist Party structures.[49] In July 1990 legislation was passed which replaced the National Committees with elected communal/municipal councils – first elected in November 1990 – and a network of District Offices (*okresní úřady*), the heads of which were appointed by the Czech Minister of the Interior. In all but the largest urban areas, District Offices were responsible for co-ordinating a range of activities including social services, environmental protection, records of births, marriages and deaths, licensing small businesses, vehicle registration, museums and larger public libraries. The regional-level National Committees (KNV), a bulwark of the old *nomenklatura* system, were abolished (*Lidové noviny*, 14 October 1990, 10), while a Czech government commission studied options for regionalization. Many central government ministries later established their own local agencies – employment offices, education authorities and tax bureaux – independently of the District offices, using a variety of mutually contradictory administrative and territorial models.

Although the 1990–2 Civic-Forum-led government had set a high priority on creating a neutral professional civil service, its efforts to take control of the state apparatus in 1990 set a precedent for future politicization by openly sharing out administrative posts on a partisan basis between the Forum and its largest Czech coalition partner, the People's Party.[50] Failure to pass early legislation defining the status, rights and responsibilities of civil servants and delineating which posts were occupied by neutral career administrators and which posts by party appointees also created uncertainty over acceptable boundaries.

When there was a change of government in June 1992, this logic was continued. Key agencies such as the boards of radio and television, the Supreme Control Office responsible for audit and anti-corruption functions, and the Czech intelligence service were headed by right-wing party political appointees. At lower levels, the power to appoint the head (*přednosta*) of a District Office and the directors of government ministries' disparate local agencies represented an important further source of party patronage. Conversely, the ability to recruit the head of a District Office or other influential local official represented an important resource for parties. Unsurprisingly, far from being politically neutral professional administrators, District Office heads or those heading educational or other authorities often were (or became) party political appointees and, in many cases, active local politicians. Press reports record a number of cases where partisan

District Office heads used the resources of their office (usually indirectly) to support local party activity (*Mladá fronta Dnes*, 13 October 1996, 5 and 29 January 1998). Such patronage resources were, however, shared, between ODS and smaller right-wing parties and, more unequally, between the government parties and the emergent centre-left opposition.[51]

Delaying state reform

In a transitional society the absence of necessary new institutions– or the creation of dysfunctional, partially reformed ones – can represent a failure to overcome historical legacies or resolve ongoing political struggles. However, it may also represent a conscious power-enhancing strategy by dominant groups to avoid the constraints that formal institutions could impose (Grzymala-Busse 2006). As the dominant governing party in national government, Klaus's ODS had strong incentives to block the emergence of the countervailing institutions that the decentralization of the Czech state would create. Moreover, the right's approach to 'large privatization' relied heavily on the centralized state structures inherited from communism to achieve *rapid* implementation central to economic transformation strategy.

However, even after the break-up of Czechoslovakia, the limited strength of the Czech right as a bloc and the divisions between ODS and its two smaller partners made maintenance of a centralized state problematic. In order to gain the enhanced majority required to pass the Czech Constitution of December, ODS agreed as a concession to Moravian regionalists and the two Christian Democratic parties in the governing coalition that the principle of regional government should be written into the constitution. However, it quickly emerged that both Václav Klaus and much of ODS were sceptical of regionalization, inclining towards a system of weak regional assemblies with chief executives appointed by central government (*Lidové noviny*, 1 November 1993; *Respekt*, 31 May 1993, 6; *Respekt*, 11 October 1993, 2). Although sometimes citing the need first to professionalize public administration or the complexity of fiscal arrangements, ODS concerns centred more on fears that regional government would serve as a platform for vested interests and opposition parties to slow economic reform and impinge upon individual freedom (Klaus 1995: 75–8, 149–51). In 1993 the party proposed the postponement of regionalization until 'no later than 1996' (*Lidové noviny*, 8 November 1993, 3) and blocked cabinet discussion of regionalization plans drawn up by the Office for Legislation and Public Administration headed by ODA leader Jan Kalvoda.

Having initially favoured a small number of large regions and later toyed with the idea of transforming the existing 77 districts into 'regions', in June 1994 Klaus's party pushed through a proposal for 17 weak regions as government policy, overriding the preferences of its smaller coalition partners for a smaller number of more powerful regions (*Respekt*, 4 July 1994, 3). However, a bill was not submitted to parliament until June 1995, following pressure from coalition partners and President Havel and the publication of alternative regionalization proposals by a parliamentary commission. In a series of votes ODS deputies blocked the bill by voting against or failing to vote. In April 1996 the party's legislators also prevented the passage of a regionalization bill presented by the former ODS deputy Josef Ježek (*Mladá fronta Dnes*, 25 April 1996).

The passing of legislation to create a Senate, the new upper chamber of parliament provided for in the Constitution, was similarly delayed because of disagreements between ODS and its smaller coalition partners. In this case, however, ODS's incentives to block the creation of a new institution were less clear cut. The powers of the upper chamber were limited and the use of a majoritarian electoral system stipulated in the Constitution to elect the Senate would potentially benefit ODS as one of the larger parties. Although Václav Klaus was reportedly sceptical of the need for a Senate, as a party ODS opposed moves by left-wing parties and the far-right to amend the Constitution and abolish the upper chamber (Pehe 1993, 1994c).[52] In September 1995, ODS's proposed compromise – single member constituencies with a second run-off round of voting between leading candidates – was accepted (*Respekt*, 30 September 1996, 9–11).

The break-up of Czechoslovakia as fillip for the right

There is a large literature examining the reasons for the break-up of the Czechoslovak federation in 1992–3. Factors examined include political-cultural differences between Czechs and Slovaks; economic and social differences between the two republics (Whitefield and Evans 1999); and the defective nature of federal institutions designed under an authoritarian political system (Kopecký 1999; Bunce 1999b). Some authors also cite the role of party development and party competition in undermining efforts to reach a constitutional compromise by acting as a conduit for – and multiplier of – nationalist sentiments (Olson 1993; Innes 1997), which were an effective means of mobilizing mass electorates. Others note the pragmatism of Czech and Slovak governing elites in quickly opting to terminate the federal state in mid-1992 (Innes 2001) or their different values and understandings of politics (Eyal 2003).

It is difficult to assess the extent to which Czech right-wing elites involved in dismantling the federal state were power seeking and the extent to which they were motivated by policy considerations such as the need to maintain a coherent state structure capable of administering the economic reform and privatization strategies chosen. The purely pragmatic consideration that there were few mutually acceptable compromise options may also have been relevant. Nevertheless, in contrast to the interregnum of partial reform and partial decentralization of public administration, the division of the federal state and the creation of an independent Czech state was a definitive, irreversible institutional choice permanently strengthening the Czech right.

Had the Czechoslovak federal system been preserved, the power of the Czech right, whatever its dominance in the Czech lands, would have severely circumscribed. The gains made by the ODS-KDS coalition in the Czech lands in the June 1992 elections were more than offset by the collapse of the pro-market liberal parties in Slovakia. Indeed, after the June 1992 elections Klaus's party and Benda's allied Christian Democrats were the only liberal pro-market groupings represented in the Federal Assembly, in which they held a mere 28 per cent of seats. Even if able to ally with disparate Czech, Slovak and Hungarian Christian Democrats – an unwieldy and unlikely coalition – the centre-right would have fallen far short of a federal majority.

The challenge of ODA and the Christian Democrats

Czech politics during the 1990s has often been presented as clash between Prime Minister Klaus and President Havel centring on rival views of civil society and the Czech place in Europe (Potůček 1999; Bugge 2000; Pontuso 2004; Myant 2005). In reality, even as a heuristic exercise, the strategies for post-communist transformation debated in Czech politics were far from reducible to the contrasting liberalism of Havel and Klaus, encompassing such diverse alternatives as neo-communism, anti-communist populism, several forms of democratic corporatism and a pallet of alternative liberal and ecological positions (Machonin *et al.* 1996). Despite his international and domestic prominence, after 1992 Havel was, as President, a relatively weak political actor, whose power was overshadowed by that of the principal parties and party blocs. Conflicts *within* the Czech right were, therefore, arguably of greater significance than the Havel–Klaus conflict. Party political division on the centre-right were reinforced and exacerbated by the experience of government in 1992–6 and conflicts over the implementation of transformation policies. In addition to challenging Klaus's ODS over policy issues, its two smaller coalition partners developed broader strategies based on alternative visions of transformation intended to make inroads into ODS's dominant position on the centre-right.

On replacing Josef Bartončík in November 1990, the new People's Party leader Josef Lux quickly abandoned the idea of building up a large bloc of Christian-oriented voters linked to the party by mass organizations. In April 1992 the KDU coalition structure was abolished and the party renamed itself the Christian and Democratic Union–Czechoslovak People's Party (KDU-ČSL). Lux argued that in a largely secular society, historically lukewarm towards Catholicism, Christian Democrats should focus on overcoming their limited traditional support bases by appealing to voters in broad programmatic terms. This implied a move towards centrally run media-based campaigning projecting the party as a 'tranquil force' in Czech politics with a distinct Christian Democratic vision of a social market economy, civil society and 'social peace' (KDU-ČSL 1996, 1998). Rather than being polarized into two large blocs of left and right divided by distributional issues, the party system should, Christian Democrats argued, be 'triangular' in form with the liberal right and social democratic or communist left complemented by a third Christian Democratic pole with a distinct agenda embracing both socio-economic questions – focused primarily on the interests of families with children, pensioners, disabled people and the embryonic Czech middle classes – and moral issues (*Lidové noviny*, 10 May

1995; Lux 1996; *Respekt*, 2 December 1996, 13; *Respekt*, 20 April 1998, 3). In this vision, Czech politics would come to resemble the three-cornered party systems of Belgium and the Netherlands.

The Civic Democratic Alliance, by contrast, presented its differences as a principled liberal critique of Klaus's 'ideology of pragmatism' (*ZpraODAj*, February–March 1993, 2–3; *ZpraODAj* no. 1994/4, April, 1–2; ODA 1996). In this view, socio-economic transformation under Klaus was insufficiently liberal and was losing impetus because unprincipled etatism and vested interests were eroding the reformist élan of Klaus's party. Further measures such as radical deregulation, further privatisation, administrative decentralisation and the promotion of civil society were needed, the Alliance argued, to avoid a slide into semi-reformed 'bank socialism'.

Of the two parties, ODA initially seemed the more dynamic and dangerous competitor. In 1993–4 the Alliance's opinion poll ratings rose rapidly and were consistently above 10 per cent, at one point rising high as 15 per cent (*Lidové noviny*, 21 September 1995, 5). However, as private polling for the party made clear, for much of the electorate ODA's image was vague. Voters saw it at best as a 'companion and helper' to ODS, rather than an alternative to it (*ZpravODAj*, February–March 1993, 2). Moreover, much of the ODA electorate was composed of 'floating voters' who were closer to the political centre than ODS supporters. This left the party vulnerable to the impact of events. There was a marked drop in ODA support in early 1995 following revelations about the purchase of the party's large debt in September by the (now bankrupt) KPB bank, whose owner Antonín Moravec was under investigation for suspected embezzlement of the bank's funds. A deal brokered by Moravec in December 1992 had effectively written off the debt at the bank's expense (Reed 1996: 252–3; *Respekt*, 25 September 1995, 5).[53] Accusations by the ODA leader, Jan Kalvoda, of a plot against the party by the Czech intelligence service ('the BIS affair') were widely ridiculed as a means of distracting attention from the scandal (Rychlý 1995). The Alliance subsequently accepted that its debt to KPB had never been repaid properly and was still owed to institutions that had taken over KPB's assets.

1996 as critical election

Until 1995 most opinion polls suggested the centre-right coalition would not only retain its parliamentary majority but would gain sufficient seats to gain the enhanced majority required to pass constitutional laws (120 seats in the lower house) (*Lidové noviny*, 21 June 1995, 5). The decline in ODA support and the resurgence of the Czech Social Democratic Party (ČSSD) under the more assertive leadership of Miloš Zeman in 1995–6 suggested a more even contest. However, despite the emergence into the public domain of numerous scandals connected with the privatization process (Reed 1996), Czech public opinion appeared broadly satisfied with the progress of economic reform, and few outside a fringe of radical anti-communist groups saw the Czech left as an electoral challenge comparable to that of the reformed communist parties that had displaced centre-right governments in Poland and Hungary in 1993 and 1994.

In contrast to the feverish realignment on the fractured Polish and Hungarian centre-right before both parliamentary elections (Fowler 2004; Kaminski 2003; Szczerbiak 2004), on the Czech right there was therefore only a very limited resumption of the intense merger discussions and alliance building of 1991–2. The most concrete move towards centre-right consolidation was the integration of the tiny Christian Democratic Party (KDS) into Klaus's ODS. Although it had ten deputies and two ministerial portfolios, polling had consistently shown that KDS's independent support did not exceed 1 or 2 per cent. Despite the replacement of the party's dissident founder, Václav Benda, by the younger, more pragmatic Ivan Pilip in December 1993, the 1994 communal elections confirmed that the party lacked even localized support (*Lidové noviny*, 11 October 1994, 5). Despite the defection of five Catholic-oriented KDS deputies to the Christian Democratic Union–Czechoslovak People's Party (KDU-ČSL) in May 1996, a merger was smoothly concluded in April 1996. However, plans to bring the Club of Committed Non-Party Members (KAN) into ODS, by first merging it with KDS, failed after being rejected by delegates to a special KAN conference, which considered Klaus's party too compromised on decommunization issues (*Lidové noviny*, 2 November 1995, 16 November 1995; Pšeja 2004b: 1082–5).

The ODS campaign for the 1996 elections used the slogan 'We've shown that we can do it' (*Dokázali jsme, že to dokážeme*) and stressed the Czech Republic's unique success in post-communist economic transformation. Nevertheless, neither the campaign nor the party's lengthy programme – essentially a compilation of policy positions developed by separate ministerial teams – gave any sense that the party was offering more than a continuation of the *status quo*. ODS campaigning was also badly organized. Many experienced ODS Head Office staff had left the party for more influential or better-paid positions in government or the private sector and, in contrast to 1990 and 1992, regional campaign events featuring Klaus and other leaders were poorly co-ordinated and lacked active support from the party's (by now) demobilized grassroots. The Social Democrats' 1996 campaign, by contrast, was considerably more professional and well organized than its expensive but ill-focused campaigning in 1990 and 1992, making use of billboard advertising and foreign consultants for the first time. Whilst national advertising stressed the honesty and straightforwardness of its more popular and better-known leaders and concern for inclusiveness and fairness, its regional campaigning – centring on a battlebus used by Social Democrat leader Miloš Zeman (skilfully contrasted with Klaus's use of a private jet) – targeted small and medium-sized communities in Moravia which had made only limited gains during the transformation process (Pečinka 2003a).

The results of the election were a major surprise. The popular vote was won by Klaus's ODS with a share similar to that which it had gained in elections to the Czech parliament in June 1992, although it failed to match the somewhat higher levels of support achieved in 1992 in the poll for the federal parliament.

Table 5.6 Elections of 31 May–1 June 1996 to the Chamber of Deputies of the Czech Parliament

Party	No. of votes	% of vote	No. of seats
Civic Democratic Party (ODS)	1,794,560	29.62	68
Czech Social Democratic Party (ČSSD)	1,602,250	26.44	61
Communist Party of Bohemia and Moravia (KČSM)	626,136	10.33	22
Christian Democratic Union–Czechoslovak People's Party (KDU-ČSL)	489,349	8.08	18
Association for the Republic–Republican Party of Czechoslovakia (SPR-RSČ)	485,072	8.01	18
Civic Democratic Alliance (ODA)	385,369	6.36	13
Pensioners for a Secure Life (DŽJ)	187,455	3.09	0
Democratic Union (DEU)	169,796	2.80	0
Free Democrats–National Social Liberal Party (SD-LSNS)	124,165	2.05	0
Others	241,436	3.22	0
Total	6,105,588	100.00	200

Source: www.volby.cz.

Note
Turnout: 76.41%.

The unexpected large gains made by the Social Democrats, who polled over 26 per cent, coupled with increased support for the far-right Republicans, narrowly deprived the centre-right coalition of its parliamentary majority. Although the Christian Democrats gained votes and seats and the Civic Democratic Alliance (ODA) marginally increased its support, the three parties of the centre-right coalition gained only 99 seats in the 200-member Chamber of Deputies. As neither the Republicans nor the Communists were acceptable coalition partners for the Social Democrats, an informal agreement was negotiated allowing the continuation of the Klaus-led centre-right coalition as a minority administration in exchange for concessions to the Social Democrats in parliament, such as the election of Miloš Zeman as speaker of the lower house and the sharing of parliamentary posts such as committee chairmanships – previously monopolized by governing parties – between government and opposition. The second Klaus government also saw an important shift in the balance of power between ODS and its smaller coalition partners, who insisted that, regardless of relative electoral support, ODS should no longer hold a majority of cabinet posts, an arrangement which had always ensured it a majority in government deliberations in the first Klaus administration.

Conclusions

In successfully taking over the resources, electorate and pro-reform mission of Civic Forum and stabilizing itself through a stratarchical division of power between elite and grassroots, Václav Klaus's Civic Democratic Party (ODS) established itself as the dominant force on the Czech right. In doing so it denied small ex-dissident parties resources and opportunities, so condemning most to political marginality, although one – the Civic Democratic Alliance (ODA) – narrowly succeeded in accumulating sufficient resources to break into parliament as a liberal-conservative competitor. The early electoral and organizational consolidation of ODS also ensured that rivals with alternative models of right-wing politics, such as the Christian Democrats and the populist anti-communist Republicans, remained minor parties. ODS's effective monopolization of party building resources for the centre-right thus produced a strong 'logic of increasing returns' locking-in its initial dominance in relation to right-wing competitors.

The design of Czech transformation policies such as decommunization, privatization and regionalization was largely the product of the political compromises of 1990–2 period, rather than a neo-liberal blueprint. However, their *implementation* offered the incumbent parties of the civic right considerable resources and opportunities to consolidate their organization and power. This was particularly the case after the June 1992 election when the first Klaus government took office and the break-up of Czechoslovakia dissolved the federal political system. Nevertheless, the politics of transformation exacerbated political and party differences on the incumbent Czech centre-right, supplying resources and opportunities for competition between them rather than durable political compromise or cartel-like division of spoils. Trade-offs between liberal goals of marketization and individual freedom and demands for historical justice helped fracture the alliance between neo-liberals and anti-communists, which had briefly held at the time of ODS's foundation, leaving the civic centre-right unable to incorporate the small anti-communist constituency represented by groups such as KAN, the Democratic Union and, to a lesser extent, the Republicans. Had the civic right been able to draw on even a part of this constituency it would have retained its parliamentary majority in 1996. Conflicts over privatization policy, in part rooted in inter-ministerial rivalries, aggravated tensions between Klaus's ODS and ODA which had been politically and ideologically close. As in Poland and Hungary, however, ideological and cultural divisions between neo-liberals and conservatives also coloured such conflicts. In the Czech case, however, the neo-liberal right was the dominant partner. Moreover, the liberal-conservative fissures which opened up between ODS and its two more conservative partners centred on disputes over restitution, regionalization and civil society, rather than moral issues.

Despite their early advantages, the parties of the Czech centre-right lacked sufficient initial power to 'lock-in' their political dominance over the fragmented centre and left-wing forces and, subsequently, lacked sufficient internal cohesion and concentration to out-compete the centre-left when it belatedly coalesced around the Czech Social Democratic Party. Klaus's party was able to block regionalization, but was unable to enforce its own preference for a more centralized constitutional system with weak regions. Opportunities for party corruption seem to have brought the incumbent right significant, but ultimately limited resources. In the absence of a bourgeoisie or bourgeois civil society willing or able to align with parties of the right, the only alternative was a reliance on public subsidy linked to election results, making political competition more open.[54] Access to patronage resources and any further advantages that might be accumulated from incumbency remained dependent on the uncertain prospect of winning elections. This a complacent Czech centre-right narrowly failed to do in June 1996

6 Beyond the politics of transformation
Declining and realigning 1996–2006

Introduction

The 1996 election marked an end to centre-right majority government in the Czech Republic, beginning a pattern of political stalemate characterized by a succession of minority or weak majority governments sustained by unstable left–right co-operation, which lasted until 2006. Many accounts of Czech politics attribute the decline of the Czech right in the late 1990s to exogenous factors such as the unravelling of its economic policies or the belated consolidation of the centre-left. However, as discussed in Chapter 5, the difficulties of Czech transformation strategy were apparent at an early stage. Moreover, in both electoral and parliamentary terms support for centre-right parties remained relatively stable throughout across the 1990s, falling sharply only in 2002, six years and two parliamentary elections *after* the Social Democrats had first established themselves as a major party.

This chapter will suggest that of equal or greater importance to the displacement of the Czech right after 1996 were divisions and realignments between, and within, centre-right parties driven by a series of overlapping debates about the identity and role of the centre-right in the Czech Republic. These debates and divisions concerned issues such as the boundary between the politics of transformation and the development of more settled forms of right-wing politics; the relationship of the right to Czech society and to local interests within its own party structures; and the question of whether (and how) the right could broaden itself sufficiently to win durable majorities or seek the best possible *modus vivendi* with the left and other Czech proponents of a social market.

Although catalysed by developments such as electoral competition or economic difficulties, such debates and divisions originate in the early 1990s when the right was organizationally stable and political dominant. This chapter tracks these debates and the (re-)alignments surrounding them from 1992–3 to the fall of the second Klaus administration in November 1997 and then examines the series of close or inconclusive elections that followed in 1998, 2002 and 2006, each of which blocked the return of a centre-right coalition to power, whilst offering limited political influence to parts of the right.

Realigning after 1996

From post-communist transformation to 'everyday politics'?

Despite the apparent success of reform and the smooth division of Czechoslovakia, internal discussions about ODS's future role began almost immediately after its June 1992 election victory. Former ODS deputies in the defunct Federal Assembly were an early source of discontent, criticizing the party's failure to transform them into a temporary upper house of the Czech parliament; ODS's support for Václav Havel's presidential candidacy; and the slowness of the Klaus government in passing decommunization laws or health and tax reforms. Observers spoke of the emergence of a 'conservative democratic' faction which felt that ODS – like Civic Forum – lacked ideological clarity and was too broad in its appeal (*Telegraf*, 25 January 1993, 3; *Český deník*, 7 October 1993).

Others argued that the flagging party required less an injection of radicalism and militancy than a strategy oriented to everyday politics, which would ensure its long-term stability. Although he consistently opposed this view, Václav Klaus himself appears to have triggered these ideas in 1993 by making a series of remarks suggesting that the most significant and painful economic reforms had already been completed (*Respekt*, 15 March 1993, 2; and 18 October 1993, 2). Although probably intended as a tactic to deflect criticism of government policy, the remarks were widely interpreted as a claim that social transformation was effectively at an end – raising questions as to what 'post-transformation' might entail (*Respekt*, 18 October 1993, 2). The argument for a right-wing transition to 'everyday politics' was taken up especially strongly by Josef Zieleniec, the most influential of the party's four Deputy Chairmen, who responded to Václav Klaus's apparent comments that transformation had basically been completed by arguing that the ODS should retain its breadth, but learn to 'master practical everyday problems' (*Telegraf*, 26 November 1993). At ODS's fourth congress in Kopřivnice in November 1993, and in contrast to Klaus's confident endorsement of ODS's achievements, Zieleniec warned the party that its 'transition from the heroic era to that of a more or less normally functioning party is in no case self-evident' and proposed the adoption of a long-term political programme of aims and values paving the way for an election programme stressing 'everyday policies' (*politika pro všední den*) to ensure that the party did not stand or fall with specific leaders (*Respekt*, 29 November 1993, 3). However, Václav Klaus opposed these ideas as premature, arguing that the weakness of the Czech left concealed further fundamental battles over transformation, and the congress rejected Zieleniec's proposal. Elite criticism of Klaus did not, however, subside. By mid-1994 supporters of Zieleniec such as ODS deputy Richard Mandelík were again openly speculating about the possible formation of a conservative faction, reportedly supported by 11 of ODS's 65 deputies, which sought 'everyday policies' attuned to issues such as housing, law and order and banking reform (*Lidové noviny*, 17 June 1994). Zieleniec chose to lobby within the party leadership rather than mount an overt challenge. In September 1994 he

succeeded in persuading the party's Executive Council that a political programme should be formulated, a proposal accepted by the party's fifth congress
in Karlovy Váry in December 1994. Klaus, it should be noted, voted against the
resolution and in his opening address to the congress implicitly dismissed Zieleniec's arguments that a long-term programme was needed to establish a
'common denominator' between liberal and conservative voters.

Although a Political Programme reflecting Zieleniec's more conservative
concerns with social and community cohesion was duly drafted and adopted, it
had little practical impact on the party's strategy or campaigning. After ODS's
disappointing 1996 election results, Zieleniec publicly resumed the debate,
arguing in a newspaper interview (*Mladá fronta Dnes*, 5 August 1996, 4) that
ODS needed to become a more pluralistic party with several distinct political
currents (*názorové proudy*) represented. A clash of ideas, Zieleniec claimed,
would both generate more effective and appealing policies and enable a wider
range of voters to identify with the party. Reiterating his view that ODS should
begin to address issues beyond macro-level economic transformation such as
corruption, the rule of law, the position of small businesspeople and the quality
of community life, he argued for a more explicitly social dimension to Czech
right-wing politics, arguing that the right must understand that 'society is more
than a set of individuals and not be ashamed of the values upon which social
cohesion rests' and that ODS should not primarily be a party for 'entrepreneurs
with big (often borrowed) money'. Through a process of 'broadening out'
(*rozkročení*) towards both the political centre and conservative anti-communist
voters on the right, Zieleniec suggested, ODS could become a powerful centre-
right force appealing to 'voters similar to those of the German CDU' across
some 40 per cent of the Czech electorate, thus blurring the existing division of
the Czech right into liberal and Christian-conservative wings stressed by Klaus
and his supporters (Klaus 1993a: 64).

In the following months Zieleniec's analysis was debated both within ODS
and in the Czech right-wing press in a series of contributions by politicians,
intellectuals and academics. However, many in ODS, including Klaus, rejected
both the substance and the assumptions of Zieleniec's critique. Klaus argued that
a political party could not be re-engineered like a commercial organization. As
both Klaus and others (*Lidové noviny*, 21 August 1996, 9; *Lidové noviny*, 11
September 1996, 11) noted, previous initiatives to spur policy debate within
ODS had foundered on a lack of interest among local ODS members and officials (*Lidové noviny*, 11 September 1996, 11). A new political party with a relatively small membership and limited backing from the intelligentsia such as ODS
could not be expected to have the political breadth or the ideological depth and
diversity of established centre-right parties in Western Europe. Instead, Klaus
claimed, ODS's problems required limited organizational reform focusing on the
party's managerial structures and handling of media relations.

Zieleniec's vision of making ODS into a broader, more socially rooted party
was an indirect response to the challenge posed by Josef Lux's project of
making the Christian Democrats into a 'Czech CDU' more attuned to the

Central European character of Czech society and traditions. Klaus also rejected these strategic arguments by suggesting that Zieleniec's 40 per cent target was arbitrary, over-ambitious and even dangerous. The experience of right-wing blocs in post-communist Hungary and Poland and the record of Austrian and German Christian Democratic parties, Klaus suggested, demonstrated that transforming ODS into a 'typical Central European "People's Party"' would make it incoherent and unstable and tend over time to force out liberal forces and allow the left to take over the mantle of socio-economic modernization. Instead, the Czech premier argued, the Civic Democrats should seek to match (and marginally exceed) their support in 1992, aiming for 33–34 per cent of the vote (*Lidové noviny*, 11 September 1996, 11). When the ODS Executive Council met in August 1996 to discuss the issues raised by Zieleniec's interview, it was evenly divided between supporters of his position and those accepting Klaus's more limited diagnosis, and recommended a compromise package of organizational reforms reflecting the views of both sides (*Lidové noviny*, 14 August 1996).[1]

Economic problems and political pressures

Despite these difficulties, divisions among opposition parties seemed to make the second Klaus administration a relatively strong minority government. Not only was there a significant divide between the Social Democrats and the more radical Communists and the far-right Republicans, but the Social Democrats themselves were divided and disunited following the party's unexpectedly large electoral gains. In early 1997 two Social Democrat deputies broke ranks with their party by voting for government budget proposals and subsequently left the party, one through expulsion, the other defecting directly to ODS. By working with the now independent ex-Social Democrat Jozef Wagner, the ODS-led coalition enjoyed a narrow and unstable, but workable two seat parliamentary majority.

From spring 1997 the Czech Republic's increasingly evident economic problems put political pressures on the coalition. Budget and trade deficits grew, unemployment rose and growth stagnated as public opinion polls detected an increasing sense of public disengagement and malaise, famously described by President Havel as Czech society's sinking into a 'foul mood' (*blbou náladu*) (*Mladá fronta Dnes*, 2 April 1997, 2). On 16 April 1997 the incipient crisis came to a head when the government finally announced a package of austerity measures to curb spending and hold down public-sector wages (*Mladá fronta Dnes*, 17 April 1997, 1). Yet the package did little to address the underlying problems of the economy or political responsibility for them.

In May 1997 the previously stable Czech crown came under sustained pressure from currency speculators, prompting the Czech National Bank to raise interest rates and spend US$3 billion defending the national currency. Despite these measures and the departure from the government, at the insistence of the ODS executive, of the Industry and Trade Minister Vladimír Dlouhý (ODA) and Finance Minister Ivan Kočarník (ODS), the Bank was finally forced to allow the crown to float, resulting in an immediate 10 per cent devaluation against the US dollar. The government then introduced a second, more far-reaching set of austerity measures accompanied by a declaration, read by Klaus at a televised press conference, which admitted for the first time that 'mistakes in economic policy' had produced long-term problems such as low productivity, the subsidizing of inefficient enterprises, an ineffective banking system and an opaque, poorly functioning legal system (*Mladá fronta Dnes*, 29 May 1997, 3 and 15). Although scarcely an original diagnosis, this *mea culpa* reflected the growing leverage of ODS's two smaller coalition partners, who, having gained increased cabinet representation in the second Klaus administration, now insisted that their criticisms of Czech transformation policy be publicly acknowledged as the price of their continuation in the coalition.

Although the government won a parliamentary vote of confidence called by Klaus on 10 June, the fiscal and currency crisis of April–May 1997 further exacerbated tensions between the coalition parties and triggered a further wave of discussions with ODS. In May, ODS's Central Bohemian region, supported by Interior Minister Jan Ruml, called for a special party congress.[2] In June, further conflict erupted publicly between Klaus and ODS deputy leader and Foreign Minister Josef Zieleniec, who claimed that Klaus had withheld from ministers critical assessments of the Czech economy by the International Monetary Fund. Although the conflict was quickly smoothed over, on 23 October 1997 Zieleniec unexpectedly resigned as Foreign Minister and as an ODS deputy chairman.[3] However, his opaque resignation statement, which complained of 'not being informed of grave decisions concerning the management of the party' taken without the knowledge or authorization of executive bodies, left it unclear whether he was speaking out against malpractice or acting from political pique and his resignation was received unsympathetically by other ODS ministers (*Respekt*, 1 December 1997, 9–12). Efforts by Miroslav Macek, who despite the privatization scandals of 1992 had again been elected as an ODS Deputy Chairman at the party's 1996 congress, to take over Zieleniec's mantle as the main voice for reform were even less successful.[4] Although Macek and the new ODS Finance Minister Ivan Pilip agreed to step down as ODS deputy chairmen at the party's forthcoming congress, thus enabling all four posts to be newly elected, most senior ODS figures seemed happy to endorse Klaus's view that ODS merely required a change of image (*Mladá fronta Dnes*, 10 November 1997, 2).

'Sarajevo' and the fall of the Klaus government

In late 1997 two overlapping party funding scandals engulfed ODS. The first concerned concealed donations connected with the privatization of the Třinecké železárny steelworks in 1995. In November 1995, the Moravia Steel group, co-owned by the former professional tennis player Milan Šrejber, won the tender to buy the steelmaker Třinecké železárny. The heavily leveraged bid was facilitated by advantageous credit terms from the partially state-owned Česká spořitelna savings bank (Terra 2002: 203–8; Myant 2003: 199–200). Some weeks before the privatization decision Šrejber met ODS's Executive Deputy Chairman Libor

Novák to discuss a donation of 7.5 million crowns (US$250,000) to the party.[5] As Czech law required that the identity of donors giving more than 100,000 crowns be published in an annual financial report, Novák advised making the donation through an intermediary to avoid the appearance of corruption (*Právo*, 28 November 1997, 2). In circumstances that remain unclear, Šrejber's donation was subsequently recorded by ODS as two donations of 3.75 million crowns from clearly fictitious individuals: 'Láos Bacs' of Budapest and 'Radjiv M. Sinha' of Mauritius,[6] a crude subterfuge which both concealed the origin of the money and reduced the party's tax liability.

In April 1996 journalists from the news magazine *Respekt* began to investigate the origins of the donations. As they were unable to establish the real source of the donations, their report (*Respekt*, 9 April 1996, 5) had limited impact. ODS stated that it had acted in good faith, had correct documentation for both donors and set up a party commission to investigate the donations. Some ODS leaders however were already aware of the donations' origins. Fearing a potential scandal in the run up to 1996 elections, Novák had brought in an external media consultant, Michal Kuzmiak, to manage the situation.[7] In this role, Kuzmiak informed the ODS Deputy Chairman, Josef Zieleniec, the party's election campaign co-ordinator, about the situation. According to his own subsequent account, Zieleniec was so shocked that he immediately spoke to Klaus, who, Zieleniec claimed, seemed already aware of the situation (for which he blamed Novák), but otherwise appeared unperturbed.[8] In late 1997, journalists who had learned Šrejber's identity as the donor reinvestigated the affair. Despite efforts by Libor Novák to shield others,[9] between 22 and 27 November 1997 details of the affair were revealed to the Czech press and subsequently confirmed by Zieleniec, his former aide Petr Kolář, Kuzmiak and Šrejber (*Mladá fronta Dnes*, 22 November 1997, 1–2, and 25 November 1997, 2; *Lidové noviny*, 22 November 1997, 3, and 27 November 1997, 1).

Far more serious allegations were reported in *Mladá fronta Dnes* on 28 November 1997 at the height of the Šrejber affair. According to the newspaper, ODS controlled a secret bank account in Switzerland containing 170 million crowns (US$5.75 million) – a sum sufficient to cover the costs of a national election campaign – allegedly accumulated since the early 1990s in secret donations from firms involved in privatization.[10] As with the Šrejber affair, the main source of information about the secret account was the ODS elite itself. The account's existence seems to have been revealed inadvertently by ODS's Head Manager, Tomáš Ratiborský, on 26 September 1997 at a meeting of the party's *gremium* – an informal weekly co-ordinating committee made up of Klaus, ODS's four deputy chairmen and the leaders of its two parliamentary groups.[11] These reports were then confirmed by three others present at the *gremium* meeting, Josef Zieleniec, Ivan Pilip and Jan Stráský (*Mladá fronta Dnes*, 29 November 1997, 1–2; *Respekt*, 1 December 1997, 9–12). Despite subsequent investigations by police and prosecuting authorities which concluded that an account probably had existed and a forensic audit conducted at ODS's own request by Deloitte and Touche (1998), little further concrete evidence publicly emerged. It now became clear that Zieleniec's unexpected resignation stemmed from his frustration at Klaus's failure to address the issue of the account satisfactorily. Ivan Pilip chose to remain in office, maintaining in public that ODS finances were in order until the scandal broke in November.[12]

Despite incomplete evidence both cases suggested clear violations of laws on political party financing, tax and foreign currency regulations and legislation against false accounting. Both also contained strong circumstantial evidence adding to the picture of extensive party corruption during the privatization process. The subsequent Deloitte and Touche (1998) study concluded that ODS's accounts had been routinely falsified by party officials to conceal the identity of donors, avoid tax or siphon resources to firms they themselves controlled. In addition to the 7.5 million crowns donated by Šrejber, the identities of the donors of a further 11.1 million of the 24.9 million crowns of donations recorded in the ODS's annual financial statement for 1995 were false (Deloitte and Touche 1998: 24–5). The study also found that large sums of money had never been entered into the party's accounts – in 1995 at least 2,367,000 crowns of additional donations were not entered into the party's's accounts (Deloitte and Touche 1998: 26–7, 37–8). Most damagingly of all, the accounts given by Zieleniec and others suggested that Klaus had condoned illegality and lied or dissembled about his knowledge of it for months, perhaps years. Klaus himself vigorously denied all the accusations against him and the allegation that ODS or anyone linked to the party had ever held a Swiss bank account,[13] but offered no explanation as to why his recollection of conversations in April 1996 and the crucial *gremium* meeting in September 1996 differed from those of Zieleniec, Pilip and Stráský.[14]

The political impact of the two scandals was immediate. When allegations of a Swiss bank account broke on the morning of 28 November 1997, the ODS *gremium* agreed that the whole party leadership including Klaus should resign at the forthcoming party congress. Klaus then announced that he would seek re-election as party leader before departing for a summit of Central European leaders in Sarajevo. A group of ODS politicians, dissatisfied with Klaus's failure to take greater responsibility, then took pre-emptive action. On the evening of 28 November, Ivan Pilip and former Interior Minister Jan Ruml, supported by the current Interior Minister Jindřich Vodička and Social Affairs Minister Stanislav Volák, called on Klaus to resign as party leader at a televised press conference.[15] Klaus, the ministers declared, 'had been unable to refute exceptionally serious allegations convincingly' and his lack of credibility 'threatened public trust not only in ODS but in this country's whole political system' (*Mladá fronta Dnes*, 29 November 1997, 2). Later the same evening the Christian Democrats withdrew from the coalition government, giving similar reasons for their decision. The Civic Democratic Alliance (ODA), now under its newly elected leader, Jiří Skalický, quickly followed suit (*Mladá fronta Dnes*, 29 November 1997, 1). On 30 November 1997 Klaus resigned as Prime Minister, formally triggering the fall of the government (*Mladá fronta Dnes*, 30 November 1997, 2). On 9 December 1997 in an address to the Czech parliament, President Havel (1997) set the seal on the fall of the Klaus government, delivering a stinging critique of Czech transformation as based on flawed privatization policies backed by 'petty-bourgeois provincialism' and an economistic view of the world that set little store on moral values, which had undermined public trust in democracy and the market.[16]

It was initially assumed that the existing centre-right coalition would be reconstituted under a new Prime Minister, such as Ivan Pilip or Christian Democratic leader Lux. However, Klaus announced that he still intended to seek re-election as ODS leader at the forthcoming congress and, if re-elected, would lead ODS into opposition, rather than attempt to renegotiate the three-party coalition. Moreover, although opposed by a narrow majority of his own deputies, Klaus enjoyed the solid support of ODS Senators and – as became apparent, after an initial period of disorientation – of a clear majority of ODS district organizations (*Lidové noviny*, 1 December 1997, 4).[17]

Klaus termed his resignation a 'forced move' dictated by opponents, who had ignored his political achievements and impugned his personal integrity (*Lidové noviny*, 1 December 1997, 3). Klaus's supporters argued more bluntly that he had been the victim of an 'internal putsch' by disloyal, self-seeking politicians, who had conspired against him, quickly dubbing Ruml and Pilip's televised appeal the 'Sarajevo assassination'. Aware of the divisive impact of their actions, Pilip and Ruml had both initially ruled themselves out as potential leadership candidates. However, when no challenger of any stature emerged, Ruml agreed to challenge Klaus. Although Ruml's forthright political style and anti-communist radicalism, which dated back to dissident activism of the 1980s, had previously made him popular among the ODS grassroots, his appeals to restore credibility and trustworthiness of the party were ignored by delegates to the ODS special congress in Poděbrady on 13–14 December 1997; they re-elected Klaus by three to one – a majority only a little lower than previous (uncontested) congress votes electing Klaus leader in earlier years.

The disintegration of the Civic Democratic Alliance

In late 1997 a party financing scandal also overtook the Civic Democratic Alliance as cases of concealed donations from beneficiaries of privatization covertly channelled through offshore companies and bank accounts came to light (*Mladá fronta Dnes*, 7 February 1998, 1 and 2). As in ODS, the timing and impact of the scandal related more to factional tensions than to any surprising new information about the Alliance's finances. Despite breaking through to become a parliamentary competitor to ODS in June 1992 and maintaining its position in the June 1996 elections, questions had long been asked about the rationale for the Alliance's independent existence, given the similarity of its 'civic democratic' outlook to that of ODS. Despite its small size (see Table 6.1) the Alliance was also subject to a range of internal political and organizational tensions between its Prague-based founding elites and its well-educated grassroots members, who, in contrast to ODS's stratarchically divided membership base, were willing and able to participate in debates on high policy.

Table 6.1 Membership and organization of smaller right-wing parties 1990–2003

Party	Christian Democratic Union–Czechoslovak People's Party (KDU-ČSL)		Civic Democratic Alliance (ODA)		Freedom Union–Democratic Union (US-DEU)[1]	
	Members	No. of local branches	Members	No. of local branches	Members	No. of local branches
1990	48,037	n/a	13	n/a	–	–
1991	95,435	n/a	10	12	–	–
1992	88,737	2437	350	27	–	–
1993	100,000	n/a	1350	n/a	–	–
1994	n/a	n/a	2050	70–80	–	–
1995	80,000	n/a	2409	178	–	–
1996	n/a	n/a	2755	190	–	–
1997	n/a	n/a	2782	192	–	–
1998	60,460	2635	2925	208	2400	
1999	55,616	n/a	2162	n/a	3118	
2000	55,306	n/a	1889	n/a	2933	
2001	51,453	n/a	1668	n/a	3570	
2002	50,657	2218	1550	131	3152	90
2003	49,441	n/a	n/a	n/a	n/a	n/a

Source: Hanley (2000) and Linek (2003) using party records and press reports.

Note
1 Freedom Union (US) 1998–2001.

First, ODA's intellectual ex-dissident leaders and officials saw themselves as occupying a privileged position in keeping and interpreting these principles and their attempts to 'educate' newer, less intellectual members often took the form of abstract philosophical expositions, sometimes delivered with undisguised condescension. Second, the stress on the autonomy of the party's parliamentarians, in fact, served to insulate the leadership from criticism and accountability, as the party's leadership and its parliamentary group were largely overlapping. As party membership and organization grew, these tensions increased. Newer members tended to be more centrist and pragmatic than the intellectual founding group, and to be liberal rather than neo-conservative in outlook.[18]

This 'pragmatic' wing of the party, identified with Vladimír Dlouhý, the Industry and Trade Minister, argued that ODA's intellectualized approach to politics would always lack broad appeal (*ZpravODAj*, August 1992, 1–2) and suggested that ODA should orientate itself towards concrete social groups such as small businesspeople and the emergent middle class (*ZpravODAj*, 1995/5 July, 15) and build a more extensive party organization to gain wider legitimacy as a 'real' party (*ZpravODAj*, July 1992; 4.) Other 'pragmatists' stressed that the diversity of the ODA membership and its views should be recognized, criticized the elitism of the party's leaders and founders and attacked its strategy 'of being a party of crafty little imps kicking the big fellows in the shins' as a hypocritical political failure, leaving ODA weak and unviable as an independent party (*ZpravODAj*, November 1996, 9). While advocating the decentralization of the state and the emergence of civil society, critics noted, ODA leaders avoided issues of centralism within ODA itself. However, supporters of the 'fundamentalist' wing of the party such as ODA deputies Čestmír Hofhanzl and Ivan Mašek saw the 'pragmatists' as representing only careerism and illegitimate sectional interests, which were subverting the party's principles. The unexpected resignation of Jan Kalvoda as ODA Chairman in January 1997 – apparently as a matter of honour because he had used an academic title he was not entitled to – allowed the 'pragmatists' to elect a relative newcomer, the former Czech ambassador to Washington Michal Žantovský, as leader. In response, the 'fundamentalists' formed an organised 'Right Faction' (*Týden* no. 12/97, 19–22; *Respekt*, 12 May 1997, 3), whose leading members made thinly disguised accusations of financial impropriety against the party when its November 1997 conference replaced the divisive figure of Žantovský with a compromise candidate, Jiří Skalický. In December 1997 and January 1998 journalists began to investigate the shell companies and intermediaries listed as donors in the ODA's financial statements, rapidly identifying prominent domestic and foreign companies involved in privatization as the real source of donations to the party. The suspicions raised by this information precipitated ODA's disintegration. With the exception of Daniel Kroupa, many of the Alliance's prominent leaders, including Jiří Skalický, left the party.[19] In the aftermath of splits and scandal, ODA's opinion poll ratings collapsed to 1 per cent and, faced with electoral oblivion, the rump party decided not to contest the 1998 parliamentary elections.

The foundation of the Freedom Union

By January 1998 the 99 deputies elected for the three parties of the Czech centre-right in June 1996 had split into five groupings.[20] The anti-Klaus right commanded only 61 seats in the 200-member Chamber of Deputies (*Lidové noviny*, 15 January 1998, 3). Given the left-wing opposition parties' insistence on early elections, there was little option but to negotiate a caretaker government, which would hold office until the (constitutionally complex) process of calling early elections could be agreed. Following negotiations involving both the Social Democrats and President Havel, a government headed by the Governor of the Czech National Bank, Josef Tosovský, which included both non-partisan technocrats and ministers from ODA, the Christian Democratic Union and the anti-Klaus wing of ODS, took office on 2 January 1998.[21]

After the Poděbrady congress, Klaus's opponents within ODS had initially formed a 'platform' (*názorová platforma*). When the new pro-Klaus ODS executive instructed the platforms' supporters to cease organized activity and withdraw from the Tosovský government or leave the party, it was clear that a new centre-right grouping would emerge. Some figures on the anti-Klaus right such as Jindřich Vodička and Klaus's former aide Petr Havlík argued for the creation of a loose electoral coalition of the ex-ODS politicians and small existing right-wing parties as a so-called 'Right Alternative' (*Lidové noviny*, 10 January 1998, 2). Although accepting the need for co-operation with other groups, the leaders of the anti-Klaus platform saw little alternative but to create a new party (*Lidové noviny*, 9 January 1998, 3). On 17 January 1998, the Freedom Union (US) held its founding congress in Litomyšl and was officially registered five days later (*Lidové noviny*, 19 January 1998, 3; *Respekt*, 19 January 1998, 4; *Týden*, no. 5/98, 20–2).

Although the conflicts of November–December 1997 had centred on the personality and integrity of Klaus, the Freedom Union quickly took up a familiar palette of alternative centre-right policies previously outlined by Zieleniec and other ODS reformers and ODS's two former smaller coalition partners: a culture of 'openness', 'trustworthiness' and 'communication'; more deregulation and market reform; closer attention to legal and regulatory structures; greater decentralization, more emphasis on culture, education, the environment and social policy; and an acceptance that social cohesion underlay individual and market freedoms, and acceptance of concepts such as civil society and the social market economy as valid concerns, not surrogate forms of collectivism (*Lidové noviny*, 19 January 1998, 3; *Respekt*, 19 January 1998, 4). The Union's programme and statutes also revisited other themes overlooked by ODS in office such as the development of a Czech middle class and the institutionalization of party platforms representing different social and political concerns as advocated by Zieleniec.[22]

The Union's launch attracted considerable sympathetic media and public interest and its early opinion poll ratings were high. An initial poll found that 58.3 per cent of respondents were sympathetic to the new party and 23.7 per cent would consider voting for it.[23] It thus briefly seemed that the new party's political élan might allow it to displace a discredited and scandal-ridden ODS as the leading party of the Czech liberal right. Polls in February 1998 seemed to confirm this, recording the Union's support at 16–18 per cent – ahead of Klaus's ODS, whose support sank in one poll to a nadir of 9 per cent. The Freedom Union's local and national founding events also rallied support from a range of influential social and elite groups such as small business associations and prominent figures from academia, business and the media.

The new party quickly faced political and organizational difficulties. The Union's initial membership stood at 2400, of whom an estimated 40 per cent were former ODS members and 60 per cent political newcomers. Tensions between experienced ex-ODS members and newcomers were soon evident at both national and local level. Although founded by former ODS politicians, the Union's leadership was concerned that it should not appear an 'ODS mark II'. Political newcomers were thus favoured over ex-ODS figures vulnerable to accusations that they were responsible for the failures of the 1990s or acting purely from political opportunism. Former ODS members occupied only a third of places on the newly elected party executive, and few former ODS deputies did well enough in internal party primaries to gain 'electable' positions on the

Union's lists for the June 1998 elections, although several re-entered parliament after they were selected for the reserved top positions chosen, as in ODS, by the party leadership, rather than by grassroots delegates (*Mladá fronta Dnes*, 28 April 1998, 2).[24]

More problematic still were the party's identity and role in Czech politics. Early debates over the party's new name had highlighted that, although not devoid of policy ideas, it was essentially defining itself *against* the model of centre-right politics established by Klaus and ODS (*Lidové noviny*, 19 January 1998, 3). It was unclear whether the Union was a reconstituted party of the 'civic' right, seeking to replace ODS as principal bulwark against the left, or a centrist modernizing force seeking to transcend the established left–right divide. This ideological dilemma was thrown into sharper relief by opinion polls, which showed that, even when its support was highest, the Union would need to form a coalition with either the Social Democrats or Klaus's ODS to enter government (*Mladá fronta Dnes*, 16 March 1998, 2).

As the election approached, the Freedom Union's support in opinion polls started to decline. Although the newness and diversity of its leadership and its stress on honesty in politics initially made it a focus for hopes of political renewal, many voters quickly found the party vague. Support for both the Social Democrats and the Civic Democrats rose. In the competition for right-wing voters the Civic Democrats' aggressive campaign calling for 'mobilization' against the left seems quickly to have marginalized the Freedom Union, which was handicapped both by the organizational weaknesses of its regional campaigning and by the decision of its leader, Jan Ruml, not to stand again for election to the lower house of parliament (*Mladá fronta Dnes*, 6 June 1998, 4).

The 1998 elections – left turn

The parliamentary elections of 14–15 June 1998 were convincingly won by Miloš Zeman's Social Democrats, who polled over 32 per cent of the vote, defeating the Civic Democrats by a clear margin to become the largest Czech party for the first time (see Table 6.2). Despite unresolved financial scandals and the political splits of 1997–8, Klaus's party succeeded in rallying the bulk of its electorate, polling almost 28 per cent support. Although the Freedom Union entered parliament, gaining almost 9 per cent support, its performance fell far short of initial expectations, effectively establishing the party merely as a substitute for the Civic Democratic Alliance. Despite receiving their highest vote since 1990, the Christian Democrats, too, remained essentially a minor party, having failed to expand sufficiently beyond their core rural electorate.

As widely anticipated, the election failed to produce a viable majority coalition. In purely arithmetical terms – largely as a result of far-right Republicans' failure to win any seats – the three parties of the centre-right had gained a narrow parliamentary majority and could in principle have formed a coalition government. The acrimonious disintegration of the Klaus government, Klaus's continued leadership of ODS, and the Freedom Union's origins as a party

Table 6.2 Elections of 19–20 June 1998 to the Chamber of Deputies of the Czech
Parliament

Party	No. of votes	% of vote	No. of seats
Civic Democratic Party (ODS)	1,665,550	27.74	63
Czech Social Democratic Party (ČSSD)	1,928,660	32.32	74
Communist Party of Bohemia and Moravia (KSČM)	658,550	11.03	24
Christian Democratic Union–Czechoslovak People's Party (KDU-ČSL)	537,013	9.00	20
Freedom Union (US)	513,596	8.60	19
Association for the Republic–Republican Party of Czechoslovakia (SPR-RSČ)	232,965	3.90	0
Pensioners for a Secure Life (DŽJ)	182,900	3.06	0
Democratic Union (DEU)	86,431	1.45	0
Green Party (SZ)	67,143	1.12	0
Others	97,388	1.63	0
Total	5,969,926	100.00	200

Source: www.volby.cz and *Svobodné slovo*, 22 June 1998.

Note
Turnout: 74.03%.

formed in reaction against Klaus's record, made such a coalition a political
impossibility. A second option favoured by President Havel, Miloš Zeman and
the Christian Democrat leader Josef Lux was that of a left–right majority coalition of Social Democrats, Christian Democrats and Freedom Union united by a
positive commitment to rapid integration with the EU, decentralization, civil
society promotion and the modernization of public administration. The prospects
of such a government foundered when a narrow majority of the Freedom
Union's executive endorsed Jan Ruml's conception of the party as a right-wing
anti-socialist formation, which should respect his pre-election commitment not
to ally itself with the left.

The 'Opposition Agreement'

The unexpected political denouement of post-election negotiations was a third
option: the signature of a formal written political pact between Klaus's ODS and
the Social Democrats which allowed a minority Social Democratic administration
to take office. The so-called 'Opposition Agreement', signed by representatives of
the two parties on 9 July 1998, committed ODS to support the continuation in
office (but not the legislation) of a minority Social Democratic government by not
participating in an initial vote of confidence and not voting for any subsequent
motions of no confidence. The agreement also guaranteed ODS posts in parliament, such as the speakerships of both houses, chairs of key parliamentary committees and (informally) positions in the management structures of public bodies

and state-owned companies. However, although it contained a vague provision for political consultation, the only other politically substantive point in the Agreement was a commitment for the two parties to co-operate in introducing constitutional amendments to 'define the competences of certain constitutional bodies more precisely ... and strengthen the importance of the results of party competition'. Such amendments, both parties acknowledged, would entail the restriction of presidential powers and the introduction of a more majoritarian voting system for parliamentary elections likely to increase the representation of the two largest parties at the expense of smaller competitors[25] (*Lidové noviny*, 10 July 1998, 1 and 5).

The Opposition Agreement was presented in its preamble as a framework to maintain political stability necessary for reform. Critics, by contrast, viewed it as a cynical exercise in clientelistic power politics which made a nonsense of pretended ideological divisions (Roberts 2003; see Chapter 7). Internal discussions on the right, however, advanced an additional set of justifications for the arrangement as exercising a 'braking' effect upon the Social Democrats and allowing the party to discredit itself in government. In this view, the Agreement did not mark the suspension of left–right competition, but merely transferred it to a new setting (Klaus 2000a: 76–7 and 82–4). As Roberts (2003) argues, for ODS the Opposition Agreement represented a rational trade-off of short-term loss of office, albeit retaining an unusual degree of political influence for an opposition party, against the longer-term prospect of exercising single-party majority under a new electoral system. In attempting to reduce the representation and thus curtail the political influence of smaller right-wing parties, the Agreement thus represented a new solution to the problem of creating a broad, cohesive centre-right, which ODS reformists had sought to address through alliance building and policy change.

The realignment of ODS

Grassroots support for Klaus almost regardless of the circumstances of the funding scandals, but consistent with the stratarchial relationships described in Chapter 5, can be viewed as a break-down of the institutionalization process, in so far as it missed an opportunity for the party to outgrow its charismatic founder and adopt a set of values going beyond the concerns of the period in which it was founded. Instead, in choosing to support Klaus almost regardless of the circumstances of the funding scandal or the party's record, the majority of ODS delegates in effect chose to make the party a formation based increasingly on a bond of trust with its charismatic founder and leader.

This outcome did not mean, however, that ODS ceased to become a programmatic party. Indeed, the 1997–2002 period was characterized by a conscious search for forms of right-wing ideological renewal under Klaus, which could offer an alternative to the reformist agenda of the Freedom Union and its antecedents. In March 1998 party leaders met with ODS mayors and regional representatives to agree four broad themes on which the party would campaign (the 'Poděbrady articles'): 'inviolability of privacy', 'a cheap state', 'a future

without debt' and 'solidarity between responsible citizens' (ODS 1998) implying a wave of further liberal economic reforms based on lower, flatter taxation; a
major restructuring of public expenditure; a scaling back of state power and
bureaucracy; and a more individualized approach to pensions and welfare.
Although the new focus on the state and public service represented a concession
to reformist centre-right agendas of the 1990s, the 'Poděbrady articles' retained
a strongly neo-liberal emphasis on economic and fiscal transformation and individualist anti-statism. Beyond a commitment to a 20 per cent flat tax and single
universal welfare benefit, the 'Poděbrady articles' were not translated into distinct policies and were soon overshadowed by other themes. Principal amongst
these were the defence of Czech national interests in European integration
process and the defence of ODS in domestic politics.

Such policy renovation was backed by a reassertion of ODS's political identity and record rejecting both centre-left and centre-right critiques of Czech
transformation. The Civic Democrats thus stressed their distinctness and consistency as a historically new Czech liberal right-wing tradition, besieged by forces
hostile to market-led transformation. In this view, both centre-left and centre-
right critiques of the Klaus governments' record were distortions of political
history intended primarily as attacks on the legitimacy of transformation and the
'civic' right *per se*. The economic difficulties of 1997 were thus viewed as an
outcome less of flawed transformation policies than of a short-term currency
crisis caused by extraneous or technical factors such as cyclical recession and
the restrictive monetary policy of the Czech National Bank. Similarly, the fall of
the Klaus government was interpreted as the overturning of the 1996 election
result by self-seeking small parties and disloyal individuals – supported by
President Havel and a hostile media – which had undemocratically excluded the
winning party from office.

Accordingly, the party's successful 1998 election campaign had stressed anti-
socialism and anti-communism, asking for a 'Mobilization' against the left
given the supposed choice of going 'With Klaus or to the left!', and sought to
cultivate a sense of combative defiance among erstwhile ODS voters using
slogans such as 'Head Up' and 'If you believe in yourself, vote for Klaus'. From
mid-1999 the party began to rethink its identity and relationship with Czech
society. Although some ODS documents still paid lip service to the importance
of the middle class (ODS 1998), the party began to stress the importance of the
nation, the homeland (*vlast*) and other 'natural communities'. The significance
of the ODS turn to 'national interests' in relation to European integration is discussed in detail in Chapter 8. In domestic politics, however, it brought a
national-populist tinge to the party's neo-liberal individualism, rejecting the
'mythologization of the middle classes' as a form of 'rehashed Marxism
(*zástydlý marxismus*)', which, it claimed, merely served to justify welfare policies redistributing resources from rich and poor to middle-income groups to
engineer an majority of the centre (Nečas 1999b; see also Hanley 2004b).
Indeed, for some social conservatives in the party, such as Petr Nečas, the
renewal of 'family values' and 'national cohesion' was an alternative to tradi-

tional social policy in overcoming the divisions between generations, social groups and regions opened up by market forces.

Short-term management of the complex political situation created by the Opposition Agreement posed more immediate problems. Contrary to the views of some commentators, the Agreement fell far short of an (implicit) Grand Coalition in both formal scope and actual operation. Far from ushering in two-party cartellization, it led to a period of fluid ad hoc parliamentary coalitions, which saw the governing Social Democrats vote more often with the Christian Democrats, Freedom Union or Communists than with their co-signatory to Opposition Agreement (Roberts 2003). Even the Agreement's specific provisions for the two larger parties to co-operate over electoral and constitutional reform proved difficult to implement as the Social Democrats' declining poll ratings and unexpected ability to govern through ad hoc majorities led them to prevaricate. Internal debates in ODS canvassed a range of responses, ranging from withdrawal from the Agreement to seek rapprochement with the Christian Democrats and Freedom Union, to entering a formal coalition with the Social Democrats giving ODS direct influence in government. On 16 October 1999, however, Klaus's party sought to combine the two strategies, unexpectedly suggesting the formation of a 'supergrand' or 'rainbow' coalition of all non-communist parties to supplement the Opposition Agreement ostensibly to address high levels of public discontent at the ineffectiveness of minority government. However, Christian Democrat and Freedom Union leaders questioned the likely legitimacy of a 'supergrand' coalition and rejected any scenario involving a continuation of the Opposition Agreement (*Mladá fronta Dnes*, 19 October 1999, 2 and 14 December 1999, 2). Ultimately, in January 2000, the Social Democrats and ODS signed a more explicit agreement ('Patent of Toleration'), which included a timetable for the passage of legislation reforming the electoral system ('Toleračni patent' 2000).

The rise of the Quad-Coalition

The Civic Democratic Alliance (ODA) and Christian Democrats (KDU-ČSL) had often found themselves in joint opposition to ODS in the 1992–7 Klaus governments and, partly because of this, their political positions on issues such as regionalization, civil society promotion and European integration significantly overlapped. The two parties had also successfully co-ordinated their campaigns for the November 1996 Senate election to overcome the disadvantages of the first-past-the-post system, standing down candidates in constituencies where the other party was stronger. This strategy significantly reduced the gains made by ODS. Relations between the Freedom Union (US) and the Christian Democrats (KDU-ČSL) were initially cordial but detached. The Christian Democrat leader, Josef Lux, had initially hoped to draw former ODS politicians into his own party in the same way that he had attracted conservatively minded liberals such as Petr Pithart from the defunct Civic Movement in 1995–6. The founding of the Freedom Union not only blocked this strategy but created a potential competitor of wider appeal.

Nevertheless, the signing of the Opposition Agreement in July 1998 prompted Josef Lux to speculate about the possibility of an alliance between his party and the Freedom Union (US), laying the basis of a new 'credible conservative party of a Christian Democratic type' (*Mladá fronta Dnes*, 14 July 1997, 1). The Union responded positively to these overtures by suggesting that the two parties might form a joint 'Shadow cabinet' to offer 'real opposition' to the Opposition Agreement (*Mladá fronta Dnes*, 15 July 1997, 3). The two parties quickly reached an arrangement for co-operation in the November 1998 local and Senate elections, which also took in the Civic Democratic Alliance and Democratic Union (now shorn of much its earlier radical anti-communism), creating the Quad-Coalition (Čtyřkoalice, or 4K).

In the 1998 Senate elections 4K enjoyed considerable success, winning 13 of the 27 seats due for re-election. For the first year of the Opposition Agreement, relations between Czech parties remained fluid and appeared at some points to be polarizing into new blocs of centre-left and centre-right. Some Freedom Union leaders, including Ruml (1999), began to rethink the rationale of establishing a new party of the liberal right and started to rebuild relations with ODS. In May 1999 the Freedom Union's executive even went as far as to empower Ruml to open negotiations with ODS about a possible electoral coalition between the two parties.[26] In January 1999 Christian Democrat deputies, by contrast, had worked with the minority Social Democrat government to pass a budget bill rejected by the 'civic' right (Dimun 2002).

Developments elsewhere in Czech politics gave further impetus to the development of the Quad-Coalition into more a united third force. The election of the businessman Václav Fischer to the Senate as an independent in August 1999 in a by-election occasioned by the death of ODS Senator Václav Benda highlighted the unpopularity and political vulnerability of the Opposition Agreement. Although the Quad-Coalition candidate came a distant third, Fischer won the election in a wealthy district of central Prague with an overwhelming majority on a platform of direct opposition to the Agreement. Moreover, his election deprived the Civic Democrats and Social Democrats of the 60 per cent majority in the Senate required to pass constitutional changes envisaged in the Agreement (*Mladá fronta Dnes*, 30 August 1999, 1 and 2).

When in 1999–2000 the Social Democrats and Civic Democrats finally began the process of negotiating legislation for a more majoritarian electoral system the Quad-Coalition parties decided to transform their loose electoral alliance into a more integrated bloc. On 28 September 1999 the parties signed the 'St Wenceslas Day Agreement' setting out a commitment to long-term electoral co-operation,[27] a political rationale for the coalition and a rudimentary co-ordination structure. Twelve months later this was elaborated into a more detailed coalitional structure, programmatic statement and schedule to agree a joint Prime Minister designate and 'Shadow cabinet' and programme for government.

As Lux had foreseen shortly before leaving politics through illness, the grouping seemed to have the potential to create an influential fusion of liberalism and moderate conservatism based on shared commitments to civil society, decentralization and European integration. In November 2000, 4K enjoyed further success in regional and Senate elections, making sufficient gains in the upper house to block further amendments to the electoral law which, unlike other legislation, could not be passed without approval in both houses (*Mladá fronta Dnes*, 21 November 2000). The Quad-Coalition's growing support, which according to the STEM polling organization peaked in January 2001 at 30.9 per cent, not only enabled it to block the institutional changes envisaged under the Opposition Agreement but allowed it to challenge ODS as the dominant force on the Czech centre-right and begin to rival both ODS and the Social Democrats as principal actors in Czech politics, in effect creating a form of the 'triangular' politics advocated by Josef Lux in the mid-1990s.[28]

In May 2000 after much delay, ODS and ČSSD legislators passed a new electoral law. As they were now unable to amend the constitution which enshrined the use of proportional representation (PR) for elections to the lower house, the two parties agreed a bill which respected the outward forms of PR, whilst modifying it to produce significantly more majoritarian outcomes.[29] The probable net impact of the law would have been to enable a winning party or bloc to win a majority in the lower house with 30–35 per cent support (Kostelecký 2000; Birch *et al.* 2002: 81–3). Although the Quad-Coalition's high poll ratings suggested that it could be a principal beneficiary of the new electoral law,[30] as a weakly integrated bloc of small parties formed to overturn the Opposition Agreement it continued to oppose it. Although President Havel's July 2000 vetoing of the electoral law was easily overturned in parliament, his referral of the new electoral law to the Constitutional Court had greater effect. On 24 January 2001 the Court struck down most of its provisions as unconstitutional. In January 2002 all three principal party actors agreed a compromise revision of the electoral law, which introduced a slightly higher degree of disproportionality by adopting the d'Hondt formula and increasing the number of electoral districts, mirroring the 14 elected regional units agreed in 2000 (see Chapter 5) (Birch *et al.* 2002: 85–6).

In November 1999 and December 2001 civic initiatives against the perceived political stagnation, brought about by the Opposition Agreement and the apparent 'partification' of the media by its two signatories, triggered mass demonstrations on the streets of Prague. The 'Thank You, Now Leave' petition launched by six former leaders of the student protests of 1989 as the tenth anniversary of the Velvet Revolution approached initially appeared destined to be as ineffective and limited in impact as many similar previous civic initiatives (Dvořáková 2002). However, the petition's articulation of an underlying sense of frustration and malaise at the symbolic tenth anniversary of the Velvet Revolution – a period when support for the hardline Czech Communists was also unexpectedly growing – saw it rapidly gain 200,000 signatories. Demonstrations organized by 'Thank You, Now Leave' attracted 50,000–70,000 in Prague and several thousand in provincial centres, the largest since the fall of communism in November 1989.

A second wave of civic mobilization occurred in late 2000 and early 2001. On 12 December 2000 the governing body of Czech Television (ČT), the Czech state-owned public broadcaster, replaced its chief executive. Subsequent changes made to ČT's troubled news and current affairs section provoked a strike by journalists, who occupied their studios, forcing normal programming off air. Czech Television's governing body was (by law) appointed by parliament and composed of representatives of political parties. Having been most recently appointed in February 2000, the board was dominated by nominees of the incumbent Social Democrats and Klaus's Civic Democrats The striking journalists and their supporters alleged that the two parties were attempting to partify and censor the media. Spontaneous demonstrations in support of the strikers outside television studios in Prague and Brno rapidly escalated into mass protest on a scale similar to that in November 1999 bringing more than 100,000 demonstrators on to the streets of the Czech capital.

Although partly driven by the political ambitions of civic activists and sectional interests in the Czech broadcasting industry (Stroehlein 2001; Čulík and Pecina 2001), the protests' focus on the Opposition Agreement as a source of social and political stagnation fitted the Quad-Coalition's discourse, which depicted its two larger rivals as nationalistic and clientelistic leftovers from the past with a 'communist' approach to governing (see Chapter 7). Striking journalists were known to be sympathetic to the Quad-Coalition, whose support they successfully solicited, and 4K politicians maintained regular contacts with the leaders of 'Thank You, Now Leave' and other 'civic initiatives', urging them not to form a new political party but to view the Quad-Coalition as a political partner. This suggested that the Quad-Coalition might be able to form a wider societal coalition linking conventional electoral politics with social movements to articulate a powerful public mood for change. However, despite organizing further rallies and meetings and, in the case of the journalists' strikes achieving their main goal of forcing the resignation of the chief executive of Czech Television, mass support for both movements rapidly waned, leaving little more than a handful of small new civic associations.[31]

Tensions within the Quad-Coalition

Even leaving aside its failure to build links with civic protest movements, the Quad-Coalition faced significant organizational and political challenges. Almost from its inception, 4K was undermined by divisions of the type that had plagued similar centre-right coalition groupings in Poland and Slovakia. These centred on rivalries between member parties, aggravated by their disproportionate size, and the weakness of coalition leadership structures to enforce decisions. Politicians in the four member parties were inconsistent and divided over the extent to which 4K should be integrated into a single party or bloc. In the case of 4K, it was the strongest coalition partner, namely the Christian Democrats (KDU–ČSL), whose mass membership, long party tradition and distinct electorate marked it out from other smaller, liberal and anti-communist coalition members – that became a source of instability. Rival factions within KDU–ČSL tended to use the coalition framework as an additional means of pursuing their own intra-party conflicts.[32] More significantly, however, the Christian Democrats, who had long favoured the model of a two-party liberal-Christian bloc or merger based on their own party structure, became increasingly unwilling and unable to meet the programmatic and political demands of 4K's smaller parties. Following the absorption in October 2001 of the Democratic Union (DEU) by the Freedom Union (US), creating US–DEU, the Christian Democrats intensified pressure on the smallest 4K member, the Civic Democratic Alliance, to resolve its long-running debt problems, dating back to the Moravec affair, or to merge with US–DEU. When ODA refused this perceived ultimatum and withdrew from 4K, the Quad-Coalition framework collapsed. Although replaced by a looser alliance between the Christian Democrats and the Freedom Union–Democratic Union ('Coalition'), the potential for a broad liberal–conservative bloc to rival ODS had dissipated.

No right turn: the 2002 elections

Despite unexpected success in progressing Czech EU accession and implementing legal and constitutional reforms, such as the establishment of regional authorities, the 1998–2002 Social Democrat government largely failed to achieve the investment and improvement in public services stressed in the Social Democrats' 1998 campaign. Nevertheless, after the Miloš Zeman's resignation as Social Democrat leader in April 2001, following his decision to retire from politics, the Social Democrats again successfully campaigned on social and economic issues under a new chairman, Vladimír Špidla, the former Minister of Social Affairs. Špidla ruled out any extension of co-operation with Klaus's ODS under the Opposition Agreement. While the Social Democrats campaigned on domestic issues, the ten key electoral themes unrolled at intervals in the ODS campaign devoted significant space to the defence of Czech national interests against both EU encroachment and German demands for the revision of the Beneš Decrees (ODS 2002a; see also Chapter 8), as well as other themes outlined at Poděbrady such as cutting taxes and slashing bureaucracy. In other respects, the ODS campaign, particularly in its final phases, resembled that of 1998 centring heavily on Václav Klaus and using strident, anti-communist and anti-socialist rhetoric. ODS slogans urged voters to 'Stop the Socialists! The Nation is Voting Klaus'. The fact that Klaus had not only sustained a 'socialist' minority centre-left administration in office but was willing to contemplate the possibility of further pragmatic co-operation with the Social Democrats as a post-election scenario undermined its credibility.

The elections of 14–15 June 2002 were, however, won by the Social Democrats (ČSSD). Although all parties other than the Communists saw a decline in their vote share, ČSSD maintained sufficient support to significantly outpoll Klaus's Civic Democrats, whose support fell markedly in comparison with 1998 (see Table 6.3). A dramatic fall in turnout (from 74 per cent in 1998 to 58 per

Table 6.3 Elections of 14–15 June 2002 to the Chamber of Deputies of the Czech Parliament

Party	No. of votes	% of vote	No. of seats
Civic Democratic Party (ODS)	1,166,464	24.47	58
Czech Social Democratic Party (ČSSD)	1,439,797	30.20	70
Communist Party of Bohemia and Moravia			
(KSČM)	882,477	18.51	41
'Coalition'	680,420	14.27	31
of which			
Freedom Union (US)	–	–	(8)
Christian Democratic Union–			
Czechoslovak People's Party (KDU-ČSL)	–	–	(21)
Independents	–	–	(2)
Association of Independent Lists (SNK)	132,699	2.78	0
Green Party	112,929	2.36	0
Others	353,220	7.41	0
Total	4,768,006	100.00	200

Source: www.volby.cz.

Note
Turnout: 58.00%.

cent); a fall in support for all mainstream parties; and a very significant advance for the hardline Communist Party of Bohemia and Moravia (KSČM) seemed to confirm high levels of popular dissatisfaction with the political drift and cartel-like behaviour of the two main parties during the Opposition Agreement. Unlike 1998 there was no arithmetical possibility of a majority centre-right coalition, and the Freedom Union (US) had little difficulty in agreeing to work with the technocratic, modernizing Špidla, who had disavowed the Opposition Agreement. The Social Democrats were thus quickly able to form a coalition government with the two parties of the 'Coalition' controlling 101 seats in the 200-member lower house, a government welcomed by many observers as a majority administration with an unambiguously pro-European orientation.

Realignment on the right after 2002

Defeat in the 2002 elections came as a political shock to the Civic Democrats. Having maintained high levels of support in the crisis year of 1998 and withstood the challenge of the Quad-Coalition (4K), many Civic Democrats had assumed that the party would make further gains, allowing a smooth transition from the temporary containment policy of the Opposition Agreement to a majority right-wing coalition formed on their terms. In ODS the post-election period was thus one of recrimination against Václav Klaus and the wider party leadership. Resisting calls for immediate resignations, Klaus refused to speak of his party's 'defeat', merely acknowledging 'lack of success', but announced that he and the rest of the party leadership would formally resign at the party's next congress in December.[33] For many powerful provincial ODS organizations, this response was inadequate. In September 2002 the widely respected ODS governor of the Moravian-Silesian region, Evžen Tošenovský, announced that he would stand at the forthcoming congress, raising the possibility of a challenge to Klaus, whose intentions were unclear. Tošenovský seemed to embody a new type of practical, regional ODS politician, whose success in the 2000 regional elections seemed to offer an alternative strategy to the grand ideological politics of the Klaus era. Although he was not widely expected to defeat Klaus, Tošenovský's candidature posed a serious challenge likely to undermine Klaus's authority and divide the party to a far greater degree than the essentially elite-based 'platform' that had challenged Klaus in 1997–8.

In October 2002 Klaus announced that he would not stand for re-election as ODS chairman in order to contest the Czech presidency due to be vacated by Václav Havel in February 2003 when his final term of office expired. Although now the clear favourite, Evžen Tošenovský unexpectedly withdrew his candidacy as a result of pressure from Klaus, media scrutiny and the hostility of many ODS parliamentarians. A number of new candidates then entered the contest: Jan Zahradil, ODS's Shadow Foreign Minister and one of the party's four deputy chairs; Petr Nečas, its Shadow Defence Minister, who was also a deputy chair; Miroslav Topolánek, the leader of the ODS group in the Czech Senate; and the parliamentary deputy, Miroslava Němcová, a deputy speaker in the Chamber of Deputies. Of the five candidates, Zahradil, who combined uncompromising euroscepticism with liberal views on social issues, and Nečas, the leading voice of social conservatives within the party, were the best-known and gained the most (non-binding) endorsements from the party's regional organizations. Both were young and had entered high-level ODS politics after working as Prague-based policy specialists.[34] Miroslav Topolánek, who was politically close to Tošenovský with whom he shared both a background in municipal politics in Ostrava, emerged as the next best placed candidate.

The election results had also raised wider questions about the position of the liberal and neo-liberal centre-right in Czech politics. Despite their entry into government, the results of the 'Coalition' were also poor. Indeed, the 14 per cent won by the joint Coalition list not only fell short of the 17–18 per cent forecast by pre-election polling but was less than the combined total its two member parties received separately in 1998. The Freedom Union–Democratic Union (US-DEU) fared particularly badly. Several of the party's leading candidates failed to gain election[35] and, with eight deputies, it was unable to form a parliamentary faction without the addition of two independents elected on the 'Coalition' list.[36] For the Christian Democrats the results were disappointing, but less disastrous. The party retained the bulk of its traditional support in its Catholic heartlands; with 21 deputies its parliamentary representation remained unchanged and, as a junior partner in the new coalition government, it gained the key Foreign Affairs portfolio in the new Social-Democrat-led government.

ODS: debating the post-Klaus era

The 2002 election result enhanced the position of historic parties committed to some form of social market such as the Social Democrats, Christian Democrats and Communists. To some this suggested that the Czech lands were reverting to the corporatist, state-centred Central European tradition characteristic of Czech politics before communism. The prospect of such a historic setback prompted much soul searching on the Czech right. The Civic Democratic Party's congress in Františkovy Lázně on 13–15 December 2002 saw some of the most open and wide-ranging debate about the party's identity and role since its foundation. Although most speakers showered Václav Klaus with praise and backed his bid for the presidency, few accepted his explanation that the June 2002 election defeat was merely a consequence of the Social Democrats' populist campaign and local ODS politicians' being distracted by the prospect of Senate and local elections later in the year. In a fragmented and sometimes tense set of exchanges dominated by deputies and regional leaders, many contributors echoed ODS's own official post-election analysis of the inadequacies of the election campaign (ODS 2002b) as too focused on Klaus and unable to communicate a coherent political vision.[37] These were often combined with blunt criticisms of the party's longer-term strategy during the Opposition Agreement as negative and preoccupied with past achievements. The party's policies after 1997, some suggested, had offered at best a return to the status quo of the early 1990s and at worst an underdeveloped set of slogans (ODS 2002c: 66–8, 76–7, 84–90).

Such views echoed the diagnosis and agenda of Zieleniec and his allies in 1993–7. ODS should, it was said, move from being a party of transformation to a 'standard party reacting to the development of the Czech Republic' (ODS 2002c: 76–7), an 'everyday ODS' (ODS 2002c: 68–9). Although some speakers suggested building on the liberal Poděbrady themes of fiscal reform and reduced state activity (ODS 2002c: 102–4), many speakers, like the centre-right reformists of the 1990s, suggested that the party needed coherent policies in areas 'stolen' by the left such as the environment, healthcare, welfare and education (ODS 2002c: 84–7, 96–7, 102–4). To this end, some suggested, the party should embrace the notion of a conservative civil society as an alternative provider to the state (ODS 2002c: 94–6, 101–4). Some speakers also criticized the Opposition Agreement or stressed the need for ODS to become more acceptable to potential coalition partners such as the Christian Democrats and Freedom Union with whom the party was now frequently allied in regional government (ODS 2002c: 69–70).

As at previous congresses, organizational deficiencies were also a major preoccupation. Inadequate elite–grassroots communication and a consequent lack of real discussion and internal competition had, it was claimed, reduced the quality of the party's membership and policy-making leading to stagnation (ODS 2002c: 66–8, 76–7). Some argued for members to participate *directly* in selecting leaders and candidates through primaries, rather than electing them indirectly through delegate conferences (ODS 2002c: 105–7). Others advocated greater co-operation with intellectuals and independent policy experts outside the party (ODS 2002c: 69–70, 87–90). A number of speakers called for success-ful local ODS politicians to play a more prominent role in its national leadership (ODS 2002c: 66–8, 75–60).

The outgoing leader and the three principal candidates to replace him offered contrasting responses to these concerns, all of which largely ignored demands for a more pragmatic, pluralistic, centrist party. In his opening and keynote addresses Klaus rejected the idea that ODS was at a crossroads and warned against avoiding public defence of the transformation politics of the 1990s, which had defined the party. Tempting but spurious notions of neutral non-ideological solutions to polit-ical problems based on analogies with local politics would risk, he argued, the 'gradual erosion and consequent destruction of the liberal-conservative world-view we have introduced to this country' (ODS 2002c: 37)

Both Nečas and Zahradil endorsed Klaus's arguments about the dangers of a retreat from ideology and the corrosive effect of local sectional interests. Although acknowledging the need to rebalance national and regional interests within the party and focus on reform of public services, Zahradil, for example, spoke of the need to prevent ODS becoming 'a corporatist federation of inter-est groups, each cancelling each other out', thus losing sight of bigger issues such as European integration (ODS 2002c: 44–7). Petr Nečas, while agreeing with the need for a clear ideology, offered a bolder strategy, which recast some of Josef Zieleniec's arguments in far more radical and populist terms. Building on his earlier rejection of middle-class development as a strategy for the right, Nečas urged the Civic Democrats not to become a bourgeois party 'representing better-off strata and high-income groups from larger towns, tending to defend the interests of businesspeople and better-qualified, better-paid employees' (ODS 2002c: 41–4). In Czech conditions, he argued, this would represent a passive strategy of retaining a loyal electorate of 20–25 per cent sufficient only to force occasional power-sharing agreements on the Social Democrats, who would in time come to dominate Czech politics as their sister parties had done in Scandinavia. Instead, Nečas advocated the trans-formation of ODS into a 'People's Party' representing a diverse range of social groups by emulating some of the organizational strategies, but not the policies, of the German CDU and becoming a broader catch-all party (ODS 2002c: 82–4). In strategic terms, Nečas argued, ODS should accept the risks of programmatic vagueness and populism and be prepared to make alliances with all non-socialist parties setting aside the divisions of 'Sarajevo' to create a right-wing 'pole of liberty, responsibility and activity' capable of driving the Social Democrats from office. Like a number of speakers, Nečas also urged the party to become more socially conservative by taking up issues such as law and order and social and family policy and extending its organization into small rural communes (ODS 2002c: 62–3, 102–4). Nečas's policy of electoral expansion and 'zero tolerance' for the centre-left also led him openly to condemn the clientelistic practices catered for in the Opposition Agreement, arguing that party policy would lose any credibility if it continues the practice of preferring parliamentary seats or seats on the boards of public corporations or partially state-owned companies ... if we support our own party members in every privatization.

(ODS 2002c: 42)

The third principal candidate, Senator Miroslav Topolánek, painted an optimistic picture of ODS as a financially solvent party with rising opinion poll ratings and a growing membership, whose success would depend on political will rather than fundamental political realignment (ODS 2002c: 48–50). Nevertheless, he rejected Klaus's arguments for a political strategy rooted in a defence of transformation policies of the 1990s as too distracting and too complex for voters. In contrast to Klaus, Zahradil and Nečas, Topolánek presented himself as a practical political manager capable of uniting diverse ideological currents in the party, not a thinker and ideologue in his own right. Although paying lip service to problems raised in the discussion, such as the need for organizational reform or the importance of euroscepticism and anti-collectivism, Topolánek concluded that at bottom the party needed no new ideology and no new policies. In his view ODS's 'new start' would consist mainly in the fact that it would no longer be led by Klaus.

In the first round of voting, delegates' support was split almost evenly between the three leading contenders. Zahradil, who narrowly came third, was eliminated. In a second run-off round between the two leading candidates, Topolánek narrowly defeated Nečas, reportedly as the result of a political deal with Zahradil's supporters, which saw the Shadow Foreign Minister elected first deputy leader. Topolánek's victory over the two better-known candidates reflected a number of factors: his status as the candidate least associated with (and least favoured by) Klaus; his reassuring, if blandly optimistic, assessment of the party's position; and his promise to move beyond the Klaus era, while maintaining the status quo, which contrasted markedly with the radical but unpredictable future outlined for the party by Nečas. Topolánek's background as a politician with a regional base, a background in business and local politics; and greater experience of political leadership, which contrasted with the relative youth and inexperience of his two principal challengers, also enhanced his credibility with delegates (Pečinka 2003b).

ODS under Topolánek: a Blue Chance for the right?

The Civic Democrats entered the post-Klaus era with an immediate and unexpected political success when Václav Klaus was elected President by the Czech parliament in February 2003. After several inconclusive rounds of voting, Klaus sought and gained the support of Communist deputies – attracted by his resolute defence of the Beneš Decrees and promise to normalize relations with their party – and dissident Social Democrats hostile to Prime Minister Vladimír Špidla (Urban 2003; Pečinka 2003a). The election was a personal triumph for Klaus and his informal team of advisers, marking the beginning of a more detached relationship between ODS and its founder (see Chapter 7). Longer-term electoral trends, however, still appeared unfavourable for the Czech centre-right. ODS's support had declined in every parliamentary election since 1992. Moreover, calculations of the combined votes and seats won by liberal free-market parties suggested that, although until 1998 this bloc's support remained significant, it had been static at about 35 per cent of the electorate.[38]

Despite questions over Topolánek's authority, grasp of policy and media performances, ODS formulated a new set of policies, the 'Blue Chance' programme, based on detailed policy papers drawn up by its 'Shadow Ministers'. In substantively addressing areas such as education, welfare, the environment and family policy, the programme represented a move in the direction long advocated by critics of Klaus. Its centrepiece was fiscal and tax reform along the lines advocated in 1998 in the Poděbrady articles: a 15 per cent flat tax combined with a universal basic income payment ('guaranteed income') to all adults, which would replace most existing welfare benefits, and a progressive reduction in the value of the state pension offset by anticipated growth in private pension provision.[39] Although its scheme for calculating taxable income was complex, the net effect of the ODS programme would have been to boost the income of the economically active population through cuts in taxation. Such measures, ODS argued, would spur economic growth and reduce unemployment by lowering the tax burden, which, it was argued, would improve tax collection, reduce bureaucracy and create incentives for the unemployed to enter low-paid work, as had occurred in Slovakia and a number of other Central and East European countries which had already begun a second wave of liberal market reforms. Less clear, however, was how large increased deficits in public finances would be made up.[40]

The resilience of the Social Democrats

In 2002–6 the political fortunes of the Social Democrats followed a cycle similar to that experienced during the previous parliamentary term: rapidly falling popularity followed by internal splits and late electoral recovery under a new leader as the economy improved. In September 2002 the party had enjoyed a commanding poll lead over ODS. However, internal divisions, the aloof style of Prime Minister Špidla and difficulties in relations with the Freedom Union deputies, who were divided over the Social Democrats' spending priorities, deprived the coalition of a functional parliamentary majority. By May 2003 Social Democrat support had fallen to 15 per cent (CVVM cited in *Lidové noviny*, 16 March 2006), half the party's level of support in the June 2002 election. Although the 2003 EU accession referendum passed smoothly (Hanley 2004a), the disastrous performance of the Social Democrats in the 2004 Euroelections in coming fifth with 8.78 per cent of the poll prompted Vladimír Špidla to resign as Prime Minister and Social Democrat leader (Rulíková 2004).[41] As widely anticipated, Špidla was succeeded by the popular 36-year-old Interior Minister Stanislav Gross. Despite this, the Social Democrats suffered crushing defeats in the November 2004 regional and Senate elections.

In early 2005 Gross's premiership was itself dramatically terminated when he was engulfed by scandal regarding his personal and family business links.[42] On 25 April 2005 Gross resigned as Prime Minister, stepping down as party leader shortly thereafter. In the wake of the Gross affair, the Social Democrats' poll rating fell to 10.5 per cent. Gross was replaced as Prime Minister by the Minister of Local Development, Jiří Paroubek, a relatively unknown figure whose competence and lack of an internal party power base made him an acceptable caretaker. As Prime Minister, Paroubek took an uncompromising attitude towards the opposition Civic Democrats and President Klaus, co-operating more freely with the Communists in parliament to pass a number of pieces of legislation, opposed by the Social Democrats' more right-wing coalition partners. These tactics proved politically effective. Under his leadership voter perceptions of ČSSD's effectiveness and credibility recovered (CVVM press release, 3 May 2006) and the party's poll ratings gradually increased as Paroubek established himself.[43]

For much of the 2002–6 parliamentary term, a clear right-wing victory in 2006 had seemed certain leading ODS leaders to speak confidently of implementing a 'blitzkrieg' of economic and social reforms in 2006 (*Právo*, 13 December 2004) in coalition with the Christian Democrats (KDU-ČSL), many of whom were increasingly unhappy with the their party's relationship with the Social Democrats. Accordingly, Miroslav Topolánek set an ambitious target of 35–6 per cent of the vote (*Lidové novinyz*, 25 November 2005; *Právo*, 28 November 2005) – significantly above ODS's highest ever vote in parliamentary elections – and stressed that his party would enter government only as part of a majority coalition. The centrepiece of ODS's 2006 election campaign was the flat tax and benefit proposals developed in the Blue Chance programme. Its campaign focused on allaying public concerns that the reforms would benefit only small groups of high earners – a concern perhaps reinforced by the defeat of the liberal Civic Platform (OP) in the Polish election of 2005 by conservative opponents attacking the social consequences of flat tax proposals (Szczerbiak 2006). The ODS campaign also reclaimed the theme of middle-class development, stressing the importance of the self-employed and family-owned businesses for the Czech economy to whom it promised reduced regulation and new tax breaks. The Social Democrats, ODS claimed, had favoured large foreign-owned firms at the expense of small business. However, as ODS's commanding opinion poll lead eroded in late 2005, the party began an aggressively anti-communist advertising campaign warning of a tacit alliance between the Social Democrats (ČSSD) and the Communists (KSČM).

As the main incumbents the Social Democrats fought an essentially defensive campaign – neatly summed up in their election slogan 'Security and Prosperity' (*Jistota a prosperita*) – which appealed to voters' economic self-interest, moderation and fear of change. Paroubek stressed that his party was at the centre of Czech politics standing between economically damaging extremes represented by the Communists, on one hand, and ODS on the other (*Lidové noviny*, 7 April, 20 April and 2 May 2006). Towards the end of the campaign, however, the two major parties moved away from socio-economic issues entirely and began to trade increasingly hyperbolic accusations of corruption, criminality and a totalitarian desire to pervert democracy and dominate the state (Hanley 2006).

The eclipse of centre-right alternatives

The 2002–6 period saw the growing eclipse of the parties of the former Quad-Coalition (4K) as competitors to ODS. Both the Christian Democrats (KDU-ČSL) and Freedom Union (US) suffered a decline in support, internal splits and changes of leadership, related in part to the difficulties of their collaboration with the Social Democrats. Under the leadership of Foreign Minister Cyril Svoboda, the Christian Democrats were among the most energetically pro-European parties in Czech politics. However, in successive elections the party had failed to expand its electorate beyond its traditional Catholic heartlands (Šaradin 2002/3). For many traditionally minded Christian Democrats, however, the success of the 2003 EU accession referendum undermined the rationale for further co-operation with the Social Democrats. Svoboda's focus on European affairs at the expense of more traditional Christian Democrat concerns with social and regional policy weakened his position as leader. On 8 November 2003 the Christian Democrat party's congress voted to replace him with Miroslav Kalousek, a pragmatic politician more acceptable to conservative and right-wing groupings in the party. Although their 2006 election programme contained a number of market-oriented reforms, the Christian Democrats presented themselves, as in the 1990s, as the 'Quiet Force' of Czech politics standing between 'socialism' and the Blue Chance programme of the right.

The Freedom Union–Democratic Union (US-DEU) was in a state of permanent crisis almost from its entry into Vladimír Špidla's Social-Democrat-led coalition in July 2002. Despite the Union's pro-Europeanism, many leading members – including its then leader Hana Marvanová – found the fiscal and social policies of the government difficult to support. The Union's opinion poll ratings thus fell precipitately to 1–2 per cent and its support and (limited) grass-roots organization quickly eroded. The party's decline was accelerated by its failure – even in short-lived alliance with other liberal groups – to gain a single MEP in the June 2004 European Elections (Rulíková 2004).

The 2006 elections: right turn, dead end?

The June 2006 elections were, as widely expected, won by ODS with a vote of 35.38 per cent, the highest level of support for the party in its history. The party's 81 seats, nevertheless, fell far short of the 101 seats required for a parliamentary majority (see Table 6.4). Moreover, the Social Democrats under Paroubek also polled strongly receiving 32.22 per cent, an increase in both votes and vote share compared to 2002 and the party's highest ever percentage vote.[44]

Smaller parties performed poorly. On the centre-right the Christian Democrats received their lowest share of the vote since 1990 and their lowest number of votes in any parliamentary election since the fall of communism and saw their parliamentary representation halved. Liberal groupings fared far worse. Despite

Table 6.4 Elections of 2–3 June 2006 to the Chamber of Deputies of the Czech Parliament

Party	No. of votes	% of vote	No. of seats
Civic Democratic Party (ODS)	1,892,475	35.38	81
Czech Social Democratic Party (ČSSD)	1,728,827	32.32	74
Communist Party of Bohemia and Moravia (KSČM)	685,328	12.81	26
Christian Democratic Union–Czechoslovak People's Party (KDU-ČSL)	386,706	7.22	13
Freedom Union–Democratic Union (US-DEU)	16,457	0.31	0
Green Party (SZ)	336,487	6.29	6
Association of Independent Lists–European Democrats (SNK-ED)	111,724	2.08	0
Others	190,972	3.57	0
Total	5,348,976	100.00	200

Source: www.volby.cz.

Note
Turnout: 64.47%.

a last-ditch youth-oriented rebranding of the party, the Freedom Union polled less than half a percent of the vote and dropped out of parliament. The European Democrats–Association of Independent Lists (ED-SNK), headed by the former Civic Democrat mayor of Prague, Jan Kasl, and Josef Zieleniec, despite polling 11 per cent in the 2004 Euro-elections (Rulíková 2004), also failed to enter parliament. However, the Czech Greens (SZ), who seemed to have benefited from the electoral collapse of the Freedom Union, did narrowly exceed the 5 per cent threshold for parliamentary representation and indicated a willingness to work with all parties other than the Communists (Hanley 2006).

The 2006 election results reproduced a familiar pattern of political deadlock. Given the Communists' unacceptability as a coalition partner to all other parties, the only viable majority administration was a grand coalition of Civic and Social Democrats, possibly supplemented by other parties. Although the Greens quickly agreed a coalition with the Civic Democrats and Christian Democrats, the resultant 100-seat coalition fell one vote short of a majority. Negotiations with the Social Democrats for the 'toleration' of a minority government led by ODS proved fruitless. Efforts to reach agreement on a short-term Civic Democrat minority administration under Topolánek also foundered. Although formally appointed to office by President Klaus in September 2006, Topolánek's first government lost a vote of confidence a month later. Any minority Social Democrat administration supported by the Communists would similarly only command 100 votes. At the time this book was completed, President Klaus was brokering further negotiations about the formation of a caretaker government to lead the Czech Republic to early elections.

Conclusions

The circumstances that led to ODS's rapid formation and early dominance subsequently limited the concentration and consolidation of the centre-right in the Czech Republic. As well as being divided from the small Christian Democratic right and populist far-right by ideological and cleavage differences, the tightly organized, charismatically led Civic Democrats consistently failed to incorporate or fully marginalize smaller centre-right liberal groups, which rapidly became competitors with distinct alternative policies. In electoral and social terms, despite having a committed core vote based in a broad constituency of pro-market transition 'winners', the Civic Democrats' underlying appeal – even in 2006 at the moment of their greatest electoral triumph – lagged behind that of the centre-left.[45] In this respect, the party's failure to win over a 4–5 per cent group of well-educated, urban voters with both pro-market views *and* quality of life and governance concerns, who had gravitated to the Greens in 2006, having previously supported the Civic Democratic Alliance (ODA) and the Freedom Union (US), seems highly significant.

However, the divisions on the Czech right, so central to its decline in the decade after 1996, were attributable to more than historic cleavages, failures of organizational concentration or the dynamics of party competition. They also reflected unresolved – or inadequately resolved – divisions over the strategy and identity of the political right in post-communist Czech society. The scandals over 'civic' right-wing parties' illegal financing practices that led to the collapse of the Klaus government and subsequent fracturing of the Czech centre-right in 1997–8 were less the inevitable political culmination of flawed economic transformation than the denouement of conflicts present within both ODS and ODA almost since their foundation in the early 1990s, which intensified as economic problems and the electoral challenge of the centre-left became more apparent. Although Klaus supporters' conspiratorial view of a well co-ordinated strategy to 'assassinate' the former Prime Minister seems wide of the mark, as elite and party cohesion broke down, leakage of information about party financing and party management became an important factor in the political struggles over the direction of the right.

A loose centre-right reformist agenda quickly emerged. Reformists aspired to develop a moderate centre-right bloc with deeper social roots and greater electoral breadth than ODS with 'everyday' rather than transformational policies, which embraced more than economics. In many ways, such aspirations amounted to a project to create a form of secularized Christian Democracy. However, Klaus and his co-thinkers remained wedded to their founding vision of ODS as a party of the neo-liberal right confronting collectivism and the left and, supported by a majority of the party's grassroots, rejected realignment along the lines proposed by the reformists. Instead, under Klaus's continued leadership ODS addressed the question of developing a broad appeal in an era of post-transformation politics by combining economic neo-liberalism with a form of national-populism distantly reminiscent of the Polish or Hungarian right. The

'Blue Chance' programme developed under Miroslav Topolánek dropped these more nationalistic accents and developed the neo-liberal fiscal and tax reform developed under Klaus's leadership in 1997–8, but did not innovate further. Despite tensions between liberals and Christian Democrats, the small parties and politicians of the reformist right had little difficulty in agreeing a new centre-right agenda centring on issues of governance, public sector reform and social cohesion. However, as the experience of the Quad-Coalition demonstrated, they lacked the ability to create a strong political vehicle capable of uniting the Christian Democrats and elite-dominated liberal, anti-communist groups on the durable basis necessary to compete against the Civic Democrats.

The realignment of the Czech centre-right resulting from the Opposition Agreement, although allowing both Klaus and then his centre-right opponents to have some influence on Social-Democrat-led governments of 1998–2006, further divided the Czech centre-right, providing a focal point for ideological rethinking which led the Civic Democratic Party and the Quad-Coalition parties to stress differences within the right, rather than differences between right and left.[46] Although the first stillborn ODS–Christian Democrat–Green coalition agreed after the 2006 elections represented a partial healing of rifts on the centre-right, the electoral weakness and internal divisions of two smaller parties made the prospect of a centre-right majority administration as uncertain as ever. Despite the Civic Democrats' significant success in local and Senate elections in October 2006, it remains to be seen whether the Czech centre-right will reassert itself more successfully in early parliamentary elections likely to take place in 2007 or 2008 and whether (and how) it will broaden and renew its appeal.

7   Conservatism, nation and transformation

Building a new ideology of the right

Introduction

Early analyses of 'Thatcherism Czech-style' (Rutland 1992–3) viewed it as a set of policy prescriptions or strategies whose underlying beliefs could be straightforwardly understood as a form of East European liberalism or neo-liberalism. Such analyses usually argued that the Klaus governments' pragmatic pulling of economic punches, combined with relatively high living standards and macroeconomic stability, legitimized the Czech right for much of the 1990s (Orenstein 1994; Dangerfield 1997). However, such approaches are of limited usefulness for understanding the political appeal of the new Czech right. They do not explain, for example, why Czechs' support for Klaus and his party was high in 1991, when the post-1989 transformational recession was deepest and living standards in the Czech lands fell most sharply (Myant 1993b: 182–205; Večerník 1996: 80), nor why this support was sustained at relatively high levels for more than decade, much of it spent in ineffective opposition, despite the gradual unravelling of the Czech 'economic miracle'. As subsequent cross-national research has confirmed, trajectories of political support and economic reform strategies in post-communist states are hard to explain fully in terms of economic welfare, the relative strengths of domestic interest groups (Appel 2000, 2004) or even the wider geo-political balance between states (Abdelal 2001).

Later discussions of the Czech right showed more concern with its ideology. However, much early writing reduced Czech right-wing ideology and its mass appeal to a set of underlying sociological and historical *causes*. Some saw the Czech case as an extreme illustration of how the social atomization and economistic thinking induced by communism had created fertile ground for neo-liberal individualism in Eastern Europe (Wainwright 1994; Srubař 1996). Later authors more sensitive to national context highlighted greater public hostility to the communist regime in the Czech lands after 1989, which, unlike its Polish and Hungarian counterparts, had remained highly repressive until its ultimate collapse and given rise to a hardline successor party suffused with nostalgia for the past (Pickel 1997: 223; Appel 2004). In this view, neo-liberalism as before 1989 represented a 'neglected path of anti-communism, by offering a theoretical blueprint of the free market as the polar opposite of totalitarianism and central planning' (Szacki 1995: 148–9; Pickel 1997: 223). A further set of arguments viewed the ideological strength of the Czech right as a (temporary) side-effect of specific patterns of transition politics. The ideological appeal of parties of the Czech right could thus be interpreted as a product of their success in becoming a vehicle for Czech national self-assertion against Slovakia in the unfolding negotiations to agree a new constitutional settlement (Stein 1997; Innes 1997). Alternatively, the Czech centre left's slowness to unite politically or offer a coherent alternative narrative of transformation can be seen as allowing the right to become the only credible vehicle for ideologies of reform (Vachudova 2005).

However, while relevant, none of these explanations adequately addresses the intrinsic ideological appeal of the Czech right. First, as noted in Chapters 4 and 5, as elsewhere in the region Czech anti-communism initially took more direct, obviously populist forms than demands for free market economics. Second, the appeal of the right in the Czech Republic cannot simply be deduced from the partial ideological vacuum on the centre-left. Nor, despite Czechs' well-established tendency to define their identity in contradistinction with that of Slovaks (Holy 1996: 102–13), can the Czech right's ideological appeal be seen as essentially a manifestation of anti-Slovak nationalism. As noted in Chapter 4, the rise of the Czech right took place in mid to late 1990 at a time when the notion of conflicting Czech and Slovak interests was still not widely accepted in the Czech lands and when it seemed unlikely that elite disagreements over constitutional technicalities would result in the division of the state (Stein 1997: 98).[1] In this context, while clearly a Czech party, Klaus's ODS projected itself as a disinterested guardian of the federal state, rather than a vehicle for Czech interests (Innes 2001: 64–8), and seemed to one writer to reflect a 'blankly materialistic understanding of national conflict' (Innes 2001: 174; see also Stein 1997: 333). Only *after* the split of Czechoslovakia had become a fait accompi did the Czech right *retrospectively* incorporate the defence of Czech national interests against Slovak demands into its ideological discourse, viewing the crisis of Czech–Slovak relations in hindsight as one of the many 'crossroads' faced on the path of national transformation.

The impacts of Czech right-wing ideology

A more recent set of writing has focused more on the effects and function of Czech right-wing ideology, rather than its causes, drawing on wider academic literatures on ideas and ideology.[2] Appel (2000, 2004), for example, argues that, having overcome more moderate liberal alternatives less amenable to anti-communism, the Western oriented neo-liberal ideology of the Czech right was a crucial factor enabling the adoption of extensive voucher privatization in the Czech Republic. It did so, she suggests, by disempowering institutionally powerful managerial lobbies and trade unions, who were unable to assert their interests, and serving a 'compliance mechanism' securing popular consent and legitimacy by offering a long-term vision of security, prosperity and belonging

(Appel (2000; 2004). Where, as in Slovakia and Russia, such ideologies were not adequately formulated and lacked resonance with national traditions, she suggests, different political outcomes ensued (Appel and Gould 2000; see also Abdelal 2001). As suggested in Chapter 4, similar arguments can also be developed in relation to the overcoming of collective action problems inherent in party formation in 1990–1 where the formulation of a new ideological vision of right-wing politics, supplemented by Klaus's charisma, provided a focus for various groups within the unwieldy Civic Forum movement to co-ordinate and coalesce around.

However, although the *roles* of Czech right-wing ideology have been clearly stated, the specific *content* of the Czech right's ideological discourse and the process through which it emerged have not, thus undermining the value of much analysis of its supposed causes and effects. Many analyses of Czech right-wing ideology in fact highlight only *general* aspects of the Czech liberal-democratic national political discourse, which predominated after 1989. While right-wing neo-liberal ideologies clearly drew legitimacy from their obviously 'Western' character (Pickel 1997: 222), the same should have been true of Social Democracy and Christian Democracy, which were politically well established in neighbouring West European states. Similarly, stating that Václav Klaus appealed to 'Czechs' self-perception as Europeans and willingness to shoulder collective sacrifices' (Rutland 1992–3: 128) and justified voucher privatization by combining anti-communism, pro-Europeanism and pro-Czech sentiments 'playing on the notion of a European property system was organic to Czech soil' (Appel 2004: 175) offers little enlightenment, as the same could be said of virtually all leading Czech politicians, including Klaus's defeated centrist and centre-left opponents, after November 1989.[3] Similarly, the argument that the Czech 'ideological climate' of the early 1990s was strongly characterized by anti-communism (Appel 2000, 2004) does not explain why the 'civic' Czech right was able to frame its ideology in anti-communist terms more successfully than others who deployed anti-communist discourses, nor so precisely how it did so.[4] Other studies, such as the work of Hadjiisky, focus more narrowly on the ideologies of specific professional elites that formed the Czech right. However, although they offer acute snapshots of the builders and building blocks of Czech right ideology, such studies do little to address its construction as a more complex and wide-ranging ideology with resonance for both elites and mass publics. Indeed, perhaps because so much of the literature is focused on empirically disentangling the relative importance of ideology, interests and (sometimes) institutions,[5] it largely reduces the *process* of ideological construction to asides about the 'will and skill of leaders' (Appel 2000: 539), offset by a truistic acknowledgement of the importance of aligning ideology with existing political culture and national identity. In practice, many such accounts merely fall back on discussions of Václav Klaus as an individual, either lauding his personal political acumen[6] or fruitlessly attempting to resolve the psychological conundrum of whether Klaus was an ideological neo-liberal who recognized the need for pragmatism or a pragmatist who recognized the need for ideology.[7]

Building a new ideology of the right

Ideologies of transformation

This chapter will therefore consider the *emergence, construction* and *evolution* of the ideology of the Czech right, which, it will argue, should be seen as a specific ideology of social and national transformation shaped (and reshaped) in the course of political struggle from a range of earlier discourses. Ideology plays an important role in any period of rapid or profound socio-political change. Previous periods of regime change in Czech history thus invariably generated distinct ideologies of political transformation, often associated with a dominant party or bloc. During the struggle for national autonomy in the nineteenth century, for example, this role was taken by the Young Czech Party and its ideology of national liberalism (Garver 1978; Urban 1995). The era of post-1945 reconstruction, when the Communist Party of Czechoslovakia gained mass support, was defined by ideas of socialism as the apogee of Czech democratic and national traditions (Sayer 1998; Abrams 2004). However, ideology can be seen as particularly important in post-communist social transformation. While communist one-party systems suppressed the public sphere and monopolized the political discourse, the more pluralistic and democratic political arrangements that replaced them after 1989 made securing long-term *consent* by a range of social groups a newly important aspect of holding power. Moreover, the sudden extinction of the old (communist) regime required not only the building of new institutions but also the construction of new understandings of politics and of new political identities to provide a meaningful framework for political action. Indeed, the *very absence* of civil society, well established institutions and interests (Pickel 1997: 224, 227; Appel 1998; 2004) or well articulated alternative ideologies created a vacuum that could be filled by new ideologies (Salecl 1994; Lester 1995).[8]

However, as noted above, much analysis of ideology in post-communist societies tends to discuss broad *national* discourses, rather than the ideologies of specific parties and movements. There is, moreover, a lack of literature on the centre-right as an ideological vehicle for social transformation. A partial exception can be found in Gramscian analyses of British 'Thatcherism' of the 1980s developed by Stuart Hall (1988) and others. Hall argues that the coming to power in Britain of Margaret Thatcher's Conservative Party in 1979 was not a 'swing of the pendulum', reflecting the conventional logic of postwar British party competition, which would be reversed when the left mobilized or the economy deteriorated, but the implementation of a 'historic project' for far-reaching transformation backed by a powerful, newly formulated populist ideology, which had percolated into popular 'common sense' from elite settings via the media and party politics. Disconcertingly for many on the left, Hall argued that Thatcherism was not so much imposed or foisted on people as *accepted*, *consented to* and *supported* by them even when their 'real' interests lay elsewhere because of its ability not only to address and explain apparent national decline but also to (re-)define the interests and identities of heterogeneous new popular constituencies by drawing on aspirations for social mobility and personal advancement, rather than established class identities.

Despite the clear differences of context between 'British Thatcherism' of the 1980s and its supposed Czech imitator of the 1990s, there are a number of parallels, which make Hall's framework relevant.[9] Both right-wing projects sought to redefine and radically transform the relationship between market, state and civil society as a means of reversing long-term economic stagnation and perceived moral and national decline by breaking with the past. Both legitimized and explained themselves through innovative popular (or populist) ideologies, which combined seemingly new neo-liberal ideas with established discourses of national identity and projected their policies as a historical imperative. Finally, both enjoyed periods of intellectual and political dominance before suffering sudden decline, expressed not only in policy failure and electoral reverses but expressed, too, in a search for ideological renewal. Like its British precursor 'Czech Thatcherism' can be understood as a 'hegemonic project'. However, as this book suggests, contrary to many of the more hyperbolic accounts of the dominance of neo-liberalism in Central and Eastern Europe (see Ganev 2005), the Czech right never achieved a durable political hegemony, nor can its success be seen as comparable to that of the British Conservative Party in the Thatcher era.

Gramscian analysis of the type used by Hall has been further developed by post-Marxist discourse theorists.[10] As well as radically challenging conventional social science ontologies, such thinkers reconceptualize Gramsci's ideas of the ideology and politics of crisis and transformation in less class-bound terms more congruent with the fluid social structures and identities experienced in post-communist Central Europe. Rather than an 'organic crisis' of material structures of (capitalist) state and economy, periods of political and social transformation, it is argued, are better understood in terms of 'a proliferation of antagonisms and … a general crisis of identities' (Laclau and Mouffe 2001: 136). In this perspective (Smith 1994; Laclau and Mouffe 2001), ideologies are less artefacts of class struggle than unattached, but powerful, discourses, which seek to naturalize certain meanings as enduring (sometimes universal) truths. They do so by defining *social antagonisms* and *political frontiers*, which generate political identities and meanings by defining a threatening, excluded, alien 'other' outside normal politics and *chains of equivalence* or *chains of difference* explaining the relationship between different ideas and meanings.

In this chapter, I loosely employ the tools of (post-)Gramscian analysis to analyse the development of the ideology of the Czech right during the 1990s across a number of key discourses, most associated with Klaus and ODS: the nature of transformation and its political supporters and (hidden) opponents; 'civicness' and democracy; the right as a 'conservative' force; and right-wing understandings of Czech national identity and its relationship to transformation. I then consider how centre-right forces reformulated their ideological appeals in the period after the fall of the Klaus government in 1997. While Klaus's centre-right opponents largely rearticulated the original right-wing project of liberal transformation and Europeanization in more 'genuine' terms, ODS reinterpreted post-communist changes in terms of the defence of the nation and the national statehood.

The rejection of 'Third Ways'

Despite its responsiveness to populist anti-communist discourses of excluding Communists and their collaborators and 'old structures' from political life, in ideological terms the anti-communism and neo-liberalism of the new Czech right were brought together in the discourse of avoiding 'Third Ways' first publicly presented by Klaus in his Olomouc speech of December 1990 challenging the erstwhile Civic Forum's leadership view of the movement's future discussed in Chapter 4. Those resisting party organization and party politics by promoting a loose inclusive civic movement were, Klaus had argued, consciously or unconsciously drawing on the heritage of the 'Prague Spring' in seeking a 'Third Way' between capitalism and socialism and thus repeating the worst Czech traditions of utopianism and messianism. Civic movements, he argued:

> do not correspond to European political culture. The concept is basically an attempt to find a Third Way, this time in the political sphere.
> ... neither in economics nor politics does the Third Way lead [to a modern European state] ... attempts at any kind of symbiosis ... of specific state regulation of the market do not lead there, and neither do any kind of experimental ideas concerning civic initiatives ... trying to be a shining example, either in domestic or foreign policy, to anyone, ..., does not lead to being a modern European state. We do not want to blaze a false trail (*být falešnými průkopníky*). [T]he date that we should draw on in seeking our interrupted continuity with European history is in no case 1968 and the ideological constructions linked with it, but exclusively the period before 1948.
>
> (Klaus 1991: 206)

ODS's 1992 election programme was similarly sceptical of 'ideas that a country which has just escaped the Russian colonial yoke can enrich a tired democratic Europe with new and original initiatives and approaches' arguing that these were 'third ways ... which do not mean a return to communism, but which do not mean a return to Europe either' (ODS 1992: 7). The discourse of 'Third Ways' redefined the nature of the 'communist' threat to transformation by constructing a new identity for the right's centrist and centre-left competitors, depicting them as opponents of transformation. This also provided an enduring right-wing ideological frame for left–right competition in the Czech Republic and bolstered the right's own identity.

The notion of 'Third Ways' between capitalism and socialism as potentially dangerous to liberal democracy as full-blown totalitarianism was scarcely new. Similar constructions can be found in Hayek's *Road to Serfdom*, the writings of von Mises and other canons of 'Austrian School' neo-liberalism. Klaus's identification of the reform of state socialism as a 'Third Way', although more novel, drew directly from debates on the Czech left which had followed the collapse of the Prague Spring. Writing in exile in Switzerland, Ota Šik, the architect of the 'market socialist' reforms of the 1960s, reinterpreted the Prague Spring as precisely as such a 'Third Way' between Soviet socialism and Western capitalism (Šik 1976). As noted in Chapter 3, in the more immediate context of 1990 much grassroots hostility to ex-dissidents was framed in anti-communist terms. Critical undercurrents of public opinion locating the 'experimental' nature of Civic Forum's beliefs *between* communist utopianism and mainstream European politics can also be detected in the Czech press of the time.[11] However, only with Klaus's Olomouc speech were such themes melded into a coherent ideological discourse.

The right's discourse on Third Ways, however, did not merely combine ideas drawn from the varied reading and experiences of neo-liberal technocrats. It modified and reworked the earlier liberal anti-communist discourse of Civic Forum. First, it identified the danger to transformation stemming from the communist past as an *ideological* threat, rather than one rooted in the administrative structures and mentalities of the old regime or the enduring strength of the Communist Party, as Havel had done in his August 1990 speech. Second, following the lead of grassroots anti-communists (see Chapter 4), it redrew the political frontier, locating the threat to reform *within* the democratic coalition that had coalesced within Civic Forum by establishing a chain of equivalence between the 'civic' politics of former dissidents and the more conventional social-democratic and social-liberal positions of left-wing technocrats.

In doing so, however, it constructed the shared 'Third Wayism' of the two groups in quite different ways. The non-ideological 'civic' discourse of Havel and the ex-dissidents *did* have prototypical elements found in other historical 'Third Way' discourses. These included claims to transcend old divisions at a moment of rupture and crisis; an appeal to ethics, rather than material interests; a stress on a partially present, but yet to be fully reconstituted community ('civil society'); and a focus on a special set of agents destined to bring about change ('civic initiatives', 'independent intellectuals') (Bastow and Martin 2000, 2005).[12] Through the dichotomy of 'Third Ways' and 'standard' 'tried and tested' Western institutions, the right established a new political frontier between the 'experimental' and 'messianistic' traditions of a failed national past threatening to hold back transformation and the modernizing, Europeanizing project of the right.

Prototypical elements of Third Way ideological thinking were, however, less present in the positions of the more conventional social democrats in Civic Forum, who tended to sympathize with Klaus's calls for 'standard' party politics (see Chapter 4). The Third Wayism of these groups was therefore constructed *biographically* by identifying them as former reform communists, who had retained the 'Third Way' thinking implicit in the Prague Spring.[13] Finally, in the early to mid-1990s, the chain of equivalence linking 'Third Ways' was extended to include political and intellectual challenges as diverse as calls to preserve the Czechoslovak federation; the policies of both Czech Social Democracy and the Quad-Coalition; US-inspired communitarians; President Havel's calls for civil society development; ecological activism; 'Europe-ism' and the current direction of European integration. Rather than a specific feature of the politics of early transition, 'Third Ways' were, Klaus argued, a constantly reccurring phenomenon, reflecting the temptation of collectivism for intellectuals and politicians in general and Czech elites in particular (Klaus 1995: 27–30; 1996: 288–91; 2006a, 2006b).

'Two basic alternatives'

The discourse of 'Third Ways' remained part of the Czech right-wing ideological repertoire into the late 1990s and beyond, but was used increasingly selectively, typically as a defence of the right's legitimacy as the principal architect of democracy and capitalism in the Czech lands (Klaus 2006a) or, in 1999–2000, to attack the Quad-Coalition's claims to be a more genuine vehicle of liberal transformation (see Chapter 6).[14] However, from the mid-1990s in response to the rise of the Social Democrats and the subsequent growth in the influence of the Czech Communists, the right adopted a modified form of this discourse which largely dispensed with the notion of Third Ways, instead stressing polarized, irreconcilable opposites of left and right, individualism and collectivism. Addressing the Civic Democratic Party's December 1996 conference Klaus abandoned the earlier rhetoric of 'Third Ways' to argue that that year's election result had

> made Czech politics more transparent … The elections have proved what I have often and repeatedly said: that there are two basic paths, two basic visions for the further development of our country … represented, on one hand by ODS and, on the other by the Social Democrats.
>
> (Klaus 1997a: 110–20)

In a domestic context, this discourse of 'two basic alternatives' translated into a more explicitly anti-communist or anti-socialist framing of politics, which paralleled the rhetoric of Hungary's Fidesz or the Polish right. In this construction, which was repeated in essentially the same terms in its 1998, 2002 and 2006 election campaigns, left–right electoral competition was no longer represented as a search to avoid ideologically misguided 'Third Ways' but as a direct continuation of the process of regime change in which the task of the right was to prevent a creeping left-wing 'counter revolution' (Říman 2005). The Social Democrats and Communists, the right's rhetoric suggested, represented a quasi-totalitarian threat to democracy and reform and consequently the Czech Republic found itself in a position of national emergency like that of 1938 or 1948.[15] As with all other instances of this discourse, the precise nature of the 'socialism' of the contemporary Czech left and the threat it posed to freedom and democracy were left implicit, to be 'self-evidently' understood by readers and listeners.[16] The totalitarian threats evoked by the ideology of the right were also vague enough to allow pragmatic co-operation with the left as with the signing of the Opposition Agreement with the Social Democrats in 1998 or the unspecified understandings reached with the Communists in February 2003 when Klaus was elected president by the Czech parliament (Pečinka 2003a).

As with the notion of 'Third Ways', the discourse of two 'basic alternatives' was deployed more widely as a means to explain new challenges and integrate them with more familiar opponents. This pattern can, for example, be seen in Václav Klaus's response to the terrorist attacks on New York and Washington on 11 September 2001, which, he argued, were an 'extreme, insane act, but one falling logically into a certain pattern' (*do jistého celku*) as a new manifestation of collectivism and the ideology of group rights. Other more familiar variants of collectivism, Klaus claimed, such as 'lack of respect for success, efficiency (*výkonu*), property, wealth' or anti-globalization movements, campaigns for fair trade, and the criticisms of technology and the consumer society made by well-known Czech ecological activists were thus 'directly related' (*mají ... přímou souvislost*) to the attacks on 11 September. The challenge of radical Islam was for Klaus not an indication of new divisions in a post-Cold-War world but merely the 'continuation of the struggle against human freedom, capitalism, the market and technological progress', confirming once again the 'deep, fundamental and irreconcilable clash of two fundamental views of the contemporary world', individualist liberalism and state-oriented collectivism (Klaus 2001a).[17]

Right-wing redefinition of the 'civic'

Some writers see parties with liberal roots such as ODS and Hungary's Fidesz–Hungarian Civic Alliance and Poland's Civic Platform (OP) as sharing a common identity because of their use of the label 'civic' (Sitter 2001a). This is somewhat misleading, obscuring the extent to which concepts of citizenship are embedded in national cultures and the ways in which right-wing ideological entrepreneurs have *crafted* specific (and changing) understandings of civil society and the 'civic' through political struggles.[18] As seen in Chapter 3, the concept was the 'civic', expressed in concepts such as the 'parallel polis' or Pithart's discussion of the 'homeland', was central to the thinking of a number of leading dissidents and naturally framed the movement they came to lead in November–December 1989, Civic Forum (*Občanské fórum*). Indeed, the movement's initial rationale, of enabling the inclusive participation of Czechs in public life as citizens rather than subjects of the communist one-party state, makes 'Civil Forum' or 'Citizens Forum' a better rendition of the movement's name at this time.[19] Even the Civic Democratic Alliance (ODA), the first proto-party to define itself as right-wing in terms of neo-liberalism and Anglo-American conservatism, also understood its 'civicness' primarily in terms of its commitment to citizen empowerment against the state (ODA 1989).

However, as Civic Forum was drawn into fulfilling the functions of a political party during the course of 1990 and discussion turned to its possible transformation into some form of 'civic party', the term was increasingly redefined to mean the broad, non-communist middle ground in Czech politics favouring democracy, marketization and Europeanization, *not allied to any of the small historic parties.* The emergence of the right within Civic Forum in late 1990 further redefined the 'civic' in Czech politics. The Civic Democratic Party (ODS) used the label 'civic' to indicate that it was one of Civic Forum's 'successor parties' and aspired to take up its role as the main political vehicle for post-communist reform. The identification of 'civic' reform with the centre-right was reinforced by the electoral competition and the evolution of the party system. The electoral failure in 1992 of Civic Movement (OH) eliminated all notion of a centrist 'civic party', and the subsequent emergence of the Social Democrats, a 'historic' party which had remained outside Civic Forum, further confirmed the identification of 'civic' with the liberal right.

However, like their counterparts elsewhere in the region, ODS leaders crafted a deeper right-wing meaning for the term. For Klaus and his ODS colleagues, the 'civicness' of the party also indicated its breadth of appeal in both being secular and non-confessional and committed to individualism, rather than to class or sectional interests. ODS's first electoral programme thus pointedly stressed that, in its view, politics and society began with 'the citizen, the individual as a source of initiative' (ODS 1992: 2). Speaking to ODS's first regular Congress, Klaus asserted that 'we do not restrict our membership, our sympathizers and supporters or our voters to certain specific politically, socially, economically, geographically or generationally defined groups' (*Sobotní telegraf* no. 27, 4–10 December, 1).

The electoral failure of Civic Movement (OH) had a further consequence, indirectly triggering the long-running controversy over whether it was necessary to build a strong civil society as a counterweight to party politics as President Havel and others insisted (Pehe 1994a). ODS's 'civicness' was thus further defined through its opposition to such conceptions of civil society and any channels such as referenda as a recipe for a 'corporatist or syndicalism state' of 'corporations and institutions which are under the control of particular groups of citizens' (ODS 1996b: 11), whether vested economic interests or self-appointed intellectual and cultural elites lacking democratic legitimacy. Similar points are made many times in Klaus's writings, which reject the notion that a genuinely public or 'civic' interest can be formulated below the level of national party politics. Indeed, Klaus does not contest the use of the term 'civil society' by political opponents, pointedly replacing it with his own concept of a 'society of free citizens'. In stressing citizens as free individuals *within* natural local communities, rather than participants in organized local associations, ODS discourse rearticulated the notion of citizenship, civic virtue and the civic sphere in terms of *economic* (specifically market) participation, industriousness and self-reliance, rather than discussion and collective decision-making. The 1998 ODS programme thus characteristically asserted that

ODS is a *civic* party. It is an open party that during the seven years of its existence has become a ... part not just of big politics but also of community and public life in the regions and districts. It is oriented towards hardworking enterprising and responsible people. It is convinced that it is precisely on such people that the Czech national community rests.

(ODS 1998: 1, emphasis in original)

Finally, the right's construction of the citizen as relatively isolated bearer of individual interests and preferences can also be seen as part of a modernizing discourse challenging Czech traditions of romanticism and collectivism. The philosopher Václav Bělohradský, one of the few Czech intellectuals supportive of the 'civic' right during the early 1990s, argued that its liberal conception of politics as trading-off the conflicting priorities and interests of a multitude of individuals imported a 'realism' largely absent from traditional Czech thought, whose origins in German-influenced romanticism of the nineteenth century had, he claimed, led it to see politics as an exercise in seeking consensus through overarching values, metaphysics and morality (Bělohradský 2000). He viewed Klaus's thinking as a return to the American-influenced pragmatic liberalism of the Czech essayist and writer Karel Čapek appropriate for the fragmenting values and identities of the postmodern liberal market society the Czech Republic would inevitably become (Bělohradský 1995, 2000).[20]

Liberalism, democracy and technocracy

The Czech right's construction of its 'civic' political identity and of the 'free citizen' connects with wider discourses on democracy. As many observers have noted, the Czech 'civic' right was broadly consistent with its proclaimed commitment to classical liberalism in viewing democracy in Schumpeterian or Downsian terms as adversarial elite competition between professional politicians competing in a political market of individual citizen-voters (Hadjiisky 2001; Pehe 2004). 'Non-civic' social, class and group identities and organizations were rejected as illegitimate actors in democratic politics, as were unelected elites not organized in professionalized party structures. Such models are usually contrasted with consensus-based or participatory models of democracy implicit in the thinking of Václav Havel and his political allies, often seen as part of a civic republican tradition traceable to de Tocqueville, Rousseau and Machiavelli (Pehe 1994a; Dryzek and Holmes 2000; Myant 2005). However, we should be cautious of viewing ideological discourses as neatly fitting categories in intellectual history or of accepting at face value the arguments of Klaus (following earlier neo-liberals such as Hayek) that their neo-liberalism was a mere restatement of classical liberalism in a contemporary context.

As many writers have noted, there is a tension between liberalism and democracy in most liberal-democratic ideologies. The discourse of the British and US New Right of the 1980s, for example, has thus been widely analysed as highlighting this tension, disarticulating links between liberalism and democracy in order to create a reduced sphere for democratic political contestation (Laclau and Mouffe (2001: 171–6). Such a view is less sustainable in any analysis of the Czech new right, whose ideology sought to *link* liberalism, capitalism and democracy in specific ways in a context where a diminution of the scope of politics was widely accepted as part of the transition from totalitarianism. Indeed, as Pavlik (1999) convincingly argues, far from thinking in terms of a Constitution of Liberty to entrench liberal rights against excessive democracy, ODS saw legal and constitutional structures in a transitional society as a malleable work-in-progress, reflecting the current balance of power and interests and hence subject to democratic majorities.

Others have suggested that ODS offered 'technocratic democracy' (Hadjiisky 2005) where expertise and scientific certainty, rather than liberal constitution-making constrained the legitimate sphere of democratic politics. Such readings of ODS ideology have led to some of the hyperbolic accounts of the Czech right, which see it as a quasi-totalitarian inheritor of the scientific certainties of communism.[21] Technocratic legitimacy undoubtedly gained neo-liberal and other economists an entrée in politics in November 1989 (see Chapter 3). Styles of policy-making after 1989 by Czech governments of right and left were undoubtedly elite-driven and technocratic, rather than consultative (see Chapter 5). Václav Klaus's speeches and writings are frequently peppered with technical, academic references, graphs, equations, foreign-language terms and neologisms. However, if, adapting Centeno's (1993) definition, we see technocratic discourses as those which represent as legitimate and imperative the apolitical application of rational techniques by technocrat-politicians or technocratic institutions, ODS ideology appears technocratic in only a weak and limited sense. Hadjiisky (1996), for example, rightly notes the 'ideology of political professionalism' developed by politicians and managers within ODS in 1990–1 which served as a form of legitimation for those who had been uninvolved in the opposition before 1989 and played a marginal role during the Velvet Revolution itself. Managerialist discourses of ODS as a rational, efficient organization run on businesslike lines, similar in character to a private company, can also be found in the party's wider presentation of itself. Internal party relationships, for example, were depicted in 'professional' and 'business' terms, which were contrasted with the 'provisional revolutionary character, amateurism and chaos (*živelnost*)' of Civic Forum.[22]

As the quote above suggests, such discourses were essentially concerned with the political *identity* of party members, rather than the broader state–society relationship. Moreover, rather than being an expression of 'technocratic democracy', this representation of the party as a professionally run commercial organization shades into its wider discourse of citizenship and political participation as an extension of market activity.

The ideology of the Czech right did not offer a depoliticized technocratic vision of politically neutral expert decision-makers insulated from society as the key legitimate actors in social transformation, as in some South American contexts (Centeno 1993). Instead, technocratic strains in its ideology were overlaid by anti-communist, liberal and democratic discourses, which stressed the transformation of mere 'experts' into professional politicians with a distinct political identity (the 'civic right') legitimized by support gained in electoral competition.

The meaning(s) of conservatism

The mass appeal after 1989 of a neo-liberal ideology able to accommodate popular anti-communism is at one level not difficult to state: economic efficiency, prosperity, the freedom to pursue one's own individual goals and interests denied under communism. While the 1990 Civic Forum programme had promised a vague 'Return to Europe', the 1992 ODS programme offered the benefits of a liberal order: 'Freedom and Prosperity'. The neo-liberal promise of an economic miracle also recognized and catered for the consumerist appetites fostered by both late communism and the geographical and cultural proximity of Western consumer societies.[23] However, as discussed in Chapter 3, Anglo-American neo-liberal ideas – and especially those of Hayek – had a deeper appeal in the Czech post-communist context than simply abstract efficiency or getting-rich-quick. The Hayekian idea of market and market society as a 'spontaneous order' allowing the emergence of a stable, well-ordered and moral society through individual action, rather than state coercion, was deeply appealing to many Czechs, who had retained both a Central European sense of petit-bourgeois propriety and a suspicion of the state rooted in the experience of both communism and foreign rule before 1918 (Holy 1996: 180–94).

Conservatism and conservative conceptions of social order were, however, also keenly debated among Czech intelligentsia and politicians in 1991–2. These debates were in part a continuation of the dissident explorations of the subject in the 1980s (see Chapter 3) and in part a reaction to the unanticipated rise of the right within Civic Forum. Although much writing on the subject merely repeated conventional understandings of conservatism and liberalism in Western contexts, a number directly addressed the question of what 'conservatism' could or should mean in relation to Czech post-communist transformation. The Catholic–conservative group around *Střední Evropa*, despite a certain following within the intelligentsia, found that radical deconstruction of Czech national identity and nostalgic Central Europeanism implied little in practical political terms after 1989 beyond close alignment with Germany and a commitment to a Christian Democratic 'Europe of the Regions'. As Czech Prime Minister (1990–2), Petr Pithart enjoyed a more advantageous platform from which to develop his dissident 'Toryism' of the 1980s. However, his opposition to the 'Jacobin radicalism' of militant grassroots anti-communists; his view that transformation 'would be slow, [and] necessarily "impure", that is not very fair'; and his appeals to establish a new sober, self-critical national consciousness better able to accommodate Slovak aspirations, left him politically isolated. Other dissidents influenced by British Toryism, sharing Pithart's concern with the lost virtues of decency, hard work and civic mindedness embodied by past generations of

Czechs, argued for a socially conservative vision of transformation focusing on family and morality, rather than history and national identity. In this view, moral permissiveness, relativism and mass consumerism supposedly fostered by both Western liberalism and ex-*nomenklatura* 'mafias' alike were the main obstacles to successful transformation and Europeanization (Hromádková 1991). By contrast, for Bohumil Doležal, the founder of the defunct Liberal Democratic Party (LDS), the central problem remained that Czechs, as in the 1980s, had been denationalized through a mixture of historical processes, including Russian communist imperialism. Intervening in the debate on conservatism, Doležal argued against the importation of foreign models, arguing that the nation was 'one of the pillars of our domestic traditions and Czech conservatism must honestly come to terms with it' by renewing historic liberal-nationalist traditions (Doležal 1997: 13, 14).

Václav Klaus as conservative ideologist

As with the anti-communist discourse of 'Third Ways', the conservatism of the Czech right was most publicly and influentially framed by Václav Klaus through a reworking of existing discourses. When he had emerged as a national political figure in 1990 Klaus played no part in debates on conservatism, initially defining his Hayekian pro-market politics as a right-wing 'genuine liberalism' (*Literární noviny*, 8 November 1990). He began to identify himself as a 'conservative' only after his election as Chairman of Civic Forum in October 1990 (Klaus 1991: 176–81) and his initial definitions of conservatism as a 'standard right-wing position' putting the individual before the state were vague and seemed entirely to overlap with liberalism (*Fórum* no. 43/90, 12; *Mladá fronta Dnes*, 22 December 1990). Klaus, nevertheless, encouraged delegates at ODS's April 1991 founding congress to see the new party as a Czech equivalent of the British Tories and even toyed with the notion of including the word 'conservative' in the new party's name, before rejecting it because of its lack of resonance with grassroots ODS supporters (Stoniš and Havlík 1998: 84). Nevertheless, the erstwhile neo-liberal Klaus and other ODS politicians and supporters subsequently made a sustained intellectual effort to represent their party as the bearer of a new form of Czech conservatism. The 1992 ODS programme accordingly identified the party as 'a conservative party attempting to preserve and renew for our future the fundamental values of European Christian civilization and Czechoslovakia's democratic traditions' (ODS 1992: 3) coinciding with an essay by Klaus entitled 'Why I Am a Conservative', which self-consciously reversed the title of Hayek's famous postscript to *The Constitution of Liberty* – 'Why I Am Not a Conservative'.[24]

Given the marginal influence of ex-dissident conservatives such as Pithart, Bratinka, Kroupa and Hromádková; the neo-liberals' rejection of historic Czech political tradition and hard-headed recognition of the appeals of consumerism and radical anti-communism; and the inherent difficulties of 'Czechizing' ideas derived from Anglo-American contexts, well understood by Klaus and other neo-liberals at an early stage,[25] why and how did ODS articulate a Czech conservative ideology, rather than simply fuse anti-communism with free-market liberalism? The choice cannot be reduced to the presence of an external model in the British Conservative Party – although Klaus undoubtedly admired its free market policies and broad integrative role on the British right (Klaus 1993b: 55; 1997b: 109–16, 147–50) – nor to the conjunctural use of the 'liberal' label by groups of Klaus's opponents. Both the 'conservative' and the 'civic democratic' labels later used by Klaus's party were already in use by prominent minor parties.[26]

Despite its emphasis on meeting the future-oriented tasks of post-communist transformation, the new ideology of the right had to be legitimized as more than a fast route to economic prosperity and freedom, or even as the surest means to break with the communist past or navigate around crypto-communist Third Ways. It had to be *naturalized* as the seamless, inevitable and logical outcome of Czech history and culture. This was problematic given that the right presented its main ideological reference points in Western neo-liberalism as a new 'main-stream' set of modernizing ideas *superseding* the provincialism and messianism of both dissident and traditional (pre-communist) Czech political thought. Czech neo-conservatives faced a similar problem from a somewhat different angle. As elsewhere in Central and Eastern Europe, it was difficult in the Czech context to identify what (if anything) was genuinely 'traditional', a problem which had already occurred in more intellectualized form in the dissident discussions of the 1980s. Interwar Czechoslovakia, whilst broadly inspiring as a democratic, Western-style market economy, was, however, too socially progressive and etatistic to offer inspiration to either neo-conservatives or neo-liberals. Despite its anti-communist commitment to focus on 'exclusively the period before 1948' (Klaus 1991: 206), the 1945–8 interregnum was seen as a period of archetypical 'Third Ways', seeking to reconcile Western pluralism and market economics with Soviet-style economic planning and 'managed democracy'. Moreover, as Daniel Kroupa conceded in 1990, even a conservatism of values rather than institutions inspired by US neo-conservatism was problematic because 'we have very few values we should conserve, in the past forty years most of them have been shattered' (*Fórum* no. 46 /1990, 16).

'Revolutionary conservatism'

This ideological dilemma was partly resolved through the formulation of the dis-course of a 'revolutionary conservatism' defined by the special circumstances of post-communist transformation, concerned not with evolutionary change and continuity but with recovering 'values' via a revolutionary break with the imme-diate past (Znoj 1994). As Klaus put it:

> The credo of conservatism is not a longing to hold on (*uchovávat*) at all costs to everything old, but an attempt to conserve (*zachovat*) the genuine, tried and tested values on which our civilization was for a long time based

and on which we want it to be based in the future ... when society rests firmly on well-anchored pillars of 'conservative' values, when it senses them thoroughly and is governed by them (...) conservatives act in a very 'unrevolutionary' way, as guardians of what exists, in such situations they want in the true sense of the word to conserve what is. However, in a society in which true values have been violently interrupted ... the goal of conservatives is to return to true values, and their means of doing so is to make every possible effort to re-establish them. It is for this reason that the conservatism of our time, of our present time, is revolutionary in the extreme (*navýsost revoluční*), and for this reason that it is wholly, and as a matter of principle (*programově*), lacking in moderation (*neumírněný*).

(Klaus 1996: 224–5)

The special situation of post-communism thus justified the temporary and special dispensation of using 'revolutionary' means for conservative ends. The discourse of 'revolutionary conservatism' built on two key ideas. First, it drew on the widely shared Czech liberal-national reading of communism as an ahistorical 'unnatural order' (Klaus 1996: 225) which represented 'the isolation of Czech society from its natural cultural sphere (*civilizačniho okruhu*) ... a deviation from our tradition and historical continuity' caused by external pressures and the failings of Czechs at a particular historical moment in 1945–8 (ODS 1996b: 8). Although the civic right echoed dissident rhetoric of communism's legacy of 'declining morality, social solidarity (*sociálního cítění*), education, general cultivation and basic decency' (ODS 1992: 3), its underlying view was that communism had neither fundamentally changed Czechs nor left them morally corrupted as dissident thought often suggested. Rather, communism was seen as merely placing a different set of incentives before the usual mix of human motivations (Klaus 2001b: 173–4).

Although stigmatized as a naive search for 'Third Ways', the relatively democratic and popular character of 1960s reform communism posed particular problems for right-wing ideology. Some right-wing anti-communists dismissed 1968 as simply a power struggle between communist elites taking place over the heads of a 'democratic' non-communist nation. Drawing on Hayek, Klaus, however, presented a more nuanced picture of a society which both 'wanted and didn't want' socialism and was led astray by reform communist intellectuals (Klaus 1996: 113–16). The strong public support for the Communist Party or socialism in 1945–8 or 1968 and the tacit mass collaboration with 'normalization' so central to dissident conservatism were thus glossed over.

Second, it defined the market and liberal institutions as 'traditional values' (and vice versa). Liberal institutions including legal and economic structures and other 'normal' institutions such as 'standard' political parties were traditional not only because, as one ODS billboard put it in 1992, 'Doing Business Is Natural' but rather, as Hayek had argued, because they were the 'tried and tested' product of a long evolutionary process. In Klaus's view this resolved the contradiction between liberalism and conservatism (Klaus 1996: 226, 229). For this reason, the ideology of the Czech civic right is often identified by its supporters as a 'liberal-conservative' (*liberálně konzervativní*) orientation.

'Active patriotism': hard work and common sense as national tradition

The discourse of 'revolutionary conservatism' served firmly to delegitimize the notion of Czech tradition producing a 'socialist nation', so successfully constructed by Communists and the left after 1945 (Abrams 2002). However, as Pavel Bratinka (1991: 209) observed, a revolutionary break with the immediate past also implied a process of active re-engagement with a more distant past 'to dig back more than 41 years into the past to find a time when parliamentary democracy, the rule of law, market economics and civil society were established features of this country'. However, the nature of the 'certain traditionalism' and 'moral values of the past', which the new Czech conservatism would excavate remained unclear.

Indeed, as Doležal had suggested, in the Czech context the only well-established moral and historical tradition was nationalism. Indeed, the articulation of liberalism and national identity was arguably central to Czech right vision of transformation (Williams 1997b) as well as to a range of competing centrist and centre-left positions (Auer 2003). However, despite – or perhaps because of – its Central European origins, Hayekian neo-liberalism sat uncomfortably with discourses of national identity. Hayek was in much of his writing at pains to stress that the liberal tradition he defended was a product of Western and European civilization, rather than any particular national culture. Indeed, Austrian school neo-liberals such as von Mises (1938/2002: 315–20) and Hayek (1944/1997) regarded nationalism as a dangerous form of collectivism and were among the earliest advocates of the dissolution of national states in a European federation.[27]

The right therefore adopted (and adapted) the conventional Czech view, which stressed the affinity between national tradition and liberal institutions. The free market and the liberal society, it argued, were not only efficient, natural and 'traditional' in Hayek's sense, but also an expression of Czech national character and traditions, which underlined Czechs' strongly Western and European culture. However, the right constructed this affinity in particular ways. As the main force in government in 1992–7, it naturally embraced the theme of a uniquely successful 'Czech Way' (*Česká cesta*) of reform combining radical market policies and low social costs. Following the break-up of Czechoslovakia this discourse of national economic superiority became more explicit. The dissolution of the federation into two independent states allowed the liberal Western oriented identity of the Czechs to be contrasted with the apparent populism and nationalism of independent Slovakia (Holy 1996).

As it became clear following the 1992 elections that an independent Czech state would come into existence, Klaus began explicitly to address questions of Czech national identity and its relationship to the market liberalism and

anti-communism that had hitherto been the most distinct elements in the ideology of the Czech right. The break-up of Czechoslovakia, Klaus argued, should
be seen not in terms of loss or political failure, as the Czech left and centre
maintained, but as one episode in a longer tradition of Czech statehood which
could now be rediscovered and redefined (Klaus 1993a: 65–6; 70–2).[28] For
Klaus, however, national tradition was not primarily embodied in the ideas or
political activities of Czech elites or the flawed, if partially successful,
Czechoslovak state institutions they had created and still less in any universal
values that the Czech nation might represent but – as for Pithart and Hromádková – in the hard work, entrepreneurialism and common sense of anonymous
ordinary Czechs, which was to be contrasted with the unrealistic hubris of intellectual and political elites. Klaus argued that this tradition had historically sustained and underpinned elite politics and the building of democratic political
institutions.[29] Speaking in 1993 at the Říp hill near Prague, the mythical point of
origin of the Czech nation, about the Czechs' supposedly unique experience of
transformation, Klaus argued that

> Permanent success depends on us alone, on our hard work, inventiveness
> and enterprise and on our common sense ... The glory and gravity (*vážnost*)
> of our country will not be renewed or guaranteed by ... gestures or grand
> words, but by the everyday ... and perhaps slightly subterranean work of
> each of us. This is practical, *active patriotism.*
>
>   (Klaus 1996: 95; emphasis in original)[30]

This discourse of 'active patriotism' reversed the usual juxtaposition of the
Švejkian 'Little Czech' removed from great historical processes and the 'Great
Czech Nation' of culture and intellectual achievement (Holy 1996). It was sup-
ported by a selective appropriation of Czech political tradition, which erased
much of the established left-liberal construction of Czech democratic identity.[31]
This can be seen clearly in Klaus's interpretation of the interwar Czechoslovak
Republic and the legacy of its revered founder and first President, T.G. Masaryk.
In reflections on Czech statehood in 1992–3, Klaus (1993a: 66–7) had interpreted Masaryk as a pragmatic liberal politician, like himself, committed to
'European individualism' and critical of the Czech traditions of his day, but ultimately concerned to 'realize the interests of Czech society' and unafraid to
create a new state structure for the Czech nation when confronted by new realities. This interpretation naturally erased much in Masaryk's thinking: his stress
on the universal meaning of the 'Czech Question'; his sympathy for social
democracy and concerns with the position of the working class and the 'Social
Question'; and his view of politics as an extension of ethics and religious morality. Indeed, the only distinct Masarykian idea Klaus embraced at this time was
that of 'small-scale work' (*drobná práce*) which he saw in terms of the anonymous 'active patriotism' of ordinary people described above (Klaus 1996: 67).[32]

The discourse of 'active patriotism' and avoidance of Third Ways rejected
what they termed the 'messianism' of Masaryk and the broader Czech liberal-

nationalist tradition: the belief that Czech democratic development was in advance of developments elsewhere and had broader historical, perhaps universal significance.[33] For the right such traditions were harmful, crypto-socialist and outdated as a form of national identity (Budil 1992). Any 'imaginary higher idea' for Czech statehood was, ODS argued, unnecessary, as the assertion of national identity and national continuity was a sufficient justification of statehood in itself (ODS 1996b).[34]

Ideologies of 'post-transformation'

The fall of the Klaus government in 1997 and the economic problems that preceded it triggered ideological as well as strategic debates on the Czech right. The sharpest and most radical interventions came from the intellectual hinterlands of the centre-right. While Catholic conservatives (along with the Czech left) blamed the problems of the 1990s on excessive economic liberalism and a neglect of morality, social cohesion, state authority and law-and-order (Janata 1998; Vystrčil 1998), neo-liberals in the media, the economics profession and the influential Liberal Institute (LI) think-tank saw the period as one of half-hearted compromise, unprincipled pragmatism and state intervention – a missed opportunity for genuinely radical free market reform – and looked to the full-blooded unleashing of market forces into the Czech economy and public sector. However, from 1997 to 1998 a number of alternative centre-right ideologies began to emerge from the parties and politicians who later coalesced into the Quad-Coalition, and ultimately from ODS itself

Christian Democratic alternatives to liberal transformation

As noted in Chapters 4 and 5, the Christian Democratic Union and Czechoslovak People's Party (KDU-ČSL) initially struggled to find a coherent ideological response to the politics of post-communist transformation beyond exaggerated anti-communism and appeals to historic party traditions and vaguely defined Christian values. By early 1992, however, the party had adopted the mainstream West European notion of the 'social market', an emphasis marking it out both from the civic right's stress on the 'market without an adjective' and the more morally or culturally defined agenda of small Christian niche parties elsewhere in Central and Eastern Europe (Enyedi 1996; Haughton and Rybář 2004). Thus, according to its Chairman Josef Lux speaking to the 1992 party Congress in Jihlava, KDU-ČSL's vision was 'a social market economy based on Christian solidarity ... the co-operation of all social classes in the interests of prosperity and maintaining social peace and stressing respect for the individual' (*Zprav-ODAj* no. 14, 10 April 1992, 5–6). Marketization was thus to be tempered by active, individually empowering social policy to protect vulnerable groups such as the sick and elderly, families with children, disabled people or the unemployed, supported by a broad social consensus. In allying itself with ODS in 1991–2, KDU-ČSL had pragmatically accepted policies with national-liberal and anti-communist rationales such as voucher privatization and lustration. Despite sharing in the material and political gains of office, the Christian Democrats nevertheless retained an ideological rationale for allying themselves with the 'civic' right: to advance reform whilst acting as a check on excessive social or economic liberalism (*ZpraODAj* no. 38, 1992, 3–4). From 1994, however, KDU-ČSL began to emphasize its commitment to a German- or Austrian-style social market economy (Lux 1995a, 1995b) as an *alternative*, rather than a mere corrective to the 'civic' right. In doing so the Christian Democrats directly challenged the legitimacy of Klaus's conservatism, which they presented as an '-Anglo-Saxon' import inappropriate to the Czech lands and their Central European traditions (Lux 1996), de-emphasizing the notion of a distinct Catholic Czech identity in favour of a stress on 'self-evident' geo-political and cultural affinities and more widely acceptable Czech corporatist and 'social' traditions. Indeed, Josef Lux suggested, neo-liberal parties such as ODS and ODA, Christian Democrats argued, were inauthentic and inappropriate in a Central European context like that of the Czech lands because these parties were based on ideas imported from Britain and the US (*Lidové noviny*, 11 May 1996).[35] Just as a Central-European-style 'social market economy' would be more in keeping with Czech traditions than unfettered economic liberalism, so, it was argued, the 'European model' of three-cornered party system with 'a plurality of views directly linked to a variety of political parties' was preferable to 'Anglo-Saxon' (two-party) models (*Respekt* no. 49, 2–8 December 1996, 13).

Anti-establishment liberalism

As the right fragmented from the mid-1990s, small 'civic' right-wing parties such as the Civic Democratic Alliance (ODA) and (later) the Freedom Union (US) began to formulate an alternative ideology of liberal transformation, which stressed that transformation, while partially or initially successful, had been left uncompleted (and was thus endangered) because of the failures of established politicians. This drew a further political frontier within the right between a failing pseudo-liberal establishment represented by ODS and genuinely liberal reformist outsiders. Its somewhat contradictory diagnosis was that Czech society required both 'genuine' radical market liberalization and a greater anchoring of the market in morality and society. The discourse of genuine market liberalization stressed that established politicians had failed to liberalize sufficiently or legislate for institutions that would create competitive markets and that measures such as tax cuts, deregulation, further privatization and the decentralization of the state were needed. Reform was said, in a characteristic phrase, to have 'stopped half-way (*na půli cesty*)' (Unie svobody 1998). However, the threat to transformation was identified less in the fatal misconceptions of establishment reformers than in more traditional liberal bugbears of vested bureaucratic and economic interests. These, it was argued, created a 'reform trap' which threatened to bring transformation to a halt, locking-in the status quo of partial reform. Finally, characteristically for Czech centre-right discourses, anti-reform forces and the danger they posed were represented as a form of regression into the communist past. The ODA leader Jan Kalvoda (1996b, 1996c), for example, spoke of cross-ownership structures and problems of corporate governance characteristic of the Czech Republic during the 1990s (see Chapter 6) as threatening the emergence of 'bank socialism' resting on an 'extremely strong stratum of managers ... former directors of state-owned firms and their deputies'.[36]

The second theme stressed that the difficulties of the Czech economy – and hence the problems of Czech transformation overall – stemmed from a failure to ground the market and the individual in morality and society. Such ideas – in part derived from US neo-conservatism, in part from dissident readings of Hayek – were present in the thinking of ODA at an early stage.[37] They also emerged as an undercurrent in ODS's long-term Political Programme (ODS 1996b) formulated in 1995–6 under the auspices of the Foreign Minister Josef Zieleniec. They were most fully developed, however, in 1997–8 by the Freedom Union (US), which stressed the need a Czech middle class (*střední stav*), represented as both a dynamic economic actor *and* a repository of ethical values and civic mindedness, making it an ideal bulwark against an over powerful post-communist state (Večerník 1999a, 1999c).

'Czech Mečiarism' – the discourse of the Quad-Coalition

The formation of the Quad-Coalition in 1999 generated a further critical centre-right discourse.[38] Although deeply critical of Klaus's ODS, the Quad-Coalition (4K), like ODA and the Freedom Union, framed its identity squarely within the liberal, anti-communist discourse of reform, modernization and Europeanization which had defined the Czech centre-right since early 1990s. Its founding 'St Wenceslas Day Agreement' of 28 September 1999 thus pledged it to 'tackling political drift (*marasmus*), effectively countering growing communist influence, solving our country's current problems and leading it to the European Union' (Čtyřkoalice 1999). Like ODS, the Quad-Coalition defined itself by highlighting a threat to transformation and the liberal Western-oriented Czech identity stemming from 'non-standard' politics, 'Third Ways' and provincialism *within* the broad democratic camp, which unconsciously echoed ideas rooted in the communist past. For the Quad-Coalition, however, it was the Opposition Agreement and its two signatories which posed the threat, having, it was claimed, lapsed into dangerous forms of illiberal democracy and clientelism – a 'pretend quasi-democracy' founded on vested interests (Lobkowicz 1999) – blocking the successful completion of reform (Unie svobody 1998; Pehe 2002a: 12)

The Quad-Coalition re-articulated the ODS discourse of 'standard' politics and 'Third Ways' claiming that it was an alliance of 'classic European currents' (liberals and Christian Democrats), challenging the experimental 'Third Way' and 'non-standard' politics of the Opposition Agreement, which they claimed, as a denial of left–right competition, had no parallels in Western Europe, only in the failed politics of interwar Czechoslovakia (Pehe 1999: 258–61). Like ODS,

4K's discourse also emphasized the origins of such 'non-standard' politics in thinking developed in the communist period.[39]

However, the Quad-Coalition and its members stressed that the Opposition Agreement was dangerous not merely because it delayed necessary change and lowered the quality of democracy but because it threatened Czech identity as an advanced, Western-oriented liberal nation. A Civic Democratic Alliance statement of 4 September 1999 thus described the Opposition Agreement as 'a threat to pluralism, individual liberties, legal certainties and the European orientation of the Czech Republic' before claiming still more starkly that 'the policies (*politika*) of the current government and its Opposition Agreement partner [ODS] are leading the Czech Republic to catastrophe, away from Europe and towards Asia' (cited in Hamerský and Dimun 1999: 224, 225).

As in many Czech discourses, the Quad-Coalition also used comparison with neighbouring Slovakia to highlight Czech identity and threats to it. In 1992 comparison of Czech and Slovak election results had been used to stress that majority support for the 'civic' right was an affirmation of Czechs' liberal-democratic, Western identity, while Slovak voters' endorsement Vladimír Mečiar revealed a more 'Eastern' culture of populism and nationalism. In 1999, however, such comparison was used by the Quad-Coalition to highlight how flagging reforms and the Opposition Agreement threatened Czech identity by reversing this 'natural' state of affairs. The Czech Republic's patchy implementation of the EU *acquis* thus not only threatened Czechs' sense of identity but risked conferring on a Slovak identity on them. As an ODA statement of 12 March 1999 put it, there was 'a threat that we will fall out of the first group of countries [for EU accession] *and assume the role of Slovakia*' (cited in Hamerský and Dimun 1999: 227, my emphasis). The notion of Czechs falling behind the 'naturally' less advanced Slovaks was further underlined by the Slovak elections of June 1998, which coincided with the Czech elections that had given rise to the Opposition Agreement and saw the pro-European Slovak Democratic Coalition (SDK) displace the government of Vladimír Mečiar.

In so doing, commentators close to the 4K constructed 'Mečiarism' in a quite specific way. It was in Pehe's (2002a: 265) words 'far from the product of some specific "Eastern" factor, but rather of the legacy of normalization which the Czechs and Slovaks share'. This reinterpretation of Mečiarism as a form of 'neo-normalization' (Šiklová 2003), not, as more commonly argued, a product of Slovakia's longer historical experience as a nation or the dynamics of the Czech-Slovak relationship, rendered the prospect of 'Czech Mečiarism' more credible and immediate to a Czech audience and – like ODS's discourse on 'Third Ways' – framed opponents as pseudo-democrats shaped by communism outside the world of acceptable transformation politics.[40]

Defending the nation – ODS ideology after 1997

The dominant tendency in ODS's ideological discourse from its foundation in 1991 had been to break with or radically rearticulate historically derived categories of Czech political thought, viewed as provincial, utopian or left-wing and in need of transfusion from mainstream, 'tried and tested' Western ideologies. However, when Klaus and other ODS leaders returned to the theme of Czech national identity in the aftermath of the political crisis of 1997–8, their discourse differed significantly from that of the early 1990s.

First, ODS began to incorporate the traditional Czech nationalist paradigms it had once eschewed. This was most clearly illustrated in the new stress on 'national interests' (see Chapter 8) and the party's growing tendency to define Czechs and Czech interests against Western Europe, Germany and the EU, rather than less successful post-communist neighbours. However, it was also a more open assertion that ODS's identity as an 'Anglo-Saxon' liberal-conservative party was an expression of Czech national identity against the dominance of Austro-German Christian Democratic models of centre-right politics in Central Europe (ODS 1998; ODS 2002b). [41] Second, ODS stressed that the Czech nation itself, rather than transformation, was under threat. In 1992–3 Klaus had depicted Czech tradition as grounding the politics of right-wing liberal transformation, defining the Czech nation inclusively as 'a community that includes all democratic diversity and gives it meaning' (Klaus 1993a: 72). Although the same emphases on shared history, culture and national values of hard work and common sense (*Mladá fronta Dnes*, 27 October 1998) were still present, in the late 1990s Klaus began to stress the notion of internal and external *threats* to the Czech nation and the politically divisive nature of Czech national identity In a series of reflections written in January and February 1998, for example, he argued that the politics of the 1990s had not merely divided free-marketers from proponents of Third Ways, but divided those who identified with and valued the Czech nation and those who did not (Klaus 2002d: 47–9).[42]

His opponents, Klaus asserted, saw the national state not as a 'natural unit', embodying national and human identity and autonomy, but as an artificial and accidental creation, which could be dismantled for the sake of a 'universalistic left-wing dream' such as 'vacuous Europeanism' or notions of 'global egalitarianism' (*Lidové noviny*, 3 June 1999; Klaus 2002b: 48). This discourse again linked Czech national autonomy with the free market, but this time through the construction of a common threat to both: a class of supra-national bureaucrats 'who do not believe in the market and want to manage regulate and plan, this time globally' (Klaus 2002b: 49). As Klaus himself naturally noted, in threatening both national independence and economic freedom the new threats were reminiscent of communism. He also constructed a chain of difference, which excluded political opponents from the national community by constructing a chain of ideas linking them to past Czech capitulations, which had supposedly resulted from a lack of patriotic sentiment. Speaking in 2000, Klaus, for example, described Czech Europhile politicians supporting EU integration as a manifestation of a historically rooted lack of Czech national self-confidence:

> a constantly returning feeling that our state and national existence is not self-evident ... not only in underestimating ourselves and accusing

ourselves, and in submitting to great powers and strong allies on the other, but in accusing and denouncing domestic political opponents for a lack of devotion to foreign countries.

(Klaus 2000b)

This was an allusion to the so-called 'Czech Question' of the nineteenth century, a debate centring the character and meaning of Czech national identity. Klaus's description in the same speech of Czech Europhile politicians as having a 'Protectorate mentality' – was a reference to the acceptance by some of the liquidation of Czech statehood and national identity under German occupation (Klaus 2000b).

In contrast to his earlier robustly optimistic vision of liberal nationhood, Klaus now questioned the existence of a deeply rooted Czech liberal-democratic tradition, noting the lack of societal resistance both to Munich in 1938 and to 'normalization' after 1968 which, he claimed, demonstrated the Czech public's trusting attitude towards domestic elites and foreign powers. After 1997–8 Klaus thus took a more overtly critical stance towards Masaryk and interwar Czechoslovakia. He now presented the 1918–38 'Pre-Munich Republic' – the pejorative Communist-era label – not as an example to be followed but as a society wracked by economic crisis, ethnic conflict, instability and corruption, which should serve as a warning for the contemporary Czech Republic (Klaus 1999: 50–1; 2000a 126–7). Klaus also openly challenged what he termed the myth of Masaryk as a moral and political giant. Far from embodying and protecting Czechoslovak democracy and statehood or acting as a pragmatic liberal, Masaryk, Klaus now suggested, had merely been a partisan politician of the left, more comfortable with elite pacts than open competition, who had underestimated the threats of ethnic divisions and the extreme left and compensated for a lack of real international stature with grandiose, but irrelevant, political visions (Klaus 2000a 297–302: also Klaus 2001b: 117–19). As contemporary listeners understood, these remarks also summed up Klaus's view of the presidency of Václav Havel, who identified strongly with the Masarykian tradition. Klaus himself underlined this point dismissing contemporary use of a 'distorted Masarykian ideal' consisting of 'a democratic commitment of pretty words (*verbální libivý demokratismus*); the underestimation of ethnic problems, [and] efforts to impress foreign countries more than the domestic public' (Klaus 2000a: 302).

Such thinking thus marked a turn to a historically grounded rhetoric of nation-building and national renewal, which stressed the weakness or incompleteness of Czech national identity – an idea echoing Czech dissident conservatives or the anti-communist national populism of the centre-right in Hungary and Poland (Fowler 2004). However, Klaus's response was not to question traditional concepts of Czech nationhood but to call for the reinforcement of

values such as patriotism and national pride [which] are under-valued or even mocked and presented as something unmodern, old fashioned and even slightly dangerous. It is sad that awareness of national togetherness (*národní sounáležitosti*) is almost concealed and that we are only unashamed of it at ice hockey matches and football internationals.

(Klaus 1999: 51)

National liberalism versus multi-culturalism

The concept of 'national interests' and the defence of the Czech state was tentatively extended from the European to a domestic political arena by Klaus and some other ODS politicians. Petr Nečas (1999), for example, argued that national interests should be asserted not only against 'cheap pseudo-Europeanism' but as a means of preserving social cohesion against the destructive effects of social, economic and generational differences. Klaus and other ODS leaders initially distanced themselves from such notions of 'national cohesion' (*národní soudržnost*), whose echoes of interwar integral nationalism sat uneasily with the party's commitment to (neo-)liberalism and Western-style conservatism (*Lidové noviny*, 3 June, 1999). However, by 2002 the ODS election programme (ODS 2002d) had extended the notion of 'national interests' to areas such as the regulation of illegal immigration and the status of Vietnamese migrants legally resident in the Czech Republic, where it argued for more restrictive measures (*Hospodářské noviny*, 28 May 2002).

Once again linking the 'civic' and the 'national' but now focusing on the 'problem' of social order, rather than economic and political transformation, Václav Klaus continued to explore this theme by arguing that immigration into the Czech Republic could risk the 'loss of a certain civic coherency (*koherence*) ... of consistency (*konzistence*), of the homogeneity (*homogenity*) of the world I live in' (*Hospodářské_noviny*, 28 May 2002). In subsequent speeches and writings Klaus extended such thinking into an explicit critique of multiculturalism, which he understood as 'the idea that every difference is valuable and must be preserved at all costs' (Klaus 2001b: 117. In this later writing, liberal concerns with 'civic coherency' in a multicultural society and conservative preoccupations with multiculturalism's threat to 'the homogeneity (*homogenity*) of the world I live in' would emerge more distinctly.

Consistent with discourses of 'Third Ways', Klaus attacked multiculturalism as an *anti-liberal* collectivist ideology which not only entailed the political recognition of minority groups as special interests but was also damaging to market efficiency. The newly elected Czech President published a sympathetic review of a working paper criticizing multi-culturalism because it allegedly eroded the social capital created by shared national identity (*Lidové noviny*, 18 February 2003).[43] He also attacked multiculturalists' supposed neglect of the historical and cultural embeddedness of liberal rights in communities with a 'natural' shared sense of national identity and concrete legal and political institutions to enforce them (*Lidové noviny*, 18 June 2005; *Mladá fronta Dnes*, 27 February 2006). Echoing the arguments of British Tories such as Scruton, Klaus argued that – problematically for the human rights discourses of Havel and other ex-dissidents – in the absence of an enlightened world dictatorship – few rights were meaningful or enforceable at the global level.

However, Klaus developed a parallel set of a conservative-national arguments, unusual on the Czech right, which claimed that multiculturalism was a threat not just to liberal rights but also to social cohesion and national identity. His arguments focused on the warning for the Czech Republic represented by the (supposed) disintegration of Western societies. Although the ethnically diverse societies of Western Europe were a point of reference – like the British populist anti-immigration discourses of the 1960s and 1970s (Smith 1994) – Klaus saw the dangers of multiculturalism illustrated most starkly in the United States. Indeed, he seems to have first publicly highlighted the 'problem' of multiculturalism in reflections on visits to the US in 1999 and 2000, in which he expressed concerns over the balkanization of US society and the US media along ethnic and linguistic lines (Klaus 2000a: 116–18).[44] Finally, after '9/11', Klaus also took up the argument that the openness of all Western societies to migration made them vulnerable to terrorism and that the ideology of multiculturalism was therefore – albeit at several removes – a cause of terrorism. To reverse these trends, he suggested, migrants should fully assimilate with host societies (*Lidové noviny*, 18 June 2005; *Mladá fronta Dnes*, 16 July 2005, 4–5), perhaps along the lines of the US 'melting pot' model, which he claimed had successfully instilled a sense of US patriotism in earlier waves of East European immigrants (*Mladá fronta Dnes*, 21 February 2006).

In a Western context New Right discourses on 'race' and national identity have often emerged in response to political events which challenged established identities, rather than demographic change *per se*. Britain's postwar retreat from Empire or the success of the US civil rights movement are both argued to have been events which had such a galvanizing effect on right-wing discourses (Smith 1994). The same is true of the Czech right's explorations of the 'threat' of multiculturalism. Despite some growth in the 1990s, the Czech Republic had low levels of inward migration and only a small number of foreign-born residents, and the question of immigration had previously had almost no political salience (Kopeček 2004). The main focus for previous debates on cultural pluralism and Czech identity centred on the position of the country's Roma minority, the most identifiable minority group within Czech society, who could be represented as outsiders and 'invaders'. Czech popular and media discourses often operate in precisely these terms contrasting Roma fecklessness, criminality and childlike dependency with supposedly archetypical Czech qualities of rationality, industriousness, orderliness and respect for education. Klaus has in the past reacted with irritation to criticisms of the position of Roma irritation made by both domestic human rights advocates and international organizations.[45] However, unlike the populist far right, the new Czech right's conservative discourses of Czech identity and its defence against multi-culturalism, consistent with much popular historiography (Čaněk 1996), largely ignored the Roma, in favour of hypothetical immigrant minorities. Given its limited salience with Czech voters, other right-wing politicians followed the President's lead, but showed little enthusiasm for the theme.[46] The Czech right's discourse on 'multi-culturalism' thus seems more a representation of the threatening possible consequences of an insecure hostile world for a small homogeneous nation connected with the right's growing concerns over European integration and globalization.[47] These concerns are explored in more detail in the next chapter.

Conclusions

This chapter has argued that the ideology of the new Czech right was neither an imported blueprint incubated by technocratic elites nor a simple legacy of the social structures or mentalities of communism. Rather, it was a rearticulation of a range of existing discourses of Czech post-communist transformation and identity, which redefined the nature of that transformation and those who stood outside it as its enemies and defining 'other'. The chapter thus noted how in the early 1990s the discourse of 'Third Ways' rearticulated the notion of a 'civic' transition from communism to a liberal-democratic market society by redrawing political frontiers to identify the liberal centre and social democratic centre-left, rather than the Communist Party and *nomenklatura* networks, as transformation's principal 'socialist' enemies. 'Civicness' was similarly redefined as a secular liberal politics of individual participation in economic and electoral markets supported by – but not embodied in – local communities and serviced by a professionalized party political elite. However, although in part an adaptation of classical liberalism or Anglo-American neo-liberalism, Czech new right ideology differed from its Western reference points. Its discourse on democracy, for example, did not seek to narrow the scope of the political to defend established market institutions against the predations of democratic majorities, but instead stressed the need for democratic majorities to be relatively unconstrained to achieve the historically imperative goals of post-communist transformation.

The chapter then considered the new Czech right's attempts in 1992–3 to define itself as 'conservative'. This, it was argued, was partly a response to the break-up of Czechoslovakia and the dislocation of Czechoslovak identity. However, it also served to ground the right's modernizing discourse contrasting 'standard', 'mainstream' neo-liberal approaches to a failed, collectivist 'provincial' national past, in a newly reworked narrative of Czech identity and history. This was created by eclectically rearticulating discourses of Czech conservatism formulated by former dissidents whose own forays into party politics had quickly foundered. The notion of conservatism as a radical 'revolutionary' force drew on ideas of the Civic Democratic Alliance and thus, indirectly, on American neo-conservatism; the concept of Czech tradition as embodied in the hard work and common sense of ordinary people, rather than the humanism and 'messianism' of elites echoed the thinking of dissident conservatives such as Pithart or Hromádková; and the notion of a revived Czech (not Czechoslovak) liberal-nationalist tradition and the focus on statehood and identity reflected the influence of Bohumil Doležal, both in the 1980s and, more briefly, in 1992–3 when he was a political adviser to Klaus.[48]

The economic problems of the late 1990s and the political crisis of 1997–8 dislocated key aspects of ODS's ideology of right-wing transformation generating a range of competing centre-right-wing discourses of 'post-transformation', all focusing in different ways on the socio-cultural bases of the market society. Discourses of 'critical liberalism' associated with small right-wing parties like the Civic Democratic Alliance and the Freedom Union retained much of the structure of ODS ideology in seeing politics as a process of market-led transformation blocked by pseudo-reformers whose thinking was shaped by the communist past. However, in their construction, Klaus and ODS, rather than the ex-dissident centre and the centre-left, were principal villains of the piece. This attained its most elaborated form in the ideology of the Quad-Coalition, which denied a modern, liberal right-wing identity to Klaus and ODS, whom it assimilated both with the Czech left and with 'backward' Slovakia in its discourse of 'Czech Mečiarism'. The Quad-Coalition thus represented itself, as ODS had previously done, as the only force capable of safeguarding Czech society against the enemies of genuine transformation, who threatened its very identity as a relatively advanced liberal European nation. Christian Democrat discourses offered a more fundamental challenge in stressing Czechs' Central European identity and affinity with corporatism rather than liberal politics and economics. To a considerable extent, it represented an economized and outwardly secular variant of older Catholic conservative discourses challenging the assumption of a liberal, Western identity for the Czechs.

ODS's own ideology of 'post-transformation' focused less on threats to liberal transformation than on new threats to nation and statehood *per se*. In this vision, neo-liberalism was reinterpreted as an expression of Czech national identity and autonomy in an inhospitable German-dominated Europe, rather than as a tool of economic reform. Although often expressed in the Czech right's euroscepticism, examined in detail in the next chapter, it also generated a new conservative-national strand in the ideology of the Czech right seen in Petr Nečas's ideas of 'national cohesion' or President Klaus's reflections on multiculturalism.

8 From neo-liberalism to national interests

Europe and the new Czech right

Introduction

As across Central and Eastern Europe, membership of the European Community (later the European Union) was a key priority for all mainstream Czech parties and governments after 1989. This goal was finally achieved with the accession of the Czech Republic and nine other candidate states on 1 May 2004. However, despite a widely shared pro-Western orientation, by the mid-1990s European integration and EU accession had become increasingly divisive issues in Czech party politics. This was largely due to the growing euroscepticism of the Civic Democratic Party (ODS) under Václav Klaus. The euroscepticism of Klaus and his party has been widely remarked upon, but with a few exceptions (Bugge 2000; Kopecký and Učeň 2003; Kopecký 2004) rarely analysed in detail. More surprisingly, ODS's shift in the late 1990s to a more strident euroscepticism committed to defend Czech national interests against the European Union, if necessary to the point of remaining outside the EU, has scarcely been remarked upon in scholarly writing. This is surprising, given that ODS does not fit the typical profile of eurosceptic parties in East and Central Europe, which are typically groupings of the far right or left, which remain outside normal coalition-building politics, or traditionalist conservative forces rooted in historical nationalism (Taggart and Szczerbiak 2002). ODS, by contrast, was a relatively new party with a free market vision, a key political actor in Czech transformation politics and a credible contender for office throughout the period since its foundation in 1991.

Many analysts have accounted for the euroscepticism of Klaus and his party as an 'instinctive' position resulting from their neo-liberal 'Thatcherite' ideology and identification with British conservatism bolstered by a growing awareness of the asymmetrical power relations between the EU and accession states (Robejsek 2002). Others have seen it as a 'nationalist card' prompted by electoral opportunism and a self-interested desire to preserve clientelistic networks threatened by the prospect of accession (Pehe 1999, 2002b, 2002c). Such commentaries have a certain validity. However, leaving aside the contradiction in viewing Klaus's party as simultaneously nationalistic, dogmatically committed to imported free market models *and* politically opportunistic, they leave much unexplained. They fail, for example, to explain why ODS should take up 'Thatcherite' euroscepticism, when other aspects of the British New Right agenda such as 'family values' and welfare reform were largely ignored (see Chapter 7). Nor do they explain why ODS, but not the incumbent, europhile Czech Social Democrats (ČSSD), who, after entering government in 1998, were also frequently accused of practising a similar mixture of etatism and clientelism (Pehe 2002c), should turn to euroscepticism. Nor do they account for the *changing* nature of the euroscepticism of the Czech centre-right or coherently link them with Czech electoral politics or the development of ODS as a political organisation. This chapter seeks to address these questions. It begins by mapping the evolving euroscepticism of ODS and its leaders across the changing domestic and European contexts after 1989. After briefly noting the contrasting europhile views of ODS's rivals on the Czech centre-right, it then seeks to explain the party's euroscepticism in terms of wider comparative literature on the subject and to assess its impact on the Czech Republic's participation in the European integration process.

The centre-right and the road to Czech EU accession

The Czech debate on European integration and Czech political parties' positions on the issue passed through a number of phases: in the early 1990s closer integration with Western Europe was welcomed enthusiastically by all parties other than the Communists, without detailed debate of the Czech–EU relationship. What debate did exist was largely driven by the interest of individual politicians in 'Europe' as an issue, principally Václav Havel and Václav Klaus. After the EU committed itself in principle to enlargement in the mid-1990s, Czech parties started to adopt general positions on the models of European integration and the Czech Republic's role within them. Following the launch of the formal accession process in 1998, these became clearer detailed positions, addressing the current and future direction of the EU in terms of specific aspects of the *acquis* and offering detailed pre- and post-accession strategies for the Czech Republic. Most parties produced specific programmes dealing with European integration and EU accession. After 1997 Czech accession to the EU gained in prominence as a political issue in the Czech media and featured for the first time as a significant election issue in 2002.

Czechoslovakia and the EU

Before 1989 relations between Czechoslovakia's highly conservative communist regime and the European Community (EC) were poorly developed. Diplomatic relations were only established in 1988 and, although a trade agreement was signed in December 1988, it was less extensive than those signed by the EC with some other East European states. Czechoslovakia was, moreover, excluded from the PHARE technical assistance programme established in July 1989 for reforming regimes in Hungary and Poland. In the euphoria following the collapse of communism, Czechoslovak foreign and European policy, under Foreign Minister Jiří Dienstbier, initially flirted with a utopian vision of dismantling all existing European institutions and replacing them with a loose confederal structure. This reflected the notion of a 'Europe without Blocs' developed by Dienstbier and other dissidents before 1989 as a strategy for reducing Soviet domination of Eastern Europe.

However, Czechoslovak policy quickly evolved a more hard-headed strategy of establishing ties with the European Community (EC) with a view to eventual membership, which centred on securing an Association Agreement ('Europe Agreement') with the Community. A Trade and Co-operation Agreement between Czechoslovakia and the EC was concluded in March 1990 and Czechoslovakia was incorporated into the PHARE programme shortly afterwards. In late 1991 a Czechoslovak Europe Agreement was successfully concluded and signed at a joint ceremony with Hungary and Poland in December of that year. The Agreements established a more open and full trading relationship between CEE associate states and the EC; committed associate states to approximate domestic legislation to the *acquis communautaire*; and established a political relationship of 'dialogue' between the EC and associated CEE states without making any specific commitment to accept them as members of the Community. In this period Czechoslovakia's foreign and European policy, was closely co-ordinated with those of Hungary and Poland, with whom it formed the so-called Visegrad Group (Wallat 2001). Czechoslovakia also gave a high priority to improving relations with Germany, which had historically been problematic and remained difficult into the 1970s and 1980s, largely because of unresolved issues surrounding the expulsion of Czechoslovakia's 2.5-million-strong ethnic German population after the Second World War under the 'Beneš Decrees' (Stroehlein 1998; Bazin 1999). Consistent with the views of non-socialist dissidents, in 1990 President Havel made his first official foreign visit to Germany and later sought to promote Czech–German reconciliation by taking the unpopular step of publicly apologizing for Czechs' brutal treatment of the country's Sudeten German minority in 1945–6.

Integration with Western Europe as a rejection of 'Third Ways'

As noted in Chapter 4, the divisions within Civic Forum that led to the emergence of the Czech right and the foundation of ODS centred almost entirely on domestic issues of post-communist transformation (see Chapter 4). The desire for closer integration with Western Europe, by contrast, was an uncontroversial ideal with few immediate concrete policy implications shared, with the partial exception of the Communist Party, across the whole of the Czech political spectrum. However, to the limited extent that 'Europe' did become a matter of mainstream domestic political contestation in the immediate post-transition period, it did so as an extension of the emerging Czech right-wing critique of dissident-led 'civic' policies of domestic reform, viewed as a 'Third Way' threatening Czechoslovakia's Europeanization (see Chapter 7). The equivocation of Jiří

Dienstbier's European policy as it evolved from advocating the dissolution of all existing blocs towards seeking co-operation with, and eventual membership of, the European Community made it a logical target of the right, which saw the existing West European institutional architecture as another set of 'standard', 'tried and tested' institutions to be embraced by post-communist democracies as quickly and fully as possible. The 1992 ODS programme, therefore, advocated 'a pragmatic foreign policy, free of empty gestures, moralizing and lecturing others' in which NATO membership and 'the integration of Czechoslovakia into the European Community is our most important and immediate goal' (ODS 1992: 13–14). Although strongly supporting the active participation of the US in Europe and hostile to the EC-sponsored notion of Central Europe as a potential bridge for trade between the West and the USSR, neither the programme nor the public statements of ODS leaders at this time contained any substantial criticism of EU policies or institutions. Indeed, it was characteristic of the right's position on European integration in the early 1990s that it saw any questioning of the institutional status quo in Europe as ideologically suspect.

The ODS-led centre-right coalition government, which took office in June 1992 – and in which ODS held the Foreign Affairs portfolio – retained the commitment of its Czechoslovak predecessor to rapid integration with Western Europe and eventual membership of the EU and NATO. It rapidly negotiated a Europe Agreement for the independent Czech Republic, which was signed on 4 October 1993 and took effect on 1 January 1995. In other respects, however, its approach to European integration was very different. Having dispensed with the less reform-minded and geographically (and supposedly culturally) less Western Slovaks, the new Czech government believed that its radical reform policies – widely believed at the time to have successfully combined rapid marketization, high growth and low social costs – would mark the Czech Republic out as an early candidate for admission to the EU. This rested on the assumption that EU enlargement when it took place would be an essentially 'political' process reflecting Western geo-political considerations, rather than strict criteria for membership, and would take place on a piecemeal basis with negotiations with 'advanced' states going ahead first.

The euroscepticism of Václav Klaus

At the same time, the Czech right began to develop more detailed and critical understandings of the EU as an institution and of its relationship with the Czech Republic. ODS programmatic documents of the early to mid-1990s consistently favoured EU entry – but tended to balance positive evaluation of the EU with mildly expressed concerns over the preservation of diversity and national sovereignty. The 1996 ODS election programme, for example, while promising to 'consistently base ourselves on the Czech national interest' and insisting that integration 'should not artificially suppress the diversity of nations and cultures', identified EU membership as the party's main foreign policy goal. EU membership, it was argued, would bring 'peace, security, stability and economic prosperity' to citizens of all member states (ODS 1996a: 7). The only specific position taken on the institutions of the EU was a wish that 'the sovereignty and powers of the Union should be derived from the sovereignty and powers of individual states' (ODS 1996a: 11). However, from 1992, in a series of speeches and articles for both domestic and international audiences, the new Czech Prime Minister Václav Klaus, whose public pronouncements tended to overshadow official Czech diplomacy under Foreign Minister Josef Zieleniec, developed a more assertive and acerbic critique. This contained three interrelated sets of arguments: an 'Anglo-Saxon' neo-liberal economic critique of the EU as an inefficient, over-regulated and 'socialist' structure dominated by self-seeking bureaucratic elites with far-reaching political ambitions to challenge the United States, undermining the original, economic rationale for its foundation; a moralistic 'Central European' critique of the EU's self-interest and bad faith in the enlargement process and in its relations with East and Central Europe; and a 'national' critique of the EU as a threat to Czech national sovereignty and identity, both through its existing policies and in its plans for further political integration, sometimes depicted as reflecting German (or Franco-German) domination of the Union.

'Continentwide dirigisme'

As a politician committed to neo-liberal positions Klaus saw the EU as an institution based on the collectivist 'ideological paradigm of the first part of the twentieth century' and traditions of 'continentwide dirigisme' (Klaus 1997b: 107) which reflected the political concerns of postwar French Gaullism and German Christian Democracy. He also detected left-wing and collectivist tendencies in the Union's current practice, and specifically in 'excessive regulation and bureaucratization' and 'ballooning welfare states' which he viewed the EU as both supporting and extending. Like many neo-liberals, he therefore argued that the Union needed internal reform not so much to facilitate enlargement as to maintain Europe's global competitiveness (Klaus 1997a: 347–54). Such neo-liberal criticisms were, however, relatively unfocused, sometimes failing to distinguish between the EU and domestic social and economic arrangements determined by national governments. The one key exception can be found in Klaus's detailed critique of the Euro and its political implications. Klaus argued that, because in fiscal terms EU states did not constitute an optimal currency zone, EMU was therefore 'above all a political project' (Klaus 1997a: 357–65), but one, crucially, which lacked an adequate political basis. Citing the break-up of Czechoslovakia as a negative example, and the unification of Germany as a positive counter-example, Klaus argued that, when economically diverse states united into a single currency zone, large transfers from richer to poorer regions were usually necessary. This presupposed political solidarity based on a strong shared identity, usually a national identity. While in 1990 a common national identity had, he believed, successfully underpinned currency union and political unification in Germany, divergent Czech and Slovak national identities revealed after the fall of communism had made the maintenance of an integrated Czechoslovak federation impossible. The EU, he argued, lacked precisely such a strong common political identity. The result, he suggested, of such a currency union would be that economically less developed regions – regions such as East and Central Europe – would become caught in a cycle of backwardness, as had occurred with southern Italian regions following the unification of Italy in the nineteenth century (Klaus 1997a: 354–7; 2002b: 219–22).

European integration and the experience of Central Europe

However, as with other aspects of the politics of the Czech 'civic' right, Klaus's euroscepticism of the 1990s was more complex than a simple transposition of Anglo-American neo-liberal arguments to post-communist Central Europe. It also contained a distinctly 'Central European' strand. Klaus and ODS rejected the institutionalization of 'Central Europe' after 1989 in the Visegrad group as a Third Way attempting to create 'interval stages, an interval society [which] revived some kind of ideas of bridges between East and West' (Klaus 1997a: 386–9, citation 388) with echoes of the ill-fated and unrealized project of President Beneš for postwar Czechoslovakia. Klaus also rejected the Visegrad framework as *politically* counterproductive, because it failed to address the question of EU membership for Central and East European states or take into account their divergent interests, instead favouring a purely economic model of integration of markets through the Central European Free Trade Area (CEFTA) (Wallat 2001). Despite such interest-based arguments, aspects of Klaus's euroscepticism clearly drew on a sense of Central European identity and experience. This can be seen, for example, in his moralistic arguments that the EEC was a product of the Cold War which, in effect, benefited its West European members at the expense of Central Europe (Klaus 1997a: 119–25; Bugge 2000: 25–9). This line of argument echoed the thinking of more self-consciously 'Central European' writers such as Kundera and Havel. Moreover, Klaus argued, the historical experience of Central European states, which were dominated by larger, centralized, supranational bureaucratic regimes – first under the multinational dynastic empires and later under Nazi rule and Soviet domination – left them acutely sensitive to the dangers of over-centralization and excessive supra-national harmonization inherent in the current European project. More significantly, he suggested that history had left the Czech Republic and other states in the region facing a 'double task' in post-Cold-War Europe, one of integrating participating in European integration *and* maintaining and rediscovering national identity and national independence (Klaus 1997b: 105–8). This view is summed up in Klaus's famous remark, first made in 1994 (*Respekt* no. 21, 23 May 1994, 10), that the Czech Republic faced the task of 'how to be European without at the same time dissolving into Europeanism like a lump of sugar in a cup of coffee' (cited in Bugge 2000: 24).

Safeguarding national distinctiveness

The concern with the Czech nation and its character and interests evident both in ODS's ideology and aspects of its reform policies also informed its approach to European integration and European identity. While politicians such as Havel viewed European, national and local identities as concentric and overlapping, rather than conflicting, and addressed the relationship between them through a mixture of metaphysical reflection and suggestions for institutional compromises, Klaus and ODS saw the relationship in markedly zero-sum terms. They consequently sought to mount a vigorous defence of the Czech national state as a guarantee of national identity and political self-determination against supranational or regional institutions promoted by the EU, both of which they viewed as inefficient, undemocratic and irreparably lacking political, cultural and historical legitimacy (Klaus 1997b: 101–4). Czech 'Europeanism' (*evropanství*), Klaus suggested, should, therefore, be interpreted as 'obligations to safeguard and preserve our distinctive features' (Klaus 1997a: 354–7). Although at this time, however, neither Klaus nor ODS as a party specified in any detail precisely what this implied in terms of a model of European integration, it was clear that they wished to proceed on the basis that nations and national states were to remain the essential building blocks of the Union.

The Klaus government's accession strategy

Accordingly, the Klaus government gave priority to integrating the Czech Republic into the global economy through membership of international bodies such as the Organization for Economic Co-operation and Development (OECD) and the General Agreement on Tariffs and Trade (GATT), rather than developing a concrete strategy for managing accession. It also delayed the Czech Republic's formal application for EU membership until 23 January 1996, making it the last but one CEE associate state to apply. The Klaus government largely abandoned the co-ordination of European policy with Visegrad neighbours, viewing the Visegrad Group as an artificial West-European-inspired creation intended to delay rather than facilitate enlargement, which was liable to hold back the advanced Czech Republic's prospects for membership. It downgraded the importance of improving relations with Germany, seeking to assert Czech interests within a framework of mutual accommodation. This was most clearly illustrated in negotiations over the so-called Czech–German Declaration, signed in December 1997, which attempted, with some difficulty, to reach an agreed position on the divisive and emotive events of the Second World War and its immediate aftermath. At this time, Prime Minister Klaus also took up a high-profile eurosceptic stance similar to that of the British Conservatives stance, criticizing the EU as over-regulated and inefficient, irritating many EU policy-makers. Exasperated by Klaus's criticisms of EU agricultural subsidies, EU Commissioner Hans van den Broek famously remarked that 'the Czech Republic is joining the European Union, not the other way around' (*Carolina* no. 189, 9 February 1996).

By 1995–6, the Czech government appears to have realized that its assessment of both the enlargement process and the strength of the Czech Republic's position within it were over-optimistic. The EU's December 1995 Madrid Summit set an approximate date for accession negotiations to begin and requested that the European Commission prepare a formal Opinion (*avis*) on each applicant state's readiness for membership. It also made it clear that the EU intended to deal with all CEE applicants within a *single* framework. Moreover, the June 1995 EU White Paper on the Single Market suggested that the accession process would be based on the fulfilment of detailed legislative, administrative and economic criteria reflecting the *acquis*, rather than ad hoc assessment of the broad Copenhagen criteria of democracy, a functioning market economy and appropriate administrative and legal capacities. Finally, it became clear that the Czech Republic's size and location gave it considerably less geo-political leverage than larger, more strategically located states such as Poland. The Klaus government, therefore, adopted a less abrasive approach in its dealings with the EU, evident, for example, in the conciliatory tone adopted in the Memorandum that accompanied the Czech Republic's application for membership. It also belatedly started to establish structures to manage European integration, principally the inter-ministerial Government Committee for European Integration and its associated working groups (Jacoby 2004: 44–5).

From neo-liberalism to national interests

Europe and the fall of the Klaus government

The fall of the Klaus government coincided with the EU's decision at its December 1997 European Council meeting in Luxembourg to open formal accession negotiations with the six best prepared candidate states identified in the Commission's formal Opinions (*avis*) on applicant states of July 1997. The Czech Republic was included with Hungary, Poland, Slovenia, Estonia and Cyprus in this group. Negotiations would proceed on the basis of the enlargement strategy set out in the accompanying *Agenda 2000* report. At the bilateral Czech–EU conference of 30 March 1998, which established an Accession Partnership as a new framework for Czech–EU relations and Czech adoption of the *acquis*, the Czech side was thus represented by the caretaker Tošovský government, which formally opened accession negotiations with the EU on 31 March 1998.

The European Commission's initial *avis* of July 1997 had painted a broadly positive picture of the Czech Republic as a reforming state, which could be considered for membership. However, it further punctured the notion that the Czech Republic was a front-runner whose domestic reforms merited the immediate 'reward' of EU membership. Its judgements also highlighted as obstacles to EU accession a number of legacies linked to the policies of the Klaus governments. Although the Czech Republic broadly met the broad human rights conditions of the Copenhagen Criteria and was judged a functioning market economy, sectors such as banking, securities trading, telecommunications, energy and steel required either restructuring or the creation of more competitive, better regulated markets. The Commission also identified major problems with the administrative and legal capacity of the Czech state to implement the *acquis communautaire*, noting that key institutions such as the civil service, police and judiciary were under-resourced, inadequately trained and in some cases subject to political pressure and that other institutions necessary to implement EU policies such as regional government and agricultural payments agencies had barely been created.

After the early elections of June 1998 Czech European policy passed to the minority Social Democratic government under Foreign Minister Jan Kavan. The Opposition Agreement, which enabled the Social Democratic government to take office, had been partly justified as necessary to provide the stability needed in the years before EU accession. However, although it provided for parliamentary consultation between Civic and Social Democrats on domestic and foreign policy matters, the text of the Agreement made no direct reference to accession and, as noted in Chapter 6, in practice the two parties' collaboration was uneasy and limited. Nevertheless, the Commission's first annual reports in 1998 and 1999 were highly critical, noting a lack of progress in addressing many accession related issues (European Commission 1998, 1999). At this time, the Czech Republic's readiness for EU membership appeared significantly less advanced than that of other candidate states such as Hungary and Estonia, leading Commission officials to hint that its accession might ultimately be delayed. Despite poor initial progress in adopting the *acquis* (see Chapter 6), in subsequent years the minority Social Democratic government successfully implemented a range of reforms related to EU accession. These included the creation of regional authorities, reform of criminal procedure and structural measures required for accession such as full privatization of state-owned banks. Despite their lack of a formal parliamentary majority, where the passing of accession legislation was required, the Social Democrats were often able to rely on the parliamentary support of the pro-European Quad-Coalition parties. From 2000 to 2002 the Commission's annual reports recorded steady progress in the meeting accession criteria, with the final major outstanding issue, the passing of a Civil Service Law, finally addressed in May 2002 (European Commission 2000, 2001, 2002).

Europe and the 'new' ODS

ODS's political realignment following its traumatic exit from government in 1997 saw the party develop its existing eurosceptic positions into a more strident and higher-profile euroscepticism, which later defined a right-wing strategy for approaching Czech membership of the EU.[1] There was a much heavier stress on patriotism and defending national interests and identity against the European Union. These were justified in terms of the doctrine of 'realism', which tended to displace neo-liberal and 'Central European' critiques of the EU. The party also began to contemplate scenarios for Czech non-membership of the EU, either because of the postponement of enlargement or because an offer of 'second-class membership' to Central and East European states might in some circumstances make a Czech medium-term future outside the Union preferable. Finally, the party formulated explicit models for the reform or transformation of the EU linked to strategies for building a 'reformist current' in the EU through realignment in the European Parliament and developing new coalitions of member governments in the European Council. Although the changes in ODS views of integration had their roots in wider realignment after 1998, the Kosovo crisis appears to have acted as a catalyst for their radicalization. Despite its strong support for Czech membership of NATO, ODS forcefully criticized allied air strikes against Yugoslavia as a politically counterproductive and unacceptable on principle as a violation of national sovereignty (Klaus 2000a: 113–15). ODS fears that the European Commission or coalitions of EU states might impinge upon the sovereignty of small, newly admitted members by seeking to influence their domestic politics were further illustrated by the party's outspoken opposition to EU sanctions against Austria adopted in response to the entry into government in early 2000 of Jörg Haider's far-right Freedom Party (FPÖ). Despite Haider's hostility to the EU's eastern enlargement and the Czech government's plans to complete the Temelín nuclear power plant (Fawn 2006), Klaus considered his party's domestically unpopular stance 'the lesser evil' (*Lidové noviny*, 4 February 2000; see also Mareš 2000; Klaus 2000a: 161–6), a view endorsed by the party's new foreign affairs spokesman, Jan Zahradil (*Právo*, 10 March 2000).

The turn to national interests

The notion of a 'national interest' is commonplace in English-language political discourse. However, despite the centrality of the nation as a category in Czech political discourse since at least the mid nineteenth century, Czech nationhood has usually been expressed in terms of historical rights; the juxtaposition of a Czech (or Slavonic) civilization to the German-speaking world; or a Czech(slovak) 'state idea' embodying certain ethical and moral values (Rak 1994; Holy 1996). In 1992 even Václav Klaus had argued that the notion of Czech 'national interests' was academic, abstract and removed from real politics, concluding that defining them was 'a never ending task for political scientists and historians, not for practical politicians' (Klaus 1993a: 53–4) in the tradition of 'philosophy with a big P' which had framed outdated historical debates on the 'Czech Question' (*Respekt*, 29 June 1992, 4).[2]

Klaus did, however, think that politics should be informed by 'pragmatism, realism, [and] tangible comprehensible goals' (*Respekt*, 29 June 1992, 4) and the Klaus government's European policy had clearly been based on the assumption that international politics in Central and Eastern Europe primarily involved self-interested competition between states. Indeed by 1994 Klaus himself recognized that his priority for the 'rediscovery of lost national identity and not immediately losing it on joining Europe' or succumbing to the notion of liberalism as 'boundless, phoney cosmopolitanism' was 'the Czech interest, if you like' (*Respekt*, 23 May 1994, 10). References to Czech 'national interests' first appear in ODS programmatic documents in the mid-1990s (ODS 1996a: 6–9, 10–15) supplementing the notion of a Czechoslovak 'state idea'. The term seems to have entered political usage as a result of overlapping debates in academic and policy communities following the unexpected emergence of an independent Czech state after the break-up of Czechoslovakia in 1992 (Valenta 1992; Krejčí 1993; see also Drulák and. Königová 2002). However, the idea of national interests was relatively unimportant in ODS's 'balanced' euroscepticism of this period and hardly features explicitly in Klaus's writings and speeches of the time. Moreover, where a Czech national interest was evoked in relation to European integration, the national interest of the Czech Republic was almost always used to *justify* joining the EU, rather than to highlight costs and conflicting interests (ODS 1992: 10–13).

The notion of European integration as *centring* on conflicting 'national interests' first emerged as a theme in Václav Klaus's speech to the extraordinary ODS Congress in Poděbrady on 13–14 December 1997 and was developed at the party's congress in Jihlava in April 1998, which incorporated it into its election programme of that year (ODS 1998). However, these speeches and documents gave equal or greater prominence to other themes of the 'Poděbrady Articles' such as individual freedom and a 'cheap state'. ODS's more 'national' standpoint towards integration was first presented as a *key* plank of party policy at the party's first Ideological Conference held in June 1999, a shift signalled to the wider public by Klaus and ODS's new foreign affairs spokesman Jan Zahradil in newspaper interviews (*Mladá fronta Dnes*, 2 June 1999; *Lidové noviny*, 3 June 1999). At this time, Václav Klaus also once again stressed the concept of European integration as a clash of identities, contrasting the 'natural entities of human societies with which a person identifies' with the 'vacuous Europeanism' upon which a 'certain organization' was being constructed (*Lidové noviny*, 3 June 1999), and arguing that these conflicts were becoming more acute as the Czech Republic's accession to the European Union became a more concrete prospect.

However, while Klaus's comments essentially represented change of emphasis and a clarification of his well-known objections to political integration, the 'euro-realist' position set out by Jan Zahradil and his team, was more radical and specific, combining a critique of European integration with proposals to reform the EU and modify Czech accession strategy (*Mladá fronta Dnes*, 2 June 1999; *Hospodářské noviny*, 10 June 1999).

Czech 'eurorealism'

Václav Klaus first used the term 'eurorealism' in mid-1994 (*Respekt*, 23 May 1994, 10) reviving it in June 1999 when he took up the issues of European integration and national interests more intensively (Klaus 2000a: 144–6). However, ODS's new 'eurorealism' was most fully developed in the *Manifesto of*

Czech Eurorealism presented by Zahradil and his team to the third ODS Ideological Conference in April 2001. The *Manifesto*, which was the fullest and most sceptical assessment of European integration produced by any mainstream political party in Central Europe after 1989, was to shape ODS policy until 2006. In many ways, the *Manifesto* echoed and amplified Klaus's criticisms of the EU as a product of postwar corporatism and vested interests manipulated by West European states seeking to restore their lost great power status.[3] Its vision of integration, like Klaus's, was of inter-governmental co-operation between sovereign states, extending mainly to economic co-operation, with limited political co-ordination.[4] Like Klaus (2002c), the *Manifesto* argued that current trends towards greater political integration in the Union should be frozen (Klaus 2002c).

However, other aspects of the *Manifesto* developed ODS thinking on the EU on more radical lines. Consistent with ODS's 'realist' foreign policy doctrine, the *Manifesto of Czech Eurorealism* depicted the EU as a 'gladiatorial arena' (*kolbiště*) of conflicting interests, opposing existing members, candidate states, national interest groups and the EU bureaucracy itself. This, it suggested, made it necessary to reassess the accession process and the prospect of EU membership. Czechs, it suggested, 'can no longer settle for a blanket interpretation of our entry to the EU as a final, symbolic end to our being part of (*pobyt v*) the former socialist empire or today's temporary state of post-communism' (Zahradil *et al.* 2001a: 3). Nor, it argued, should EU accession be regarded as a politically neutral, technical and administrative process of adapting to the *acquis communautaire*. Rather, the *Manifesto* stressed, enlargement should be viewed in terms of conflicting self-interests as

> concerned not with the acceptance of candidate countries as rapidly as possible but with using the accession process to the advantage of current members. The EU sees the candidate states above all as markets for its products, sources of beneficial opportunities (*výhodné uplatnění*) for its surplus professionals, as well as a source of raw materials and cheap and skilled local labour and a possible buffer zone against political and security risks in the East and the Balkans.
>
> (Zahradil *et al.* 2001a: 5)

Given such a zero-sum clash of interests, the *Manifesto* concluded, Czech accession required a careful political appraisal of the conditions and costs and benefits of entry and the taking of a clear position both on accession and on the future shape of the Union, reflecting and maximizing the Czech national interest.[5] This new ODS approach to EU accession was bluntly summed up by the party's Defence spokesman Petr Nečas in a speech to its 2001 Ideological Conference in which he urged Czechs to

> gain everything possible from the EU ... let us not give it a fraction more than we have to. Let us say fairly, openly and loudly to the Czech public

that for us entering the European Union is not, and will not be, a love match, but a marriage of convenience.

(Nečas 2002)

The 'realist' stress on interest maximization led the *Manifesto*'s authors to a further significant conclusion: that the Czech Republic and other candidate states were committing a 'strategic error' in giving priority to the rapidity of EU accession, at the expense of the quality of the terms of entry (Zahradil *et al.* 2001a: 6–7).

Alternatives to EU accession?

This view of accession, and the *Manifesto*'s 'realist' view of the enlargement process as based largely upon national states and other actors pursuing conflicting self-interests, led its authors to conclude that the EU side lacked a strong interest in enlargement. This logically implied either a significant delay in enlargement or the offering of a diluted 'second-class membership' (*České slovo*, 14 November 2000. This in turn necessitated the exploration of alternative scenarios to (rapid) Czech EU accession. The *Manifesto* envisaged three such scenarios: (1) a delay in Czech accession initiated by the EU because of the Czech Republic's robust defence of its national interests; (2) a Czech decision to review EU membership if it 'was unfavourable from the point of view of foreign policy or national interests'; and (3) a rejection of EU membership by the Czech public in a referendum. The *Manifesto* specified several instances in which 'unsatisfactory' membership in the EU might prompt a Czech review of accession to (or membership of) the EU. These included the consistent marginalization of the Czech Republic within the decision-making processes of an enlarged EU; a growth in anti-Americanism and the scaling back of transatlantic links resulting from the Common Foreign and Security Policy; or a 'revision of the results of the Second World War' through an EU-enforced cancellation of the postwar Beneš Decrees expelling ethnic Germans from Czechoslovakia.

The *Manifesto* concluded by exploring a number of alternative strategies for what Jan Zahradil termed elsewhere 'the theoretical possibility of not joining the EU' (Zahradil 2001, response to question 6). These included (1) the Czech Republic's participation in the European Single Market without adopting the full legislative and administrative burden of the *acquis*, either through membership of EFTA and the European Economic Area as in the case of Norway, or through bilateral treaties with the EU on the Swiss model; and (2) the development of closer economic and political links with Great Britain, Scandinavia and the USA in a 'broad Euro-Atlantic space linked in security, economic and political terms, rather than a Fortress Europe ranged against the USA' (Zahradil *et al.* 2001a: 12–13).

Germany, Europe and the defence of the nation

ODS's ideological shift from a modernizing discourse of breaking with a provincial national past to a form of national liberalism drawing heavily on historical nationalist paradigms juxtaposing Czech and German interests and values (see Chapter 7) is also evident in its view of European integration. Thus, for example, although on one occasion Václav Klaus quoted remarks by Tomáš Masaryk, Czechoslovakia's revered first President, on the need for a diverse Europe in which small states are not dominated by larger, centralizing powers (Klaus 1997b: 124), Klaus initially based the bulk of his critique of the EU on a neo-liberal euroscepticism inspired by British and American thinkers. After 1997, however, both Klaus's and ODS's views of European integration began to incorporate traditional Czech nationalist paradigms. This is most clearly illustrated by their growing tendency to view European integration in terms of a clash of German and non-German interests. A veiled anti-German undercurrent can be detected in many ODS statements on European integration throughout the 1990s.

Nevertheless, ODS when in government between 1992 and 1997 had sought to neutralize the emotive and divisive potential of the Czech–German relationship. Bilateral negotiations between the Czech and German governments thus led to the signature in 1997 of a 'Czech–German Declaration', which agreed a compromise formula, addressing the issue of the postwar 'transfer' of Czechoslovakia's ethnic German population (Stroehlein 1998). From 1999, however, the 'realist', international relations-based concept of 'national interests' was reshaped into a more traditional Czech nationalist paradigm, explicitly defining the Czech nation and its interests in opposition to those of Germany and the German-speaking world. First, ODS leaders such as Klaus and Zahradil explicitly linked existing trends in European integration with a (supposed) preponderance of German interests in the EU, referring to 'German' visions of a federal Europe or to a 'dominant German conception of the EU' (*Večerník Praha*, 7 July 2000; *Respekt*, 19 February 2001). The *Manifesto of Czech Eurorealism* took this a step further by attempting to align ODS's preferred neo-liberal model of European integration with the Czech national tradition, claiming that liberal-nationalist thinkers of the nineteenth century such as Havlíček, Palacký and Masaryk were 'strikingly close to Anglo-Saxon liberal-conservative thought' (Zahradil *et al.* 2001a: 8). This claim was intended to legitimize ODS's preferred neo-liberal model of integration by grounding it in the Czech political tradition, and to delegitimize euro-federalist models by associating them with what Czech thinkers including Masaryk had traditionally seen as its antithesis: authoritarian, centralizing German designs for hegemony in Central Europe (Zahradil *et al.* 2001b). This implied the sceptical view that despite the postwar changes in the Federal Republic 'today's big "Europeanization" on Germany's part is nothing more than part of a long-term German policy strategy. It is not part of some civic European policy, but a clear national policy' (Klaus 2001b: 136).

Second, the *Manifesto* took up the defence of the Beneš Decrees as a Czech national interest explicitly linked to Czech EU accession which could give cause to contemplate Czech withdrawal from the accession process or the Union. ODS's June 2002 election programme also paid considerable attention to the defence of the Decrees, challenges to which it depicted as 'property and perhaps also territorial claims against the victims of past Nazi aggression' which could 'call Czech statehood into question' (ODS 2002a: 14–15). During the course of the 2002 election campaign, this position was radicalized by Václav Klaus in a demand that the retention of the Decrees be legally guaranteed as part of Czech EU accession (*Právo*, 26 May 2002; *Hospodářské noviny*, 28 May 2002). Such shifts in the party's position on 'national interests' were accompanied by radicalization of its political rhetoric in relation to both domestic rivals and foreign countries.

The rise of the europhile centre-right

From the late 1990s ODS's strident and detailed eurosceptic critiques provoked responses from both the opposition Social Democrats and its own centre-right liberal and Christian Democratic coalition partners (*Respekt*, 30 October 1995, 3). Despite their very different historical experience after 1945, the Czech KDU-ČSL drew on the same Catholic traditions as sister parties in Germany and Austria with which they had close ties and it adopted europhile positions with little debate as part of the mainstream Christian Democratic identity. ODA engaged relatively little with European integration until late 1995 when it started to criticize Klaus's pronouncements on the EU as unrealistic, premature and counterproductive given the Czech Republic's status as a small candidate state with little political leverage (*Respekt*, 30 October 1995). These europhile centre-right positions were developed when ODA and KDU-ČSL were allied in the Quad-Coalition (4K) in 1999–2002. The Coalition favoured the most rapid possible accession by the Czech Republic to the EU, and, like the Social Democrats, was strongly supportive of almost all EU integration processes,[6] advocating the gradual development of a federal political structure for the EU with a transformed European Commission acting as a European government accountable to the European Parliament. It argued that rapid accession was a vital Czech national interest, because of the economic and political benefits that EU membership would bring and because the balance of EU opinion was shifting against enlargement (Koalice 2002). However, the Quad-Coalition stressed that EU membership was not simply dictated by economic and geopolitical constraints but was a positive choice that Czechs had made, which would reinforce and accelerate post-communist reform (Čtyřkoalice 2001).[7]

The convergence of diverse small centre-right groupings around a common europhile position reflected a range of ideological and strategic considerations. For the Christian Democrats, it stemmed from the well-established sympathy of West European Christian Democratic parties for supra-national co-operation and the European social model, which fitted well with Catholic principles (Marks and Wilson 2000). For the Freedom Union, its europhile stance was a part of its wider political break with ODS and its attempts to think through obstructions to liberal economic and political reform. Neo-conservatives in the declining Civic Democratic Alliance (ODA) justified their support for European integration in conservative terms based on ideas of civilizational conflict, a declining Europe and the dangers of democracy in a small nation with weak right-wing traditions such as the Czech Republic (Kroupa 2003).[8]

ODS and the accession referendum: 'Yes, but ...'

The Czech right's divisions and ambiguities over Europe were amply illustrated during the Czech EU accession referendum campaign in 2003 Although all parties other than the Communists supported accession, unlike in other acceding states, the referendum generated little cross-party co-operation (Hanley 2004a). The Civic Democrats' referendum 'campaign' was officially launched by Miroslav Topolánek in a keynote speech in mid-February 2003, concluding with the party's fourth ideological conference in May, which was entirely devoted to the EU. Topolánek suggested that the arguments in favour of accession only narrowly outweighed those against (CEVRO 2003) and that, although he expected ODS supporters to vote 'Yes', accession could not be regarded as an issue above party politics because ODS endorsed EU membership for reasons different from those of the Social Democrats (*Lidové noviny*, 9 June 2003). The ODS accession referendum 'campaign' was largely confined to internal party discussion and criticism of political opponents. It undertook virtually no organized national or regional campaigning directed at voters in connection with the referendum.[9] ODS also failed to make any formal appeal to party supporters to vote 'Yes' until two hours before polling was due to begin on 13 June, when Jan Zahradil issued a press release urging them to do so on the grounds that the Czech Republic would be better able to defend its national interests from within the Union (*Lidové noviny*, 14 June 2003).[10] Moreover, ODS claimed, the pro-accession campaigners were missing the point that the *form* of the EU mattered far more than mere accession to it. The growing trend towards the EU becoming 'a centralized European superstate' dominated by larger nations, the party argued, urgently required the formulation of a 'Czech policy' to assert and defend national interests, rather than a bombastic official 'Yes' campaign (ODS 2003c). A number of ODS figures, including two of its 'Shadow Ministers', Ivan Langer and Martin Říman, and Miloslav Bednář, a co-author of the *Manifesto of Czech Eurorealism*, publicly opposed accession, a divergence from the party's policy that its new leader seemed to accept with equanimity (*Respekt*, 19 March 2003, 4).

In his first weeks in office, President Klaus showed a similar ambiguity to EU accession, insisting on his right as head of state to be one of the three Czech co-signatories of the Athens Treaty of Accession in April 2003, but telling *Die Zeit* that Czech accession was 'a marriage of convenience, not a love match' and expressing scepticism about the feasibility of a European foreign policy (*RFE/RL Newsline* Part II, 11 April 2003). In an eve-of-poll newspaper interview, he repeated his doubts over the viability of both democracy above the level of the nation-state and the Eurozone, criticized Czech intellectuals who, he claimed, saw EU membership as a panacea for all social and political ills and expressed regret that Czechs had not been able to enjoy the national independence regained in 1989 for longer (*Lidové noviny*, 11 June 2003). More significantly, Klaus declined to publicly advocate a 'Yes' vote – or to say how he would be voting in the referendum – and confined himself to an appeal to citizens to turn out to vote.[11] As such he was the only head of state in the nine new EU states holding referendums on accession in 2003 not to call for a 'Yes' vote. Ultimately, however, the cultural predisposition of most Czech voters to see themselves as part of (Western) Europe; the widespread perception of EU membership as the next step on the path of post-communist modernization; and the fact that Czech politicians' disagreements centred *on* accession, but were not *about* accession, ensured that, as elsewhere in Central and Eastern Europe, the 'Yes' camp in the Czech Republic scored a convincing victory in line with long-term trends in public opinion. In the referendum 77 per cent of voters supported accession (Hanley 2004a). Exit polling confirmed that despite their party's 'eurorealism', ODS's better educated, more urban supporters – like those of the liberal Freedom Union – voted overwhelmingly for accession and did so by a greater proportion than supporters of the governing Social Democrats and Christian Democrats (Hanley 2004).[12]

Post-accession euroscepticism

The EU Constitutional Treaty and the Czech right

Like many political actors across Central and Eastern Europe, the Civic Democrats saw accession as bringing an important change of national status from 'undignified, passive recipient' of integration (ODS 2004a: 1) to a full participant with influence over the future direction of the Union. An early focus of the Czech right wing on post-accession issues was the European Constitutional Treaty. The Treaty, initially drafted in 2002–3 by the Convention on the Future of Europe and approved in modified form by EU heads of government on 18 June 2004,[13] was intended to consolidate and modernize the institutional structure of the EU, both improving decision-making and adding democratic legitimacy. For ODS, however, as for many other eurosceptics, it represented an unacceptable step towards federalization and centralization. Even during the 2003 accession referendum campaign, the party was already demanding the holding of a second referendum on any proposed EU Constitution (*RFE/RL Newsline*, 11 May 2003). On 30 May 2003, Jan Zahradil, one of the three Czech delegates to the European Convention, joined five other eurosceptic delegates, including a representative of the British Tories, in producing a dissenting Minority Report calling for a 'Europe of Democracies', an 'association of free and self-governing European states and an open economic area ... organized on an interparliamentary basis ... open to any democratic European state' (European Convention CONV 773/03, CONTRIB 347). On 12 June 2003 Zahradil walked out of the Convention in protest against the 'unacceptably federalist' character of the draft Constitutional Treaty being finalized. ODS also unsurprisingly rejected the modified text agreed at the EU Intergovernmental Conference in June 2004 (*Právo*, 23 August 2004). In January 2005 ODS MEPs joined the Czech Communists and the two Czech independents in voting against the Constitutional Treaty when it was presented to the European Parliament for symbolic ratification.[14]

Although most EU states, both new and established, chose to ratify the Treaty by parliamentary vote, the Czech Republic's Social-Democrat-led coalition government announced that it would, as demanded by ODS, seek to ratify the Treaty by referendum in 2006.[15] As early as December 2004 the Civic Democrats therefore prepared campaign materials outlining arguments against the Constitutional Treaty (ODS 2004b). These spanned both the fairness of the European constitution-making process[16] and the substance of the Treaty itself which, ODS claimed, reduced the national sovereignty of all member states,[17] but put smaller member states at a special disadvantage by decreasing their voting weight in the European Council. In tandem, the party argued, such measures would increase the influence of large states such as Germany at the expense of small states such as the Czech Republic (ODS 2004a). In granting the EU features of statehood such as legal personality, a President, flag and anthem, ODS argued in common with other eurosceptics, the Constitution was paving the way for its ultimate transformation into a federal superstate. These views were shared by President Klaus who, taking a more historical perspective, argued that supranational European structures had always resulted in centralization leading to a lack of freedom, ethnic oppression and the dominance of large powers. Universalistic principles used to justify such structures as an alternative to nationalism and the national state, he claimed, served merely to mask the vested interests of elites and larger nations (*Lidové noviny*, 14 February 2004).[18] A distant 'federal government' in Brussels, he contended, would leave Czechs with virtually no influence and accelerate pressures for still further harmonization and unification. Klaus therefore refused to sign the Treaty on behalf of the Czech Republic in Athens in October 2004, delegating his powers of signature to Prime Minister Gross.

ODS's 'pause for reflection'

The rejection of the EU Constitutional Treaty in referendums in France and Holland on 29 May and 1 June 2005 changed the political climate in Europe, effectively stalling the ratification process and inaugurating an official 'pause for reflection' on the Union's future institutional architecture. In the Czech Republic, the Social-Democrat-led government quickly postponed plans for a referendum (*Prague Post*, 27 July 2005) as it became clear that in the aftermath of the French and Dutch referendum votes there had been a marked decrease in Czech public support for the Constitution, breaking a pattern of public support for further integration paralleling levels of support for EU membership itself. Polls from June and July 2005 suggested that Czech public opinion had reversed from clear support for the Constitution to narrow opposition.[19] Polling also recorded a marked drop in support for the Constitution among ODS voters from 73 per cent in February 2005 to 43 per cent in July 2005 with a corresponding growth in opposition from 27 per cent to 53 per cent (STEM cited in Úřad vlády 2006: 14), suggesting that, for the first time, the views of Civic Democrat voters had moved into line with its 'eurorealism'. However, Eurobarometer polling in late 2005 suggested a more complex picture, finding that a majority of Czechs agreed that a Constitution would make the EU more efficient, transparent and democratic, but favoured the negotiation of a new document. In addition, stable majorities continued to support the trend towards the European political union, expressing a willingness to transfer further powers to the EU level in fields such as security, foreign policy or environmental protection, while retaining taxation and welfare policy at national level (European Commission 2006: 36–43).

The 'pause for reflection', nevertheless, created a sense of possibility among Czech eurosceptics. Václav Klaus responded by calling for a full-scale reappraisal of the direction of European integration in the previous half century and the re-establishment of the EU in a wholly new form, the Organization of European States (OES). Despite the vagueness of his arguments,[20] this marked a further radicalization of Klaus's position. As the Czech President himself accepted, he was thinking no longer of merely freezing existing levels of EU political integration but of reversing it through 'the abolition all kinds of things that have emerged (*zrušensí lecčeho, co vzniklo*) in the last twenty years' (*Lidové noviny*, 18 June 2005).[21] On the domestic stage, Klaus adopted a Masarykian turn of phrase by speaking of 'our current European crisis' (*Newsletter CEP*, October 2005, 8; see also Klaus 2005c) and calling for a new national debate to agree a common Czech position on the future of the EU. However, his invitation to Czech politicians of all parties to meet under the auspices of the Presidency to formulate such a policy met with little enthusiasm, as it both bypassed existing contacts between party leaders on European issues[22] and, given the President's own well-developed and contentious views, lacked credibility.

ODS and 'flexible integration'

Official ODS thinking on the future of the EU after 2004, influenced by Jan Zahradil, evolved in a different direction, moving from radical counter-visions of a Union transformed into a 'Europe of Democracies' to the seemingly more mainstream concept of 'flexible integration'. Even before the French and Dutch referendum votes, ODS had officially abandoned the view that the EU was becoming a federal superstate, arguing instead that talk of 'federalization' merely served to disguise a 'renationalization' of EU policies by large states (ODS 2004a: 2). The party's critique of the EU moved from a near exclusive focus on national interests to arguments about European responses to economic globalization and structural limits on further integration in an enlarged EU. Unlike Václav Klaus, who tended to see international markets as a constant, Zahradil accepted that economic globalization was an important challenge. However, he saw EU *responses* to globalization – and the conflicting interests of

EU member states that determined it – as more problematic than globalization itself to which he felt small states were especially well placed to respond. As well as allowing democratic accountability and recognizing the reality of national identities, the national state, argued Zahradil was also a 'useful tool' for success in a globalized world for small states with open economies, because it allowed them to react quickly and flexibly to a complex, rapidly changing environment (Zahradil 2004: 4–5).[23] Zahradil also rejected the argument that small Central European states gained in geo-political terms from membership in a politically integrated EU. The EU's very influence in global politics, which made membership attractive to small states, he argued, was being gradually undermined by enlargement, which was making the Union unwieldy and unable to function effectively as an international actor (Zahradil 2004). Instead, he suggested, the EU's Common Foreign and Security Policy (CFSP) highlighted the limits of 'sustainable integration' (Zahradil 2005b: 3).

EU decision-makers, claimed Zahradil (2005b), overlooked the potential of flexible forms of integration based on the principle of choice, rather than a uniform fixed *acquis*. Accepting varying levels of national commitment to integration through opt-outs was, he argued, a precondition to effective decision-making and in the longer term could even *increase* the overall momentum of integration. The ultra-flexible *à la carte* Europe he favoured would not aim to produce a common form of integration nor would it have a core membership or core *acquis* (Zahradil 2005a). Instead it would represent a 'context of complex interdependence, rather than the creation of a closed regional power bloc' better able to meet the challenges of the dynamically changing twenty-first century world (Zahradil 2005b: 7; see also ODS 2004a).

EU enlargement and the Czech right

Most political Czech parties took a broadly positive attitude towards further enlargement of the EU (Hanley 2002; Král 2005). Consistent with their visions of a decentralized, flexible EU of markets and nation-states, the Civic Democrats favoured wide ranging enlargement going far beyond current EU policies. In an interview with *Frankfurter Allgemeine Zeitung* (15 March 2005), Václav Klaus, for example, spoke of enlarging the EU to include Turkey, Ukraine, Morocco and even Kazakhstan. Although partly intended as a strategy for blocking further political integration, these views also reflected more complex understandings of the relationship of European identity in the EU and the place of Europe in the wider world, understandings which sharply divided the Czech centre-right. The question of Turkey's application for EU membership, and the broader debate about the West's relationship with the Islamic and Arab world, threw such division into particularly sharp relief. Czech Christian Democrats, neo-conservatives and conservative liberals largely rejected Turkish claims for EU membership on the grounds that Turkey's non-European culture and poor human rights record would dilute the EU's democratic values and identity.

As his views on multiculturalism and national identity demonstrate (see

Chapter 7), Václav Klaus was far from rejecting the political importance of culture and identify. However, just as he viewed Europe as a diverse patchwork of more or less homogeneous national units (*Lidové noviny*, 17 May 2005), he also saw civilizations and cultures as self-contained entities capable of institutionalized co-operation for mutual benefit. In contrast to Czech Christian Democrats and europhile liberals, Klaus and other ODS 'eurorealists' viewed European identity as weak – and to some extent artificial – and considered conflicting national interests *within* Europe more significant than civilizational divides.[24] The EU, Klaus argued, was not an expression of European culture or identity but merely a 'temporary institutional structure created by people', like other international organizations (Klaus 2005b).

The strongly Atlanticist inclinations of the Civic Democrats led the party to endorse US and British views that the end of the Cold War had created new security threats such as rogue states, organized crime, ethno-religious extremism and international terrorism (ODS 2004a: 5). ODS endorsed US-led intervention in Iraq (Nečas 2003) and supported the *co-ordination* of national security and asylum policies within the EU (although not the further development of common European Justice and Home Affairs policies or EU law enforcement agencies) (Král and Pachta 2005). Václav Klaus, however, developed a different view on security issues, taking his party's stress on national, not civilizational divisions to its logical end. Klaus's rejection of any notion of a *clash* of civilizations in international politics led him to a refusal to identify Al-Qaeda-inspired terrorism with Islam or to perceive Islamist terrorism as a global threat to Western civilization (*Mladá fronta Dnes*, 25 February 2006; see also Klaus 2006b).[25] The absence of powerful external civilizational threats in turn nullified the geo-strategy rationale for a politically integrated EU with common defence and security policies, refocusing attention on conflicting national interests central to ODS's understandings of integration.[26] A similar logic led Klaus to a highly critical view of US-led intervention in Iraq, which departed from the official position of his party.[27]

'*A Blue Chance for Europe*': the right's post-accession strategy

Although rejection of the European Constitution in the French and Dutch referendums denied ODS a domestic battle over European integration, in 2004 the party proceeded to present a detailed post-accession strategy as part of the Blue Chance programme. The strategy, largely drawn up by Zahradil, linked the 'realist' pursuit of Czech national interests with broader projects to reform the EU. The Blue Chance paper on integration argued that EU membership would not in itself deliver economic prosperity, noting that many established EU member states were suffering from economic stagnation. It therefore concluded that the Czech Republic should seek space to develop a competitive domestic economy by pursuing independent national policies such as the flat tax and welfare reforms outlined elsewhere in the Blue Chance programme and should avoid the 'hard core' of integrationalist states which, in ODS's view, were merely using integration as a means of avoiding domestic structural reform and resisting competition by forcing the harmonization of fiscal, tax and social policy on new member states.[28]

In practice, the strategy described above amounted to a stress on building coalitions with like-minded countries and parties within the European Parliament. The Blue Chance programme identified the UK, Ireland, Scandinavia, the Baltic states and Portugal as natural allies in such a 'reform current' (Zahradil 2004: 9–10, 14). Consistent with earlier ODS positions, Germany – still viewed as wishing to 'export' its own federal political system to Europe – was presented as the main obstacle to reform. Indeed, Zahradil (2005a) suggested, the political deadlock in Germany resulting from the 2005 election offered eurosceptics a political opportunity to assert alternative visions of integration. Although ODS stressed its identity as a 'standard' West European party, its euroscepticism left it isolated on the wider European centre-right where the British Conservatives were its only significant allies on European issues. For this reason, like the British Tories, ODS had remained outside the formal structures of the Christian-Democrat-led European People's Party (EPP) preferring to join the European Democratic Union (EDU), of which it became a full member in October 1992.

However, the effective absorption of the EDU into the European People's Party in 2002 and ODS's entry into the European Parliament in 2004 posed dilemmas. Given its hostility to the pro-integration stances of the EPP's Christian Democratic founder parties, ODS considered joining the newly formed Alliance for a Europe of Nations (AEN) group in the European Parliament, which united a range of parties committed to the defence of national sovereignty including the Gaullist RPF of Charles Pasqua, Italy's post-fascist National Alliance (AN) and Ireland's Fianna Fáil.[29] However, the illiberal, etatistic leanings of many members of the Alliance for a Europe of Nations persuaded ODS leaders that it would be best to follow the British Conservatives in joining the European People's Party faction as part of the European Democrats sub-grouping, whose members retained a statutory right to express 'distinct views on constitutional and institutional issues in relation to the future of Europe'.[30] ODS's admittance to the EPP-ED group, negotiated with leading West European Christian Democrats in Budapest in 2004, was, however, also made conditional on the party moderating its views on the EU Constitutional Treaty and Czech–German relationship (Sokol 2006).[31]

ODS was, however, active in efforts to develop new anti-federalist 'eurorealist' groupings on the European centre-right, which could draw in larger right-wing parties from Central and Eastern Europe. To this end, Civic Democrat representatives attended four regional conferences bringing together key centre-right formations, which included the Civic Platform (PO) and Law and Justice (PiS) parties from Poland, Hungary's Fidesz and Bulgaria's Union of Democratic Forces. At the last such conference in Prague in 2002, the Civic Democrats were instrumental in drafting a common declaration arguing for an East European centre-right view on European integration stressing the importance of the national state, the individual and the free market, which reproduced passages from the *Manifesto of Czech Eurorealism* almost verbatim (Sokol 2006: 87–9). In the event, the diverse groupings had little interest in sustained regional co-operation or a common 'eurorealist' agenda and the meetings were discontinued.[32] A more focused initiative in July 2003 saw ODS, the British Tories and Poland's Law and Justice (PiS) party issue the 'Prague Appeal' rejecting the draft European Constitution as a step towards a 'centralised and federal European superstate, which serves the interests of bureaucrats and politicians, rather than those of the people' ('Pražská výzva' 2006: 91). However, the appeal had little wider impact and was endorsed by only one other party, the small extra-parliamentary Civic Conservative Party (OKS) of Slovakia.[33]

2006: scepticism about euroscepticism

Under Miroslav Topolánek, ODS strategy increasingly focused on domestic reform, downplaying its views on the EU after private polling had showed the party's 'eurorealism' was off-putting to some potential right-wing voters (ČTK press release, 19 April 2004). After the 2006 elections Topolánek's pragmatic approach to European issues brought him into increasing conflict with Zahradil, who was passed over for the post of Foreign Minister in the short-lived minority ODS government of September–October 2006, in favour of the diplomat and former adviser to President Havel Alexandr Vondra. Vondra argued explicitly for a new middle way in Czech European policy steering between over assertive 'eurorealism' and unfocused enthusiasm for European integration (*Lidové noviny*, 10 July 2006). Topolánek was also unenthusiastic about Zahradil's strategy of building an anti-federalist coalition and effectively ruled out ODS participation in the revived notion of an anti-federalist grouping in the European Parliament mooted by British Conservatives after the election of David Cameron as Tory leader in 2005.[34] For Topolánek and his team Zahradil's high-profile euroscepticism was increasingly seen as a distraction from priority issues of domestic reform and an unnecessary complication in relations with the party's preferred coalition partners, the pro-European Greens and Christian Democrats, and the Social Democrats whose 'tolerance' was needed to make any centre-right minority government viable (*Lidové noviny*, 8 June 2006).

Explaining the euroscepticism of the Czech right

Both the official positions of ODS of the early to mid-1990s and the more strident eurosceptic views expressed by Václav Klaus remained squarely within the limits of what Taggart and Szczerbiak (2002: 7) term a ' "soft" euroscepticism' – qualified opposition to the EU based on hostility to certain policies and a negative assessment of the overall costs and benefits of joining. This contrasted with the 'hard' eurosceptic position characteristic of radical forces on left and right such as the Czech Communists and Republicans based on ideological opposition to EU membership *per se* (or demands which amount a de facto rejection of membership). At no time did Klaus or other ODS leaders call into question, even in hypothetical terms, the necessity or desirability of Czech membership of the EU. Nor was it directly suggested that any of the Union's fundamental institutions or any aspects of the *acquis*, even those of which he was critical (such as the Euro), should be reformed or rejected. ODS's position clearly 'hardened' from 1999 when, for the first time, the party suggested that *in certain circumstances* non-membership of the EU would be preferable to accession.[35] It briefly moved still further in the direction of 'hard' euroscepticism when in 2001–2 it made its support for EU entry conditional on the guaranteeing of the Beneš Decrees, a demand impossible or unlikely to be met. [36] However, despite this pre-election gesture the party's position still essentially remained within the 'soft' eurosceptic category as it did not reject EU membership outright.

However, a simple static dichotomy between 'soft' and 'hard' euroscepticism defined by attitudes to membership arguably fails to capture either the complexity of evolving party positions on Europe, or the multi-faceted and changing nature of integration and enlargement. Other writers stress that euroscepticism, whatever its overall 'hardness' or 'softness', must be seen in terms of opposition to *specific policies* within a multi-faceted and often contradictory EU project encompassing liberalization *and* regulation, selective political integration and enlargement (Hooghe and Marks 1999; Hooghe *et al.* 2002). Party positions, they suggest, are rooted in and given coherence by competing ideologically derived models of European political economy, which respond to a kaleidoscopic, constantly evolving European project.[37] Liberal-conservative parties such as the British Tories under Margaret Thatcher, for example, moved from enthusiastic support for European integration to euroscepticism as the nature of European integration changed. When integration was mainly a liberalizing project centring on the creation of a single European market, they embraced it. However, as the EU followed the implications of market integration by establishing European regulatory structures and developing common policy frameworks for social policy, foreign policy, and justice and home affairs, liberal-conservative parties opposed it as an assault on the national state. ODS's early trajectory on the question of European integration seems to fit this model well. Václav Klaus's speeches and writings repeatedly highlight that, for him, as for liberal-conservative leaders in Europe, the signing of the Maastricht Treaty in 1992 represented the turning point at which European integration turned away from its original liberalizing mission and took on an unacceptable federalist course. The role of party family identity is further confirmed by the obvious transfer of ideas on Europe from an Anglo-American context to ODS.[38]

Strategy, ideology and interests

Parties' positions on European integration are, however, more than a function of a fixed ideology. They also reflect competitive pressures, the incentives of opposition or government status and the need to represent and accommodate the interests of social and electoral constituencies.[39] In one of the more sophisticated treatment of these issues, Sitter and Batory (2004) explain varying stances on integration through a 'three-stage model'.[40] In the first instance, they argue, parties may have a cleavage-based predisposition towards euroscepticism, reflecting the preferences of a party electorate or, in cases where the historical cleavages defining the party are residual, a party's identity, values and ideology. This basic stance, argue Sitter and Batory, is subsequently modified by a party's medium- to long-term strategic orientation, which reflects its competitive position within a given party system.[41] Finally, short-term tactical considerations, usually reflecting the imperatives of coalition formation, may further modify a party's stance on specific issues. This three-stage model works well for a party family with a well-defined core constituency and historical identity such as Scandinavian and Eastern European farmers' parties, which are minor actors operating in a strategic context largely determined by bigger parties. It can also be extended with relatively little difficulty to large de-ideologized West European catch-all formations which have emerged from historic parties and movements with clear social and ideological roots such as Social Democracy or Christian Democracy (Sitter 2001b).

Some classic, structural-historical divisions, such as centre–periphery, rural–urban and religious–secular cleavages, have persisted in post-communist Central and Eastern Europe, often sustaining small historic or interest-based parties with well defined subcultures (Werning 1996; Enyedi 1996; Szczerbiak 2001; Sitter and Batory 2004) for whom the three-stages model works well. However, for a broad catch-all party of the right, formed to meet the exigencies of post-communist transformation such as the Civic Democrats, the 'stages' model works less well.

Euroscepticism in post-communist Europe has often been linked to divisions between 'winners' and 'losers' in socio-economic transformation. This division also tends to overlap with socio-cultural divisions between younger, better-educated, more metropolitan voters and more traditional rural or provincial communities. While transition 'winners' tend to be Europhile given that European integration reinforces the market and liberal institutions and values from which they benefit, 'losers' are more eurosceptic, given their perceived disempowerment by such institutions and values (Henderson 2001; Ágh 1998; Mudde 2005). While the strong euroscepticism of parties of the far left and far right – in the both the Czech Republic and East and Central Europe more generally – corresponds to their electorates of elderly, unskilled, rural and economically deprived transition 'losers' (Kreidl and Vlachová 1999; Gzymala-Busse 2002) this is clearly *not* the case with ODS and its relatively young, wealthy, educated urban electorate.

In Central and East European states such as Poland and Hungary centre-right parties' scepticism towards European integration can be related to long-standing socio-cultural and historical cleavages dividing Westernizing liberals from national-populist conservatives discussed in Chapter 1. Again, this is not the case in the Czech Republic. Despite the more nationalistic and conservative positions explored by some in ODS after 1997, the Czech party system has been overwhelmingly defined by a single axis of left–right competition over the extent to which resources should be allocated by the market or the state (Kitschelt *et al.* 1999; Vlachová 1999). Opinion polls have, moreover, consistently showed that, in so far as Czech voters' views on EU membership coincided with a left–right division, it was supporters of the *right*, including the overwhelming majority of ODS supporters, who strongly favoured EU accession (Mišovič 2000; Česal 2000; Hartl 2000).

Euroscepticism as political strategy

The hardening of ODS euroscepticism after 1997 does, however, confirm expectations that opposition parties will be less constrained in their opposition to European integration than incumbents. Nevertheless, when considered more closely, the Civic Democrats' position, which took the party to the verge of rejecting EU membership, lacked strategic rationale. It served to divide the party from potential coalition partners on both the centre/centre-right and the centre-left and failed to match the preferences of its electorate on European integration.[42] In comparative perspective, the party's euroscepticism is surprising given its position in the Czech party system. Comparative surveys of party euroscepticism suggest that broad, programmatically based, catch-all parties of centre-left and centre-right, which are (or are likely to be) actors in governing coalitions, tend not to be strongly eurosceptic or to adopt only milder forms of euroscepticism when faced with competitive pressures to do so (Taggart 1998; Taggart and Szczerbiak 2002; Sitter 2001b). Where 'harder' euroscepticism is found within such parties, it tends to be confined to factions of limited influence. ODS, like the British Conservatives (Baker, Gamble and Seawright 2002), therefore appears an anomalous case both in the (increasing) 'hardness' of its euroscepticism and in the fact that euroscepticism was part of the party mainstream. While there are clear historical factors, such as the role of Empire, marking out British conservatism and the British party system as a special case (Baker *et al.* 2002), there are no such distinguishing features explaining the stance of the Czech Republic's post-1989 centre-right. Taken together, this suggests that ODS euroscepticism has been an ideologically driven product of party elites largely disconnected from underlying social divisions and has reacted mainly to the unfolding dynamics of integration and enlargement. This finding is consistent with the elite-defined nature of Czech right-wing politics, the low salience of integration issues for Czech votes and the relative weakness – or disengagement – of civil society in shaping Central European states' preferences on integration issues (Haughton and Malová 2006).

Politics of transformation and integration

Relationships between euroscepticism, party strategy and ideology were arguably more complex in post-communist Central European accession states than in established EU states in Western Europe, where stable parties with well-defined, if eroding, historical constituencies and ideologies can be assumed to be central to party systems. This assumption is made by both 'ideological' and 'strategic' analysts of party-based euroscepticism. Far from being de-ideologized teams of office seekers on the pattern of West European catch-all parties – or even technocratic post-communist social democrats (Grzymala-Busse 2002) – centre-right parties in East Central Europe, such as ODS, were often highly ideologized not to say ideologically militant (see Chapter 7). Most, like ODS, were the successors of opposition movements, whose rhetoric and identity were defined by the experience of regime change and the intense and polarized politics that followed when fundamental issues such as regime type, political identity or the direction of post-communist transformation were contested. As relatively new parties formed in the absence of civil society or conventional interest groups, all such centre-right formations faced problems of problems of stabilization and institutionalization stemming from their weak social implantation, limited organization and dependence on open electorates (see Chapters 5 and 6). ODS's use of 'harder' euroscepticism in the late 1990s can thus be viewed as a political strategy seeking to repeat the party's successful transformation mobilizations of 1992 and 1998 in a period – that of the Opposition Agreement – when it could no longer credibly present itself as the sole vehicle for successful market reform or guarantor against an irresponsible centre-left.

The internal balance of power in ODS (see Chapter 6) also shaped the party's evolving European policy. Despite his role as the dominant public face of ODS from its foundation and the passivity of the party's grassroots on matters of high policy, Václav Klaus was constrained by others figures in the leadership group such as Josef Zieleniec, who exerted countervailing pressures on Klaus on questions of European integration (*Lidové noviny*, 9 May 1994).[43] Younger politicians, such as Petr Nečas and Jan Zahradil, elected to the ODS leadership after 1997, and who had formed their views during the ideologically charged politics of mobilization lacked both the political authority and the ideological inclination to challenge Klaus on Europe. This may explain the divergence between Klaus's own markedly eurosceptic agenda and the more balanced positions of official ODS documents during the early 1990s. The growing influence within ODS of regional politicians with a direct and pragmatic appreciation of the political usefulness of EU structural programmes may now be exercising pressure for a more pragmatic European policy.[44]

Impacts of Czech right-wing euroscepticism

Viewed in wider perspective, the impact of ODS 'eurorealism' was limited. The party's misreading of the nature of the accession process and critical stance towards the EU model of integration arguably slowed the Czech Republic's initial progress and complicated the position of the 1998–2002 minority Social Democratic government in implementing the *acquis*. Under ODS influence, Czech debates on the EU became highly contested, running ahead of the accession process, as the party's 'eurorealist' critique spurred europhile competitors to formulate detailed responses. Despite its lack of enthusiasm for EU membership, ODS formed part of a wide consensus favouring Czech accession, which took place as scheduled in 2004.

ODS euroscepticism had very limited impact on Czech public opinion. Until 2005, polls suggest, the Czech public remained strongly supportive of further political integration and did not endorse unconditional defence of national sovereignty. Moreover, ODS's own voters have consistently been more supportive of integration than those on the centre-left. ODS euroscepticism also contributed to the division and disunity of the Czech centre-right, providing a political rationale for anti-ODS projects such as the Quad-Coalition and the 2002–6 coalition government. At a European level too, the party found itself relatively isolated on integration issues and, like other Central and East European eurosceptic groupings, was too small to affect the EU party political balance in any fundamental way. Its entry into the European Parliament in 2004 did, however, provide British Tories with a credible, like-minded European partner, keeping the prospect of a pro-market, mainstream anti-federalist grouping open in the longer term.

The Europeanization of ODS?

A related question is the extent to which ODS has itself been 'Europeanized' by the enlargement and integration process. The emerging literature suggests that the 'Europeanization' of parties and party systems can take several forms: the emergence of European integration as a new cleavage (re-)shaping party competition; changes in the programmes of national parties resulting from Euro-parties' influences and bilateral contacts with West European parties or the need to react to ongoing integration; the use of European integration by party politicians to legitimize their own preferences, discredit opponents or gain partisan advantage from new policies and institutions stemming from EU membership.

ODS was clearly 'Europeanized' in the weak sense in seeking to emulate Western conservative models and align itself with European party groupings and in adopting detailed and high-profile policy stances on European integration, seen as significant for domestic party political competition. It is more difficult, however, to detect Europeanization constraining or reshaping ODS's programme and preferences other than in the sense that the mere fact of the EU's existence obliged the party to support membership in a Union in which forms of integration and overall trajectory were considered less than optimal because the costs of non-membership would be too high (Vachudova 2005). The accession process did *not* lead the party to moderate its initial position or seek consensus. Indeed, on the contrary, ODS's sense that Czech accession was as a *fait accompli* led it to explore eurosceptic positions centring on *post*-accession issues. The party was, however, forced to accept limitations on expressing its views as a condition of membership in the European People's Party faction in the European Parliament. A further Europeanization mechanism that may be significant for the case of ODS is the indirect impact of regionalization reforms required to meet the EU *acquis*. As noted above, regional reform triggered important internal organizational and political changes in ODS, all of which seem to have contributed to a moderation of its position on integration after the departure of Klaus. The extent to which Czech regionalization was the product of EU leverage is, nevertheless, open to question and ODS's turn from 'eurorealism' in 2006 can equally well be attributed to the difficulties of coalition building.

Conclusions

This chapter has mapped the evolution of the Civic Democratic Party's positions on European integration, distinguishing the relatively restrained euroscepticism of 1992–7 from more elaborated post-1997 critiques, critiques which flirted with the idea of non-membership of the EU, developed the concept of 'national interest' and stressed a more traditionally nationalist view of the Czech state. It also distinguished the euroscepticism of Václav Klaus from the more moderate official position of the party before 1997. As the accession process was completed, ODS euroscepticism refocused on the European Constitution and its failure. The party initially presented sweeping demands for the wholesale reshaping of a Union it regarded as a technocratically driven superstate in the making, but later revised this view into a more concrete strategy of 'flexible integration' to promote European competitiveness, resolve the contradictions of an enlarged EU and secure the rights of smaller member states such as the Czech Republic.

The driving forces behind ODS euroscepticism seem to be the ideologically conditioned reactions of its party elite to an integration process over which they initially had no influence. The intersection of the growing domestic weakness of the Czech right and the acceleration of European enlargement and integration in the mid- to late 1990s created a context favouring a 'hardening' euroscepticism, and the renewed personal dominance of Václav Klaus and related circulation of party elites after the split of 1997–8 allowed his euroscepticism to be rapidly diffused throughout the party as official policy. In broader comparative terms, ODS's development between 1991 and 2002 suggests that for 'new' parties of the Central European centre right the relationship between ideology, identity and the imperatives of party competition may not be the straightforward trade-off between deep structures and shorter-term electoral strategies suggested in the emerging literature. For such parties, ideology (and identity formation) and party strategy appear more parallel tracks than the hierarchical 'stages' detectable in older, more institutionalized political formations.

Notes

1 Getting the right right in post-communist Europe

1 Shields (2003) offers a detailed historical reconstruction of the origins of Polish neo-liberal elites in the 1970s and 1980s. However, his application of the Transnational Capitalist Class (TCC) perspective to Poland ignores the challenge that such historical evidence poses for such approaches.

2 This echoes Enyedi's (1996) conceptualization of Hungary's Christian Democratic People's Party (KNDP) as 'sub-cultural party'.

3 Here I draw on Pete Učeň's presentation at the workshop on 'Hollow cartels or embedded institutions? The centre-right and civil society', Leiden University, 3 February 2006.

4 For example, in Romania the pro-Western Justice and Truth Alliance (DA) belongs to the 'moderate right' while its main rival the Social Democratic Party (PSD) is part of the 'communist right'; in Slovakia the Movement for a Democratic Slovakia is one of the 'independence right' parties, whereas its rivals who made up the former Slovak Democratic Coalition (SDK) are on the 'moderate right'.

5 As Kitschelt (1995) notes, such patterns of competition resemble the threefold division between socialist, liberal and Catholic blocs in party systems such as those of the Netherlands and Belgium.

6 A similar pattern seems observable in Serbia. However, here the oppressive nature of the Milošević regime and a historic split between liberals and traditional nationalists made opposition alliances more unstable and thus lacking even a loose 'right-wing' identity (Garton Ash 1999: 254–74).

7 In Scandinavia, however, Christian Democratic parties were founded on the basis of Protestant organizations and remained small niche groupings stressing moral issues, rather than the social market, with support bases limited to a rural periphery.

8 In this respect the Romania case is perhaps closer to states, such as Slovakia or Croatia, undergoing a 'second transition' (Deegan-Krause 2002; Ottaway and Malz 2001) where a modern centre-right bloc is formed as part of a broader 'democratic' opposition seeking to displace semi-authoritarian elites.

9 The small Agricultural Party (ZS), which functioned largely as a lobby group for former agricultural co-operatives, was briefly represented in the Czech parliament between 1992 and 1996, as a result of its participation in the Liberal Social Union (LSU) electoral list.

10 I assume that broad integrated parties of the right are generally more effective in electoral competition and government co-ordination than a larger number of small to medium-sized right-wing parties. As Roper (1998) suggests, there may be certain circumstances in which – or a certain threshold after which – this generalization no longer applies. For a longer discussion see Hanley *et al.* (2006).

11 In Poland, for example, the 1997–2001 coalition government between the liberal

Freedom Union (UW) and the larger, conservative-national Solidarity Election Action (AWS) bloc proved fraught and collapsed in 2000, ultimately resulting in the electoral demise of both parties (Szczerbiak 2002). Similar tensions emerged after the 2005 elections when the socially conservative Law and Justice (PiS) proved unable to agree a coalition with the liberal conservative Civic Platform (OP) grouping. Similar, although less acute, tensions emerged in Slovakia's 2002–6 centre-right coalitions between the liberal, pro-business Alliance for the New Citizen (ANO) and the Christian Democratic Movement (KDH) over proposed changes to the country's abortion law (*RFE/RL Newsline*, 25, 29 April and 20 May 2003).

12 However, as Zake (2002) suggests, in small states with open economies, globalization and Europeanization can open opportunities for new parties of the (centre) right, by creating new social constituencies with an interest in maximizing integration into the global economy.

13 The war in Iraq threw these divisions into sharp relief. Conservative nationalist formations such as FIDESZ-MPP in Hungary and the League of Polish Families (LPR) opposed US–British intervention and their own governments' support for the Anglo-American coalition (*RFE/RL Newsline*, 21, 24 March and 6 May 2003). Liberal anti-communist, centre-right groupings, by contrast, such as Bulgaria's ODS and – with the notable exception of President Klaus – the Czech Civic Democrats (ODS) firmly supported the Coalition, criticizing their governments' stances on Iraq as half-hearted.

2 Historical legacies and the Czech right

1 The third historic pathway that Kitschelt *et al.* identify is that of states in Eastern Europe, such as Bulgaria and Romania, with extremely low levels of pre-communist modernity, which led to 'patrimonial communist' regimes. Such regimes, they argue, used clientelistic networks to control weak unmobilized societies. Communist successor parties in these states in 1989 underwent only superficial reform and were able to dominate both the transition from communism and early post-communist politics through the use of nationalism and economic populism. Faced with strong ex-communist elites, centre-right groupings in these states, it is suggested, fuse pro-market stances with militant anti-communism.

2 In the bibliography of Kitschelt *et al.* (1999) approximately one-tenth of the works cited refer to *historical* patterns of development of the national cases. Most of these works are general histories published in West European languages. Kitschelt and his collaborators (1999: 26; Kitschelt 2002: 25–6) themselves concede there is a lack of empirical evidence concerning the precise extent of clientelism and patronage politics in pre-communist Central and Eastern Europe.

3 Critics of Kitschelt's (1992b) initial model objected that he had failed to consider the impact of ethnic divisions (Evans and Whitefield 1993). This is addressed in theoretical terms in his later writing (Kitschelt 1995) but not tested in his empirical work (Kitschelt *et al.* 1999) which ignores cases such as Slovakia or the Baltic states.

4 As Kitschelt and his co-authors point out (1999: 42), comparative methodology does not exclude the possibility that only one empirical example of a general category may exist (or indeed, that no empirical examples of a category may exist, making counterfactual analysis necessary). Some commentators have suggested, however, that, despite including East Germany, the 'bureaucratic-authoritarian' path appears tailored around the Czech historical experience (Lewis 2000b).

5 Despite the absence of a Czech national state, the centre–periphery cleavage identified by Lipset and Rokkan also impacted on how the Czech party developed. This resulted from the administrative separation of the two historic Czech provinces, Bohemia and Moravia, and the emergence of Prague as the centre of Czech cultural and political life and Moravia as the periphery (Garver 1978; Pernes 1996; Řepa 2001; Šedo 2002).

6 A key difference between the Czech and Scandinavian contexts is the divided nature of the Czech left, which reflected both the divisive effect of the National Question and the strength of the Communist Party of Czechoslovakia. An additional peculiarity is the highly unusual presence of both a Catholic and an agrarian party.

7 Czechoslovak National Democracy was known from 1935 to 1938 as National Unity (*Národní sjednocení*) after the party merged with two small extreme right-wing groups.

8 Two other minor non-communist Slovak parties were permitted, the Freedom Party (SS) and the Party of National Renewal (SNO).

9 A number of former National Democrats joined the National Socialists after 1945 attracted by their nationalism which acquired a more illiberal, anti-German, integralist character in the postwar period (Kocian 1994).

10 After 1948 exile groups representing the People's Party, National Democrats and Agrarians were formed. All were intensely fractious and split into different factions. The issue of co-operation between non-communist National Front parties in exile and exile groups of the banned 'historic right' was especially contentious. With the exception of the exiled Social Democrats and National Social groups, most Czech 'historic' parties in exile seem to have become defunct by the 1970s (Mrklas 2004).

11 Most estimates of the numbers persecuted or imprisoned in Czechoslovakia between 1948 and the mid-1950s reviewed by Blaive are in the region of 100,000 (2001: 187–90).

12 Further confusion was caused in the 1960s by the labelling of both non-communist activists and radical reform communists as 'rightist' and the subsequent use of the term 'conservative' to describe communist opponents of Dubček's (and Gorbachev's) reforms.

13 After choices made at critical junctures, a certain pattern is then 'locked-in' for a prolonged period through a self-reinforcing logic of 'increasing returns' (Pierson 2004).

14 They also speak of 'a party elite unwilling to make concessions for the sake of greater popular inclusiveness and economic efficiency' without indicating whether this characterization refers to the *whole* duration of the regime, or only post-1968 'normalization' (Kitschelt *et al.* 1999: 27; see also Kitschelt 2002: 17).

15 The Czechoslovaks appear to have underestimated the importance of personal trust for Soviet leaders. Not only was the Soviet regime more patrimonial in character than that in Czechoslovakia, but Brezhnev and his comrades belonged to a generation steeped in the Stalinist culture of seeking out internal enemies (Williams 1997a: 36–7).

16 For example, they note that '[r]egardless of pre-existing state traditions and communist regime practices the founders of new states may succumb to powerful temptations to pack the new state apparatus with personal followers and thus nurture clientelistic patronage networks' (Kitschelt *et al.* 1999: 52). This argument is raised only in connection with new, post-communist states, however.

17 Kitschelt *et al.* (1999: 35, 38) allow that the geo-strategic position of some communist states might have had some impact on regime characteristics, citing the possible linkage between the 'front line' position of Czechoslovakia and the GDR and the intransigence of their regimes. They also accept the effect of 'changing external constraints on power relations' within communist states (1999: 29) in relation to the more laissez-faire attitude of Gorbachev's reformist leadership in the USSR after 1985 towards domestic change in Central and Eastern Europe.

18 I am indebted to Brigid Fowler (2004) for this insight.

3 'Normalization' and the elite origins of the Czech right

1 Kitschelt (2002: 35–6) provides similar counterfactual analysis of the Hungarian case when he discusses the possibility that an alliance between reform communists and

national-populist elites might have produced a form of populist 'chauvino-communism'.

2 In Slovakia, Eyal (2003) suggests, counter-elites saw themselves as rooted in a world of social and national interests and interpreted the communist era as part of a shared national past.

3 Havel (1968), for example, called for the establishment of a socialist opposition party and later signed a petition for the refoundation of the Social Democratic Party (Kusin 1972: 170–6.

4 In the late 1980s the Czech Catholic hierarchy also began to speak out openly against the regime's human rights abuses.

5 An independent demonstration, authorized by the authorities, took place on 10 December 1988 to mark International Human Rights Day. This was the only legally permitted event of its kind during the 'normalization' period.

6 The Democratic Initiative group attracted some student activists in Prague in early 1989 and even established its own student section. However, this section disintegrated in October 1989 when DI restyled itself as a political party.

7 I use this term by analogy with Szacki's concept of dissident 'proto-liberalism' (1995: 74–7, 109–11). I follow Szacki (1995: 76) in using hindsight to identify 'relatively uniform elements and to treat them as embryos of present orientations whose separateness no one doubts'.

8 Even when overtly political concepts such as conservatism were starting to be discussed in dissident circles in the mid-1980s, they were explored as intellectual themes, not as ideologies intended to inform political or social action.

9 For example, care was always taken to ensure that the choice of Charter 77's three 'speakers' reflected the major sub-groups within it. The 'speakers'' most important task was to co-sign and issue the Charter's public declarations.

10 Eyal's construction of 'reform communists' as a distinct sub-group *outside* dissent and opposed to its (supposedly 'anti-political') conceptualization of power is highly problematic. It leads to the dubious conflation (Eyal 2000: 66) of 'reform communists' in the cultural world who 'managed to stay in their jobs' through accommodation with the 'normalization' process with 'reform communist intellectuals' involved in dissident *samizdat* debates, who were mostly Charter 77 signatories.

11 Similarly, the Catholic dissident Václav Benda argued that '[t]otalitarian power has extended the sphere of politics to include everything ... the first responsibility of a Christian and a human being is to oppose such an inappropriate demand of the political sphere' (Benda *et al.* 1988: 222).

12 Interestingly, Pithart (1990c) argued that anti-politics was a hallmark of ideological movements of the *left* such as high Stalinism, the Western New Left and technocratic reform communism.

13 Patočka's rejection of politics for individual sacrifice as an existential act was so radical it denied even the exercise of 'pastoral power' central to Eyal's account. In Patočka's view Charter 77 participants were 'not even attempting to be a moral authority or the "conscience" of society' (cited in Palouš 1991: 124).

14 In a *samizdat* essay also written in 1979, Václav Benda (1985: 117) expressed a similar view that 'the slightest social groundswell may (which may mean only a few people displaying the courage to take a chance despite everything ...) may call into life processes whose tempo and consequences no one can foresee'. A decade later he repeated the point, commenting that 'a single loose pebble can cause an avalanche; an accidental outburst of discontent in a factory, in a football match, in a village pub is capable of shaking the foundations of the state' (Benda *et al.* 1988: 221).

15 Patočka's influential, if contradictory, writings on the philosophy of Czech history also stressed the importance of the spiritual unity of premodern Europe which small modern nations in Central Europe, in his view, struggled to articulate (Tucker 2000: 58–71, 89–114).

16 Václav Havel, for example, commented in 1988 that he was 'irritated with Roger Scruton, who has said in the *Salisbury Review* that I am a typical neo-conservative. It is not true, and everybody who knows me knows this' (cited in Selbourne 1990: 81).

17 Paul Wilson's rendition of the Czech as 'radical conservatism' (Benda 1985: 124) is misleading.

18 For example, the claim in 'A Right to History' that Masaryk had a humanist conception of the Czech nation, whereas the Catholic-oriented historian Pekař stressed the role of religion, is questionable. Masaryk's view of Czech development, as shaped by Christianity, was criticized by Pekař, who stressed national factors.

19 The journal reprinted writings by ultra-conservative Catholic intellectuals of the inter-war period such as Rudolf Voříšek, including articles written during the 'Second Republic' (Laruelle 1996).

20 *Střední Evropa* was especially preoccupied with the Holy Roman Empire, which, echoing Patočka (Tucker 2000: 58–71), was seen as a golden age predating the eruption of modernity, nationalism and mass politics that shaped Austria–Hungary.

21 Some members of the 'realist' group such as Bohumil Doležal did, however, sign the Charter. Others such as Mandler did not. However, the 'realists' were linked to the Charter by common networks – Mandler, for example, attended the 'Kampademia' seminar in the early 1970s and was in contact with Petr Pithart.

22 Pithart shared the realists' arguments for 'small-scale work' (*drobná prace*) – the promotion of civic values through everyday practical activities (Pithart 1990d) – as well as their concern that Charter 77 was too elitist, self-righteous and detached from society.

23 Pithart and his co-thinkers saw Czech Catholicism as too isolated and too inwardly preoccupied to attract broad national support ('Podiven' 1991).

24 Pithart and the other 'Bohemus' authors argued that the *odsun* had paved the way for communist rule by removing a significant element of Czechoslovakia's Catholic and bourgeois population who might have formed the social basis of a conservative alliance in a multinational state.

25 Pithart also valued the integral nationalists' view of politics as centring on conflicting interests, rather than moral categories (Pithart 1990a: 105–64).

26 The Havel–Kundera debate was also a point of reference for neo-liberals such as Klaus (2001b: 105).

27 For example, only one neo-conservative intellectual, Norman Podhoretz, was among the US speakers who visited Czechoslovakia as part of the Jan Hus Foundation's programme (*New York Post*, 9 December 1986; Day 1999: 283–9).

28 Indeed, as Scruton (1996) himself acknowledged, given their suspicion of nationalism and populism, when transferred to a Central European context, traditional British Tory ideas seemed *liberal* in their stress on individual freedom, private property, the market economy and civil society.

29 Arguably, the neo-conservative critique of a left-liberal 'New Class', in part derived from the Trotskyist movement's critique of the USSR, easily lent itself to readaptation as a critique of the *nomenklatura* and reform communist intellectuals. Many leading US neo-conservatives were active Trotskyists in the 1940s.

30 This vision of a moral market economy backed by a non-confessional politics informed by religious values was attractive to figures such as Bratinka, Kroupa and Ježek who were personally religious but not inclined towards political Catholicism.

31 The 'Young Economists' included, for example, Lubomír Mlčoch, who served as an economic adviser to the Christian Democrats after 1989 and become one of the most trenchant critics of Czech neo-liberalism, and Jan Klacek, who was economics spokesperson for the Social Democrats during the 1990s (Klaus 2001b: 27).

32 For example, Klaus (1996: 15–16) recalled that as a researcher in the Economics Institute in the 1960s he was 'being paid to study contemporary international economics and clearly, for a graduate of the Economic University [in Prague], which was

simply untouched by contemporary international economics, this was simply a revelation and I was completely hooked. I had entered a completely different intellectual world and toying with official Czechoslovak economics just never came into consideration'.

33 Klaus (1999: 10) recalled that he had first seen Hayek speak in August 1968 at an academic seminar in Austria, but had 'really just gone to look, I was intellectually somewhere quite different and hardly listened'.

34 Myant (2003: 18, 23) argues that, paradoxically, the conservative fiscal policies of the 'normalization' period left Czechoslovakia relatively free from such inflationary pressures.

35 Bockman and Eyal (2002) suggest that for strategic reasons both groups accepted the fiction that East European economists lacked knowledge of Western economic theory and only reported empirical findings.

36 Myant (1989: 173, 258–9) briefly discusses the work of the 1968 'Young Economists' and the neo-liberals many had become by the 1980s. He identifies 1980s neo-liberals with a view identifying problems of disequilibrium as the key to reform of Czechoslovakia's socialist economy, rather than sectoral imbalance, enterprise autonomy or management techniques. However, he dismisses the group as unimportant, arguing that an 'uncontrolled market system', implying also a fully open economy, would in practice have such obviously catastrophic economic and social consequences as to stand only a minimal chance of winning significant support' (Myant 1989: 253–4).

37 During the 1980s some Polish liberals anticipated and welcomed the possibility of authoritarian market reform, seeing marketization as a more effective guarantee of freedom than political democracy and as an economic prerequisite for eventual democratization (Szacki 1995).

38 Gellner (1988: 26–30) argues that the anti-totalitarian liberalism of Popper and Hayek reflects the experience of 'the individualistic, atomized, cultivated bourgeoisie of the Habsburg capital [which] had to contend with the influx of swarms of kin-bound collectivistic, rule-ignoring migrants from … the Balkans and Galicia'.

39 Until the 1970s the People's Party usually had one or two ministerial portfolios. However, these posts afforded the party little real influence, as key policy decisions were always taken within the Communist Party.

40 The existence of 'bourgeois' satellite political parties – as opposed to 'patriotic' fronts consisting only of mass social organizations – was unusual in communist Central and Eastern Europe and seems an unintended legacy of national Communist strategies to 'manage' bourgeois opponents when they briefly shared power after 1945. I owe this insight to Brigid Fowler.

41 Different authors give different estimates of People's Party membership during 1960s. Ulč (1974: 34–5) gives membership as 21,362 in 1966 and 77,566 in January 1969. Pecka *et al.* (1995: 10) cite membership as 20,642 on 1 January 1968.

42 The party leadership's uncritical endorsement in 1986 of a new law liberalizing access to abortion was a major catalyst for reformists (Daněk 1990: 52–4).

43 This replicated divisions of the interwar period between ČSL leaders, who pragmatically adapted to the Czechoslovak state, and the ultra-conservative Catholic intellectuals on whose heritage *Střední Evropa* drew.

4 From civic movement to right-wing party: the emergence of the Civic Democratic Party 1990–1

1 Kopecký (1995: 528), for example, claims that ODS 'started to develop its organization from scratch'.

2 A number of 'Civic fora' were also initially created in Slovakia but, sensitive to

Slovak sensibilities, the Co-ordinating Centre directed them towards the emerging Public Against Violence movement in Bratislava.

3 These decisions were taken on 10 December 1989 at the Prague Co-ordinating Centre by the Plenum – a kind of general meeting of activists. The decision-making bodies of the Co-ordinating Centre in November–December 1989 were a 'crisis team' (*krizový štab*) of three; an 'action group' with approximately 20 members; and the Plenum, which numbered about 150. The Plenum was later reorganized and renamed the Assembly when it included regional representatives in December 1989 (Suk 1995; Glenn 2001: 50).

4 The earliest OF document on internal organization (Suk 1998: 159–60, document 57) had suggested that supporters of local fora show their affiliation by signing a 'founding document' (article 2).

5 The Assembly met as a nationally representative body for the first time on 23 December 1989 replacing the Plenum (Suk 1995: 4, 32–6).

6 It was anticipated that Civic Fora at lower levels, although autonomous, would loosely mirror this structure, establishing their own Assemblies, Councils, 'representatives' and (at district level) Co-ordinating Centres.

7 Until 10 December 1989 the Political Commission was called the Conceptual Commission.

8 Resources were shared out between individual groups through negotiations in the Political Commission.

9 In Czech 'Strany jsou pro straníky, Občanské fórum je pro všechny'. The Czech word *straník* (party-member) has (pejorative) connotations of participation in the communist-era political system and Communist Party membership. Its opposite *nestraník* (non-party-member) is often translated as 'independent'.

10 Party members were, however, generally ranked slightly higher on the OF list than non-party-members, arguably reflecting the fact that many party leaders were prominent ex-dissidents.

11 Clearly, the interests of legislators and party bureaucrats can and do diverge on many occasions as the literature on party organization emphasizes.

12 Before the 1990 elections there were two clearly discernible concepts within the Commission preparing OF's election campaign: (1) a nationally co-ordinated centralized media-orientated campaign with a programmatic message ('The return to Europe') using modern communications and polling techniques and a network of professional 'electoral managers' and (2) a 'traditional' grassroots-based strategy based on OF activists, 'personalities', personal contacts and local campaigning ('Zpráva o zasedání sněmu KC OF dne 17.3', *Inforum* 21/90, 2 April 1990; Hadjiisky 1996: 14–15).

13 Responsibility for the managerial network was fully transferred to district Civic Fora by the Assembly of 21 July 1990. ('Zpráva o zasedání Sněmu KC OF dne 21.7.90 ', *Inforum* 33/90, 31 July 1990).

14 In the Czech lands, the Christian and Democratic Union (KDU) coalition comprised the People's Party (ČSL), Benda's Christian Democratic Party (KDS), the Free Peasant Party (SRS) and other minor groups. At federal level, the coalition also included Slovakia's influential Christian Democratic Movement (KDH).

15 Accordingly ČSL thus set up regional networks of Christian clubs for the disabled, women, young people and professional groups such as teachers and doctors and revived the Catholic Orel sports organization dissolved in 1949 (*Lidová demokracie*, 6 January 1990, 1; 8 January 1990, 2; 21 April 1990, 1).

16 Relations between the People's Party leadership and the party daily *Lidová demokracie* quickly broke down as journalists resisted attempts to use the paper as an outlet for party propaganda.

17 Pithart argued that legal procedures should remain sacrosanct and that 'the fundamental means to come to terms with our opponents is privatization' (Petr Pithart: Budu ochraňovat právní řád', *Inforum* 36/90, 21 August 1990).

18 As Hadjiisky (1996: 31–2) notes, these comments were untypical of Havel, who more often emphasized the need for general moral renewal.

19 Václav Klaus is reported to have regarded the beginning of bilateral Czech–Slovak talks in April as an 'unparalleled ambush' (Pithart and Kusáková 1992: 27).

20 Some, such as Petr Pithart, were aware of the potential contradiction between OF's organizing principles at a very early stage ('Hovoří Petr Pithart', *Infórum* 7/90, 9 January 1990, 1).

21 Accordingly, OF leaders tended to view political conflicts as 'human' problems of individual temperament rather than ideologically motivated disputes to be addressed by maintaining 'civic decency and mutual tolerance' ('Ivan Fišera: Občanské fórum – stav a východiska', *Infórum* 36/90, 21 August 1990).

22 Previously only district assemblies had had this power. Article 1.1 specifically gave district OF assemblies the right to overturn local decisions concerning 'removal from records'. The August 1990 Statutes also abolished Regional Civic Fora, leaving only local, district and national levels.

23 The idea of creating the post of OF Chairman seems to have originated with Havel. Rudolf Battěk reported to the Assembly of 21 July 1990 that Havel had spoken of the need for 'an important government figure' to be head of the Co-ordinating Centre ('Zpráva o zasedání sněmu OF dne 21.7.90', *Infórum* 33/90). Ivan Fišera gave a similar account to the OF Assembly of 15 August 1990.

24 Havel, for example, described the Forum in September 1990 as 'something halfway between a movement and a political party' ('Václav Havel: Je třeba zpevnit vedení OF', *Infórum* 40/90, 18 September 1990).

25 In a January 1990 AISA opinion poll, 77 per cent of respondents had rejected the idea of Civic Forum becoming a party, while only a quarter had favoured a political system based on small number of strong parties ('Odpovědnost za vítězství', *Infórum* 18/90).

26 Many of these groups joined the Free Bloc–Conservative Party (SB-KS) coalition that contested the June 1990 elections.

27 Klaus himself was reportedly 'allergic' to any suggestion that he might share the fate of Polish reformers (Stráský 1993: 81).

28 In subsequent interviews Klaus claimed that it was in this immediate post-election period that he and other economists perceived a need to intervene in politics (Klaus 1993a: 9–14, 1995: 11–15; Stráský 1993: 74, 81). The Civic Forum deputy, Klaus aide and later Civic Democratic Party Deputy Chairman Miroslav Macek claimed that Klaus contacted him on the day of the first meeting of the OF parliamentary group and stressed the need to organize the right and identify-right wing deputies (Čermák and Sontona 1997: 39).

29 Some observers suggest that the project of transforming OF into a right-wing party emerged as the brainchild of Josef Zieleniec in discussions with Klaus in August and September (Ježek 1997; Stoniš and Havlík 1998: 43–4).

30 The newspaper interview given by Havlík on 22 October 1990 appears to have been off-the-cuff, rather than part of a thought-out strategy. As Havlík notes, the journalist he spoke to was hostile to the right and his remarks were paraphrased. Nevertheless, he accepted that the content of article accurately reflected his thinking (Stoniš and Havlík 1998: 27).

31 Havlík had suggested in the remarks reported by *Mladá fronta* that the Presidium of the Federal Assembly should be restructured to reflect the right-wing majority within Civic Forum through the replacement of named left-wingers as Chairmen of parliamentary committees or leaders of OF parliamentary groups.

32 The programme referred only briefly 'to a market economy with a dominant role of private property' and even this was justified as a means to remove the 'corrupt and talentless'. The Assembly of the Prague Regional Civic Fora held on 25–6 October, for example, had adopted a programme whose demands were almost entirely militantly anti-communist ('Pražský sněm OF', *Infórum* 46/90, 1 November).

33 The organizational proposals passed were based on exclusive individual membership. Former secret police (StB) employees or former members of the defunct Communist Party 'People's Militia' were to be barred ('Principy organizační struktury', *Inʃórum* 56/91, 17 January 1991, 5–6).

34 The Liberal Club was initially founded as the Interparliamentary Civic Association (MOS) on 12 November 1990.

35 The Klaus aides Milan Kondr and Jiří Kolář claimed that preregistration was a form of 'recording' (*evidování*) of OF supporters and hence covered by the existing Statutes. They were, however, unable to give a clear explanation as to why those already 'recorded' also needed to 'preregister' ('Zpráva z briefingu OF 1.2.1991', *Inʃórum* 59/91, 6–7).

36 The extent of managers' support for Klaus is, however, sometimes exaggerated. A poll of 61 OF deputies and 68 OF district managers (about three-quarters of the total) showed that 53 per cent of managers (36) favoured dual membership in OF and constituent groups, with only 28 per cent (19) being in favour of exclusive individual membership. Most wanted OF to be either a more firmly structured but pluralistic body (30 per cent – 20) or a coalition of two or three currents (34 per cent – 19) ('Anketa – poslanci OF', *Inʃórum* 55/91, 12 January 1991, 8–9).

37 In addition to national co-ordinating committees dealing with property and legal issues, the 'shell' OF was to continue to maintain joint Civic Forum parliamentary and local council groups.

38 Struggles to reshape civic movements in other post-communist states generated either charismatic but inexpert leaders, such as Lech Walesa, or unpopular technocrat-politicians such as Lezek Balcerowicz in Poland or Egor Gaidar in Russia (Fish 1995; Grabowski 1996).

5 'An unrepeatable chance': the dominance of the new Czech right 1992–6

1 As the Polish experience of the 1990s demonstrated, even in the presence of weakened centre-left parties the centre-right can fragment (Szczerbiak 2004; Ost 2005).

2 Claiming procedural irregularities, Doležal and Mandler contested the decision to wind up the party. Their rump LDS organization formally ceased to function in 1994.

3 Klaus was ODS's only minister in the Federal government. ODS had two ministers in the 1990–2 Czech government, which increased to five by June 1992. The Lány accords stated that when ministerial posts were vacated they should go to an ODS nominee.

4 For example, on 27 September1991 ODS councillors voted to remove ODA's Jaroslav Kořan as Mayor of Prague (*Respekt* no. 38, 23 September 1991).

5 A last-minute overture before the 1992 election by the ODS Deputy Chairman Josef Zieleniec offering prominent and popular ODA leaders 'electable' positions on the ODS list was turned down.

6 Benda's KDS also gained two ministerial posts in the Czech government formed in June 1990. One deputy elected on the Civic Forum list joined KDS after the Forum's break-up.

7 ODS was registered as a political party on 5 February 1992 in Slovakia, where it recruited 450 members. In 1992 it stood (unsuccessfully) in Slovakia in coalition with the Democratic Party (DS) with which its Slovak branches merged after the break-up of Czechoslovakia.

8 Benda's party concluded a coalition with Klaus's ODS on 20 November 1991. Like its earlier KDU coalition with the People's Party, the KDS-ODS agreement provided for a joint electoral list guaranteeing KDS candidates a number of 'electable' positions.

9 Most other former OF voters supported the centrist Civic Movement (OH) or centre-left groupings such as the Social Democrats (ČSSD) or the Liberal Social Union (LSU) coalition.

10 According to ASIA polling in July 1991, 21 per cent of ODS's voters supported the party 'strongly' and 51 per cent 'moderately'. By May 1992, 63 per cent of ODS supporters supported the party 'strongly'. Across the Czech electorate as a whole, 40 per cent of voters identified with a party 'strongly' at this time (Novák 1997: 104–5).

11 ODS supporters, for example, strongly rejected the view that there was a trade-off between radical market reform and the successful negotiation of a new constitutional settlement with Slovakia (AISA cited in Novák 1997: 104–5; see also *Mladá fronta Dnes*, 23 April 1992).

12 ODS supporters' anti-communism was, however, closer to mainstream Czech opinion in mid-1992. Decommunization policies were supported by 66 per cent of the Czech electorate as a whole in the ASIA study.

13 Pavel Bratinka recalled that during the first six months of its existence ODA was sustained by a 200,000 crown gift from Roger Scruton (*ZpraODAj* no. 7–8, July–August 1994, 1–2). Hamerský and Dimun (1999: 333, 338) note that ODA had virtually exhausted its own cash assets by autumn 1991.

14 ODA's organizational weaknesses also reflected its Burkeian view of parties as select governing caucuses seeking the general 'civic' good and its early decision to work through individual members in Civic Forum's Prague Co-ordinating Centre.

15 The Party of Entrepreneurs' stress on promoting business interests contradicted ODA's notion of 'civic' politics above sectional interests both in principle and in its attempts to defend Jaroslav Muroň, a SČPŽR candidate, whom Ježek suspended as a deputy minister at the Privatization Ministry for alleged corruption; KAN's sweeping, anti-communism conflicted with ODA's stress on the rule of law and placed prominent ODA figures who had been Communist Party members before 1989 in a difficult position; ODA co-operation with Slovakia's VPN-ODÚ foundered because the Slovak party could not commit itself to ODA's policy of maintaining a strong federation and because a joint electoral list would struggle to meet the 7 per cent electoral threshold for coalitions (Hamerský and Dimun 1999: 36–9).

16 By June 1992 Civic Democratic Alliance representation in the Federal Assembly increased from three to eleven. The party also gained six additional deputies in the Czech parliament. The maverick anti-communist Czech Agriculture Minister Kubát also joined ODA in May 1991, seeking support in his battle with Czech Prime Minster Petr Pithart over reform of the co-operative farm sector.

17 In certain regions where ODS has strong grassroots presence, such as the Ostrava conurbation and the Morava valley, it polls relatively poorly. In contrast, towns such as Hradec Králové or Zlín, where ODS organization is relatively weak, record high electoral support for the party.

18 Between 1992 and 1996 the distinction between the 'party in public office' and the 'party in central office' was complicated by the fact that many ODS ministers, including Klaus, were not members of the Czech parliament, having been elected in 1992 to the (already defunct) Federal Assembly.

19 Many local associations chose not to nominate any candidates, but only to participate in the district selection conferences. The leading position on party lists was chosen by regional conferences from a shortlist of nationally known figures drawn up by the party's national executive.

20 The 1994 Law on Political Parties requires party statutes to define members' rights and responsibilities.

21 In practice most ODS local associations meet more often because of the need to elect delegates to district assemblies (Linek 2004: 184).

22 This tendency was reinforced by the absence (until 2000) of any unit of elected local government above commune or municipality level to set local issues in broader perspective and by the fact that in many localities ODS membership was too small to provide a full candidate list of party members in local elections, thus forcing the recruitment of independents (Linek 2004: 185).

23 Press reports suggested that ODS spent 100 million crowns on its 1994 local election campaign, a sum exceeding its expenditure on the 1992 parliamentary election campaign. ODS gave a figure of 25 million crowns (Reed 1996: 244).

24 ODS's outline programme for the November 1994 local elections advocated extensive commercialization and privatization of municipal services and property – proposals which were congruent with the party's broader neo-liberal programme but also offered the prospect of concrete gains to groups and individuals at local level.

25 A growing body of literature argues that the *alternation* of well-defined ideological party blocs in governments acts as a control mechanism on incumbents, inhibiting them from developing clientelistic power bases and abusing power, and allowing a rapid trial-and-error process of policy learning (Orenstein 2002; Vachudova 2005; Grzymala-Busse 2006). In this perspective in the Czech case, the early dominance of the right and the subsequent period without clear majority governments appear as impediments to reform (Vachudova 2005).

26 The 'small restitution' law, which provided for the return of property nationalized between 1955 and 1989, was passed in October 1990. A more extensive restitution law covering the 1948–89 period was passed in February 1991. A separate law concerning land restitution was passed in May 1991.

27 In June 1991 anti-communist right-wing liberal parties ODS, ODA and LDS had 52 deputies in the 200-member Czech parliament – 26 per cent of the total. If one includes the Christian Democrats (KDU), the total for the right rises to 74 deputies (37 per cent). If, in the Federal Assembly, liberal pro-market deputies of Public Against Violence are counted as allies of the Czech right, the corresponding figure is around 30 per cent.

28 The original government bill supported by the centrist Civic Movement, then the major governing party, provided for a confidential bureaucratic process designed to render decommunization an administrative matter outside the ambit of day-to-day partisan conflict (Williams 2003).

29 The 1991 federal lustration law – carried over into Czech law in 1993 – had temporary validity, but was extended by the Czech parliament in 1995 and made permanent in 2000.

30 Applicants for ODS membership were required to sign a declaration that they had not been members of the pre-1989 secret police and the 'People's Militia'. However, former Communist Party membership was not in itself an obstacle to membership.

31 Appel (2004) suggests that lustration in state-owned entreprises demobilized managerial resistance to voucher privatization. However, case study research suggests that lustration effects were easily bypassed through strategies such as job swapping until full private ownership removed companies from the ambit of lustration (Clark and Soulsby 1996).

32 This figure includes both screenings required by law and voluntarily screenings requested by individuals such as parliamentary and municipal candidates.

33 Williams (1999) cites an estimate of 100.

34 Positive lustration meant automatic dismissal from a post covered by the law (Williams 2003; Williams, Szczerbiak and Fowler 2005). Czechoslovak restitution was unusual in providing for the physical return of assets ('reprivatization'), not merely compensation.

35 This cut-off point, chosen to avoid addressing the sensitive question of property confiscation from ethnic Germans expelled in 1945–6, also excluded privately owned Czech industrial assets nationalized during the semi-democratic 1945–8 interlude.

36 This residency requirement was struck out by the Czech Constitutional Court in 1994.

37 My estimate is based on the fact that 2225 SPR-RSČ candidates for the November 1994 local elections were listed as members of the party. The Republicans regularly made extravagant claims of mass membership.

38 Neo-liberals were aware of the need to recapitalize and restructure Czech industry

and regulate corporate governance and companies' trading activities. However, as Klaus, Ježek and Zieleniec explained on numerous occasions (Reed 1996: 38; Ježek 1997: 146; Myant 2003: 117, 129), they believed that investment and normal structures of regulation would follow the creation of private property and meaningful market relations.

39 In addition to restructuring under state holding companies, Vrba himself appears to have favoured extensive privatization through immediate sale to foreign investors (Myant 2003: 118).

40 Karlovarský porcelain was privatized through the 'large privatization' process. Local Privatization Commissions were abolished in 1993.

41 According to figures compliled by Myant (2003: 121) just under 48 per cent of assets disposed of in 'large privatization' between 1992 and 1997 were privatized through the voucher method, the bulk (62 per cent) during the first wave of voucher privatization. Just under 27 per cent of 'privatized' assets consisted of shares held by the National Property Fund. The remaining 25 per cent was privatized through restitution and other 'standard' methods.

42 Before June 1992 the Czech Industry Ministry under Jan Vrba was able to insist as the 'founding ministry' of many state enterprises that large-scale allocation of shares to the voucher scheme should take place only if strategic foreign investors could not be found (Orenstein 2002).

43 One of the most notorious cases of privatization-related bribery concerned Jaroslav Lizner, the head of the Coupon Privatization Centre, who was apprehended by police on 31 October 1994 having received eight million crowns in cash to influence pricing of shares in a firm being auctioned in the voucher process (Reed 1996: 226–30).

44 In Czech coalition governments the first deputy minister (*náměstek*) is typically a politician from a different party to that of the Minister. In 1992–3, however, ODA held both posts in the Privatization Ministry.

45 ODS's political and practical difficulties of accessing large illicit funds allegedly held in a Swiss bank account are discussed in Chapter 6.

46 There is some dispute as to how active the Czech state was in exercising its direct ownership and indirect influence in the economy. The consensus seems to be that, although there was a political expectation that banks should lend to newly privatized companies to tide them through privatization, with the exception of strategic enterprises, there was no conscious or co-ordinated policy of slowing restructuring in order to manage social costs (Orenstein 2002: 103–9; Appel 2004: 63; Myant 2003: 121–2, 142–4, 170–1). The Czech Republic's surprisingly low rates of unemployment thus seem attributable to factors such as management conservatism and the expansion of the service sector (Myant 2003: 65–6; Scheuer and Gitter 2001).

47 Although management control was sometimes challenged by investment privatization funds, IPFs lacked the expertise and personnel to make significant changes and were more focused on acquiring lucrative majority stakes (Brom and Orenstein 1994; Myant 2003). In some cases, management groups secured control of their own enterprises by establishing investment funds or front companies to buy their shares.

48 Research suggests that the emergence of a distinct 'right-wing' electorate reflected the crystallization of a distinct *left-wing* electorate and a general decline in pro-market orientations (Večerník 1996: 217–39; Vlachová 2001).

49 A new *okres* was created on 1 January 1996.

50 See the Czech Deputy Prime Minister Antonin Baudys's response to a parliamentary question on 17 December 1990. Available online at www.psp.cz/cgi-bin/ascii/www/eknih/1990cnr/stenprot/012schuz/s012005.htm (accessed 30 August 2006). A report to the Civic Forum Assembly in October 1990 noted that 39 of the 61 heads of the District Labour Offices appointed were OF candidates and that 20 others had been appointed with OF's approval (*Infórum* 44/90, 17 October 1990, 5). Published minutes of the Forum's Collegium of 28 November 1990 concluded that

although considerations of competence were important it was 'necessary to fill these offices [District Office Heads] on the basis of the election results' with the proviso that supporters of the People's Party (ČSL) should not be concentrated in South Moravia, a bastion of ČSL support (*Införum* 51/90, 6 December 1990).

51 Few reliable figures are available concerning such politicization, although available evidence suggests that it was extensive and weighed heavily towards parties of the centre-right coalition, especially ODS. In 1996, for example, 14 of the 73 heads of district offices (18 per cent) were prominent enough in party politics to be selected as candidates for elections to the Czech Senate. Of these, 11 stood for parties of the centre-right coalition – six for ODS, three for the Christian Democrats and two for ODA (*Mladá fronta Dnes*, 14 August 1996, 4 and 26 August 1996, 4). The remaining three stood as Social Democrats.

52 The Senate was able to delay ordinary legislation; jointly elect the President; and block changes to Constitution or electoral laws. Fearing ODS domination of the upper chamber, the smaller coalition parties sought a system with weaker majoritarian effect based on three-member constitutencies. In principle, ODS favoured first-past-the-post elections using single member constituencies and a single round of voting (Pehe 1993, 1994c). In practice, as discussed in Chapter 6, the two-round system agreed enabled ODS's centre-right opponents to mobilize very effectively against the party. The majoritarian logic of Senate elections was also blunted by the fact that they were staggered – after initial elections, as in the US, one-third of Senators were re-elected every two years.

53 Much of KPB's activity consisted of making large loans to companies and individuals associated with Moravec using funds previously borrowed from large state-owned financial institutions. Although investigated by the police, neither Moravec nor his associates were prosecuted as it was difficult to prove that his bank's losses (including the elimination of ODA's debt) were the result of fraudulent intent or negligence, rather than poor commercial judgement. Moravec also had close political connections with the Christian Democrats, to whom KPB also made loans (*Respekt*, 29 January 1996, 4).

54 This East Central European pattern contrasts with that in the former Soviet Union where the absence of state funding is linked to a winner-takes-all accumulation of huge patronage and administrative resources by incumbents 'locking-in' their dominance in the form of illiberal democracy (Wilson 2005: 73–88; Kopecký 2006).

6 Beyond the politics of transformation: declining and realigning 1996–2006

1 Namely the replacement of the post of Executive Deputy Chairman with a professional head election manager and a party treasurer responsible directly to the party leader (favoured by Klaus) and the establishment of specialist ODS policy commissions, whose recommendations would automatically be discussed by the party executive (favoured by Zieleniec).

2 The ODS congress scheduled for the end of 1997 was due to re-elect the party's leadership, who served a two year term. One ODS Deputy Chairman, Jan Stráský, suggested that the party's three other deputy leaders should resign before its next congress, as he planned to do, to allow political renewal.

3 Zieleniec resigned as a parliamentary deputy on 29 August 1997.

4 Macek released to the media two critical memoranda which largely rehearsed arguments already made by ODS's coalition partners, Zieleniec and the 'conservative democratic' proto-faction of 1992–3 (*Mladá fronta Dnes*, 11 September, 2; 15 September, 6; *Hospodářské noviny*, 19 November 1997, 3).

5 Some reports suggest that Moravia Steel, in fact, donated 15 million crowns, but that the source of the remaining 7.5 million crowns was more effectively concealed. The company had previously donated 250,000 crowns to ODS in 1994.

6 Two real individuals of these names did exist, but Bács had died 13 years previously and Radjiv Sinha had no connection with the Czech Republic. Láos Bács was also the name of a character in the popular Czech thriller *Vekslák*.

7 According to Kuzmiak's account, he chaired meetings attended by ODS officials and Šrejber's representatives and advised the party to destroy clearly falsified deeds of gift from 'Bács' and 'Sinha'. In April 1996 ODS claimed that the documents had been misplaced.

8 Novák resigned as Executive Deputy Chairman at ODS's 1996 congress. Control of the party's financial management passed to Tomáš Ratiborský, who held the new, non-elected post of Head Manager.

9 Novák initially insisted that he had acted alone, but later admitted that others in the party knew of Šrejber's concealed donation. He was later tried for tax fraud but acquitted in June 2000 for lack of evidence against him. The court did, however, rule that criminal offences had been committed by persons unknown.

10 Although not held in the party's name, the account had reportedly been accessible (possibly through a foreign intermediary) to ODS Executive Vice Chairmen Petr Čermák, his successor Libor Novák and (from 1996) ODS's Head Manager Tomáš Ratiborský. It was unclear if or how the account had been used.

11 Mladá fronta Dnes's allegations of 28 November 1997, which gave details of the (unminuted) meeting of 26 September, quoted two unnamed ODS sources. Ratiborský reportedly mentioned the account in relation to ODS's difficulties raising funds to buy a new headquarters.

12 According to their own accounts, Zieleniec and Pilip pressed the party to close the account and make no use of its contents and tried unsuccessfully to raise the issue at subsequent *gremium* meetings. Zieleniec also stated that he had written to Klaus about the matter (*Lidové noviny*, 2 December 1997, 2). When the issue was finally discussed on 20 October 1997, *gremium* members were only able to agree a resolution stating that it had not authorized the opening of such an account.

13 Klaus stated that he had been unaware of the source of the Moravia Steel donations until the November 1997 press revelations, and had not had a conversation with Zieleniec about the matter in April 1996 (*Právo*, 29 November 1997, 2; *Mladá fronta Dnes*, 1 December 1997, 3; *Hospodárské noviny*, 1 December 1997, 3).

14 Tomáš Ratiborský claimed that he had merely mentioned the possibility of a donation of 170 million crowns from a foreign company, not a covert bank account. Of the three others present at the *gremium* meeting, two, Miroslav Macek and Milan Kondr, refused to answer journalists' questions, and one, Jiří Honajzer, said he could not recall what had been said.

15 Jan Ruml's own account suggests that his televised appeal with Pilip was an impulsive act which he initiated without prior consultation with Pilip, Zieleniec or Havel (Ruml 1998).

16 As in other speeches of the 1990s, Havel argued that government policies had neglected the environment, failed to decentralize, not created an adequate legal framework for civil society and not communicated the historic importance of European integration to the Czech public. In March 2000 Havel also famously spoke of the development of 'gangster capitalism (*mafiánský kapitalismus*)' in the Czech Republic as result of the ill-defined rules used to privatize large enterprises and a lack of morality in public life (*Mladá fronta Dnes*, 30 March 2000, 2; and 4 April 2000, 2).

17 A crowd of several hundred Klaus supporters gathered outside ODS headquarters on the night of 29–30 November, aggressively confronting his critics as they entered the building (*Mladá fronta Dnes*, 30 November 1997, 1). A larger, more organized demonstration addressed by Klaus's wife and some of his leading supporters was held in the centre of Prague the next day (*Hospodárské noviny*, 1 December 1997, 3).

18 An internal poll of ODA members identified three 'generations' of approximately equal size. Those who had joined ODA soon after its founding were mostly

conservative and markedly right-wing, whereas the third youngest 'generation' was largely liberal and centrist (*ZpravODAj*, October 1993, 2–3).

19 The 'Right Faction' formed the tiny Party of Conservative Accord (SKS), other ODA leaders joined the Freedom Union or the Archa political club founded by Pavel Bratinka.

20 Thirty-nine for ODS (including one defector from the Social Democrats), 30 for the Freedom Union, 18 Christian Democrats, 11 for the Civic Democratic Alliance (ODA) and two for the Party of Conservative Accord (SKS) (*Lidové noviny*, 15 January 1998, 3).

21 Voting in conjunction with the Christian Democrats, Social Democrats and Civic Democratic Alliance, the Freedom Union's deputies were instrumental in re-electing Václav Havel as President. Following his speech to the Czech parliament of 9 December 1997, Havel's candidature was opposed by ODS (which had supported him in 1993).

22 The Freedom Union also took up a variety of reformist concerns relating to party organization and democracy. Its February 1998 statutes and programme, for example, allowed registered sympathizers to participate in policy-making and stand as party candidates. It also supported direct presidential elections and the introduction of a majoritarian system for parliamentary elections.

23 Polling experts argued that the new party had the potential to draw support from the ODS and Christian Democrat electorates as well as from uncommitted voters (*Lidové noviny*, 9 January 1998, 3).

24 Of the 40 Freedom Union candidates occupying top five list positions in the eight electoral districts, ten were former ODS deputies, of whom four were first place candidates nominated by the party leadership (*Mladá fronta Dnes*, 28 April 1998, 2). Seven of the 19 Freedom Union deputies elected in 1998 were ex-ODS deputies and one, Zdeněk Kořistka, was the former ODS mayor of Ostrava.

25 Article VII of the Agreement specified that constitutional amendments and other legislation would be passed within 12 months to 'reinforce the importance of the results of competition between political parties in accordance with the constitutional principles of the Czech Republic' (*Lidové noviny*, 10 July 1998, 2).

26 In April 1998 the ODS leadership resumed the politics of alliance building by asking its regional associations to accept politicians from the rump Civic Democratic Alliance (ODA) and the Democratic Union (DEU) on their electoral lists. However, although negotiations took place, none was willing to do so.

27 In May 2000 the 4K parties reached agreement on fielding joint candidates for Senate and regional elections.

28 In STEM polling (STEM, Trendy 2000–1), the Quad-Coalition overtook ODS as the most popular party in September 2000 and enjoyed a substantial lead over both ODS and the Social Democrats until June 2001. Thereafter, it enjoyed a narrow lead, with 23–5 per cent support, until the collapse of the Quad-Coalition framework in early 2002. In opinion polls, about 40–50 per cent of 4K supporters identified directly with the Quad-Coalition, rather than one of its member parties.

29 The key changes introduced by the 2000 electoral law were an increase in the number of electoral districts from eight to 36 and the adoption of a less proportional formula for seat allocation.

30 If the 2000 electoral law had been in force in 1998, the Social Democrats would have won a narrow majority of seats in the Chamber of Deputies with small parties marginalized.

31 A small network of 'Thank You, Now Leave' associations emerged, whose activities were restricted to discussion events and the formulation of public statements. Splits within 'Thank You, Now Leave' produced two small centrist liberal 'civic' groupings, Path of Change (CZ) and Hope (*Nadeje*), whose political impact was minimal (Dvořáková 2002).

32 In January 2001 with the Freedom Union's backing the liberal Christian Democrat Cyril Svoboda was selected by the Quad-Coalition's Political Council as the 4K leader and Prime Minister designate, despite not being one of three candidates nominated for the post. Svoboda then attempted to block the appointment to the Shadow Cabinet of Miroslav Kalousek, a Christian Democrat party rival. When unable to do this, he resigned. He was replaced by the Freedom Union leader Karel Kühnl, prompting the Christian Democrats to demand a redistribution of cabinet posts or a full-scale merger of the two parties. Relations improved when Svoboda was elected Christian Democrat leader ahead of factional rivals in May 2001. Kühnl resigned as Freedom Union leader in June 2001 and was replaced by Hana Marvanová (Dimun 2002).

33 The party leadership was not due for re-election until its two-year term expired in November–December 2002.

34 Nečas (then aged 38) and Zahradil (then aged 39) had been elected among ODS's four deputy chairmen in 1999 and 2001 respectively. Having briefly led a district ODS organization, Nečas was elected to parliament in 1992, served as first deputy Defence Minister in 1995–6 and later chair of the Committee on Defence and Security. Zahradil was an OF deputy in the Federal Assembly in 1990–2, later serving as foreign policy adviser to Klaus and head of the cabinet office department on European integration. He was elected to parliament in 1998, serving as the deputy chairman of the Foreign Affairs Committee. Pavel Bém, the leader of ODS in Prague, who became Mayor of Prague shortly before the congress, was also originally a candidate, but dropped out to support Zahradil.

35 Many Christian Democrat voters were unwilling to back Freedom Union candidates and used the system of individual preference voting to advance their own party's candidates up the Coalition list.

36 Independent candidates supposedly representing civil society were substituted for those of the Civic Democratic Alliance (ODA) after ODA withdrew from the Quad-Coalition.

37 The internal study also noted that the ongoing divisions of the centre-right between ODS and the Quad-Coalition parties had left ODS isolated; that the Opposition Agreement was unpopular among the party's supporters; and that the 'traditional left-wing inclination of Czech society' put the right at a disadvantage, where it lacked effective local organization (ODS 2002b).

38 A similarly stable picture emerged for the broad Czech centre-right, including both liberal groupings and the Christian Democrats.

39 The 1998 ODS election programme talked of a flat tax in the region of 20 per cent. In 2002 it specified a flat tax of 15 per cent. However, flat tax proposals were discussed in detail by right-wing politicians and policy specialists only in 2000 under the auspices of Klaus's CEP think-tank.

40 Many independent economists regarded these claims with scepticism (*Lidové noviny*, 29 November 2005; *Respekt*, 5 December 2005).

41 Špidla was later nominated as the Czech Republic's European Commissioner receiving the Employment, Social Affairs and Equal Opportunities portfolio.

42 Press reports highlighted a loan Gross had obtained to buy a flat, whose source was difficult to establish, and business links between Gross's wife and the operator of one of Prague's large brothels, suspected of laundering the proceeds of organized crime.

43 By autumn 2005 Paroubek's trust ratings were the fourth best for any Czech politician and consistently higher than those for Topolánek (CVVM press release, 26 May 2006). He was formally elected Social Democrat leader at an extraordinary party congress on 13 May 2006.

44 The Social Democrats' absolute vote was higher in 1998, but turnout was higher.

45 A study by CVVM found that 85 per cent of ODS voters in 2006 also supported the party in 2002 – but estimated ODS's maximum potential vote at 37 per cent, while

that for the Social Democrat electorate was 40 per cent. It also found that higher turnout benefited the Social Democrats (*Hospodárské noviny*, 24 July 2006; *Lidové noviny*, 24 July 2006).

46 The Opposition Agreement also paradoxically legitimized left–right co-operation for those centre-right groupings opposed to it. In entering into coalition with the Social Democrats in 2002, Freedom Union politicians deployed essentially the same arguments, that the coalition would promote Czech EU accession and avoid making the centre-left dependent on the Communists.

7 Conservatism, nation and transformation: building a new ideology of the right

1 Indeed, it has been argued that, despite the difficulty of negotiations, a new Czech–Slovak constitutional settlement remained an attainable prospect as late as February 1992 (Stein 1997: 333).

2 Approaches taken include cultural theory (Thompson *et al.* 1990; Grenstad and Selle 1995); studies of political and organizational culture; Gramscian-inspired Marxist and post-Marxist concepts of ideology and hegemony (Laclau and Mouffe 2001; Hall 1988); policy paradigms and other meso-level conceptualizations in the 'historical institutionalist' tradition (Hall 1993; Berman 1998; Lee 1996; Blyth 1997); the 'constructivist' turn in International Relations (Checkel 1998); and the 'framing' perspectives developed in social movement theory (Tarrow 1998).

3 Appel (2004: 162) does note that other political forces shared this framing of transformation and adds that Klaus 'attempted to appropriate it as his own' (Appel 2004: 162). However, her brief discussion of right-wing ideology is largely confined to Klaus's early discourse of 'Third Ways' (2004: 162–3). In earlier work she argues similarly that 'Klaus was very effective in selling the historical appropriateness of this approach [voucher privatization]' but explains such 'salesmanship' only in terms of the widely shared Czech liberal-democratic discourse that the market would ' "return" the country to its rightful place as a member of the Western or European community ... [and] equated ... pro-European emphasis with a pro-Czech position' (2000: 537).

4 Appel's concept of 'ideological context' defined as 'the sum of all elite and mass beliefs as expressed in public opinion surveys and popular discourse' (Appel 2004: 128–9) and elsewhere 'the sum of ideas held by members of elite and mass groups that find expression in both the political discourse and formal institutions' (2000: 530) is somewhat vague. In practice, it tends to present ideology merely as a static constraint on actors akin to political culture or Hall's concept of 'national discourses' and usually seems to equate to mass 'anti-communist fervour' (2004: 138) and the 'anti-communist sentiment' (2004: 142) of public opinion and enterprise level grassroots activism.

5 The difficulties of rigorously establishing the autonomy of ideas through empirical analysis have been noted by a number of authors (Blyth 1997). Indeed, as Hay (2002) suggests, it may be impossible because different findings often reflect researchers' different *ontologies* rather than merely empirical differences.

6 Appel (2004: 50), for example, explains the spread of right-wing ideology in Civic Forum as a product of Klaus's 'skills and deep commitment' to neo-liberalism and 'keen political instincts and understanding of the dominant beliefs and concerns of Czech society', while Saxonberg (1999) stresses his powerful charisma. Ironically, such academic analysis echoes the Civic Democrats' own propagandistic depiction of Klaus as a politician of genius, who singlehandedly shaped Czech transformation.

7 Appel (2000, 2004) for example, sees Klaus as deeply committed to neo-liberalism Vachudova (2005) sees him as opportunistic and power-seeking.

8 Moreover, the subsequent stabilization of party competition in East Central Europe through 'programmatically structuring', rather than pure clientelism (Kitschelt 1995;

Kitschelt *et al.* 1999; Deegan-Krause 2006) suggests that the importance of ideology in post-communist politics is not necessarily a purely transitory phenomenon.

9 I do not suggest, as the Czech right believed (following Hayek), that Czechoslovakia's bureaucratic communist regime *should* be equated with postwar welfare capitalism and democratic corporatism in Western Europe. While Britain's 'socialist' postwar settlement rested on a more or less meaningful social and ideological consensus, Communist rule in Czechoslovakia, despite enjoying some mass legitimacy, was based on a coercive monopoly of political power, rendering ideological discourse, the 'public sphere', public opinion and popular common sense largely meaningless.

10 Gramscian and post-Gramscian analyses have also been applied to a small number of post-communist settings, mainly in relation to socialist and nationalist ideologies (Salecl 1994; Lester 1995).

11 One letter writer to the Czechoslovak Socialist Party's newspaper, for example, complained that he had 'lived in an experimental utopia for forty years ... I very much want to live like a normal European, who can be involved in politics but does not have to be, who regularly votes for a democratic party, whether conservative or social ... I want to live in ordinary, boring, tried-and-tested (*vyzkoušené*) democratic Europe' (*Svobodné slovo*, 22 May 1990).

12 Havel and other former dissidents saw such thinking as part of the mainstream Czech embrace of liberal democracy, the market and 'Europe', which paralleled (and contributed to) advanced aspects of Western political practice such as new social movements or Green politics.

13 Despite technocratic elements stressing the ideologically neutral character of science and technology, during the 1960s Czechoslovak reform communist thinking located itself squarely within the socialist and Marxist camp.

14 Klaus's (2006b) most recent writings on European politics also construct the 'meta-ideology' of 'Europeanism' as a form of Third Way concealed threat to the true values of the right, falsely subverting the distinctions between left and right.

15 In 1998 ODS election posters thus echoed the language of the 1938 Munich crisis, when the Czechoslovak Army had been briefly mobilized in preparation for possible military defence against Nazi invasion. Similarly, in the 2002 election campaign, ODS warned voters that they could go 'With Klaus, or to the left' and claimed in a prerecorded telephone messages from Václav Klaus that 'our future is in danger. Don't give any opportunity to those who are burdening us with debt and taking our freedom ... We have a fateful choice ahead of us' (ODS 2002b). In 2005–6 some ODS leaders, such as its finance spokesperson Vlastimil Tlustý (*Právo*, 23 November 2005), claimed that there were parallels between the Social-Democrat-Communist co-operation of the late 1940s and the contemporary political situation, as did Klaus's adviser Jiří Weigl (2006).

16 In this context, 'Third Ways', where mentioned, were an *empty* category used to stress the absence of compromise options. Similarly, in this discourse, the political centre was less the source of a disguised collectivism than 'nothing ... the efforts of a few politicians who have no opinions, but just want to be in politics' (Klaus and Klusáková 1997), or a 'trap' to be avoided in debates on the party's future (Nečas 1999).

17 Aware of the problems of framing post-Cold-War developments in categories derived from the Cold War (Klaus 2005d; see also *Newsletter CEPu*, May 2006, 1–2), Klaus recently reframed this familiar dichotomy in terms of the threat to individual freedom from 'post-democracy' – the risk of self-appointed groups with no democratic mandate dictating public policy. 'Post-democratic' threats include the EU (*Frankfurter Allgemeine Zeitung*, 15 March 2005) and 'NGO-ism, political correctness, artificial multiculturalism, radical human rightsism and aggressive ecologism' (*Lidové noviny*, 17 May 2005; see also Klaus 2005d).

18 In Hungarian for example the term *polgár*, like the German *Bürger*, refers both to the

'citizen' and the 'bourgeois'. In the Czech context, by contrast, the notion of the citizen/*citroyen* (*občan*) and the burgher/bourgeois (*měšt'an*, *měšt'ák*) are linguistically separate.

19 I am indebted to Prof. Robert Pynsent for this observation. A proliferation of smaller groups, such as the Romany Civic Initiative (ROI) or the Moravian Civic Movement (MOH), also identified themselves as 'civic' in this sense.

20 The popular certainties of ODS ideology were, however, far from the complexities of Bělohradský's concerns with the postmodern condition. Klaus's published writings suggest that he was not familiar with Čapek's philosophical and political writings. He mentions Čapek only once (1996: 78–9) as a popular national writer.

21 Some writers claim that the Czech right's technocratic origins, economistic view of politics and determination to break radically with the communist past echo the 'scientific' certainties of Marxism–Leninism, making ODS a 'vanguardist party' and Klaus a 'Lenin for the bourgeoisie' (Innes 2001: 174, 175; see also Perron 2001). Such arguments, which parallel partisan discourses in Czech politics, seem simplistic. Many political actors, including leading Western politicians, have taken an essentially economic view of democracy. Moreover, as the insights of discourse theory highlight, it is misleading to see post-communist ideologies as in some sense structurally determined by communism, although their appeal may depend on their *rearticulation* of existing discourses.

22 ODS would, in words of Petr Havlík, Chief Secretary of the party's Head Office, 'remove all the irrationalities and revolutionary habits and gradually establish a good system of a professional standard … We are building an enterprise (*podnik*) on a green-field site and our shareholders are our members' (*Bulletin ODS* no. 11, 15 May 1991).

23 In August 1992, shortly after leaving the post of Czech Privatization Minister, Tomáš Ježek predicted 'that just as in the 1950s and 1960s people spoke of a German economic miracle, so in five years' time, or maybe sooner, people will be talking about a Czech economic miracle' (Ježek 1997: 16).

24 The title also echoes a well-known essay of the interwar period by the writer Karel Čapek: 'Why I Am Not a Communist'.

25 Jan Stráský, an ODS Deputy Chairman, noted that

> British conservatism and the British conception of the market economy, although we might take notice of and respect them as much as possible, are things we will definitely never succeed in creating. Rather, it could be said that the Czechization (*počeštění*) of the conservative programme, which we have taken on is something which will emerge.
>
> (Stráský 1993: 75)

26 The small anti-communist grouping of former émigré Jiří Kotlas had contested the 1990 elections as the Free Bloc – Conservative Party (SB-KS) The role of the Civic Democratic Alliance (ODA) has already been noted.

27 Both Hayek and von Mises viewed European federalism as economically rational and politically necessary given inter-state rivalry, nationalist forms of collectivism and the need to embed minimal government against local democratic majorities (Kukthakas 1999; Gillingham 2003: 6–15).

28 An emblematic historical figure for Klaus was St Wenceslas who, although misused by Catholic critics of the Czechoslovak state and Nazi apologists during the 1939–45 Protectorate, he considered a possible focus for a new, historically grounded post-communist Czech identity (Klaus 1993a: 68). As Klaus himself later conceded (2001b: 105–6), he made little distinction between Czech nationhood, Czech statehood and the concept of homeland (*vlast*).

29 In a speech at Masaryk's grave in August 1992 Klaus claimed that the Czech democratic institutions had been historically

borne by the small-scale everyday activity and work of people, who will never go down in history, but who represent the proverbial invisible part of the iceberg without which the visible part would never rise above the surface of oblivion.

(Klaus 1996: 67)

30 The same point is made more directly in later speeches as, for example, in Klaus's appeal to Czechs

to rid ourselves of messianic syndromes and ambitions to become great through empty words and moralizing ... [and] ... draw on another legacy of the 'founding fathers' of our independence – their stress on small-scale work (*drobnou práci*), concern with everyday life (*civilismus*), common sense and belief in their own strengths.

(*Mladá fronta Dnes*, 27 October 1998, 14; see also Klaus 1999: 49–51)

31 This is evident also in Klaus's citation of Masaryk on the importance of national diversity in his discussions of European integration (see Chapter 8).
32 Klaus's attitude to the interwar Czechoslovak Republic was also ambiguous, sometimes stressing its importance as an illustration of liberal and pro-Western traditions, sometimes its flaws as 'neither a paradise lost nor an idyllic period of welfare and civic concord (*svornost*)' (Klaus 1996: 142).
33 Elements of this tradition can arguably be found in Masaryk's view of the Czech Question as a human question or of the foundation of Czechoslovakia as the part of the vanguard of a global democratic revolution; in Kundera's response to the Prague Spring (see Chapter 3); or in former dissidents' presentation of civic movements as a partial alternative to Western party politics (see Chapter 4).
34 Critics have suggested that, despite its rejection of universal values and the notion of Czechs as pioneers of democratic change, Klaus's vision for remaking Europe was also a form of Czech national messianism (Williams 1997b; Doležal 2006).
35 ODS's leading social conservative voice, Petr Nečas, responded by stressing that there were social traditions in British and American conservatism, but argued that the Czech right needed to formulate an appropriate *national* model of Czech conservatism, rather than choose from a menu of regional models (*Lidové noviny*, 18 October 1996, 11).
36 As early as 1991 the Czech Privatization Minister Tomáš Ježek had spoken of the possible corporate governance problems associated with voucher privatization as 'stock market socialism' (*akciový socialismus*) (cited in Appel 2004: 193).
37 ODA's founding programme *The Road to a Free Society* stressed at considerable length that both free individuals and structures of 'human interdependence' (*lidská vzajemnost*) such as the family, civil society and religion were necessary for a genuinely liberal 'free society' to exist (ODA 1989).
38 This discourse was articulated both in 4K's programmatic documents and those of its member parties and the writings of critical supporters in the media and intelligentsia such as Jiří Pehe (1999: 223–36).
39 The Opposition Agreement, it was argued, revived the exclusionary, top-down conceptions of party politics, clientelism and cynical attitudes to ideology characteristic of the 'normalization' period, as well as boosting the support for the contemporary Communist Party proper by denying voters a democratic outlet through which to express dissatisfaction (Lobkowicz 2000; Pehe 2002a: 186–7). For a critique of these arguments see Roberts (2003).
40 The parallel with the Slovak experience also served to develop 4K's identity, enabling it to redefine its status as an ad hoc coalition in positive terms by stressing that it was not a mere electoral alliance but a 'Third force' acting like the Slovak Democratic Coalition in concert with civic groups to express powerful societal needs for reform (Pehe 1999: 183).

41 ODS's more traditional nationalist constructions of Czech identity reflect the intellectual influence of the philosopher Miloslav Bednář, who joined ODS in 2000, a thinker strongly committed to defending traditional Czech political thought against intellectual paradigms imported from the West. Despite his embrace of postmodernity, Václav Bělohradský had a similar view of Czechs as bearers of a democratic liberal culture contrasting with a supposed German focus on ethnic and class community (*Lidové noviny*, 13–16 July 1993).

42 This assertion overlooks the many reflections on Czech national identity by figures such as Havel (1991) and Pithart (1990a, 1998a, 1998b; see also Auer 2003).

43 Klaus's view, expressed indirectly in a highly sympathetic review of an Australian think-tank report (*Lidové noviny*, 18 February 2003), is at odds with the more widespread neo-liberal view of migration and open labour markets as economically beneficial, if sometimes socially and politically problematic. The break-down of social solidarity through cultural diversification is more often seen as a 'progressive's dilemma' imperilling the maintenance of national welfare states.

44 Klaus's first published reflection on US multiculturalism pointedly remarked that the majority of students at a graduation ceremony he had attended in Dallas were from non-white minority groups. Characteristically, however, Klaus initially wrote that he 'would not like to make any judgement whether it is good or bad' but thought it was necessary that Czechs should be aware of it and 'think through its possible consequences' (Klaus 2000a: 117).

45 Some ODS mayors and Senators have on occasion gone considerably further in suggesting authoritarian measures to control Roma or encourage them to emigrate (Fawn 2001).

46 Miroslav Topolánek thus endorsed Klaus's linkage of security issues and immigration in Europe, which he described as 'beginning to destroy its original culture from within' (*Mladá fronta Dnes*, 18 July 2005, 2). However, he argued that migration was a natural phenomenon, which could not be stopped, merely not encouraged. The Christian Democrat leader Miroslav Kalousek accepted Klaus's arguments regarding security and the need for migrants to accept the values, not just the laws, of host societies. However, he too qualified his comments, noting that migration could be culturally enriching, as with the many sources of Catholic culture in the Czech lands (*Mladá fronta Dnes*, 18 July 2005, 1, 2).

47 Klaus linked multiculturalism to the ideology of 'Europeanism' as a threat to the 'good old Europe (*starou dobrou Evropu*)' of national states (*Mladá fronta Dnes*, 25 February 2006).

48 Other elements of ex-dissident conservatisms, such as Doležal's rejection of both anti-communism and notions of Czech national superiority, Pithart's scepticism regarding traditional constructions of Czech national identity and Hromádková's stress on personal and sexual morality, were ignored.

8 From neo-liberalism to national interests: Europe and the new Czech right

1 ODS's revised position on European integration was developed from summer 1999 at both its regular annual congresses 1999–2001 and its ideological conferences; the last, in May 2003, was specifically devoted to European issues. The positions of the *Manifesto* strongly informed the 2002 ODS election programme.

2 The article dated 14 September 1992 discusses Czech–Slovak relations and the division of Czechoslovakia.

3 The *Manifesto* also noted the lack of a European political identity, the tendency of federalist models of European integration to ignore the role of national identity as a basis for democratic institutions and the 'implicit anti-Americanism' of greater EU political integration (Zahradil *et al.* 2001a: 8).

4 The *Manifesto* opposed any extension of Qualified Majority Voting (QMV), enhancement of the powers of the European Parliament or the establishment of the European Commission in a quasi-governmental role (Zahradil *et al.* 2001a: 4, 8–10). These points were re-emphasized in a speech to the European Parliament by Václav Klaus on 4 December 2001 arguing that existing levels of EU political integration should be frozen (Klaus 2002c).

5 The *Manifesto* defines the Czech national interest as

> the maintenance and development of a clearly defined national identity: the strengthening ... of an institutional framework in which the same rules apply for big and small states; the maintenance of the territorial integrity and political sovereignty, independence and security of the Czech Republic; the mutual opening and linking of markets without excessive barriers.
>
> (Zahradil *et al.* 2001a: 8)

6 The Coalition accepted all aspects of the *acquis*, including the Euro (which it wished the Czech Republic to adopt as soon as possible); the Schengen agreement; European social and regional policies; and the Common Foreign and Security Policy (which it wished to see extended) and plans to develop an EU defence capacity, which it saw as complementing Czech NATO membership and rebalancing the alliance around both European and American poles.

7 Unlike the europhile Social Democrats – and in marked contrast to ODS's critique of the European Commission – the Coalition welcomed the tutelage exercised by European bureaucracies after EU accession as means of modernizing Czech public administration.

8 Citing the US experience, Kroupa (2003) argued that federalism was in no sense unconservative and could both guarantee states' local autonomy and counteract trends towards populism and the tyranny of democratic majorities likely to arise in small, homogeneous states such as the Czech Republic.

9 Although the Civic Democratic Party had published detailed Position Documents on the EU (ODS 2003a) and proceedings from an ideological conference dealing with integration (2003b), each over a hundred pages long, it seems to have produced only one leaflet explaining its position more succinctly to voters (ODS 2003c).

10 ODS argued that it was unnecessary for the party to campaign for a 'Yes' vote, given that the overwhelming majority of its supporters were known to favour EU membership.

11 Klaus justified his stance as necessary to underline the neutrality of his office as President.

12 Klaus showed a similar reluctance to endorse EU membership during the public celebrations of 30 April to 1 May 2004 held to mark Czech accession. Rather than attend a gala concert at the National Theatre with other leading figures in Czech public life, he joined the traditional Walpurgis Night hike to Blaník hill near Prague where, according to Czech legend, sleeping knights lie buried who one day will awake to save the nation in its hour of greatest peril. The symbolism of this gesture was widely noted.

13 The Convention was a specially convened assembly of representatives of the national parliaments and governments of existing and candidate members, the European Parliament and the European Commission.

14 In total 17 of the Czech Republic's 24 MEPs voted against the Treaty.

15 This decision reflected both the contested nature of the Treaty and uncertainty over whether ratification would be a constitutional act under Czech law, requiring a qualified parliamentary majority.

16 ODS argued that the Convention had exceeded its mandate by drafting a constitution; used an undemocratic decision-making process based on consensus, which well-placed federalists had manipulated (*Mladá fronta Dnes*, 29 September 2003; ODS 2004b) and acted unfairly by denying accession states the right to block decisions when existing member states had reached a consensus (ODS 2004b).

17 These concerns centred on (1) the incorporation of the Charter of Fundamental Rights

into the Constitution; (2) the extension of Qualified Majority Voting to budgetary issues; and (3) the Constitution's requirement that member states should 'actively and unreservedly support' the Common Foreign and Security Policy and comply with actions taken under CFSP.

18 Given the complexity of interests involved, Klaus suggested that European-level decision-making was possible only at the expense of some of its participants (*Mladá fronta Dnes*, 16 December 2003).

19 CVVM polling in June/July suggested a majority of likely referendum participants still in favour of the Constitution (56 per to 21 per cent) (CVVM press release, 23 August 2005). However, polling by Median recorded a decrease from 62 per cent support in May 2005 to 42 per cent in June and 21 per cent in July, when the largest group of respondents, 36.9 per cent, opposed the Constitution (*Mladá fronta Dnes*, 14 July 2005, 2). STEM recorded a decrease of support for the Constitution among probable referendum participants from 62 per cent in May 2005 to 42 per cent and 44 per cent in June and July 2005 with majorities opposed (cited in Úřad vlády 2006: 15). SC&C polling for *Mladá fronta Dnes* showed 19 per cent in favour, 29 per cent opposed and the remainder undecided (BBC Czech.com online news, 13 June 2005).

20 Klaus's essay on the subject (*Lidové noviny*, 18 June 2005) did little to specify the structure of such a reformed EU. His most concrete demands were that an Organization of European States should abandon trappings of statehood such as European citizenship, a flag and anthem and make all significant decisions on the basis of consensus. He did, however, allow that it should be based on a 'constitutive document' to entrench the powers of national states and appease federalists.

21 Before the French and Dutch referendums Klaus had dismissed notions of returning to the pre-Maastricht era as 'utopian' (*Frankfurter Allgemeine Zeitung*, 15 March 2005).

22 ODS and Social Democrat leaders already held regular discussions to identify areas of possible consensus on issues of far-reaching national importance such as the EU and pension reform, but reportedly made little progress (*Lidové noviny*, 6 June 2005).

23 ODS argued in classically neo-liberal terms that the competitiveness of the EU could be secured only by competition between member states' national fiscal, tax and social models (ODS 2004a).

24 Klaus noted that the Czech Republic had no deeply rooted historical antagonisms with Turkey, which had last threatened the Czech lands in the seventeenth century, 'which certainly cannot be said about many current EU member states' (*Newsletter CEP*, October 2005, 8).

25 Klaus saw Al-Qaeda-inspired terrorism as a limited and localized threat to certain Western countries (*Mladá fronta Dnes*, 25 February 2006; see also Klaus 2006b).

26 For similar reasons, Klaus also dismissed the 'civilizational' threat of Russia, arguing that partial democratization, geo-political distance and economic and demographic decline had reduced Russia's capacity to threaten the Czech Republic (Klaus 2001b: 130–3).

27 Viewing democratic rights as culturally embedded, Klaus was sceptical of the exportability of liberal democratic institutions, especially when imposed by force, and was concerned at the prospect of further preventative wars against rogue states (*Mladá fronta Dnes*, 25 March 2003; *Lidové noviny*, 26 March 2003). While sympathizing with the neo-conservatives' scepticism of international organizations and stress on national interests, he was critical of claims that the US had 'extended interests' giving it a special right to shape world order (*Newsletter CEPu* 5/2004).

28 ODS had an ambiguous position on the Euro, promising to meet the criteria for entry to the Eurozone as part of wider domestic reforms and then hold a referendum on the question of Euro entry. New member states joining the EU in 2004 and 2007 are obliged to adopt the Euro when able to do so as part of the *acquis* (ODS 2004a).

29 When parliamentarians from accession states were invited to attend the European Parliament as observers in 2002, ODS had initially wished to divide its observers

between the European People's Party and the Alliance for a Europe of Nations (AEN). Jan Zahradil also attended the AEN's founding conference on an 'exploratory' basis (*Lidové noviny*, 26 February 2002).

30 In addition to the British Conservatives, the European Democrats include MEPs from the Ulster Unionist Party (UUP), the Portuguese Popular Party (CDS-PP) and the Italian Pensioners' Party (PP).

31 Civic Democrats agreed to support a Czech–Vatican treaty, an agreed statement on Czech–German relations and the Beneš Decrees restating the content of the intergovernmental Czech–German Declaration of 1997; and not to stress their views on the European Constitution (Sokol 2006).

32 Conversation with IRI official, 2 February 2006. The parties failed even to create the functioning website promised in the 2001 resolution.

33 The project of a new anti-federal grouping was subsequently dropped by the incoming Conservative leader Michael Howard.

34 Indeed, some interpreted Topolánek's undiplomatic comments about the 'populist' character of the Polish coalition government led by Law and Justice (PiS), another member of the prospective grouping, as a calculated attempt to derail the project (*Lidové noviny*, 8 June 2006). As a compromise solution Topolánek and Cameron agreed to establish an anti-federalist grouping Movement for European Reform in 2009 after the next European Elections.

35 Both Klaus (*Hospodářské noviny*, 10 December 2001) and Zahradil agreed with critics that the economic and geo-political realities constraining the Czech Republic meant that non-membership scenarios were unlikely ever to be realized and that Czech EU membership was a virtual inevitability. Their public presentation of positive scenarios of non-membership nevertheless indicated an important shift in the ODS preferences.

36 The Beneš Decrees were effectively neutralized as an issue in Czech debates on European integration following the publication in October 2002 of a legal opinion commissioned by the European Parliament, which found that the Decrees were not an obstacle to Czech accession.

37 Even europhile parties such as the Czech Christian Democrats (KDU-ČSL) were 'eurosceptic' in their rejection of certain EU policies such as opening accession negotiations with Turkey.

38 This is clearly, for example, the case with the Manifesto of Czech Eurorealism's advocacy of the 'Hong Kong solution' of becoming a free market *entrepôt* linked to NAFTA as an alternative to EU membership, an idea canvassed by a number of leading British Conservatives including the party's then leader Iain Duncan Smith (*Guardian*, 22 August 2001).

39 Much early literature on euroscepticism sought to assess the competing influences of electoral strategy, institutional factors such as electoral systems and patterns of party competition (Sitter 2001a; Taggart and Szczerbiak 2002), ideology and interests (Marks and Wilson 2000; Kopecký and Mudde 2002).

40 This approach parallels both classic approaches to West European party formation and attempts to adapt Rokkan's model to post-communist Eastern Europe (Lipset and Rokkan 1967; Cotta 1994).

41 Debates over strategy also trade off the competing claims of internal party stability, office holding and the achievement of policy goals (Sitter and Batory 2004; Sitter 2002).

42 As polling showed, the issue of Europe lacked salience for both ODS supporters and voters generally (*Mladá fronta Dnes*, 26 June 2000).

43 In the example referred to, Klaus records that pressure from Zieleniec made him abandon a series of critical remarks on the Visegrad group.

44 Tellingly, ODS's nominee for a proposed new cabinet portfolio of European affairs in 2006 was Petr Gandalovič, the former mayor of Ústí nad Lábem, who had previously served as a diplomat.

References

Abdelal, R. (2001) *National Purpose in the World Economy: Post-Soviet States in Comparative Perspective*, Ithaca and London: Cornell University Press.

Abrams, B. (1995) 'Morality, Wisdom and Revision: The Czech Opposition of the 1970s and the Expulsion of the Sudeten Germans', *East European Politics and Societies*, 9: 234–54.

—— (2002) 'The Second World War and the East European Revolution', *East European Politics and Societies*, 16:3, 623–64.

—— (2004) *The Struggle for the Soul of a Nation: Czech Culture and the Rise of Communism*, Lanham: Rowman & Littlefield.

Ágh, A. (1988) *The Politics of Central Europe*, London: SAGE.

Aldrich, A. (1995) *Why Parties? The Origin and Transformation of Political Parties in America*, Chicago: University of Chicago Press.

Alexander, G. (2001) 'Institutions, Path Dependence and Democratic Consolidation', *Journal of Theoretical Politics*, 13: 249–69.

Andor, L. (1991) *The New Right in Central-Eastern Europe*, Budapest: Budapest Papers on Democratic Transition.

Appel, H. (2000) 'The Ideological Determinants of Liberal Economic Reform: The Case of Privatization', *World Politics*, 52: 520–49.

—— (2004) *A New Capitalist Order: Privatization and Ideology in Russia and Eastern Europe*, Pittsburgh, PA: University of Pittsburgh Press.

Appel, H. and Gould, J. (2000) 'Identity Politics and Economic Reform: Examining Industrial-State Relations in the Czech Republic', *Europe-Asia Studies*, 52: 111–31.

Auer, S. (2003) *Liberal Nationalism in Central Europe*, London: RoutledgeCurzon.

Baker, D., Gamble, A. and Seawright, D. (2002) 'Nation and Market: Modern British Conservatism and Hyperglobalism', *British Journal of Politics and International Relations*, 4: 399–428.

Balcerowicz, L. (1994) 'Understanding Postcommunist Transitions', *Journal of Democracy*, 5: 75–89.

Bastow, S. and Martin, J. (2000) *Third Way Discourse: European Ideologies in the Twentieth Century*, Edinburgh: Edinburgh University Press.

—— (2005) 'Third Way Politics Today', in Howarth, J. and Torfing, J. (eds) *Discourse Theory in European Politics: Identity, Politics and Governance*, Basingstoke: Palgrave.

Batt, J. (1988) *Economic Reform and Political Change in Eastern Europe: A Comparison of the Czechoslovak and Hungarian Experiences*, Basingstoke: Macmillan.

—— (1990) *East Central Europe from Reform to Transformation*, London: Pinter/RIIA.

Bazin, A. (1999) *Germany and the Enlargement of the European Union to the Czech Republic*, Florence: European University Institute Working Paper RSC 1999/21.

Bělohradský, V. (1995) 'Nikdo není popsaný list', in Klaus, V. *Dopočítávání do jedné*, Prague: Management Press.

—— (2000) '"Realism in Politics Worries People": An Interview with the Philosopher Václav Bělohradský', *Central Europe Review*, 2. Online. Available www.ce-review.org/00/20/interview20_belohradsky.html (accessed 12 October 2006).

Benda, V. (1980) 'Paralelní polis', in Prečan, V. (ed.) *Křest'ané a charta 77: výběr dokumentů a textů*, Cologne: Index.

—— (1984) 'Dopis Rogeru Scrutonovi', *Rozmluvy*, 3: 35–8.

—— (1985) 'Catholicism and Politics', in Keane, J. (ed.) *Power of the Powerless: Citizens against the State in Central-Eastern Europe*, London: Hutchinson.

Benda, V., Šimečka, M., Jirouš, I.M., Dienstbier, J., Havel, V., Hejdánek, L. and Šimsa, J. (1988) 'Parallel Polis or an Independent Society in Central and Eastern Europe: An Enquiry', *Social Research*, 55: 211–22.

Beneš, E. (1941) *Demokracie dnes a zítra*, London: Kruh přátel československé knihy.

Benešová, L. (2001) *Kronika ODS*, Prague: ODS.

Berman, S. (1998) *The Social Democratic Moment: Ideas and Politics in the Making of Interwar Europe*, Cmbridge, MA, and London: Harvard University Press.

Betz, H. (1994) *Radical Right-Wing Populism in Western Europe*, Basingstoke: Macmillan.

Bielasiak, J. (1997) 'Substance and Process in the Development of Party Systems in East Central Europe', *Communist and Post-Communist Studies*, 30: 23–44.

Bieler, A. (2000) *Globalisation and Enlargement of the European Union: Austrian and Swedish Social Forces in the Struggle over Membership*, London: Routledge/Warwick Studies in Globalisation.

Birch, S., Millard, F., Popescu, M. and Williams K. (2002) *Embodying Democracy: Electoral System Design in post-Communist Europe*, New York: Palgrave Macmillan.

Blackwood, L. (1990) 'Czech and Polish National Democracy at the Dawn of Independent Statehood 1918–1919', *East European Politics and Societies*, 4: 469–88.

Blaive, M. (2001) *Promarněná příležitost: Československo a rok 1956*, Prague: Prostor.

Blecha, I. (1997) *Jan Patočka*, Olomouc: Votobia.

Blejer, M. and Coricelli, F. (eds) (1995) *The Making of Economic Reform in Eastern Europe: Conversations with Leading Economic Reformers in Hungary, Poland and the Czech Republic*, Aldershot: Edward Elgar.

Blinkhorn, N. (ed.) (1990) *Fascists and Conservatives: The Radical Right and the Establishment in Twentieth Century Europe*, London: Unwin Hyman.

Bloem, F. (2002) 'The Reception of Perestroika among Czech Dissidents', paper presented at the New Contours of Legitimacy in Central Europe: New Approaches in Graduate Studies conference, St Antony's College, Oxford, 24–6 May.

Blyth, M. (1997) 'Any More Bright Ideas? The Ideational Turn in Comparative Political Economy', *Comparative Politics*, 29: 229–50.

Bockman, J. and Eyal, G. (2002) 'Eastern Europe as a Laboratory of Economic Knowledge', *American Journal of Sociology*, 108: 310–52.

Boguszak, M., Gabal, I. and Rak, V. (1990a) 'Falešné jistoty', *Lidové noviny*, 24 September, 5.

—— (1990b) 'Kde jsou skutečná sociální rizika reformy', *Lidové noviny*, 17 September, 4.

—— (1990c) *Československo – listopad 1990: postoje české a slovenské veřejnosti k politickému, ekonomickému a sociálnímu vývoji*, Prague: AISA.

—— (1996) 'Political Climate Before the Election – Attitudes, Preferences, and Expectations of the Czechoslovakian Public', in Gabal, I. (ed.), *The 1990 Election to the Czechoslovak Federal Assembly: Analyses, Documents and Data*, Berlin: Wissenschaftszentrum Berlin für Sozialforschung.

Boguszak, M. and Rak, V. (1990) 'Privatizace: dříve strašidlo a co nyní', *Lidové noviny*, 18 June, 8.

'Bohemus' (pseudonym for Brod, T., Doležal, J., Otáhal, M., Pithart, P., Pojar, M. and Příhoda, P. (1990) 'Stanovisko k odsunu Němců z Československa', in Černý, J., Křen, J., Kural, V. and Otáhal, M. (eds) *Češi, Němci, odsun: diskuse nezávislých historiků*, Prague: Academia.

Bozóki, A. (2003) 'Theoretical Interpretations of Elite Change in East Central Europe', in Dogan, M. (ed.), *Elite Configurations at the Apex of Power*, Leiden and Boston: Brill.

Bozóki, A. and Ishiyama, J.T. (eds) (2002) *The Communist Successor Parties of Central and Eastern Europe*, Armonk, NY: M.E. Sharpe.

Bratinka, P. (1991) 'Conservative Reflections on Czechoslovak Politics', in Whipple, T. (ed.) *After the Velvet Revolution*, New York: Freedom House.

Brom, K. and Orenstein, M. (1994) 'The Privatised Sector in the Czech Republic: Government and Bank Control in a Transitional Economy', *Europe-Asia Studies*, 46: 893–928.

Brudny, Y.M. (1993) 'The Dynamics of "Democratic Russia", 1990–93', *Post-Soviet Affairs*, 9: 141–70.

Bryant, C. (2000) 'Whose Nation? Czech Dissidents and History Writing from a Post-1989 Perspective', *History and Memory*, 12: 30–64.

Budil, I. (1992) 'Konec českého mesianismu', *Prostor*, 19: 17–18.

Bugge, P. (2000) *Czech Perceptions of the Perspective of EU Membership Havel vs. Klaus*, Florence: European University Institute Working Paper RSC No. 2000/10.

Bunce, V. (1999a) *Subversive Institutions: The Design and Destruction of Socialism and the State*, Cambridge: Cambridge University Press.

—— (1999b) 'Peaceful versus Violent State Dismemberment: A Comparison of the Soviet Union, Yugoslavia and Czechoslovakia', *Politics and Society*, 27: 217–37.

Burian, M. (1997) 'Prognostici v takzvané sametové revoluci', *Soudobé dějiny*, 4: 492–509.

Čalda, M. (1996) 'The Roundtable Talks in Czechoslovakia', in Elster, J. (ed.) *The Roundtable Talks and the Breakdown of Communism*, Budapest: Central European University Press.

Callinicos, A. (1991) *The Revenge of History: Marxism and the East European Revolutions*, Oxford: Polity Press.

Čaněk, D. (1996) *Národ, národnost, menšiny a rasismus*, Prague: ISE.

Carty, R.K. (2004) 'Parties as Franchise Systems: The Stratarchical Imperative', *Party Politics*, 10: 5–24.

Carty, R.K. and Cross, W. (2006) 'Can Stratarchically Organized Parties Be Democratic? The Canadian Case', *Journal of Elections, Public Opinion and Parties*, 16: 93–114.

Čechurová, J. (1999) *Česká politická pravice: Mezi převratem a krizí*, Prague: Nakladatelství Lidové noviny.

Centeno, M.A. (1993) 'The New Leviathan: The Dynamics and Limits of Technocracy', *Theory and Society*, 22: 307–35.

Čermák, M. and Sontona, J. (1997) *Klaus je mrtev, at' žije Klaus!*, Prague, DUEL.

Česal, J. (2000) 'Názory naší veřejnosti na vstup do Evropské unie', *Integrace* 2. Online. Available www.integrace.cz/integrace/clanek.asp?id=53 (accessed 13 March 2007).

CEVRO (2003). 'Start kampaně před referendum', 2/2003, 16.

Chan, K.L. (2001),'Strands of Conservative Politics in Post-Communist Transition: Adapting to Europeanisation and Democratisation', in Lewis, P.G. (ed.) *Party Development and Democratic Change in Post-Communist Europe*, London: Frank Cass.

Checkel, J. (1998) 'The Constructivist Turn in International Relations Theory', *World Politics*, 50: 324–48.

Cheles, L. (ed.) (1995), *The Far Right in Western and Eastern Europe*, London: Longman.

Chudomel, J., Kavan, J. and Konvička, L. (1990) 'OF na rozcestí?', *Fórum*, 12: 1.

Clark, E. and Soulsby, A. (1996) 'The Re-Formation of the Managerial Elite in the Czech Republic', *Europe-Asia Studies*, 48: 285–303.

Collier, R. (1993) 'Combining Alternative Perspectives – Internal Trajectories versus External Influences as Explanations of Latin American Politics in the 1940s', *Comparative Politics*, 26: 1–29.

Collier, R.B. and Collier, D. (1991) *Shaping the Political Arena: Critical Junctures, the Labor Movement and Regime Rynamics in Latin America*, Princeton, NJ: Princeton University Press.

Corley, F. (1993) 'The Secret Clergy in Communist Czechoslovakia', *Religion, State and Society*, 21:2: 171–206.

Cotta, M. (1994) 'Building Party Systems after the Dictatorship: The East European cases in Comparative Perspective', in Pridham, G. and Vanhanen, T. (eds) *Democratisation in Eastern Europe: Domestic and International Perspectives*, London and New York: Routledge.

Čtyřkoalice (1999) 'Svatováclavská čtyřkoaliční dohoda'. Online. Available www.oda. cz/clanek.asp?id=224 (accessed 1 March 2006); reprinted in Hamerský, M. and Dimun, P. (eds) *10 let na straně svobody – Kronika ODA z let 1989–1999*, Brno: Bachant.

—— (1999b) 'Deklarace Společně pro změnu'. Online. Available www.oda.cz/clanek. asp?id=397 (accessed 1 March 2006).

—— (2001), *Společně pro změnu – dokument Čtyřkoalice*, Prague: Čtyřkoalice.

Cuhra, J. (2001) 'KSČ, stát a římskokatolická církev (1948–1989)', *Soudobé dějiny*, 8: 267–93.

Čulík, J. and Pecina, T. (eds) (2001). *V hlavních zprávách: Televize*, Prague: ISV.

Cvijetic, S. (2000) 'And What Now?', *Central Europe Review*, 2. Online. Available www.ce-review.org (accessed 1 June 2003).

Dale, G. (2004) *Popular Protest in the East German Revolution – Judgement on the Street*, London: Frank Cass.

Daněk, B. (1990) *Strana lidová – její krize a obroda*. Prague: Vyšehrad.

Dangerfield, M. (1997) 'Ideology and Czech Transformation: Neoliberal Rhetoric or Neoliberal Reality', *East European Politics and Societies*, 1: 436–67.

David, M. (1986) 'Moral and Maternal: The Family in the Right', in Levitas, R. (ed.) *The Ideology of the New Right*, Cambridge: Polity Press.

Day, B. (1999) *The Velvet Philosophers*, London: Claridge Press.

De Candole, J. (1988) 'Vaclav Havel as a Conservative Thinker', *Salisbury Review*, 7: 45–9.

Deegan-Krause, K. (2003) 'Slovakia's Second Transition', *Journal of Democracy*, 14: 65–79.

—— (2006) *Elected Affinities: Democracy and Party Competitions in Slovakia and the Czech Republic*, Stanford, CA: Stanford University Press.

Deloitte and Touche (1998) 'Zpráva o výsledcích forenzního šetření financování ODS'. Online. Available www.ruzovypanter.cz/file/Zprava_o_vysledcich_forenzniho_setreni_financovani_ODS.doc (accessed 1 October 2006).

Dimun, P. (2002) 'Komentář: Taková byla Čytrkoalice', *Proglas*, 2002/2. Online. Available www.cdkbrno.cz/rp/clanky/52/komentar-takova-byla-ctyrkoalice/ (accessed 10 October 2006).

Dobal, V. (1995) 'Jak byla založena ODA'. Online. Available www.oda.cz/clanek. asp?id=6 (accessed 1 July 2005).

Doležal, B. (ed.) (1993) *Hledání naděje (1978–1987) Výběry z ineditních sborníků*, Prague: Maxdorf/Nadace Demokratické Initiativy.

—— (1997) *Nesamozřejmá politika: výběr z publicistických statí, 1991/1996*, Prague: Torst.

—— (2006) 'Klausovo tažení proti evropeismu', 9 April. Online. Available www.bohumildolezal.cz (accessed 14 April 2006).

Dostál, V. (1998) *Agrární strana: její rozmach a zánik*, Brno: Atlantis.

Drápala, M. (2000) *Na ztracené vartě Západu: antologie české nesocialistické publicistiky z let 1945–1948*, Prague: Prostor.

Drulák, P. and Königová, L. (2002) 'The Discipline of International Relations in Central and Eastern Europe', *European Political Science*, 1: 47–53.

Dryzek, J. and Holmes, L. (2000) 'The Real World of Civic Republicanism: Making Democracy Work in Poland and the Czech Republic', *Europe-Asia Studies*, 52: 1043–68.

Dufek P. (2001), 'Rozhovor s Františkem Mikšem'. Online. Available www.cdkbrno.cz/ proglas.php?clanek=dufek3 (accessed 1 August 2005).

Duverger, M. (1954) *Political Parties: Their Organization and Activity in the Modern State*, London: Methuen.

Dvořáková, V. (2002) 'Civil Society in the Czech Republic', in Kopecký, P. and Mudde, C. (eds) *Uncivil Society? Contentious Politics in Post-Communist Europe*, London: Routledge.

Earle, J. and Gehlbach, S. (2003) 'A Spoonful of Sugar: Privatization and Popular Support for Reform in the Czech Republic', *Economics and Politics*, 15: 1–32.

Earle, J., Frydman, R., Rapaczunski, A. and Turkewitz, J. (1994) *Small Privatization: The Transformation of Retail Trade and Consumer Services in the Czech Republic, Hungary and Poland*, Budapest: Central European University Press.

Eatwell, R. and O'Sullivan, N. (eds) (1989) *The Nature of the Right: American and European Politics Since 1789*, London: Pinter.

Edgar, D. (1986) 'The Free or the Good', in Levitas, R. (ed.) *The Ideology of the New Right*, Cambridge: Polity Press.

Ekiert, G. (1996) *The State against Society: Political Crises and their Aftermath in East Central Europe*, Princeton, NJ: Princeton University Press.

Enyedi, Z. (1996) 'Organizing a Subcultural Party in Eastern Europe: The Case of the Hungarian Christian Democrats', *Party Politics*, 2: 377–96.

European Commission (1998) *Regular Report from the Commission on the Czech Republic's Progress towards Accession*, Brussels: European Commission.

—— (1999) *Regular Report from the Commission on the Czech Republic's Progress towards Accession*, Brussels: European Commission.

—— (2000) *Regular Report from the Commission on the Czech Republic's Progress towards Accession*, Brussels: European Commission.

—— (2001) *Regular Report from the Commission on the Czech Republic's Progress towards Accession*, Brussels: European Commission.

—— (2002) *Regular Report from the Commission on the Czech Republic's Progress towards Accession*, Brussels: European Commission.

—— (2006) *Eurobarometr 64 – Podzim 2005. Národní zpráva – Česká republika.* Prague: European Commission.

European Convention (2003) 'Contribution by Mr David Heathcoat-Amory ...'. Document no. CONV 773/03, CONTRIB 347, 30 May.

Evans, G. and Whitefield, S. (1993), 'Identifying the Bases of Party Competition in Eastern Europe', *British Journal of Political Science*, 23: 521–48.

—— (1998) 'The Structuring of Political Cleavages in Post-Communist Societies: The Case of the Czech Republic and Slovakia', *Political Studies*, 46: 115–39.

Eyal, G. (2000) 'Anti-politics and the Spirit of Capitalism: Dissidents, Monetarists and the Czech Transition to Capitalism', *Theory and Society*, 29: 49–92.

—— (2003) *The Origins of Postcommunist Elites: From Prague Spring to Breakup of Czechoslovakia*, Minneapolis, MN, and London: University of Minnesota Press.

Fawn, R. (2001) 'Czech Attitudes Towards the Roma: "Expecting More of Havel's Country?"', *Europe-Asia Studies*, 53: 1193–219.

—— (2006) 'The Temelín Nuclear Power Plant and the European Union in Austrian–Czech Relations', *Communist and Post-Communist Studies*, 39: 101–19.

Fiala, P., Mareš, M. and Pšeja, P. (1999) 'The Development of Political Parties and the Party System', in Večerník, J. and Matějů, P. (eds) *Ten Years of Rebuilding Capitalism: Czech Society after 1989*, Prague: Academia.

Fink-Hafner D. (2002), 'Between Continuity and Change', in Toš, N. and Mihelak, V. (eds) *Slovenia between Continuity and Change, 1990–1997: Analyses, Documents and Data*, Berlin: Edition Sigma.

Fish, S.M. (1995) *Democracy from Scratch: Opposition and Regime in the New Russian Revolution*, Princeton, NJ: Princeton Univesity Press.

Fisher, S. (2000) 'The Rise and Fall of National Movements in Slovakia and Croatia', *Slovak Foreign Policy Affairs*, 1: 12–23.

Flora, P., Kuhnle, S. and Urwin, D. (eds) (1999) *State Formation, Nation-Building and Mass Politics in Europe: The Theory of Stein Rokkan*, Oxford: Oxford University Press.

Fowler, B. (2004) 'Concentrated Orange: Fidesz and the Remaking of the Hungarian Centre-Right, 1994–2002', *Journal of Communist Studies and Transition Politics*, 20: 80–114.

Gamble, A. (1986) 'The Political Economy of Freedom', in Levitas, R. (ed.) *The Ideology of the New Right*, Oxford: Polity Press.

—— (1996) *Hayek: The Iron Cage of Liberty*, Cambridge: Polity Press, 1996.

Ganev, V.I. (2001). 'The Separation of Party and State as a Logistical Problem: A Glance at the Causes of State Weakness in Postcommunism', *East European Politics and Societies*, 15: 389–420.

—— (2005) 'The "Triumph of Neoliberalism" Reconsidered: Critical Remarks on Ideas Centred Analyses of Political and Economic Change in Post-Communism', *East European Politics and Societies*, 19: 343–78.

Garton Ash, T. (1991) *The Uses of Adversity: Essays on the Fate of Central Europe*, London: Penguin (2nd edition).

—— (1993) *In Europe's Name: Germany and the Divided Continent*, London: Jonathan Cape.

—— (1999) *A History of the Present*, London: Penguin.

Garver, B. (1978) *The Young Czech Party 1874–1901 and the Emergence of a Multiparty System*, New Haven and London: Yale University Press.

Gellner, E. (1988) *Plough, Book and Sword*, London, Collins Harvill.
—— (1995) 'The Price of Velvet: Thomas Masaryk and Václav Havel', *Czech Sociological Review*, 3: 45–57.
Giddens, A. (1995) *Beyond Left and Right: The Future of Radical Politics*, Oxford: Polity Press.
—— (2002) *Runaway World: How Globalisation Is Reshaping Our Lives*, London: Profile.
Gillingham, J. (2003) *European Integration, 1950–2003 – Superstate or New Market Economy?*, Cambridge: Cambridge University Press.
Glenn, J.K. (2001) *Framing Democracy: Civil Society and Civic movements in Eastern Europe*, Stanford, CA: Stanford University Press.
Glenny, M. (1990) *The Rebirth of History: Eastern Europe in the Age of Democracy*, London: Penguin.
Gowan, P. (1996) 'Eastern Europe, Western Power and Neo-Liberalism' *New Left Review*, 21: 129–40.
Grabowski, T. (1996) 'The Party that Never Was: The Rise and Fall of the Solidarity Citizens' Committees in Poland, *East European Politics and Societies*, 10: 214–45.
Grenstad, G. and Selle, P. (1995) 'Cultural Theory and the New Institutionalism', *Journal of Theoretical Politics*, 7: 5–27.
Greskovits, B. (1998) *The Political Economy of Patience and Protest*, Budapest: Central European University Press.
Gross, J. (1989) 'The Social Consequences of War: Preliminaries for the Study of the Imposition of Communist Regimes in East Central Europe', *East European Politics and Societies*, 3: 198–214.
Grzymala-Busse, A. (2002) *Redeeming the Communist Past: The Transformation of Communist Parties in East Central Europe*, Cambridge: Cambridge University Press.
—— (2006) 'The Discreet Charm of Formal Institutions: Postcommunist Party Competition and State Oversight', *Comparative Political Studies*, 39: 271–300.
Grzymala-Busse, A. and Jones Luong, P. (2002) 'Reconceptualizing the State: Lessons from Post-Communism', *Politics and Society*, 30: 529–54.
Hadjiisky, M. (1996) *La fin du Forum civique et la naissance du Parti démocratique civique (janvier 1990 – avril 1991)*, Prague: Documents du travail du CEFRES No. 6.
—— (2001) The Failure of Participatory Democracy in the Czech Republic'. *West European Politics*, 24: 43–64.
Hájek, M. (1990) 'Co pozítří?', *Lidové noviny*, 18 June, 9.
Hájek, M., Mejdrová, H., Opat. J. and Otáhal, M. (1984) 'K "Právu na dějiny"', Charter 77 document no. 16/84, 26 September. Online. Available www.sds.cz/docs/prectete/epubl/mhk_kpnd.htm (accessed 29 August 2005).
Hall, P. (1990) 'Conclusion: The Politics of Keynesian Ideas', in Hall, P. (ed.) *The Political Power of Economic Ideas: Keynesianism Across Nations*, Princeton, NJ: Princeton University Press.
—— (1993) 'Policy Paradigms, Social Learning and the State', *Comparative Politics*, 25: 275–96.
Hall, R.A. (2003) 'Nationalism in Late Communist Eastern Europe – Comparing the Role of Diaspora Politics in Hungary and Serbia (Parts 1–3)', *East European Perspectives*, 5 March, 2 April and 30 April. Online. Available www.rferl.org/eereport/ (accessed 1 June 2003).
Hall, S. (1988) *The Hard Road to Renewal*, London: Verso.
Hamerský, M. and Dimun, P. (eds) (1999) *10 let na straně svobody – Kronika ODA z let 1989–1999*, Brno: Bachant.

Hancock, M.D. (1998) 'Sweden's Nonsocialist Parties: What Difference Do They Make?', in Wilson, F. (ed.) *The European Center-Right at the End of the Twentieth Century*, Basingstoke: Macmillan.

Hanley, S. (2000a) Book review, *Party Politics*, 6: 241–3.

—— (2000b) 'Normative Conceptions of Party and the Formation of Post-Communist Party Systems: The Czech Case 1989–1998', unpublished PhD thesis, University of Birmingham.

—— (2001) 'Are the Exceptions Really the Rule? Questioning the Application of "Electoral-Professional" Type Models of Party Organisation in East Central Europe', *Perspectives on European Politics and Society*, 2: 453–79.

—— (2002) 'The Political Context of EU Accession in the Czech Republic', Chatham House Briefing Paper. Online. Available www.chathamhouse.org.uk/pdf/research/europe/Czech.pdf (accessed 14 March 2007).

—— (2003) Book review, *Party Politics*, 9: 398–400.

—— (2004a) 'A Nation of Sceptics? The Czech EU Accession Referendum of 13–14 June 2003', *West European Politics*, 27: 691–715.

—— (2004b) 'Interest Framing Strategies of Centre-Right Parties in East Central Europe – A Czech-Hungarian Comparison', Paper presented at the ECPR Joint Sessions of Workshops, Uppsala, 13–18 April. Online. Available www.essex.ac.uk/ecpr/events/jointsessions/paperarchive (accessed 1 October 2006).

—— (2006) 'Europe and the Czech Parliamentary Elections of 2–3 June 2006', European Parties Elections and Referendums Network Election briefing no. 27 Online. Available www.sussex.ac.uk/sei/documents/epern_no_27.pdf (accessed 1 October 2006).

Hanley, S., Szczerbiak, A., Haughton, T. and Fowler, B. (2006). 'Explaining the Success of Centre-Right Parties in Post-Communist East Central Europe: A Comparative Analysis', unpublished manuscript.

Hartl, J. (2000) Evropská unie v zrcadle veřejného mínění', *Integrace*, 2. Online. Available www.integrace.cz/integrace/clanek.asp?id=55 (accessed 13 March 2007).

Haughton, T. (2001) 'HZDS: The Ideology, Organization and Support Base of Slovakia's Most Successful Party', *Europe-Asia Studies*, 53: 745–69.

—— (2003) 'We'll Finish What We've Started: The 2002 Slovak Elections', *Journal of Communist Studies and Transition Politics*, 19: 65–90.

Haughton, T. and Malová, D. (2006) 'Slovakia's Integration Strategy in Comparative Perspective', paper presented at a workshop on the Impact of the EU on Slovakia as a Case Study of a Small New Member State, School of Slavonic and East European Studies, UCL, 27 April 2006.

Haughton, T. and Rybář, M. (2004) 'All Right Now: Explaining the Successes and Failures of the Centre Right in Slovakia', *Journal of Communist Studies and Transition Politics*, 20: 28–54.

Havel, V. (1968/1989) 'Na téma opozice', *Literární listy*, 4 April, reprinted in Havel, V. *Do různých stran*, Prague: Lidové noviny.

—— 'Český úděl?' (1969) *Tvář*, no. 2, reprinted in Havel, V (1990) *O lidskou identitu*, Prague: Rozmluvy.

—— (1990) *Dálkový výslech*, Prague, Melantrich.

—— (1991) *Letní přemítání*, Prague: Odeon.

—— (1992) *Vážení občané – projevy červenec 1990 – červenec 1992*, Prague, Lidové noviny.

—— (1997) 'Speech to members of Parliament'. Online. Available www.vaclavhavel.cz/index.php?sec=3&id=1&kat=1&from=81 (accessed 1 October 2006).

Hay, C. (2002) *Political Analysis: A Critical Introduction*, Basingstoke and New York: Palgrave.

Hayek F.A. (1944/1997) *The Road to Serfdom*, London: Routledge.

Hayes, M. (1994) *The New Right in Britain: An Introduction to Theory and Practice* London: Pluto Press.

Heitlinger, A. (1996) 'Framing Feminism in the Post-Communist Czech Republic', *Communist and Post-Communist Studies*, 29: 77–93.

Hekrdla, M. (1990) 'Quo vadis, OF?', *Tvorba*, 9, 28 February, 1.

Held, J. (ed.) (1993) *Right-Wing Politics and Democracy in Eastern Europe*, Boulder, CO: East European Monographs.

Hellen, T. (1996) *Shaking Hands with the Past: The Origins of the Right in Central Europe*, Helsinki: Finnish Academy of Sciences.

Henderson, K. (2001) 'Euroscepticism or Europhobia: Opposition Attitudes to the EU in the Slovak Republic', Opposing Europe Research Network Working Paper No 5, Sussex European Institute Working Paper No 50.

Hilde, P. (1999) 'Slovak Nationalism and the Break-up of Czechoslovakia', *Europe-Asia Studies*, 51: 647–65.

Hipkins, D. (2002) 'Croatia: HDZ Confident of Revival', *Institute for War and Peace Reporting – Balkan Crisis Report*, 322. Online. Available www.iwpr.net (accessed 1 June 2003).

Hloušek, V. (2002) 'Koncept konfliktních linií ve střední a jihovýchodní Evropě', *Středoevropské politické studie*, 4. Online. Available www.iips.cz/seps (accessed 8 August 2004).

Hlušičková R. (1994) 'Úvod', in Hlušičková, R. and Císařovská, B. (eds) *Hnutí za občanskou svobodu 1988–1989 sborník dokumentů*, Prague: Ústav pro soudobé dějiny/Maxdorf.

Hlušičková, R. and Císařovská, B. (eds) (1994) *Hnutí za občanskou svobodu 1988–1989 sborník dokumentů*, Prague: Ústav pro soudobé dějiny/Maxdorf.

Hlušičková, R. and Otáhal, M. (eds) (1993) *Čas demokratické iniciativy 1987–1990 (sborník dokumentů)*, Prague: Nadace Demokratické iniciativy pro kulturu a politiku.

Hockenos, P. (ed.) (1993), *Free to Hate: The Rise of the Right in Post-Communist Eastern Europe*, London and New York: Routledge.

Holy, L. (1996). *The Little Czech and the Great Czech Nation: National Identity and the Post Communist Social Transformation*, Cambridge: Cambridge University Press.

Hooghe, L. and Marks, G. (1999) 'The Making of a Polity: The Struggle over European Integration', in Kitschelt, H., Lange, P., Marks, G. and Stephens, J.D. (eds) *Continuity and Change in Contemporary Capitalism*, Cambridge: Cambridge University Press.

Hooghe, L., Marks, G. and Wilson, C. (2002) 'Does Left/Right Structure Party Positions on European Integration?', *Comparative Political Studies*, 35: 965–89.

Hopkin, J. (1996) *The Institutionalisation of New Political Parties: A Framework For Analysis*, Birmingham: University of Birmingham, Muirhead Paper no. 9.

—— (1999), *Party Formation and Democratic Transition in Spain*, Basingstoke: Macmillan.

Horowitz, S. and Petráš, M. (2003) 'Pride and Prejudice in Prague: Understanding Early Policy Error and Belated Reform in the Czech Economic Transition', *East European Politics and Societies*, 17: 231–65.

Hradec, J. (1985), 'Tragédie střední Evropy', *Rozmluvy*, 5: 91–113

Hromádková A. (1991) 'Konservativec věří ve věcné a absolutní hodnoty', *Prostor*, 17: 111–22.

Hrubý, J. (1984) *Aféry první republiky: jak se hrálo v zákulisí*. Prague: Práce.

Hruby, P. (1980) *Fools and Heroes: The Changing Role of Communist Intellectuals in Czechoslovakia*, Oxford: Pergamon Press.

Hübl, M. (1984), 'Svár dvou pojetí českých dějin', *Informace o Chartě* 77, July–August (samizdat). Online at www.sds.cz/docs/prectete/epubl/mh_sdpcd.htm (accessed 29 June 2005).

Inglehart, R. (1997) *Modernization and Postmodernization: Cultural, Economic, and Political Change in 43 Societies*, Princeton, NJ: Princeton University Press.

Innes, A. (1997) 'The Breakup of Czechoslovakia: The Impact of Party Development and the Separation of the State', *East European Politics and Societies*, 11: 393–435.

—— (2001) *Czechoslovakia: The Short Goodbye*, New Haven: Yale University Press.

Jacoby, W. (2004) *The Enlargement of the European Union and NATO: Choosing from the Menu in Central Europe*, Cambridge: Cambridge University Press.

Janata, M. (1998) 'Český stát na prahu třetího milénia', *Prostor*, 36: 8–10.

Janos, A. (1994) 'Continuity and Change in Eastern Europe: Strategies of Post-Communist Politics', *East European Politics and Societies*, 8: 1–29.

Ježek T. (1997), *Budování kapitalismu v Čechách: Rozhovory s Tomášem Ježkem*, Prague: Volvox Globator.

Jowitt, K. (1992) *New World Disorder: The Leninist Extinction*, Berkeley, CA: University of California Press.

Kaldor, M. (1990) 'After the Cold War', *New Left Review*, 180: 25–37.

Kalvoda, J. (1996a) 'Sociální inženýři současné české vlády', *Lidové noviny*, 5 February, 11.

—— (1996b) 'Ne oslavné zpěvy, ale další reformy', *Lidové noviny*, 22 March, 11

—— (1996c) 'Bez reforem nás čeká bankovní socialismus', *Mladá fronta Dnes*, 20 February, 14.

Kalyvas, S.M. (1996) *The Rise of Christian Democracy*, Ithaca and London: Cornell University Press.

Kamenitsa, L. (1998) 'East German Social Movements After the Wall', *Comparative Politics*, 30: 314–33.

Kaminski, M. (2003) 'The Collective Action Problems of Political Consolidation: Evidence from Poland', Center for the Study of Democracy Paper 03–03. Online. Available repositories.cdlib.org/csd/03–03 (accessed 1 June 2003).

Kaplan, K. (1987) *The Short March: the Communist Takeover in Czechoslovakia, 1945–1948*, London: Hurst.

—— (1993) *Stát a církev v Československu v letech 1948–1953*, Brno: Doplněk.

Katz, R. and Mair, P. (1993) 'The Evolution of Party Organizations in Europe: The Three Faces of Party Organization', *American Review of Politics*, 14: 593–617.

—— (1995) 'Changing Models of Party Organization and Party Democracy: The Emergence of the Cartel Party', *Party Politics*, 1: 5–28.

—— (2002) 'The Ascendency of the Party in Public Office: Party Organizational Change in Twentieth Century Democracies', in Gunther, R., Montero J.R. and Linz, J. (eds) *Political Parties: Old Concepts and New Challenges*, Oxford: Oxford University Press.

Kavan, J., Uhl, P. and Rendlová, J. (1990) 'Spor o volební systém, *Fórum*, 2/90, 7.

KDU-ČSL (1996) *Volební program 1996*, Prague: KDU- ČSL.

—— (1998) *Průvodce politikou KDU-ČSL – Podrobný volební program 1998*, Prague: KDU-ČSL.

Keane, J. (1988) *Democracy and Civil Society*. London: Verso.

Kettle, S. (1995) 'The Czech Republic Struggles to Define an Independent Press', *Transition*, 6 October, 5–6.

Kiss, C. (2003) 'From Liberalism to Conservatism: The Federation of Young Democrats in Post-Communist Hungary', *East European Politics and Societies*, 16: 739–63.

Kitschelt, H. (1989) *The Logics of Party Formation*, Ithaca, NY: Cornell University Press.

—— (1992a) 'Political Regime Change: Structure and Process-Driven Explanations', *American Political Science Review*, 86: 1028–34.

—— (1992b) 'The Formation of Party Systems in East-Central Europe', *Politics and Society*, 20: 15–19.

—— (1993a) 'Comparative Historical Research and Rational Choice Theory: The Case of Transitions to Democracy', *Theory and Society*, 22: 413–27.

—— (1993b) 'Social Movements, Political Parties, and Democratic Theory', *Annals of the American Academy of Political and Social Science*, 528: 13–29.

—— (1994) *The Transformation of European Social Democracy*, Cambridge: Cambridge University Press.

—— (1995) 'The Formation of Party Cleavages in Post-Communist Democracies: Theoretical Propositions', *Party Politics*, 1: 447–72.

—— (2002) 'Constraints and Opportunities in the Strategic Conduct of Post-Communist Successor Parties – Regime Legacies as Causal Argument', in Bozóki, A. and Ishiyama, J.T. (eds) *The Communist Successor Parties of Central and Eastern Europe*, Armonk, NY: M.E. Sharpe.

—— (2003) 'Accounting for Post-Communist Regime Diversity: What Counts as Good Cause?', in Ekiert, G. and Hanson, S. (eds) *Capitalism and Democracy in Postcommunist Central and Eastern Europe*, Cambridge: Cambridge University Press.

Kitschelt, H. with McGann, A. (1995), *The Radical Right in Western Europe: A Comparative Analysis*, Ann Arbor: University of Michigan Press.

Kitschelt, H., Mansfeldová, Z., Markowski, R. and Tóka, G. (1999) *Post-Communist Party Systems: Competition, Representation and Inter-party Collaboration*, Cambridge: Cambridge University Press.

Klaus, V. (1989) 'The Imperative of Long-term Prognoses and the Dominant Characteristics of the Czechoslovak Economy at Present', *Czechoslovak Economic Digest*, 7: 31–52.

—— (1991) *O tvář zítřka (rok devadesátý)*, Prague: Pražská imaginace.

—— (1993a) *Rok málo, či mnoho v dějinách země*, Prague: REPRO-PRESS.

—— (1993b) *První zprava*, Prague: Cartoonia.

—— (1995) *Dopočítávání do jedné*, Prague: Management Press.

—— (1996) *Mezi minulostí a budoucností*, Prague and Brno: Nadace Universitas Masarykiana, Edice Heureka, Nakladatelství Georgetown and Nakladatelství Svoboda.

—— (1997a) *Obhajoba zapomenutých myšlenek*, Prague: Academia.

—— (1997b) *Renaissance: The Rebirth of Liberty in Central Europe*. Washington, DC: Cato Institute.

—— (1999) *Cesta z pasti*, Prague: Votobia.

—— (2000a) *Od opoziční smlouvy k toleračnímu patentu*, Prague: Votobia.

—— (2000b) 'Úvodní vystoupení na II. ideové konferenci ODS', Online. Available www.klaus.cz/klaus2/asp/clanek.asp?id=1JjWy8loTn5Z (accessed 7 July 2006).

—— (2000c) 'Manifest srdce a rozumu', 16 December. Online at www.ods.cz (accessed 15 January 2001).

—— (2001a) 'Izolovaný čin nebo vršíček ledovce', *Listy ODS*, 1: 1.

—— (2001b) *Václav Klaus narovinu*, Prague: Rabbit & Rabbit.

—— (2002a) 'Předmluva ke sborníku CEPu o propopulační politice'. Online. Available www.vaclavklaus.cz/klaus2/asp/clanek.asp?id=odQ6ywOImi6n (accessed 15 April 2006).

—— (2002b) *Evropa pohledem politika, pohledem ekonoma*, Prague: Centrum pro ekonomiku a politiku.

—— (2002c) *Klaus v Bruselu*, Prague: Centrum pro ekonomiku a politiku.

—— (2002d) *Občan a obrana jeho státu*, Prague: Centrum pro ekonomiku a politiku.

—— (2005a) 'Využijme "období reflexe" pro vymezení jiné Evropské unie', *Newsletter CEP*, special issue: 1–3.

—— (2005b) 'Mýtus tureckého nebezpečí', *Newsletter CEP*, October 2005, 8.

—— (2005c) 'Small Nations and Europe: 90 Years After Masaryk', speech at the School of Slavonic and East European Studies, London, 19 October. Online. Available www.ssees.ac.uk/klausspeech.htm (accessed 17 November 2005).

—— (2005d) 'Intelektuálové a socialismus', *Newsletter CEPu*, September, 1–4.

—— (2006a) 'Vystoupení prezidenta republiky Václava Klause na konferenci CEPu k 15. výročí zahájení naší ekonomické transformace'. Online. Available www.vaclavklaus.cz/klaus2/asp/clanek.asp?id=923tsDTdGXgl.

—— (2006b) 'Co je evropeismus?', *Mladá fronta Dnes*, 8 April.

—— (2006c) 'The Czech Republic in the New Artificially Unified Europe', speech to the Los Angeles World Affairs Council, 25 April. Online. Available www.klaus.cz/klaus2/asp/clanek.asp?id=CF6s61Yn1tbf (accessed 1 June 2006).

Klaus, V. and Klusáková, J. (1997) *Jana Klusáková a Václav Klaus rozmlouvají NADORAZ o osmi letech ve svobodném státu*, Prague: Argot.

Koalice (2002) *Programové prohlášení Koalice*, Prague: Koalice.

Kocian, J. (1994) 'Programy obnovy Československa v českém politickém spektru v letech 1939–1945', *Moderní dějiny*, 2: 163–70.

Kohout, L. (1984) 'Odpovědnost historika vůči dějinám i budoucnosti národů Československa', samizdat. Reprinted online. Available www.sds.cz/docs/prectete/epubl/lk_ohvdb.htm (accessed 29 June 2005).

Kokošková, Z. and Kokoška, S. (eds) (1997) *Obroda – klub za socialistickou přestavbu: dokumenty*, Prague: Ústav pro soudobé dějiny/Maxdorf.

Kopeček, L. (2002), 'Aplikace Rokkanovské teorie cleavages na české politické strany na počátku éry masové politiky', *Středoevropské politické studie*, 4. Online. Available www.iips.cz/seps (accessed 8 August 2004).

—— (2004) 'Imigrace jako politické téma v ČR: analýza postojů významných politických stran', *Středoevropské politické studie*, 6. Online. Available www.iips.cz/seps/clanek.php?ID=203 (accessed 5 May 2006).

—— (2006) 'Analýza působení Aliance nového občana ve slovenské politice', 7. Online. Available www.cepsr.com/clanek.php?ID=284 (accessed 1 December 2006).

Kopecký, P. (1995) 'Developing Party Organizations in East-Central Europe: What Type of Party Is Likely to Emerge?', *Party Politics*, 1: 515–34.

—— (1999) 'From Velvet Revolution to Velvet Split: Consociational Institutions and the Disintegration of Czechoslovakia', in Kraus, M. and Stanger, A. (eds) *Irreconcilable Differences? Explaining Czechoslovakia's Dissolution*, Lanham, MD: Rowman & Littlefield.

—— (2004) 'An Awkward Newcomer?: EU Enlargement and Euroscepticism in the Czech Republic', in Harmsen, R. and Spiering, M. (eds) *Euroscepticism: Party Politics, National Identity and European Integration*, Amsterdam/New York: Editions Rodopi.

—— (2006) 'Political Parties and the State: the Nature of Symbiosis', *Journal of Communist Studies and Transition Politics*, 22: 251–73.

Kopecký, P. and Mudde, C. (2002), 'The Two Sides of Euroscepticism: Party Positions on European Integration in East Central Europe', *European Union Politics*, 3: 297–326.

Kopecký, P. and Učeň, P. (2003) 'Return to Europe? Patterns of Euroscepticism among Czech and Slovak Parties', in Zielonka, J. and Pettai, V. (eds) *EU Enlargement and the Road to European Union – Volume II*, Manchester: Manchester University Press.

Kopstein, J. (2003) 'Post-Communist Democracy – Legacies and Outcomes', *Comparative Politics*, 35: 231–50.

Kopstein, J. and Reilly, S. (2003), 'Postcommunist Spaces: A Political Geography Approach to Explaining Postcommunist Outcomes', in Ekiert. G. and Hanson, S. (eds) *Capitalism and Democracy in Postcommunist Central and Eastern Europe*, Cambridge University Press.

Korosényi, A. (1991) 'Revival of the Past or New Beginning: The Nature of Post-Communist Politics', *Political Quarterly*, 62: 53–75.

Kostelecký, T. (1994) 'Economic, Social and Historical Determinants of Voting Patterns in the 1990 and 1992 Parliamentary Elections in the Czech Republic', *Czech Sociological Review*, 2: 209–28.

—— (1995) 'Changing Party Allegiances in a Changing Party System: The 1990 and 1992 Parliamentary Elections in the Czech Republic', in Wightman, G. (ed.) *Party Formation in East Central Europe: Post-communist Politics in Czechoslovakia, Hungary, Poland and Bulgaria*, Aldershot: Edward Elgar.

—— (2000) 'Navrhované změny volebního zákona vzešlé z dodatku "opoziční smlouvy" v roce 2000 a jejich možné důsledky', *Sociologický časopis*, 36:3: 299–306.

Kotrba, J. (1997) 'Privatizační proces v České republice: aktéři a vítězové', in Švejnar, J. (ed.) *Česká republika a ekonomická transformace ve střední a východní Evropě*, Prague: Academia.

Král, D. (2005) 'The Czech Debate on the EU Membership Prospects of Turkey and Ukraine', 1 December. Online. Available www.europeum.org/doc/arch_eur/Czech_Report_Turkey_Ukraine.pdf (accessed 1 June 2005).

Král, D. and Pachta, L. (2005) 'The Czech Republic and the Iraq Crisis: Shaping the Czech Stance', Policy paper for the Transatlantic Relations Project of the German Marshall Fund of the United States, Europeum Institute for European Policy, Prague. Online. Available www.europeum.org/doc/arch_eur/CR_Iraq_crisis.pdf (accessed 1 June 2006).

Krapfl, J. (2000) 'The Velvet Revolution's Lost Treasure: The Rise and Fall of the Public Sphere', *Slovo*, Supp: 55–67.

Krause, K. (2000) 'Public Opinion and Party Choice in Slovakia and the Czech Republic', *Party Politics*, 6: 23–46.

—— (2002) 'Once More unto the Breach: The Politics of Cleavage in Slovakia and the Czech Republic', paper presented at the Annual Meeting of the APSA, Boston, 29 August–1 September.

Kreidl, M. and Vlachová, K. (1999) 'Sociální zázemí extrémní pravice v ČR', *Sociologický casopis*, 35: 335–56.

Krejčí, O. (1993) *Geopolitika a český národní zájem*, Prague: Universe.

—— (1994) *Kniha o volbách*, Prague: Victoria Publishing.

Krejčí, J. and Machonin, P. (1996) *Czechoslovakia, 1918–92: A Laboratory for Social Change*, Basingstoke: Macmillan.

Křen, J. (1990) *Bílá místa v našich dějinách?*, Prague: Lidové noviny.

Kristol, I. (1995) *Neoconservatism: The Autobiography of an Idea*, New York: Free Press.

Kroupa, D. (n.d.) 'Počátky filosofování'. Online. Available www.danielkroupa.cz/clanek. asp?id=60&referer=http%3A%2F%2Fwww%2Edanielkroupa%2Ecz%2Ffilosof%2Eas p%3Farea%3D3 (accessed 1 July 2005).

—— (1996) *Svoboda a řád: (sváteční rozhovory)*, Prague: Éós.

—— (2003) 'Konzervatismus a sjednocení Evropy', *Střední Evropa*, 117: 1–6.

Krouwel, A. (2005), 'Right in the Centre! Space Occupancy in European Party Systems', paper presented at ESRC Seminar Series on the Contemporary Right in Europe, 21 January, University of Sussex, Brighton.

Kukthakas, C. (1999) 'Hayek and Modern Liberalism', unpublished paper. Online. Available www.pol.adfa.edu.au/resources/hayek.pdf (accessed 24 March 2006).

Kundera, M. (1968) 'Český úděl', *Listy*, 7–8, 1.

—— (1968–9) 'Radikalismus a exhibicionismus', *Host do domu*, 15: 32–6.

—— (1984) 'The Tragedy of Central Europe', *New York Review of Books*, 26 April.

Kural, V. (1994) *Místo společenství – konflikt!: Češi a Němci ve Velkoněmecké říši a cesta k odsunu (1938–1945)*, Prague: Ústav mezinárodních vztahů.

Kusin, V. (1971) *The Intellectual Origins of the Prague Spring: The Development of Reformist Ideas in Czechoslovakia, 1956–1967*, London: Cambridge University Press.

—— (1972) *Political Groupings in the Czechoslovak Reform Movement*, London and Basingstoke: Macmillan.

—— (1978) *From Dubček to Charter 77*, Edinburgh: Q Press.

—— (1979) 'Challenge to Normalcy: Political Opposition in Czechoslovakia 1968–77', in Tőkes, R. (ed.) *Opposition in Eastern Europe*, London/Basingstoke: Macmillan.

Kyloušek, J. (2005) 'ODS a její vnitřní fungování', in Balík, S. (ed.) *Občanská demokratická strana a česká politika*, Brno: Centrum pro studium demokracie a kutury.

Laclau, E. and Mouffe, C. (2001) *Hegemony and Socialist Strategy*, London: Verso (2nd edition).

Ladrech, R. (2002) 'Europeanization and Political Parties: Towards a Framework for Analysis', *Party Politics*, 8: 389–403.

Lang, K. (2000), 'Falling Down – The Decline of Liberalism', *Central Europe Review*, 2. Online. Available www.ce-review.org/00/31/lang31.html (accessed 1 June 2003).

—— (2005) 'Parties of the Right in East Central Europe', *Debatte*, 13: 73–81

Laruelle, M. (1996) *'Střední Evropa': Une autre écriture de la nation?*, Prague: CEFRES Documents de travail no. 4.

Lester, J. (1995), *Modern Tsars and Princes: The Struggle for Hegemony in Russia*, London and New York: Verso.

Lewis, P.G. (2000a) *Political Parties in Post-Communist Eastern Europe*, London: Routledge.

—— (2000b) Book review, *Europe-Asia Studies*, 52: 571–2.

—— (2003) 'Political Parties', in White, S., Batt, J. and Lewis, P.G. (eds) *Developments in Central and East European Politics 3*, Basingstoke and New York: Palgrave Macmillan.

Linek, L. (2004) 'České politické strany a jejich členové. K postupné proměně charakteru členství', in Kabele, J., Potůček, M., Prázová, I. and Veselý, A. (eds) *Rozvoj české společnosti v Evropské unii I – Sociologie, prognostika a správa*, Prague: Matfyzpress.

Linz, J. and Stepan, A. (1996) *Problems of Democratic Transition and Consolidation: Southern Europe, South America and Post-Communist Europe*, Baltimore and London: Johns Hopkins University Press.

Lipset, S.M. and Rokkan, S. (1967) 'Cleavage Structure, Party Systems and Voter Alignments: An Introduction', in Lipset, S.M. and Rokkan, S. (eds) *Party Systems and Voter Alignments: Cross National Perspectives*, New York: Free Press.

Lobkowicz, J. (1999) 'Je deset let po revoluci naše demokracie vážně ohrožena?', *Mladá fronta Dnes*, 3 August, 11.

—— (2000) 'Na jaké křižovatce stojíme?', *Mladá fronta Dnes*, 20 January, 8.

Luebbert, G.M. (1991) *Liberalism, Fascism, or Social Democracy: Social Classes and the Political Origins of Regimes in Interwar Europe*, Oxford: Oxford University Press.

Lux, J. (1995a) 'Stavba založená na dvojici pilířů', *Lidové noviny*, 31 October, 8.

—— (1995b) 'Neztrácejme orientaci', *Lidové noviny*, 8 December 1995, 10.

—— (1996) 'Politický koncept KDU-ČSL je zcela konkrétní', *Lidové noviny*, 11 May.

Luxmoore, J. and Babiuch, J. (1992) 'Truth Prevails: The Catholic Contribution to Czech Thought and Culture', *Religion, State and Society*, 20: 101–19.

—— (1995) 'Search of Faith, Part 2: Charter 77 and the Return to Spiritual Values in the Czech Republic', *Religion, State and Society*, 23: 291–304.

Machonin, P. (2004) 'K sociologii v období normalizace', *Sociologický časopis*, 42: 643–50.

Machonin P., Šťastnová, P., Kroupa, A. and Glasová, A. (1996) *Strategie sociální transformace české společnosti*, Brno: Doplněk.

McManus-Czubińska, C., Miller, W.L., Markowski, R. and Wasilewski, J. (2003) 'The New Polish "Right"?', *Journal of Communist Studies and Transition Politics*, September, 19: 1–23.

Mahoney, J. (2000) 'Path Dependence in Historical Sociology', *Theory and Society*, 29: 507–48.

Mahoney, J. and Snyder, R (1999) 'Rethinking Agency and Structure in Regime Change', *Studies in Comparative International Development*, 34:2: 3–32.

Mair, P. (1997) *Party System Change: Approaches and Interpretations*, Oxford: Clarendon Press.

Mair, P. and Mudde, C. (1998) 'The Party Family and Its Study', *Annual Review of Political Science*, 1: 211–29.

Malíř, J. (1996) *Od spolků k moderním politickým stranám: vývoj politických stran na Moravě v letech 1848–1914*, Brno: Filozofická fakulta Masarykovy univerzity.

Mandler, E. (2005) *Škodolibé úsměvy svobody z let 1955 až 1992*, Prague: Emanuel Mandler.

Marada, R. (1997) 'Civil Society: Adventures of a Concept Before and After 1989', *Czech Sociological Review*, 5: 3–22.

March, L. (2006) 'Power and Opposition in the Former Soviet Union: The Communist Parties of Moldova and Russia', *Party Politics*, 12: 341–65.

Mareš, M. (2000) 'Nová rakouská vláda a české politické spektrum', *Integrace*, 1. Online. Available www.integrace.cz/integrace/clanek.asp?id=24 (accessed 14 March 2007).

—— (2004) 'Nezávislé a "antistranické" hnutí', in Malíř, J. and Marek, P. (eds) *Vývoj politických stran a hnutí v českých zemích a Československu 1861–2004 – II. Díl 1938–2004*, Brno: Doplněk, 1653–65.

Marks, G. and Wilson, C. (2000) 'The Past in the Present: A Cleavage Theory of Party Response to European Integration', *British Journal of Political Science*, 30: 433–59.

Mašek, I. and Žegklitz, J. (1990) 'ODA – co je, odkud a kam jde?'. Online. Available www.oda.cz/clanek.asp?id=8 (accessed 2 July 2005).

Matějů, P. (1999) 'The renewal of the middle class and its political circumstances', in

Večerník, J. and Matějů, P. (eds) *Ten Years of Rebuilding Capitalism: The Czech Republic after 1989*, Prague: Academia.

Matějů, P. and Řeháková, J. (1997) 'Turning Left or Class Realignment? Analysis of the Changing Relationship between Class and Party in the Czech Republic 1992–1996', *East European Politics and Societies*, 11: 501–42.

Matějů, P. and Vlachová, J. (1995) 'Od rovnostářství k zásluhovosti, Česká republika mezi dvěma ideologimi distributivní spravedlnosti', *Sociologický časopis*, 31: 215–39.

—— (1998) 'Values and Electoral Decisions in the Czech Republic', *Communist and Post-Communist Studies*, 31: 249–67.

Middlebrook, K (ed.) (2000) *Conservative Parties, the Right, and Democracy in Latin America*, Baltimore, MA: Johns Hopkins University Press.

Minkenberg, M. (2003) 'The Radical Right in Post-Communist Central and Eastern Europe: Comparative Observations and Interpretations', *East European Politics and Societies*, 16: 335–62.

Mišovič, J. (2000) 'Podpora vstupu do EU podle jednotlivých sociálních skupin', *Integrace*, 4. Online. Available www.integrace.cz/integrace/clanek.asp?id=140 (accessed 13 March 2007).

Mlynář, J. (1978) 'Exkomunisté a křestané v Chartě 77', *Studie*, 6: 414–27.

Moore, B. (1967) *The Social Origins of Dictatorship and Democracy: Lord and Peasant in the Making of the Modern World*, Harmondsworth: Penguin.

Mouffe C. (2005) *On the Political*, London and New York: Routledge.

Mrklas, L. (2004) 'Exilová demokratická pravice', *CEVRO*, March, 11.

Mudde, C (2001) 'In the Name of the Peasantry, the Proletariat, and the People: Populisms in Eastern Europe', *East European Politics and Societies*, 15: 33–53.

—— (2005) 'EU Accession and a New Populist Center-Periphery: Cleavage in Central and Eastern Europe', Central and Eastern Europe Working Paper No. 62, Center For European Studies, Harvard University. Online. Available www.ces.fas.harvard.edu/publications/docs/pdfs/Mudde.pdf (accessed 12 October 2006).

Munck, G.L. (2001) 'The Regime Question: Theory Building in Democracy Studies', *World Politics*, 55: 119–34.

Myant, M. (1981) *Socialism and Democracy in Czecholovakia 1945–48*, London: Cambridge University Press.

—— (1989) *The Czechoslovak Economy 1948–1989: The Battle for Reform*, Cambridge: Cambridge University Press.

—— (1993a) 'Czech and Slovak Trade Unions', *Journal of Communist Studies*, 9: 59–84.

—— (1993b) *Transforming Socialist Economies: The Case of Poland and Czechoslovakia*, Aldershot: Edward Elgar.

—— (2000) 'Employers' Interest Representation in the Czech Republic', *Journal of Communist Studies and Transition Politics*, 16: 1–20.

—— (2003) *The Rise and Fall of Czech Capitalism: Economic Development in the Czech Republic since 1989*, Cheltenham: Edward Elgar.

—— (2005) 'Klaus, Havel and Civil Society', *Journal of Communist Studies and Transition Politics*, 21: 248–67.

Myant, M., Slocock, B. and Smith, S. (2000) 'Tripartism in the Czech and Slovak Republics', *Europe-Asia Studies*, 52: 723–39.

Nečas, P. (1999) 'Vystoupení na Ideové konferenci ODS'. Online. Available www.ods.cz/akce/ideovky/1.ik/clanky/pr-ideo-necas.html (accessed 10 October 2006).

—— (2002) 'Základní teze k budoucímu směřování ODS'. Online. Available www.ods.cz/docs/dokumenty/necas-listopadove_teze.pdf (accessed 1 August 2006).

—— (2003) 'Válka v Iráku a české zájmy', *Politika*, 4/2003. Online. Available cdkbrno.cz/rp/clanky/107/valka-v-iraku-a-ceske-zajmy/ (accessed 10 October 2006).

Nová, R. (1994) 'Akce "Klín" po stranicku', in Žáček, P. (ed.) *Securitas imperii: 1. sborník k problematice bezpečnostních služeb*, Prague: Ministerstvo vnitra.

Novák, M. (1990) *Du printemps de Prague au printemps de Moscou: les forces de l'opposition en URSS et en Tchécoslovaquie de janvier 1968 à janvier 1990*, Geneva: Georg.

—— (1997) *Une transition démocratique exemplaire? L'emergence d'un système de partis dans les pays Tchèques*, Prague: CEFRES.

Obrman, J. (1991) 'The Issue of Autonomy for Moravia and Silesia', *Report on Eastern Europe*, 12 April, 13–22.

Obrman, J. and Mates, P. (1994) 'Subdividing the Czech Republic: The Controversy Continues', *RFE/RL Research Report*, 4 March.

ODA (1989) *Cesta ke svobodné společnosti*, Prague: ODA.

—— (1996) *Dál na cestě ke svobodné společnosti*, Prague: ODA.

ODS (1992) *Svoboda a prosperita*, Prague: ODS.

—— (1996a) *Svoboda a prosperita*, Prague: ODS.

—— (1996b) *Politický program ODS*, Prague: ODS.

—— (1998) *Hlavu vzhůru: volební program ODS*, Prague: ODS.

—— (2000) *Národní zájmy v reálném světě – základní koncepční teze pro II. ideovou konferenci*, Prague: ODS.

—— (2002a) *Volební desatero ODS, 2002*, Prague: ODS.

—— (2002b) 'Volby PS PČR 2002 – analýza volební kampaně ODS'. Online. Available www.ods.cz/knihovna/dokument.php?ID=97 (accessed 30 July 2006).

—— (2002c) *XIII. Kongres ODS: 'Nabízíme pravici'*, Prague: ODS.

—— (2003a) *IV. Ideová konference ODS*, Prague: ODS.

—— (2003b) *Poziční dokumenty ke vstupu do EU*, Prague: ODS.

—— (2003c) 'Když do EU, tak s ODS', leaflet published by the Civic Democratic Party.

—— (2004a) *Stejné šance pro všechny – program pro volby do Evropského parlamentu*, Prague: ODS.

—— (2004b) '5 důvodů proč říci NE evropské ústavě', Prague: ODS.

O'Dwyer, C. (2004) 'Runaway Statebuilding: How Political Parties Shape States in Postcommunist Eastern Europe', *World Politics*, 26: 520–53.

Olson, D.M. (1993) 'Dissolution of the State: Political Parties and the 1992 Election in Czechoslovakia', *Communist and Post-Communist Studies*, 26: 301–14.

Orenstein, M. (1994) *The Political Success of Neo-Liberalism in the Czech Republic*, Prague: CERGE-EI Working Paper Series no. 68.

—— (1998) 'Vaclav Klaus: Revolutionary and Parliamentarian', *East European Constitutional Review*, 7: 46–55.

—— (2002) *Out of the Red: Building Capitalism and Democracy in Postcommunist Europe*, Ann Arbor: Michigan University Press.

Ost, D. (1993) 'The Politics of Interest in Post-Communist East Europe', *Theory and Society*, 22: 453–85.

—— (2005) *The Defeat of Solidarity: Anger and Politics in Postcommunist Europe*, Ithaca, NY: Cornell University Press.

Oslzlý, P. (ed.) (1993) *Podzemní univerzita*, Brno: Centrum pro studium demokracie a kultury.

Otáhal, M. (1993a) 'První fáze opozice proti takzvané normalizaci (1969–1972)', in Mandler, E. (ed.) *Dvě desetiletí před listopadem 89*, Prague: Maxdorf/Ústav pro soudobé dějiny.

—— (1993b) 'Úvod', in Hlušičková, R. and Otáhal, M. (eds) Čas demokratické iniciativy 1987–1990 (sborník dokumentů), Prague: Nadace Demokratické iniciativy pro kulturu a politiku.

—— (1994) Opozice, moc, společnost 1969/1989, Prague: Ústav pro soudobé dějiny/Maxdorf.

—— (2002) Normalizace 1969–1989: Příspěvek ke stavu bádání, Prague: Ústav pro soudobé dějiny.

—— (2003) Studenti a komunistická moc v českých zemích 1968–1989, Prague: Dokořán.

Otáhal, M. and Sládek, Z. (eds) (1990) Deset pražských dnů – 17.-27. listopadu 1989, Prague: Akademia.

Ottaway, M. and Maltz, G. (2001) 'Croatia's Second Transition and the International Community', Current History, 100: 375–80.

Outlý, J. (2003) Strany a stát: vybrané aspekty primárních voleb a financování politických stran, Olomouc: Periplum.

Paces, C.J. (1999) '"The Czech Nation Must Be Catholic!": An Alternative Version of Czech Nationalism During the First Republic', Nationalities Papers, 27: 407–28.

Palouš M. (1991) 'Jan Patočka Versus Václav Benda', in Skilling, G. and Wilson, P. (eds) Civic Freedom in Central Europe, Basingstoke: Macmillan, 121–30.

—— (2003) 'Common Sense and the Rule of Law: Returning Voegelin to Central Europe', paper presented at the 19th annual meeting of the Eric Voegelin Society, Philadelphia, PA, 28–30 August. Online. Available www.cts.cuni.cz/reports/2004/-CTS-04–10.doc (accessed 1 July 2005).

Panebianco, A. (1981) Political Parties: Organisation and Power, Cambridge: Cambridge University Press.

Pavlik, J. (1999) 'About the Misinterpretations of Hayek's Theory of Spontaneous Order and Their Negative Impacts on the Transformation Programme in the Czech Republic', E-Logos. Online. Available vse.cz/kfil/elogos/miscellany/pavlik-3.htm (accessed 24 March 2006).

Pečinka, B. (2003a) Cesta na Hrad: ze zákulisí volebních kampaní. Prague: Formát.

—— (2003b) 'Co se dělo na kongresu ODS?', Politika, 9: 1. Online. Available www.cdkbrno.cz/rp/2003/1/ (accessed 1 October 2006).

Pecka, J., Belda, J. and Hoppe, J. (1995) Občanská společnost 1967–1970: emancipační hnutí uvnitř Národní fronty 1967–1970, Brno: Ústav pro soudobé dějiny/Doplněk.

Peeva, R. (2001), 'Electing a Czar: The 2001 Elections and Bulgarian Democracy', East European Constitutional Review, 10: 51–61.

Pehe, J. (1991a) 'Opinion Polls on Economic Reform', Report on Eastern Europe, 25 January, 4–6.

—— (1991b) 'The Emergence of Right-wing Extremism', Report on Eastern Europe, 28 June, 1–6.

—— (1993) 'Constitutional Imbroglio in the Czech Republic', RFE/RL Research Report, 29 January, 1–4.

—— (1994a) 'Civil Society at Issue in the Czech Republic', RFE/RL Research Report, 19 August, 13–18.

—— (1994b) 'Legal Difficulties Beset the Czech Restitution Procees', RFE/RL Research Report, 15 July, 6–13.

—— (1994c) 'Czech Senate Election Stirs Controversy', RFE/RL Research Report, 8 April, 7–10.

—— (1999) 'Lidé z ODS: eurorealisté zvláštního ražení', Lidové noviny, 22 June.

—— (2002a) *Vytunelovaná demokracie*. Prague: Academia.

—— (2002b) 'Nationalist Platform Could Be Klaus' Last Resort', *Prague Business Journal*, 24 June.

—— (2002c) 'Hrad jako záchrana klientelského systému', *Právo*, 9 December.

—— (2004) 'The Philosopher in the Castle', *The New Presence*, 1 April. Reprinted online. Available www.pehe.cz/clanky/2004/2004–04–01-presence.htm (accessed 28 March 2006).

Pelikan, J. (1976) *Socialist Opposition in Eastern Europe*, London: Allison and Busby.

Pernes, J. (1996) *Pod moravskou orlicí aneb Dějiny moravanství*, Brno: Barrister & Principal.

Peroutka, F. (1991) *O věcech obecných II (výbor z politické publicistiky)*, Prague: SPN.

Perron, C. (2001) 'Le communisme dans les têtes: Ruptures et permanences dans la société tchèque', *Raisons politiques*, 3: 113–25. Online. Available www.ce-review.org/00/13/essay13.html (accessed 3 April 2006).

Pfaff, I. (1996) *Česká přináležitost k Západu v letech 1815–1878*, Brno: Doplněk.

Pickel, A. (1997) 'Official Ideology: The Role of Neoliberal Reform Doctrines in Post-Communist Transformation', in Pickel, A. and Wiesenthal, H. (eds) *The Grand Experiment: Debating Shock Therapy, Transition Theory, and the East German Experience*, Boulder, CO: Westview Press.

Piekalkiewicz, J. (1972) *Public Opinion Polling in Czechoslovakia 1968–69*, New York: Praeger Publishers.

Pierson, P. (2000) 'Increasing Returns, Path Dependence and the Study of Politics', *American Political Science Review*, 94: 251–68.

—— (2004) *Politics in Time: History, Institutions, and Social Analysis*, Princeton, NJ: Princeton University Press.

Pithart, P. (1968) 'Národní fronta, nebo parlament?', *Literární listy*, 18 April.

—— (1990a) *Dějiny a politika*, Prague: Prostor.

—— (1990b) *Osmašedesátý*, Prague: Rozmluvy.

—— (1990c) *Obrana politiky* Prague: Rozmluvy.

—— (1990d) 'Dizi-rizika', in Prečan, V. (ed.) *Charta 77 1977–1989 od morální k demokratické revoluci*, Scheinfeld-Schwarzenberg/Bratislava: Čs. středisko nezávislé literatury/ARCHA.

—— (1990e), 'Na začátku je dobrý skutek (rozhovor s Petrem Pithartem)', *Prostor*, 3: 115–37.

—— (1992) *Petr Pithart NADORAZ*, Primus: Prague.

—— (1998a) *Po devětaosmdesátém: Kdo jsme*, Bratislava /Brno: Kalligram/Doplněk.

—— (1998b) 'A Trip through an Unknown Past', *The New Presence*, April, 6–7.

Pithart, P. and Klusáková, J. (1992) *Petr Pithart NADORAZ*, Prague: Primus.

'Podiven' (pseudonym for Pithart, P., Příhoda, P. and Otáhal, M.) (1991) *Češi v dějinách moderní doby (pokus o zrcadlo)*, Prague: Prostor.

Pontuso, J.F. (2004) *Václav Havel: Civic Responsibility in the Postmodern Age*, Lanham, MD: Rowman & Littlefield.

Potůček, M. (1999) 'Havel versus Klaus: Public Policy Making in the Czech Republic', *Journal of Comparative Policy Analysis*, 1: 163–76.

'Pražská výzva' (2006) reprinted in Langer, I. (ed.) *15 let zahraniční politiky ODS*, Prague: CERVO.

Prečan, V. (1990) *Charta 77: 1977–1989 od morální k demokratické revoluci*, Scheinfeld-Schwarzenberg/Bratislava: ČS středisko nezávislé literatury/ARCHA.

Przeworski, A. (1991) *Democracy and the Market*, Cambridge: Cambridge University Press.

Pšeja, P. (2004a) 'Občanská demokratická strana jako hlavní "dědic" OF a "agens" stranického systému ČR (1991–1998)', *Politologický časopis*, 11: 453–71.

—— (2004b) 'Malé strany konzervativní orientace', in Malíř, J. and Marek, P. (eds) *Vývoj politických stran a hnutí v českých zemích a Československu 1861–2004 – II. Díl 1938–2004*, Brno: Doplněk.

Radosta, P. (1993) *Protikomunistický odboj: historický nástin*, Prague: EGEM.

Rak, J. (1994) *Bývali Čechové ...: české historické mýty a stereotypy*, Jinočany: H&H.

Rak, V. (1992) 'Kandidáti do parlamentních voleb v Československu v červnu 1990', *Sociologický časopis*, 28: 200–21.

Ramet, S. (ed.) (1999) *The Radical Right in Central and Eastern Europe since 1989*, University Park, PA: Pennsylvania State University Press.

Rataj, J. (1997) *O autoritativní národní stát: ideologické proměny české politiky v Druhé republice 1938–1939*, Prague: Karolinium.

Raubisko, L. (2003) 'Latvia: It's Out with the Old and in with the "New Era"', Radio Liberty Feature, 5 October. Online. Available www.rfrerl.org/nca/features/2002/10/07102002160412.asp (accessed 2 June 2003).

Reed, Q. (1996) 'Political Corruption, Privatisation and Control in the Czech Republic: A Case Study of Problems in Multiple Transition', Unpublished Dphil. thesis, Oriel College, Oxford.

Řeháková, B. (1999) 'Social stratification and voting behavior', in Večerník, J. and Matějů, P. (eds) *Ten Years of Rebuilding Capitalism: The Czech Republic after 1989*, Prague: Academia.

Renwick, A. (2006) 'Why Hungary and Poland Differed in 1989: The Role of Medium Term Frames in Explaining the Outcomes of Democratic Transition', *Democratization*, 12: 36–57.

Řepa, M (2001) *Moravané nebo Češi?: vývoj českého národního vědomí na Moravě v 19. století*, Brno: Doplněk.

Říman, M. (2005) 'Kontrarevoluce levice', *Politika*, 3. Online. Available www.cdkbrno. cz/rp/clanky/270/1998–2005-kontrarevoluce-levice/ (accessed 1 March 2006).

Robejsek, P. (2002) 'Parallel Paths East and West', *Transitions Online*, 1 March. Online. Available www.tol.cz/look/TOLrus/article.tpl?IdLanguage=1&IdPublication=4&NrIssue=32&NrSection=19&NrArticle=3732 (accessed 1 October 2006).

Roberts, A. (2003) 'Demythologizing the Czech Opposition Agreement', *Europe-Asia Studies*, 55: 1273–303.

Rogger, H. and Weber, E. (eds) (1966) *The European Right: A Historical Profile*, Berkeley, CA: University of California Press.

Rogowski, R. (1989) *Commerce and Coalition: How Trade Affects Domestic Political Alignments*, Princeton, NJ: Princeton University Press.

Rokkan, S. (1970) *Citizens, Elections, Parties: Approaches to the Comparative Study of Processes and Development*, Oslo: Universitetsforlaget.

Rona-Tas, A. (1997) 'The Czech New Wave: The Third Wave of Privatization and the New Role of the State in the Czech Republic', *Problems of Postcommunism*, 44: 53–62.

Roper, S. (1998) 'From Opposition to Government Coalition: Unity and Fragmentation in the Democratic Convention of Romania', *East European Quarterly*, 31: 519–42.

Rulíková, M. (2004) 'The European Parliament Election in the Czech Republic', European Elections, Parties and Referendums Network, 2004 European Parliament Election Briefing no. 9. Online. Available www.sussex.ac.uk/sei/documents/epernep2004 czechrep.pdf (accessed 1 October 2006).

Ruml, J. (1998) *Jana Klusáková a Jan Ruml rozmlouvají NADORAZ*, Prague: Argo.

—— (1999) 'Lepší být zticha a nebýt směšný', *Mladá fronta Dnes*, 23 September, 12.

Rupnik, J. (1981), *Histoire du parti communiste tchécoslovaque*, Paris: Presses de la Fondation nationale des sciences politiques.

—— (1988) 'Totalitarianism Revisited', in Keane, J. (ed.) *Civil Society and the State*, London: Verso.

—— (2002) 'The Other Central Europe', *East European Constitutional Review*, 11. Online. Accessible www.law.nyu.edu/eecrvol111num1–2/special/rupnik.html (accessed 8 June 2003).

Rutland, P. (1992–3) 'Thatcherism, Czech-style: Transition to Capitalism in the Czech Republic' *Telos*, 94: 104–29.

Rychlý, T. (1995) 'Kalvoda proti Devátému: Špěhovaly tajné služby politické strany', in Cinger, F. (ed.) *13 českých skandálů*, Prague: Baronet.

Salecl, R. (1994), 'The Crisis of Identity and the Struggle for New Hegemony in the Former Yugoslavia', in Laclau, E. (ed.) *The Making of Political Identities*, London: Verso.

Šaradín, P. (2002/3) 'Územní podpora KDU-ČSL ve volbách', *Politologická revue*, 9: 45–65.

Sartori, G. (1976) *Parties and Party Systems: A Framework for Analysis*, Cambridge: Cambridge University Press.

Saxonberg, S. (1999) 'Václav Klaus: The Rise and Fall and Re-emergence of a Charismatic Leader', *East European Politics and Societies*, 13: 391–418.

—— (2001) *The Fall: A Comparative Study of the End of Communism in Czechoslovakia, East Germany, Hungary, and Poland*, Amsterdam: Harwood Academic Press.

—— (2003) *The Czech Republic before the New Millennium: Politics, Parties and Gender*, Boulder, CO: East European Monographs.

Sayer, D. (1998) *The Coasts of Bohemia: A Czech History,* Princeton, NJ: Princeton University Press.

Schedler, A. (1997) 'Introduction: Antipolitics – Closing and Colonizing the Public Space', in Schedler, A. (ed.) *The End of Politics? Explorations into Modern Antipolitics*, Basingstoke: Macmillan.

Scheuer, M. and Gitter, R. (2001) 'The Rise in Czech Unemployment 1998–2000', *Monthly Labor Review*, May, 46–51.

Schöpflin G. (1991) 'Conservatism and Hungary's Political Tradition', *Problems of Communism*, 40: 60–8.

—— (1993) 'Culture and Identity in Post-Communist Europe', in White, S., Batt, J. and Lewis, P. (eds) *Developments in East European Politics*, Basingstoke: Macmillan.

—— (2002) 'New-Old Hungary – A Contested Transformation', *East European Perspectives*, 4. Online. Available www.rferl.org/eepreport/2002/05/10–150502.html (accessed 1 June 2003).

Schöpflin, G. and Wood, N. (eds) (1989) *In Search of Central Europe*, Oxford: Polity.

Scruton, R. (1981) *The Politics of Culture and Other Essays.* Manchester: Carcanet Press.

—— (1988a) 'The New Right in Central Europe I: Czechoslovakia', *Political Studies*, 36: 449–62.

—— (1988b) 'The New Right in Central Europe II: Poland and Hungary', *Political Studies*, 36: 638–52.

—— (1989) *The Meaning of Conservatism*, London: Penguin Books, 1989 (2nd edition).

—— (1990) *The Philosopher on Dover Beach – Essays*, Manchester: Carcanet Press.

—— (1992) 'Totalitarianism, Civil Society and the Nation', *Salisbury Review*, 10: 10–15.

—— (1996) 'Exporting the Tory Idea', *Salisbury Review*, 14: 29–33.

Šedo, J. (2002) 'Postavení Moravy dle Rokkanova modelu centrum-periferie', *Středo-evropské politické studie*, 4. Online. Available www.cepsr.com/clanek.php?ID=37 (accessed 13 March 2007).

Seidal, G. (1986) 'Culture, Nation and "Race" in the British and French New Right', in Levitas, R. (ed.) *The Ideology of the New Right*, Cambridge: Polity Press.

Selbourne, D. (1990) *Death of the Dark Hero: Eastern Europe, 1987–90*, London: Jonathan Cape.

Sharman, J.C. and Phillips, R. (2004) 'An Internalist Perspective on Party Consolidation and the Bulgarian Union of Democratic Forces', *European Journal of Political Research*, 43: 297–420.

Shefter, M. (1994) *Political Parties and the State: the American Historical Experience*, Princeton, NJ: Princeton University Press.

Shields, S. (2003) 'The "Charge of the Right Brigade": Transnational Social Forces and the Neoliberal Configuration of Poland's Transition', *New Political Economy*, 8: 225–44.

Shugart, M. (1998) 'The Inverse Relationship between Party Strength and Executive Strength: A Theory of Constitutional Choices', *British Journal of Political Science*, 28: 1–29.

Siani-Davies, P. (1998) 'The Traditional Parties and the Romanian Election of May 1990', in Haynes, R. (ed.) *Occasional Papers in Romanian Studies II*, London: School of Slavonic and East European Studies.

Šik, O. (1976) *The Third Way: Marxist–Leninist theory and Modern Industrial Society*, London: Wildwood House.

Šiklová, J. (1990) 'The "Gray Zone" and the Future of Czechoslovakia', *Social Research*, 57: 347–63.

—— (1997) 'Feminism and the Roots of Apathy in the Czech Republic', *Social Research*, 64: 258–80.

—— (2003) 'Neo-normalizace', in Šaradín, P. (ed.) *Desetiletí*, Oloumouc: Periplum.

Šimoník, P. (1996) 'Politické spektrum v České republice', *Sociologický časopis*, 32: 457–70.

Sitter, N. (2001a) 'Beyond Class vs. Nation: Cleavage Structures and Party Competition in East Central Europe', *Central European Political Science Review*, 2: 67–91.

—— (2001b) 'The Politics of Opposition and European Integration in Scandinavia: Is Euro-scepticism a Government-Opposition Dynamic?' *West European Politics*, 24: 22–39.

—— (2002) 'When Is a Party System? A Systems Perspective on the Development of Competitive Party Systems', *Central European Political Science Review*, 3: 75–97.

Sitter, N. and Batory, A. (2004) 'Cleavages, Competition, and Coalition-building: Agrarian Parties and the European Question in Western and Eastern Europe', *European Journal of Political Research*, 43: 523–46.

Skilling, H.G. (1976) *Czechoslovakia's Interrupted Revolution*. Princeton, NJ: Princeton University Press.

—— (1981) *Charter 77 and Human Rights in Czechoslovakia*, London: Allen & Unwin.

Smith, A.M. (1994) *New Right Discourse on Race and Sexuality: Britain, 1968–1990*, Cambridge: Cambridge University Press.

Smith, S. (2003a) 'Transformation as Modernization: Readings of Post-communist Life-worlds', in Simon, S. (ed.) *Local Communities and Post-Communist Transformation: Czechoslovakia, the Czech Republic and Slovakia*, London and New York: Routledge-Curzon.

—— (2003b) 'Civic Forum and Public and Violence: Agents for Community Self-Determination? Experiences of Local Actors', in Simon, S. (ed.) *Local Communities and Post-Communist Transformation: Czechoslovakia, the Czech Republic and Slovakia*, London and New York: RoutledgeCurzon.

Snyder, T. and Vachudova, M. (1997) 'Are Transitions Transitory? Two Types of Political Change in Eastern Europe since 1989', *East European Politics and Societies*, 11: 1–35.

Sobell, V. (1988) 'Czechoslovakia: the Legacy of Normalization', *East European Politics and Societies*, 2: 36–69.

Sokol, P. (2006) 'Zahraniční kontakty Občanské demokratické strany', in Langer, I. (ed.) *15 let zahraniční politiky ODS*. Prague: CEVRO.

Spousta, J. (2002) 'Changes in Religious Values in the Czech Republic', *Czech Sociological Review*, 38: 345–63.

Šrubář, I. (1996) 'Neoliberalismus, transformace a občanská společnost', *Sociologický časopis*, 32: 67–78.

Stein, E. (1997). *Czecho/Slovakia: Ethnic Conflict, Constitutional Fissure, Negotiated Breakup*, Ann Arbor: Michigan University Press.

Stoniš, M. and Havlík, P. (1998) *Klaus & ti druzí: Osobní inventura Petra Havlíka*, Prague: Pallata.

Stráský, J. (1993) *Jan Stráský prezident na půl úvazku*, Prague: Irma.

Strmiska, M. (2000) 'Rise and Fall of Moravian Parties', *Central European Political Studies*, 4. Online. Available www.iips.cz/cisla/texty/clanky/moravian400.html (accessed 12 December 2003).

Strmiska, Z. (1986) 'Výsledky nezávislého průzkumu současného smýšlení v Československu', *Svědectví*, 20: 265–334.

Stroehlein, A. (1998) *Czechs and the Czech-German Declaration*, Glasgow: Institute of Russian and East European Studies, University of Glasgow.

—— (2001) 'Made for TV Revolution', *Central Europe Review*, 3: 1. Online. Available www.ce-review.org/01/1/stroehlein1.html (accessed 1 October 2006).

Suk, Jaroslav (1982) 'Československá radikální levice', *Svědectví*, 67: 613–29.

Suk, Jiří (1995) 'Vznik Občanského fóra a proměny jeho struktury (19. listopad – 20. prosinec 1989)', *Soudobé dějiny*, 2: 17–42.

—— (1997a) *Občanské fórum: Listopad–prosinec 1989 1. díl – události*, Brno, Doplněk.

—— (1997b) 'Občanské fórum a problém uchopení moci (listopad 1989–leden 1990)', *Babylon*, 1 October, 6–7.

—— (ed.) (1998) *Občanské fórum: Listopad–prosinec 1989 2 díl – dokumenty*, Brno: Doplněk.

—— (2003) *Labyrintem revoluce: aktéři, zápletky a křižovatky jedné politické krize*, Prague: Prostor.

Šulc, Z. (1998) *Stručné dějiny ekonomických reforem v Československu (České republice) 1945–1995*, Brno: Doplněk.

Svasand, L. (1998) 'The Center Right Parties in Norwegian Politics: Between Reformist Labor and Radical Progress', in Wilson, F. (ed.) *The European Center-Right at the End of the Twentieth Century*, London: Palgrave.

Swain, N. (1992) *Hungary: The Rise and Fall of Feasible Socialism*, London and New York: Verso.

Szacki, J. (1995) *Liberalism after Communism*, Budapest: CEU Press.

Szczerbiak, A. (1999) 'Testing Party Models in East-Central Europe: Local Party Organization in Post-communist Poland', *Party Politics*, 5: 525–37.

—— (2001) 'The Polish Peasant Party: A Mass Party in Postcommunist Eastern Europe?', *East European Politics and Societies*, 15: 554–88.

—— (2002) 'Poland's Unexpected Political Earthquake: The September 2001 Parliamentary Election', *Journal of Communist Studies and Transition Politics*, September, 18: 41–76.

—— (2003) Book review, *Europe-Asia Studies*, 55: 483–5.

—— (2004) 'The Polish Centre-Right's (Last) Best Hope: The Rise and Fall of Solidarity Electoral Action', *Journal of Communist Studies and Transition Politics*, 20: 55–79.

—— (2006) ' "Social Poland" Defeats "Liberal Poland"?: The September–October 2005 Polish Parliamentary and Presidential Elections', Sussex European Institute working paper no. 86. Online. Available www.sussex.ac.uk/sei/documents/working_paper--social_poland_defeats_liberal_poland.pdf (accessed 1 October 2006).

Szczerbiak, A. and Hanley, S. (eds) (2006) *Centre-Right Parties in Post-Communist East-Central Europe*, London: Routledge.

Szczerbiak, A. and Taggart, P (eds). (2005) *EU Enlargement and Referendums*, London and New York: Routledge.

Szelenyi, I., Eyal, G. and Townsley, E. (1999) *Making Capitalism without Capitalists: The New Ruling Elites in Eastern Europe*, London: Verso.

Taagepera, R. (2006) 'Meteoric Trajectory: The Res Publica Party in Estonia', *Democratization*, 13: 78–94.

Taborsky, E. (1959) 'The Noncommunist "Parties" in Czechoslovakia', *Problems of Communism*, 8: 20–6.

Taggart, P. (1995) 'New Populist Parties in Western Europe', *West European Politics*, 18: 34–51.

—— (1998) 'A Touchstone of Dissent: Euroscepticism in Contemporary Western European Party Systems', *European Journal of Political Research*, 33: 363–88.

—— (2002) 'Europeanisation, Euroscepticism and Party Systems: Party-Based Euroscepticism in the Candidate States of Central and Eastern Europe', *Perspectives on European Politics and Society*, 3: 23–41.

Taggart, P. and Szczerbiak, A. (2002) 'The Party Politics of Euroscepticism in EU Member and Candidate States', Opposing Europe Research Network Working Paper No 6. Online. Available www.sussex.ac.uk/sei/documents/wp51.pdf (accessed 16 October 2006).

Tarrow, S. (1998) *Power in Movement: Social Movements and Contentious Politics*, Cambridge: Cambridge University Press (2nd edition).

Terra, J. (2002) 'Political Parties, Party Systems and Economic Reform: Testing Hypotheses against Evidence from Postcommunist Countries', *Czech Sociological Review*, 38: 277–95.

—— (2003) 'Influence, Assets and Democracy: Who Got What after the Fall of Communism in East Central Europe?', unpublished PhD thesis, Stanford University.

Thompson, M., Ellis, R. and Wildavsky, A. (1990) *Cultural Theory*. Boulder, CO, and Oxford: Westview Press.

Tilly, C. (2001) 'Mechanisms in Political Processes', *Annual Review of Political Science*, 4: 21–41.

Tismaneanu, V. (1996) 'The Leninist Debris or Waiting for Perón', *East European Politics and Societies*, 10: 504–40.

Tismaneanu, V. and Klingman, G. (2001) 'Romania's First Postcommunist Decade: From Iliescu to Ilisecu', *East European Constitutional Review*, 10. Online. Available www.law.nyu.edu/eecr/vol10num1/features/romaniafirstpostcomdecade.html (accessed 16 October 2006).

Tőkés, R. (1996) *Hungary's Negotiated Revolution: Economic Reform, Social Change, and Political Succession, 1957–1990*, Cambridge: Cambridge University Press.

'Toleranční patent' (2000) Online. Available www.ods.cz/knihovna/dokument.php?ID=10 (accessed 1 October 2006).

Torfing, J. (2005) 'Discourse Theory: Achievements, Arguments and Challenges', in Torfing, J. and Howarth, D. (eds) *Discourse Theory in European Politics: Identity, Policy and Governance*, New York: Palgrave Macmillan.

Toš, N. and Miheljak, V. (2002) 'Transition in Slovenia: Democratization and the Attainment of Sovereignty ', in Toš, N. and Mihelak, V. (eds) *Slovenia between Continuity and Change, 1990–1997: Analyses, Documents and Data*, Berlin: Edition Sigma.

Tucker, A. (2000) *The Philosophy of Czech Dissidence from Patočka to Havel*, Pittsburgh, PA: University of Pittsburgh Press.

Tworzecki, H. (2002) *Learning to Choose: Electoral Politics in East-Central Europe*, Stanford, CA: Stanford University Press.

Učen, P. (2003) 'Centrist Populism Parties and the Ingredients of Their Success', in Meseznikov, G., Gyarfášová, O., Kollár, M. and Nicholson, N. (eds) *Slovak Elections 2002: Results, Implications. Context*, Bratislava: IVO.

Ulč, O. (1974) *Politics in Czechoslovakia*, San Francisco: W.H. Freeman.

Unie svobody (1998) *Politický program Unie svobody*, Prague: Unie svobody.

—— (2001) *Evropská vize Unie svobody*, Prague: Unie svobody.

Úřad vlády (2006) *Česká republika v roce 1*, Prague: Úřad vlády.

Urban, J. (1990a) 'Czechoslovakia: The Power and Politics of Humiliation', in Prins, G. (ed.) *Spring in Winter: The 1989 Revolutions*, Manchester: Manchester University Press.

—— (1990b) 'Politické orientace OF – obnova', *Fórum*, 16 May, 1 and 4.

—— (2003) 'The Making of a President', *East European Perspectives*, 16 April. Online. Available www.rferl.org/reports/eepreport/2003/04/8–160403.asp (accessed 1 June 2003).

Urban, O. (1982) *Česká společnost, 1848–1918*, Prague: Svoboda.

—— (1995) 'Český liberalismus v 19. století', in Znoj, M., Havránek, J. and Sekera, M. (eds) *Český liberalismus: texty a osobnosti*, Prague: Torst.

Vachudova, M. (2001) 'Right-Wing Parties and Political Outcomes in Eastern Europe', paper prepared for presentation at the 97th Annual Meeting of the American political Science Association, San Francisco, CA, 30 August–2 September.

—— (2005) *Europe Undivided: Democracy, Leverage and Integration after Communism*, Oxford: Oxford University Press. Vaculík, L. (1990) *Srpnový rok fejetony z let 1988–1989*, Prague: Mladá fronta.

Valenta, A. (1992a) *Máme národní zájmy?*, Prague: Ústav mezinárodních vztahů.

—— (1992b) 'Pravice se sjednocuje', *Prostor*, 19: 11–14.

Valenta, J. (1979) *Soviet Intervention in Czechoslovakia, 1968: Anatomy of a Decision*, Baltimore and London: Johns Hopkins University Press.

van Biezen, I. (2003) *Political Parties in New Democracies: Party Organization in Southern and East-Central Europe*, Basingstoke: Palgrave Macmillan.

Vaněk, M. (1994) *Veřejné mínění o socialismu před 17. listopadem 1989*, Prague: Maxdorf/ Ústav pro soudobé dějiny, Prague.

Vávra, J. (1990), 'Kolik je kandidátů na předsedu OF?', *Fórum*, 10–16 October, 2.

Večerník, J. (1996) *Markets and People: The Czech Reform Experience in a Comparative Perspective*, Aldershot: Avebury.

—— (1999a) 'Střední vrstva v české transformaci', *Sociologický časopis*, 35: 33–52.

—— (1999b) 'Capitalist Renewal: Privatization and Business', in Večerník J. and Matějů, M. (eds) *Ten Years of Rebuilding Capitalism: The Czech Republic after 1989*, Prague: Academia.

—— (1999c) 'Etika středních tříd – zapomenutý základ transformace', *Mladá fronta Dnes*, 16 June, 13.

Vévoda, R. (1998) 'Brněnské studentstvo v poslední fázi totalitního režimu', in Tůma, O. (ed.) *Historické studie: k sedmdesátinám Milana Otáhala*, Prague: Ústav pro soudobé dějiny.

Vlachová, K. (1997) 'Czech Political Parties and Their Voters', *Czech Sociological Review*, 5: 39–56.

—— (1999) 'The Crystallization of Political Attitudes and Orientations', in Večerník, J. and Matějů, P. (eds) *Ten Years of Rebuilding Capitalism: the Czech Republic after 1989*, Prague: Academia.

—— (2001) 'Party Identification in the Czech Republic: Inter-Party Hostility and Party Preference', *Communist and Post-Communist Studies*, 34: 479–99.

—— (2002) 'Levice a pravice v České republice v letech 1996–2000', in Mansfeldová, Z. and Tuček, M. (eds) *Současná česká společnost*, Prague: Sociologický ústav.

von Mises, L (2002) *Selected Writings of Ludwig von Mises – Between the Two World Wars*. Indianapolis, IN: Liberty Fund.

Vystrčil, T. (1998) 'Smysl krize a krize smyslu', *Prostor*, 36: 17–19.

Wainwright, H. (1994) *Arguments for a New Left: Answering the Free Market Right*, Oxford and Cambridge, MA: Blackwell.

Wallat, J. (2001) 'Czechoslovakia/the Czech Republic and the Visegrad Co-operation', *Slovak Foreign Policy Affairs*, Spring: 24–35.

Weigl, J. (2006) 'Volební paralely 1946/2006', *Newsletter CEPu*, May, 1–2.

Wellhofer, S. (1990) 'Contradictions in Market Models of Politics: The Case of Party Strategies and Voters', *European Journal of Political Research*, 18: 19–28.

Wenzel, M. (1998), 'Solidarity and Akcja Wyborcza "Solidarnosc" – An Attempt at Reviving the Legend', *Communist and Post-Communist Studies*, 31: 139–56.

Werning, S.R. (1996) 'Historical Cleavages or Transition Mode? Influences on the Emerging Party Systems in Hungary, Poland and Czechoslovakia', *Party Politics*, 2: 177–208.

Whitefield, S. and Evans, G. (1999) 'Political Culture Versus Rational Choice: Explaining Responses to the Transition in the Czech Republic and Slovakia', *British Journal of Political Science*, 29: 129–55.

Williams, K. (1997a) *The Prague Spring and Its Aftermath*, Cambridge: Cambridge University Press.

—— (1997b) 'National Myths in the New Czech Liberalism', in Hosking, G. and Schöpflin, G. (eds) *Myths and Nationhood*, London: Hurst.

—— (1999) 'A Scorecard for Czech Lustration', *Central Europe Review*, 1, 19, 1 November. Online. Available www.ce-review.org/99/19/williams19.html (accessed 1 August 2006).

—— (2003) 'Lustration and the Securitisation of Democracy in Czechoslovakia and the Czech Republic', *Journal of Communist Studies and Transition Politics*, 19: 1–24.

—— (2006) 'The Prague Spring: From Elite Liberalisation to Mass Movement', in McDermott, K. and Stibbe, M. (eds) *Revolution and Resistance in Eastern Europe: Challenges to Communist Rule*, Oxford: Berg.

Williams, K. and Deletant, D. (2000) *Security Intelligence Services in New Democracies: The Czech Republic, Slovakia and Romania*, London: Macmillan.

Williams, K., Szczerbiak, A. and Fowler, B. (2005) 'Explaining Lustration in Eastern Europe: A "Post-Communist Politics" Approach', *Democratization*, 12: 22–43.

Wilson, A. (2005) *Virtual Politics: Faking Democracy in the Postsoviet World*, New Haven, CA: Yale University Press.

Wilson, F. (ed.) (1998), *The European Center-Right at the End of the Twentieth Century*, London: Palgrave.

Wolff, H.J. and Hoensch, J.K. (eds) (1987) *Catholics, the State and the Radical Right 1919–1945*, Boulder, CO: Social Science Monographs.

Wolfson, A. (2005) 'Conservatives and Neoconservatives', in Stelzer, I. (ed.) *Neoconservatism*, London: Atlantic Books.

Yee, A.S. (1996) 'The Causal Effects of Ideas on Policies', *International Organization*, 50: 69–108.

Yoder, J. (2003) 'Decentralisation and Regionalisation after Communism: Lessons from Administrative and Territorial Reform in Poland and the Czech Republic', *Europe-Asia Studies*, 55: 263–86.

Younkins, E.W. (1999) 'Michael Novak's Portrait of Democratic Capitalism', *Markets and Morality*, 2: 8–43.

Zahradil, J. (2001) Untitled online interview dated 30 March. Online. Available www.ods.cz (accessed 1 May 2001).

—— (2004) *Realismus místo iluzí: modrá šance pro českou diplomacii*, Prague: ODS.

—— (2005a) 'Pět evropských klišé české diplomacie', material prepared by the office of Jan Zahradil for presentation at 16th ODS Congress. Online. Available zahradil.cz/docs/dokumenty/5_klise.pdf (accessed 20 June 2006).

—— (2005b) 'Europe – Strength and Weaknesses', presentation at the European Forum Alpach, August. Online. Available zahradil.cz/cze/download.php (accessed 1 July 2006).

Zahradil, J., Plecitý, P., Adrian, P. and Bednář, M. (2001a) *Manifest českého eurorealismu*. Online. Available www.ods.cz/docs/dokumenty/zahradil-manifest.pdf (accessed 1 October 2006).

—— (2001b) 'Odpověd kritikům Manifestu českého eurorealismu', 4 October. Online. Available www.ods.cz/zpravy/prispevek.php?ID=1905 (accessed 13 March 2007).

Zake, I. (2002) 'The People's Party in Latvia: Neo-Liberalism and the New Politics of Independence', *Journal of Communist Studies and Transition Politics*, 18: 9–31.

Zeman, M. (1990) 'O budoucnosti OF a volebním programu', *Fórum*, 18 April, 8.

Znoj, M. (1994) 'Anatomie Klausova konzervatismu', *Listy*, 24: 69–79.

Index